The Bourdieu paradigm

MANCHESTER
1824

Manchester University Press

The Bourdieu paradigm

The origins and evolution of an intellectual social project

Derek Robbins

Manchester University Press

Published by Manchester University Press
Altrincham Street, Manchester M1 7JA
www.manchesteruniversitypress.co.uk

British Library Cataloguing-in-Publication Data
A catalogue record for this book is available from the British Library

ISBN 978 0 7190 9939 7 hardback
ISBN 978 1 5261 5600 6 paperback

First published 2019

Typeset
by Toppan Best-set Premedia Limited

For Diana

For always roaming with a hungry heart
Much have I seen and known; cities of men
And manners, climates, councils, governments,
Myself not least, but honour'd of them all;
And drunk delight of battle with my peers,
Far on the plains of windy Troy.
I am a part of all that I have met;
Yet all experience is an arch wherethro'
Gleams that untravell'd world, whose margin fades
For ever and for ever when I move.
...
Death closes all; but something ere the end,
Some work of noble note, may yet be done,
Not unbecoming men that strove with Gods.
The lights begin to twinkle from the rocks:
The long day wanes: the slow moon climbs: the deep
Moans round with many voices. Come, my friends,
'Tis not too late to seek a newer world,
Push off, and sitting well in order smite
The sounding furrows; for my purpose holds
To sail beyond the sunset, and the baths
Of all the western stars, until I die.

From Alfred Tennyson: *Ulysses* (written in 1833 and published in 1842)

Will man einen Philosophen ehren, so muß man ihn da auffassen, wo er noch nicht zu den Folgen fortgegangen ist, in seinem Grund-gedanken; (in dem Gedanken,) von dem er ausgeht.

If you want to honor a philosopher, you must catch him where he has not yet gone forth to the consequences, in his fundamental thought; (in the thought) from which he takes his point in departure.

From the Collected Works of F.W.J von Schelling, WW, Section 2, III, 60, quoted by Heidegger in the introduction to his *Schellings Abhandlung über das Wesen der menschlichen Freiheit (1809)* (lectures delivered in 1936), ed. Hildegard Feick, Tübingen, Max Niemeyer Verlag, 1971, 10, translated by Joan Stambaugh as Heidegger: *Schelling's Treatise on the Essence of Human Freedom*, Athens/Ohio/London: Ohio University Press, 1985, 9.

Er: Seit vierhundert Jahren hat alle grosse Musik ihr Genügen darin gefunden, diese Einheit als bruchlos geleistete vorzutäuschen, – sie hat sich darin gefallen, die konventionelle Allgemeingesetzlichkeit, der sie untersteht, mit ihren eigensten Anliegen zu verwechseln. Freund, es geht nicht mehr. …Was der Kritik verfällt, ist der Scheincharakter des bürgerlichen Kunstwerks, an dem die Musk teil hat, obgleich sie kein Bild macht. … Die Subsumtion des Ausdrucks unters versöhnlich Allgemeine ist das innerste Prinzip des musikalischen Scheins. Es ist aus damit. Der Ansprach, das Allgemeine als im Besondern harmonisch enthalten zu denken, dementiert sich selbst. Es ist geschehen um die vorweg und verpflichtend geltenden Konventionen, die die Freiheit des Spiels gewährleisteten.

He: ' … For four hundred years all great music has found it good enough to pretend to an achieved, unbroken unity, acquiescing in the conventional and general rules to which it subjects itself, mistaking these for its own matters of concern. My friend, it won't do any more. What criticism has fallen victim to is the specious character of the bourgeois work of art in which music participates even though it produces no image. … The subordination of expression to appeasing generality is the core principle of musical illusion. That's all over. The claim to consider the general as harmonically contained within the particular contradicts itself. It's all up with the conventions currently considered prerequisite and obligatory, those guaranteeing the freedom of the game.'

From Thomas Mann: *Doktor Faustus. Das Leben des deutschen Tonsetzers Adrian Leverkühn, erzählt von einem Freunde,* Stockholm, Bermann-Fischer Verlag, 1947, 373, copyright S. Fischer Verlag GmbH, Frankfurt am Main. Author's translation.

Contents

Acknowledgements

I am very grateful for the very helpful comments on an earlier draft made by Tim Jenkins, Jesus College, Cambridge, and by an anonymous reader for Manchester University Press.

I would like to acknowledge the support given by the librarians at the Docklands campus library of the University of East London throughout the process of reading and researching for this book, and also to express my gratitude for the assistance of staff at Manchester University Press, particularly Tom Dark.

I am grateful to Éditions Gallimard (www.gallimard.fr) for permission to use the quotation from Merleau-Ponty on page 233. All rights for this text are reserved. Without authorization, every use of this text other than for individual and private consultation is forbidden. I am also grateful to Northwestern University Press for permission to use the translation of this passage.

Every effort has been made to obtain permission to reproduce copyright material, and the publisher will be pleased to be informed of any errors and omissions for correction in future editions.

Introduction

Scope

This book is the culmination of more than thirty years of study of the work of Pierre Bourdieu. During this period I have come to believe that Bourdieu is properly understood as an intellectual whose sociological production was informed by a phenomenological orientation.[1] By reference to three key phenomenological thinkers of the first half of the twentieth century, I try to provide a background to the way in which Bourdieu's work developed in the second half. I contend, however, that there is much more at stake in this account than an exegesis of the productive process of one person. The wider issue relates to the provenance in general of intellectual productions, whether they have self-referential meanings within autonomous and universal 'fields' or discourses, or are functions of the changing and contingent circumstances within which they are generated, those of particular authors inhabiting particular societies at particular times. This issue relates directly to current social and political concerns. It engages with contemporary uncertainty, particularly in Western democracies, about the authority and validity of specialist knowledge, scientific reason, monopolized by a minority 'liberal elite', in comparison with the everyday experiences and opinions of the majority of citizens. On the international stage, it relates to the authority of universalist conceptions of human rights and of structures of governance in comparison with societal practices in culturally different contexts. Phenomenology emerged in the specific intellectual, socio-political and cultural conditions of Austria and Germany between 1900 and 1940. This book suggests that the transfer of phenomenological thought from Austro-Germany to France and the United States in the 1940s involved different kinds of cultural assimilation. Merleau-Ponty was instrumental in effecting the assimilation to a French philosophical tradition and, in turn, this enabled Bourdieu to develop a sociological practice which sought to reconcile thought and experience in action.

Philosophical preliminaries

Since this book considers the philosophy underlying Bourdieu's sociology, it necessarily uses philosophical terminology which may not be wholly familiar to those who are accustomed to using Bourdieu's work in their sociological practice. This is a short introductory note which is designed to help readers by highlighting some of the language which recurs in this text. It constitutes an outline of a historical glossary of terms. I begin with Western European philosophy as it developed in response to the breakdown of the scholastic intellectual system and the rise of science at the beginning of the seventeenth century. In order to consider the claims of the new science, Descartes embarked on a quest to subject to doubt everything that he had learnt from the 'study of letters' (see *Discourse on Method*, Part I). Famously he concluded that the only thing he could not doubt was that he was doubting and, hence, formulated the dictum: *Cogito ergo sum* [I think, therefore I am] (see Meditation II of the *Meditations on First Philosophy*). The Latin statement does not use the first-person singular pronoun and it is the case that Descartes was trying to formulate a view on **Thought** and **Being** without problematizing his **identity** as a **self** or **subject**. He was convinced that his thought provided a more reliable source of **knowledge** than his **senses**. The essence of his separation of **mind** from **body** (Cartesian 'dualism') was that the mind had autonomous existence independent of the extended bodies external to it which it sensed. Hence, his supposed **rationalism**. By contrast, Locke wrote his *An Essay concerning human understanding* specifically to deny that there could be any source of **knowledge** other than our **sense impressions**. We construct our **ideas** by associating individual sense impressions. There are no 'innate ideas'. Hence his supposed **empiricism** and **associationism**. Although he denied that his work would 'meddle with the physical consideration of the mind', his interest in **epistemological** issues (questions related to the nature of knowledge) did give rise to forms of **materialist determinism** (in La Mettrie's *L'Homme machine* or Hartley's *Observations on Man*) which, during the nineteenth century, developed towards **behaviourism**. Locke's 'way of ideas' supposed that sense impressions, the ingredients of thought, emanate from a world of self-existent **physical objects**. Locke's philosophy of knowledge is **realist** as opposed to **idealist** but he does not examine the relationship between the observing human mind and its own corporeal presence in the world of those observed objects. **Understanding** 'sets man above the rest of sensible beings' and Locke was concerned to explain the process of understanding ideationally without reference to **physiology**.

Our historiography of philosophy generates an intellectual progression from Locke through Berkeley to Hume. There was certainly an element of discourse self-referentiality in the movement to Berkeley's *A Treatise concerning the principles of human knowledge* and on to Hume's *An Enquiry concerning human understanding*. To try to account for the reliability of sense impressions without succumbing to idealism, Berkeley contended that 'esse est percipere' [to be is to be perceived], which meant that the **perception** of objects is the guarantor of their objective existence, but he prevented knowledge from being reduced simply to what humans perceive by arguing that God perceives everything. Hume took a different approach. The guarantor of human knowledge is as much **intuition** or **habit** as rational enquiry. We do not know that the sun will rise tomorrow but we organize our lives on the assumption that there is regularity in nature.

Hume's approach was indicative of a diminution in the influence of **cognition** and a rise in interest in the importance of **feeling** or **sentiment** in directing human behaviour. This trend was advanced in the work of Rousseau which, in its concern with self-identity and **subjectivity**, was influential in the rise of romanticism. Although, by his own admission, Kant's reading of Rousseau roused him 'from his dogmatic slumbers', his attempted synthesis of the empiricist and rationalist traditions only amounted to an analysis of the ways in which categories of thought interact with sense impressions to generate knowledge. His analyses of **pure** and **practical** reason (Vernunft) were designed to define the limits of reason. Kant sought to unravel the systematic attempt to amalgamate physics and **metaphysics** that had been made in **natural theology** but he did not deny that there might be a rationally unknowable realm of **things–in–themselves**. Kant offered a **logic** of understanding which he took to be an explanation of human knowledge across all times and all places. In spite of his late *Anthropology from a pragmatic point of view* (which Foucault dismissed as anthropology on the grounds that it was predicated on a view of **man** already presented in the **critical philosophy**), Kant did not relate his analyses of categories of thought to the historically changing conditions of existence of people as thinking beings.

Even before Kant's death, thinkers associated with German romanticism developed critiques of the primarily rational character of Kant's critical philosophy. Thinkers such as Jacobi or Fichte sought to emphasize the acquisition of knowledge as the consequence of the engagement of whole persons, rational and sentimental. Concentration on the **subjective** supplanted the foundational commitment to the exercise of reason which had been the hallmark of the thought of the Age of Enlightenment in both its empiricist and rationalist philosophical forms. The pre-eminent critic of Kant was Hegel. His *Phenomenology of Mind* [**Geist**] (1807) is not to be understood to be 'phenomenology' as it was later to be developed by Husserl because Hegel was primarily concerned to disclose a historical process leading to Science. He argued that 'the whole project of securing for **consciousness** through **cognition** what exists in itself is absurd'. Rejecting the legacy of primary concern with cognition, but equally not privileging the subjective, Hegel explored the progressive development of mind in history as an enactment of a **dialectical**, inter-personal relationship between **Self** and **Others**. It was a progress which was the consequence of interacting mentalities, disembodied from the material conditions of their existence. His interest in the evolution of consciousness supplanted much of the language of earlier philosophy, discarding terms such as '**absolute**', 'cognition', 'objective' and 'subjective'. The ambiguity of meaning of 'Geist', either as 'world **spirit**' or individual mentality, contributed to a labelling of Hegel as '**idealist**'.

Initially under the influence of Hegel, Marx developed instead a dialectical view of historical progress based upon the ongoing encounter between the agency of a materially deprived proletariat and the structured oppression of a capitalist class sustained in its social domination by idealist thought acting as an ideology. There was a reinterpretation of Kantianism mainly in Germany at the end of the nineteenth century which culminated in Cassirer's articulation of a 'philosophy of **symbolic forms**', whereby Kant's categories of rationality were identified in social objectifications in a range of forms, including myth, religion, arts and sciences. There was also a response to Hegel in the work of Schopenhauer. His *The World as Will and Representation/Idea* (1818), denying the separation of mind and body, was important in influencing the work of Freud and Wittgenstein in Vienna at the fin-de-siècle.

'**Positive**' or '**positivist**' social and human sciences developed in the second half of the nineteenth century, particularly with the rise of economics, sociology, political science and psychology. The supposition was that all kinds of human behaviour could be understood without recourse to any source of causal influence which might be particular to humanity. The aspiration was that it would be possible to generate **rules** or **norms** of behaviour which would offer predictability because they existed without reference to metaphysical notions of **free will** and could, therefore, be deployed in social planning or social engineering. The institutionalization of Marx's thought in communist political ideology was symptomatic of this same tendency to isolate deterministic laws. Two of the 'founding fathers' of social science – Durkheim and Weber – struggled with the problem of how to reconcile the production of social science, by analogy with natural science, with responsiveness to the peculiar nature of that science by virtue of the immanence of human social scientists within the world which they seek to analyse. Durkheim recommended uncertainly that **social facts** should be treated either 'as' things or 'as if' they are things. Weber produced a methodology for the social sciences which sought to offer an objective account of the subjective intentions of social agents. The problem which had concerned earlier philosophy about the nature of our knowledge of the external world became transposed to become the problem of the nature of human knowledge of the thoughts and actions of other humans.

The emergence of Husserl's **phenomenology** was also part of this positivist mood. Husserl rejected the endeavours of positivist science, notably disparaging **psychologism**, but he tried to resolve earlier problems of philosophy by practising philosophy itself positivistically, that is to say, by arguing that although we have no access by reason referentially to a metaphysical reality, our consciousness nevertheless has a character of being 'of' something which can be analysed immanently. There is a **transcendental** quality inherent in the process by which consciousnesses relate to presentations. This was not thought to be the same as the **holistic** dimension active in human physical behaviour. While Freud was articulating his thinking about the power of the **unconscious** or **subconscious** in determining the behaviour of the **ego**, Gestalt psychologists and physiologists were demonstrating that there are natural forces which enable the body to restore to itself some functioning **wholeness** after debilitating accidents. There was an affinity between Bergson's philosophical view that there is a **vital force**, a creative evolutionary energy in nature, and Goldstein's recognition of the existence of a restorative mechanism which revives invalids to a new medical equilibrium.

In these debates, the issue was implicitly the competitive status of philosophical or scientific explanation. In Vienna, positivism in philosophy took a more extreme form than Husserl's phenomenology. The concentration on language in the Vienna Circle meant the insistence that metaphysical language was nonsense and that there should be no vestigial attachment to referentiality as contained in Husserl's notion of 'intentionality'. Hence the development of **logical positivism**. Meanwhile, Heidegger introduced a radical challenge to the prevailing emphasis on epistemology. His **ontological phenomenology** was an attempt to subject **being** to positivist analysis without reference to the pre-history of **ontology** in the Western philosophical tradition. This attempt was undertaken within the field of philosophy without regard to the findings of contemporary science.

Some of these competing approaches were in debate at Davos in 1930. This was a *philosophical* encounter between Cassirer and Heidegger, but Carnap of the Vienna Circle was also present. This encounter between neo-Kantian epistemology, phenomenological ontology and logical positivism has been regarded as a 'parting of the ways'[2] between 'continental' and 'anglo-saxon analytic' philosophies which shaped Western thought for the rest of the twentieth century. This encounter encapsulates the intellectual situation as experienced at the time by Schutz, Gurwitsch[3] and Merleau-Ponty.

Phenomenology

More needs to be said explicitly about the place of the phenomenological movement in the historical progression I have just outlined. Although the details of Husserl's position are disputed, the essential fundamentals are straightforward. Within the tradition of post-Kantian German philosophy of knowledge which argued that we cannot know 'things-in-themselves', realities behind appearances, Husserl insisted nevertheless that the phenomenal knowledge to which we are restricted is always knowledge *of* something. This is also always *our* knowledge, knowledge as it is presented to individual persons, and, therefore, in some sense both subjective and objective. While all adhering to the common, defining view that our knowledge of the outside world and of other people is confined to representation rather than reality, some phenomenologists emphasized the 'noetic', the perceptually individual process of knowledge construction, and others emphasized the 'noematic' dimension, the meanings inherent in the structures of representation to perception.

Jean-François Lyotard published a brief introduction to phenomenology when Bourdieu was still a student. Quoting passages taken from Merleau-Ponty and Jeanson, Lyotard emphasized that it was absurd to demand an objective definition of phenomenology because it was important to recognize that phenomenologists saw themselves as continuously advancing positions based on observation in defiance of systematization. This meant that philosophy must not only be grasped 'from the outside' but worked through internally 'as problem, genesis, give-and-take movement of thought' (Lyotard, 1999 [1954], 3; 1991, 31). For Husserl, this was a quest for objectivity, for 'philosophy as rigorous science',[4] even though it ran the risk of appearing to 'lean in favour of a simplistic subjectivism' (Lyotard, 1999 [1954], 3; 1991, 31). Husserl wanted to trace 'all knowledge back to a radical non-knowledge' (Lyotard, 1999 [1954], 4; 1991, 32) but, at the same time, 'there is an ahistorical pretention in phenomenology' (Lyotard, 1999 [1954], 4; 1991, 32) which appears to be in conflict with experiential contingency. Hence Lyotard commented that 'A rationalist bent leads Husserl to engage himself in the prerational' (Lyotard, 1999 [1954], 5–6; 1991, 33), or we could say that, paradoxically, the desire to formulate a universally valid philosophical grounding of 'science' led Husserl towards a sociological understanding of the particular, 'life-world' conditions of the production of thought. In considering the relationship of Bourdieu's work to the phenomenological tradition in this book, it is important to keep in mind, therefore, that he inherited this tension philosophically from the phenomenological tradition while at the same time it experientially made sense of his social trajectory which had been achieved by means of philosophy. These two factors account for his desire to offer simultaneously a philosophy of social science and also a social history of philosophy, and for his tendency constantly to oscillate between these dispositions.

Structure

This book is presented in two parts. The first focuses on the work of three thinkers – Schutz, Gurwitsch and Merleau-Ponty – who, in different ways, regarded themselves as 'disciples' or 'followers' of Husserl. Alfred Schutz

(1899–1959) studied in Vienna. He deployed the work of Husserl to launch a critique of Weber's 'verstehende Soziologie' [interpretative sociology], arguing that Weber's 'ideal-type' was an intellectualist imposition on the self-understanding of people. Schutz's critique was published in 1932 as *Der sinnhafte Aufbau der sozialen Welt*. This was published posthumously in English in 1967 as *The Phenomenology of the Social World*. The precise meaning of the original title is important. Schutz sought to provide an account of the 'meaningful' (sinnhafte) 'construction' (Aufbau) of the *social* world. Unlike the title of the book published in 1966 by disciples of Schutz – Berger and Luckmann: *The Social Construction of Reality* – Schutz restricted his analysis to the ways in which *agents* construct their social worlds, still supposing phenomenologically that 'reality' is inaccessible.

Aron Gurwitsch (1901–73) studied in Berlin under Carl Stumpf, who had struggled there to reconcile the legacy of German idealist philosophy with the emerging sciences of physiology and psychology. The form of reconciliation attempted by Gurwitsch involved seeking to argue for the theoretical benefits to be derived from associating the emphases of phenomenology and Gestalt psychology. Gestalt psychology was intent on demonstrating empirically that there are objective networks of meaning which impinge on our perception and which are not our constructs. Gurwitsch, therefore, was primarily interested in the 'noema' and its intrinsic, autonomous structure of meaning.

Gurwitsch and Schutz met in Paris in the mid-1930s as a result of the recommendation of Husserl. They became friends from 1939 and maintained a correspondence after they had both migrated to the United States (in 1940 and 1939 respectively) in which they discussed each other's work until Schutz's death in 1959. They considered that intellectually they were tunnelling in opposite directions which would meet, that is to say, they thought they were working towards a philosophical reconciliation of their noematic and noetic, objective and subjective, perspectives.

The personal circumstances of Schutz and Gurwitsch, and the structure of the post-Second World War American intellectual field which turned away from relativism towards a universalism underpinning international, imperialist political aspirations, conspired to situate their work in a rarefied intellectual sphere. It is significant that in their correspondence there is virtually no reference to contemporary political events, such as, for instance, the impact of McCarthyism. The book is disinclined to accept the de-politicization of their thought.

Those already familiar with the work of Pierre Bourdieu (1930–2002) will see that the book seeks to offer, in Part I, an analysis of the development of thinking which, for Bourdieu, became the predispositional framework which he modified for his own research purposes in different social conditions. The purpose of Part II is to show the way in which Bourdieu appropriated the intellectual legacy of Schutz and Gurwitsch and, throughout his career, sought to politicize it. There is no intention to establish the specific influence of either Schutz or Gurwitsch on the work of Bourdieu. Part I offers an account of one reconciliation of the agency and structure impulses which itself became a component of the inherited structure of thought which Bourdieu reconciled with the personal dispositions which he had imbibed from his family background. It offers one possible genealogy of Bourdieu's sociological reflexivity. One concession to an interest in 'influence' is given in the final chapter of Part I, which discusses the work of Maurice Merleau-Ponty, who attended Husserl's *Cartesian Meditations* lectures in Paris in 1930 and collaborated with Gurwitsch during the 1930s. Consideration of the work of Merleau-Ponty provides a thematic mediation between the two parts of the book and is designed to suggest that his attempt to deploy his response to *philosophical* issues raised by Gurwitsch and Schutz in the *political* context of post-Second World War France led to a substantive position with which Bourdieu was sympathetic but, more importantly, to one which Bourdieu gradually tried to actualize *sociologically*. The importance for this book of the discussion of the work of Merleau-Ponty is that, after the writing and publication of the works which were the products of his psychological and phenomenological researches, *La structure du comportement* [the structure of behaviour] (1942) and *Phénoménologie de la perception* [phenomenology of perception] (1945), Merleau-Ponty developed a particular view of the implications of phenomenological analysis for political understanding and action. Merleau-Ponty explicitly discussed the relationship between the philosopher and sociology but he remained committed to the primary importance of philosophy, as indicated by his inaugural lecture at the Collège de France of 1953 (*L'Éloge de la philosophie* [in praise of philosophy]). Merleau-Ponty had no notion that sociological research might constitute a form of political action, whereas Bourdieu actualized Merleau-Ponty's phenomenological orientation in his research and, finally, in direct action.

Part II of the book is devoted to analysis of the development of Bourdieu's work and thought. This is offered in five chapters which focus on the decades from 1950 to 2000. This is a convenient device, but it has to be remembered throughout that this is a heuristic device which does not always correspond easily with real developments. In an interview with Yvette Delsaut shortly before his death, Bourdieu commented that he could construct for himself two completely different intellectual biographies, 'one which would make apparent all my successive choices as the product of a methodically oriented project from the beginning, the other, equally true, which would describe a chain of chances, of more or less fortuitous encounters, happy and unhappy' (Delsaut and Rivière, eds, 2002, 183). He recognized that his career had been a process of interaction between a necessary logic and contingent events and, by putting it in this way, he was endorsing the theory which he had developed within his career which recognized the continuing dialectic between 'habitus' and 'fields', between the material contingencies of social reality and the relatively autonomous fields of consciousness.

A note on method

The method adopted in the book derives from the position developed by Bourdieu, and the substance of the book is an account of that development. Hence the book gives an account of the emergence of a particular philosophy of social science while the socio-historical method used is an attempt to provide an exemplar in practice of what Bourdieu eventually meant when he called for a 'socio-genetic understanding of intellectual works' (Calhoun, LiPuma and Postone, eds, 1993, 263–75).

The implication of Bourdieu's mature position was that he recommended that intellectual understandings should be phenomenologically descriptive and that each individual understanding should contribute to a collective understanding of all possible positions. His emphasis of 'socio-genetic understanding' is a particular aspect of his conviction that 'everything is social' [tout est social]. This implied an emphasis on totality as well as on the primacy of the social. It implied the accumulation of multiple correlations between phenomena rather than any quest for determining, extra-social causations. He regarded his researches as socially conditioned contributions to an understanding of the social conditions of which he was conscious rather than as formulations of definitive and generally applicable explanations. He was insistent that individuals should recognize the limits of their endeavours in the context of limitless processes of investigation. What has been regarded as a socio-centrically 'reductive' contribution to social science should rather be seen as an attempt to deploy scientificity in the more important task of developing an inclusive inter-subjectivity between all social agents, a self-negating strategy in the interest of de-privileging specialist knowledge so as to cultivate the equal participation of people in their societies. There is a reciprocal relationship between the social conditions which enable social perspectives to occur (whether formal and professional or informal and popular) and the substance of these perspectives as explanations of those conditions.

Writing a book about Bourdieu as an adherent to the position which he advanced means I explicitly acknowledge that my understanding is delimited and is only one contribution to a more comprehensive view. Bourdieu's ambition was unrealizable by himself alone but a significant aspect of his achievement was that he fostered collective endeavour, particularly in his management of the research of the Centre de Sociologie Européenne (CSE) and in his editorial direction of *Actes de la recherche en sciences sociales*. These were both collective ventures which were grounded in the social affinities between participants and, as such, they were microcosmic exemplifications of his vision of societal cohesion to be secured by reflexive socio-analytic encounter between members/citizens. Bourdieu's ambition was simultaneously inexhaustible and limited. He was embarked upon a process which might be thought to be unrealizable only if we retain the notion that social scientific knowledge is cumulative in detached and demarcated autonomy rather than constantly adaptive in immanent involvement with the changing situations which it analyses.

Disclaimers

Lyotard recognized that at the heart of the phenomenological method was 'a refusal to proceed to explanation' (Lyotard, 1999 [1954], 5; 1991, 33), an inclination only to articulate correlations and to eschew causality. As he elaborated graphically: 'to explain the red of this lampshade is precisely to abandon it as *this* red spread out on this lampshade, under whose circle I am thinking of red; it is to set it up as a vibration of a given frequency and intensity, to set in its place "something", the object for the physicist which is not, above all, "the thing itself" for me' (Lyotard, 1999 [1954], 5; 1991, 33). In this spirit, the consideration of 'influence' in my analysis is subordinate to an attempt to disclose juxtapositions and connections, to contribute to understanding rather than to offer causal explanations.

I try to apply historically the 'field' theory developed by Bourdieu, that is to say that I relate intellectual productions to the social conditions within which they originated, recognizing at the same time that these 'social conditions' themselves are the products of earlier and contemporary political and intellectual influences. I follow early Bourdieu in assuming that the education system in any society is the medium adopted by government to reproduce earlier values and to regulate modifications. I suggest, therefore, that Schutz and Gurwitsch were both products of a common European gymnasium schooling regime, and that Merleau-Ponty (and Bourdieu) were products of the lycée system in France culminating in their acquisition of 'normalien' socio-political status. In examining the development of Bourdieu's thought in Part II it becomes evident that he realized that this model was becoming moribund and that the privileging of education in the inter-generational transmission of knowledge and values was becoming analytically inadequate. These remarks are therefore intended to substantiate the specific disclaimer which is that my selection of authors for discussion is a reflection of my disposition to attend to the relations between the philosophy and the practice of social science and that my selection of topics by which to contextualize the work of these authors is both methodologically and historically contingent. To put this graphically, a different characterization of the work of Bourdieu would have emerged if I had, for instance, focused on the contextual significance of the work of Gaston Bachelard or Simone de Beauvoir or on the relations between social science and literature and the arts.

A different kind of selection is imposed by constraints of length. The ideal of phenomenological analysis is that there should be exegesis of texts without preconception. In discussing authors, I try to provide comprehensive chronological information about their publications in relation to their social trajectories before isolating specific texts for detailed attention. Of course, the choice of these texts is governed by the latent argument but I try to offset this partiality by enabling the reader to perceive the omissions in my detailed accounts. This problem is particularly acute in respect of my discussion of the work of Pierre Bourdieu in Part II. Bourdieu published about three hundred articles and forty books in a period of just over forty years. Most of these texts are densely argued and complex. I have chosen to pursue my argument by emphasizing moments of apparent transition in Bourdieu's thinking, focusing on illustrative texts rather than embarking on any attempt to provide a comprehensive exegesis. The inevitable effect is that some major texts receive disconcertingly slight attention. Equally, I have not attempted to analyse in detail the extent to which his thought was always 'conjunctural',[5] in instinctive dialectical relation to the conditions which produced it. The consideration of the work of Merleau-Ponty is designed to give a representation of the milieu from which Bourdieu's work originated, but I have not attempted in Part II the ambitious task of depicting the ways in which Bourdieu strategically steered a path among the political developments of post-1960 France and in the context of the published work of contemporaries such as Althusser, Foucault, Lyotard or Deleuze, to name only a few.[6] To this extent, I have only suggested a method, still to be applied further, by examining Bourdieu's production implicitly in terms of his originating habitus more than in terms of his subsequent position-taking adaptations.

Finally, the phenomenological orientation of my discussions entails strict adherence to chronology. The disclaimer here is that I have to admit to dependence on scholarly editors. Although I am greatly indebted to the editorial work of scholars such as Lester Embree, Helmut Wagner and Claude Lefort in respect of the posthumous publication of the works of, respectively, Aron Gurwitsch, Alfred Schutz and Maurice Merleau-Ponty, and am also indebted to the various editors who have rescued some of Bourdieu's work for posthumous publication, this dependence has generated a tension. I have been obliged to work with prior selections of editors from archival sources at their disposal. I have tried to retrieve the immanent meanings of the authors but I have been working against the grain of the efforts of editors who were disposed to de-historicize what they found in archives in order to re-present past intellectual productions as universally relevant.

Engagement with the reader

The integrity of the book in its two parts derives from Bourdieu's view of historical change, which I share. There is no necessary progress independent of the ongoing achievements or constructions of humans. Bourdieu was attracted by the thinking of the Pre-Socratic philosophers, particularly Heraclitus. We do not put our feet in the same river twice. All individuals in all generations either adapt the values which they inherit to fit the prevailing system of values or attempt to modify that system so as to preserve their inheritance. There is a continuum of adaptation and modification, and positions on that continuum are determined by the extent to which we have the power to project future change and to implement it. Bourdieu inherited the traditional values of rural, agricultural, provincial France, overlain with his father's commitment to social-ist solidarity and republican egalitarianism. He recognized that his personal tra-jectory was one from traditionalism to modernity and postmodernity. During his career he realized that the power of the inter-generational transmission of values was diminishing and that, instead, people were beginning to make life-style choices with reference to a market of possible options rather than by reference to an inherited sense of identity. He tried to adapt his inherited values to the new social situation by developing an emphasis in sociological research designed to expose the extent to which the structured options at our disposal are social constructs imposed upon us in ways which depend on the degree of our possession of power. By developing a sociologically 'reflexive' critique of structures and a methodology which sought to be dialogical and 'maieutic', Bourdieu sought to remain faithful to egalitarianism by recommending social constructivism.

The book tries to show how Bourdieu adapted his habitus to his changing circumstances by developing a theory which enabled him to deploy sociologi-cally the noetic/noematic, subjective/objective elements of the Western Euro-pean epistemological tradition that he imbibed as a student. Just as Bourdieu's preface of 1988 to the English translation of *Homo Academicus* invited readers to respond to his text by analysing their own situations rather than by treat-ing it as a representation of Parisian reality, so readers of this book are invited to consider in what ways the case-study of Bourdieu's trajectory vis-à-vis the indicative ideas of Schutz and Gurwitsch can offer a model of how we, in turn, should respond to Bourdieu's conceptual constructs. Bourdieu always said he intended that his post-structuralism should go beyond structuralism, not negate it. The 'socio-analytic' encounter between social agents which Bourdieu recommended as the foundation for a democratic society was predicated on a shared Gestalt of the social system (which almost unconsciously Bourdieu tended to identify with his model of a socially and culturally reproductive society). Contemporary cross-cultural encounters in the 'social media' are, perhaps, immediate, without reference to any shared system of meaning. A sub-text of the book is that it indicates the migration of ideas between cul-tures. Anyone familiar with Karl Kraus's two essays on Heinrich Heine of 1910 and 1911[7] will be aware of the complexity of the crisis of the period in respect of Austrian, German, French and Jewish identities and cultures. If you subscribe to the primacy of life-world experience in constituting intel-lectual objectivities (the view which is in contention in the debates discussed), the book provides the suggestion that the noetic/noematic or subjectivist/ objectivist dichotomy takes its particular form in accordance with the socio-historical conditions of its development. It follows the progression of the opposing positions from Austrian/German cultural origins to North American assimilation and to French appropriation, leading to the conclusion that Bourdieu's adaptation of this intellectual inheritance was a function of his position within French society and in relation to French culture. What is exposed is a constantly shifting correlation between experiential, indigenous cultures and universalizing, intellectualist discourses.[8] As such, the intention is that the book should invite reflexivity on the part of readers from whatever cultural tradition. The exploration of the social and intellectual trajectory of Bourdieu in implicit response to the legacy of Schutz, Gurwitsch and Merleau-Ponty is an invitation to diverse readers to study that response with a view to considering to what extent it should be imitated in their own situations. Hence the title of the book is 'The Bourdieu paradigm' and not 'The Bourdieu prescription'.

Technical information

As I have indicated, Bourdieu was committed to the encouragement of collective endeavour. Many of his publications were co-authored. Elsewhere I have tried to identify the contributory emphases made by some co-authors to joint texts.[9] In this book, I make no such attempt. For convenience, I assign the meaning of all co-authored texts to Bourdieu alone.

Most of the quotations in the book are from non-English sources. Although I have some German-language competence, all of the quotations from German sources are taken from published translations. I normally read French texts first in the original language. In quoting French texts with a published English translation I cite the date and page reference of the original French publication and, separated by a semi-colon, the date and page reference for the English translation, for example (Bourdieu, 1979a, 189; 1986a, 169), which indicates the page references for a quotation from *La distinction/Distinction*. Where no translations have been published, I make my own translations and give page references to the French texts (e.g. Bourdieu, 1979b, 3), which indicates that this is my translation of a passage on page 3 of the untranslated 'Les trois états du capital culturel'. In respect of both languages, I sometimes provide the original text in parentheses when the particular language use is intrinsic to the discussion.

I use square brackets on occasion to indicate the date of first publication. The following example from above: (Lyotard, 1999 [1954], 3; 1991, 31) means that the quoted passage uses the 13th (1999) edition and the English translation of 1991 (actually of the 10th edition of 1986) of the book by Lyotard which was first published in 1954.

After the first mention of the Centre de Sociologie Européenne (CSE) above, I always refer to it as CSE.

I never add italicization to quotations.

Notes

1 See, most recently, chapter 1 of Robbins, ed., 2016.
2 See Freedman, 2000.
3 Gurwitsch attended the Davos conference. See chapter 2.
4 The title of an early Husserl publication of 1910–11.
5 See Boschetti, 2006, 135.
6 My *French Post-War Social Theory* (Robbins, 2012) was an attempt to correlate chronologically the production and reception of the work of Althusser, Aron, Foucault, Lyotard and Bourdieu, but, partly for lack of space, even this became a historiography of texts rather than the historical sociology of textual production that I had envisaged.
7 See 'Heine and the Consequences' and 'Afterword to "Heine and the Consequences"' in Franzen, 2014, 3–133 and 262–293.
8 See Robbins, 2015b.
9 See Passeron, ed. Robbins, 2013 and Robbins, 2014b.

I
Origins

The legacy of the Western European thought of the nineteenth century was a disjunction between idealist and materialist world-views. This is to state the issue in philosophical terms but the real tension was between the truth claims of philosophy and science. 'After Hegel, ... philosophical foundations in science, or for science in general, suddenly came to seem dispensable' (Schnädelbach, 1984, 67). The phenomenological movement tried to heal the rupture by representing philosophy as scientific, and the development of Gestalt psychology, emanating initially from Berlin, was an attempt, from the opposite direction, to identify the intrinsic importance of the mind in physiological processes. A tendency of one Austrian movement, evident in its school of economic theory, was to emphasize the agency of self-determining individuals, unconstrained by normative laws. This Part follows the development in these terms of the thought of Schutz in Austria and Gurwitsch in Germany and France. It then explores the incorporation of their thinking into the American context after 1940, an incorporation which accentuated formally the idealist intellectualism about which both were substantively sceptical. It concludes with a chapter on the work of Merleau-Ponty, who worked with Gurwitsch in Paris in the 1930s. Merleau-Ponty resisted the appropriation of phenomenology by existentialism as advanced by Sartre but he shared Sartre's commitment to political action. He tried to develop a philosophy of action which correlated with a denial of a mind/body dualism. This can be seen to have been an attempt to reconcile opposing dispositions within the phenomenological movement but he could not resist undertaking this reconciliation within the field of philosophy rather than actualizing it in socio-political action. Consideration of his resigned refuge in philosophy leads the way to an exploration, in Part II, of the affinities between the thinking of Bourdieu and Merleau-Ponty, focusing on the evolution of Bourdieu's intellectual social project which represented a sustained effort to put into practice the theoretical resolutions which he inherited.

1

Schutz in Vienna, 1899–1938

This chapter offers a brief outline of Schutz's career in the first half of his life and then considers in detail the texts, published and unpublished at the time, which he produced in this period. It concludes with a summary of the correlations between these social and intellectual trajectories, both in relation to the Viennese context.

The career

Alfred Schutz[1] was born in Vienna on 13 April 1899. After several years of elementary schooling, he attended the Esterhazy Gymnasium. This offered a classical curriculum. He studied Latin and Greek for eight years, graduating in January 1918, *summa cum laude*. According to Helmut Wagner, adolescence, for Schutz, 'was a period of *Sturm und Drang*, a time of great inner unrest and search for personal identity' (Wagner, 1983, 5). He joined the loose groups which formed in 1915, which became known as the Viennese Youth Movement: 'Politically and socially progressive, they consisted of passionate hikers, who often met in a central assembly hall for lectures, discussions, and artistic performances' (Wagner, 1983, 5).

Schutz graduated early from the Gymnasium, taking an emergency examination one year before he should have taken the 'Abitur' to qualify for university entrance. After already suffering heavy losses, the Austrian army was in urgent need of replacements and Schutz was drafted immediately, attached to an artillery regiment and sent to the Italian front with the rank of 'Fähnrich' (second lieutenant). After spending ten months at the front, he qualified for furlough. He took the last train back to Vienna. As Barber puts it succinctly: 'The rest of his regiment were taken prisoners, the war ceased, and the Central

Powers had been defeated' (Barber, 2004, 5). Wagner concentrates on the estrangement Schutz felt on returning from the front to his home city, which had suddenly ceased to be the capital of a powerful empire, likening Schutz's experience to the account which he later gave in 'The Homecomer' (1945) of the responses of American soldiers returning after service abroad in the Second World War. Wagner comments that Schutz's 'estrangement from the new social order of postwar Austria lasted and, perhaps, never left him completely' (Wagner, 1983, 6).

In 1919, Schutz matriculated as a student of Law at the University of Vienna. As a war veteran, he was allowed to rush through a shortened curriculum, with the result that he received the title of Dr. Jur. (LL.D) in December 1921. He concentrated on International Law. During 1919 and 1920, he also studied at the Business School of the Institute for International Trade. A few weeks before his final examinations, he was offered the job of executive secretary of the Austrian Bankers' Association. Wagner contends that the socio-political estrangement Schutz felt on his return from military service persisted in a new form as he embarked on a career in banking while at the same time maintaining a separate intellectual life. As Wagner puts it: 'From the outset, Schutz settled for a split existence' (Wagner, 1983, 9).

In his banking position, Schutz carried out research on banking problems in Central European countries and acted as an economic advisor to affiliated firms. In 1929,[2] he joined the private bank of Reitler and Co., where he continued his research and advisory work throughout Central and Western Europe. Still emphasizing Schutz's estrangement, Wagner argues that Schutz was attracted by Weber's insistence on the value neutrality of social science because it legitimized his intellectual detachment, but that the obverse of estrangement was a disposition to rely on affective attachment to friends and family. Wagner identifies 'two bridges' which led Schutz from experience to his intellectual position: 'One issued from the experience of estrangement and led to the stance of "scientific detachment"; the other guided him from strong, intimate, Thou-feelings to the consistent intersubjective approach of his social-science concerns' (Wagner, 1983, 10).

Schutz assigned particular significance to the influence of five of his university teachers. In International Law, these were Hans Kelsen and Alfred Verdross. In Economics, they were Friedrich von Wieser and Ludwig von Mises, while, in Sociology, it was Othmar Spann. Wagner argues that only Kelsen and von Mises exerted permanent influence. Schutz's period of formal study at the university was short, but, as a result of personal contacts established there, he participated between 1921 and 1933 in the activities of two of the lecture and discussion circles ('Kreise') which were characteristic of Viennese socio-intellectual life at this time. He became involved in the 'Geistkreis' and in the Mises seminar. He was not a member of the Vienna Circle, nor of the group which gathered around Hans Kelsen. Wagner suggests that Schutz was drawn towards the study of the work of Max Weber, not so much through the influence of his tutors as that of his fellow students who had spent the last year of the war at the university and had attended the lectures which Weber gave there during the first semester of 1918. Wagner affirms that Schutz studied carefully the two volumes of Weber's *Wirtschaft und Gesellschaft* and his *Gesammelte Aufsätze zur Wissenschaftslehre*, both of which were published posthumously in 1922. As a result, 'Schutz became a Weberian sociologist' (Wagner, 1983, 14), but one who set himself the task of clarifying Weber's 'conception of a sociology of understanding' (Wagner, 1983, 15). To remedy the shortcomings of Weber's understanding of subjectivity with a view to grounding it with more philosophical adequacy, Schutz turned first to the work of Bergson. There was a short Bergsonian period in the mid-1920s, but Schutz soon turned instead to the work of Husserl. According to Wagner, 'The Bergsonian period of Schutz lasted from 1924 to 1928' (Wagner, 1977, 187). This is documented 'by a set of fragments of one to four handwritten pages each, and by three unfinished manuscripts: *Lebensformen und Sinnstruktur* (166 typed pages: started 1925), *Sinnstrukturen der Sprache* (49 handwritten pages: summer 1925), and *Sinnstruktur der Novelle: Goethe* (42 typed pages: also mid-twenties)' (Wagner, 1977, 187). Wagner was subsequently responsible for making some of this documentation public by, first, translating and introducing the *Theorie der Lebensformen* which had been published in German in 1981 (Schutz, ed. Srubar, 1981) as *Life Forms and Meaning Structure* (Schutz, ed. Wagner, 1982),[3] and then by including a translation of Schutz's early seminar text on 'Thou and I' in Volume IV of Schutz's *Collected Papers* (Schutz, ed. Wagner, Psathas and Kersten, 1996).

Schutz developed his ideas within the Mises Circle. According to Barber, it was in this context that Schutz 'expounded on such topics as Max Weber's methodology, the economic thought of Wieser and Sombart, Scheler's approach to the social sciences, the Thou and I, group soul and group spirit, and understanding and acting' (Barber, 2004, 14). Wagner argues that some manuscripts, probably dating from 1927–28, on 'relevance' illustrate Schutz's thought in transition from Bergsonian to Husserlian influence, and these fragments were given prime position in the *Collected Papers*, Volume IV. The editors of the *Collected Papers*, Volume IV, also assembled texts which are based on the notes for lectures which Schutz gave to the members of the Mises seminar circle in 1928–29. Four of these lectures are given the title: 'Toward a Viable Sociology'. Another lecture, prepared for a seminar in June 1930, is given the title: 'Understanding and Acting in Political Economy and Other Social Sciences'. There is, therefore, now some evidence for the development of Schutz's thought during the 1920s, but it remains the case that *Der sinnhafte Aufbau der sozialen Welt: Eine Einleitung in die verstehende Soziologie* [the meaningful construction of the social world: an introduction to the interpretative sociology], published in 1932 by Springer Verlag, Vienna, was Schutz's first publication.

Schutz spent the summers of 1936 and 1937 'deepening his own philosophical position' (Barber, 2004, 63). He produced four manuscripts making a set entitled 'The Problem of Personality in the Social World', but an edited version of these was published only later in English in the United States in *Philosophy and Phenomenological Research* as 'On Multiple Realities' (1945c). He reviewed two of Husserl's texts in the early 1930s, von Mises's *Grundprobleme der Nationalökonomie* [basic problems of political economy] (1933) in 1934, and Otaka's *Grundlegung der Lehre vom sozialen Verband* [the foundation of the doctrine of social association] in 1937, but he published nothing else in German before his enforced departure from Western Europe. The *Collected Papers*, Volume IV, contains an unpublished essay in response to von Hayek of 1936 which is given the title: 'Political Economy: Human Conduct in Social Life'. Either late in 1938 or in the spring of the following year, von Hayek (then editor of *Economica* at the London School of Economics) invited Schutz to review Talcott Parsons's *The Structure of Social Action* (1937) for the journal (see Grathoff, ed., 1978, xvii). Schutz wrote a critique but it was not then published. As we shall see, he did send it to Parsons and there followed a short correspondence between the two men from November 1940 until April 1941. The critique and the correspondence were published in 1978 (Grathoff, ed., 1978).

Schutz was in Paris on business when the Anschluss (the annexation of Austria into the Third Reich) was formally promulgated on 13 March 1938. He was advised to stay there. His bank terminated his contract at the end of August 1938. According to Barber, Schutz had already met Aron Gurwitsch on a business trip to Paris in 1935. In Paris, the Schutzes moved in a circle of Jewish emigrants which included Gurwitsch and his wife, and Hannah Arendt. Alfred Schutz was 'familiar with Lucien Goldmann, Gaston Berger, Alexander Koyré, Gabriel Marcel, Hélène Metzger ..., Jacques Maritain, Maurice Merleau-Ponty, Jean Wahl, and Raymond Aron and Louis Rougier' (Barber, 2004, 81). Paris was, however, only a temporary resting place. On 14 July 1939, the Schutz family set sail for New York, arriving there on 22 July.

Schutz's early thought

Life Forms and Meaning Structure

This was the title which Schutz gave to the first of three parts of a study which he was proposing in the period between 1925 and 1927. According to his introduction, Schutz was intent on exploring 'Life and cognition', which he specified as an exploration of 'Sciences of Life and *Geisteswissenschaften*' and of the 'crisis of epistemology and logic' (Schutz, ed. Wagner, 1982, 11). This was further specified to involve consideration of the 'applicability of modern epistemological tendencies to the social sciences' (Schutz, ed. Wagner, 1982, 11). He proposed, on the one hand, to examine 'Weber's theory of a sociology of understanding' and to offer an outcome of this examination, and, on the other, to explore Bergson's 'intuitionist philosophy' (specifically 'the *not* biological part') with a view to finding a resolution of the life/cognition problem 'by way of Bergson and the philosophy of duration' (Schutz, ed. Wagner, 1982, 12).

The first manuscript, dated 1924–25, was entitled 'Soziale Aspekte der Musik als Artform' [social aspects of music as art form] and rendered by Wagner as 'Meaning Structures of Drama and Opera' as the third component of Part II. Schutz begins his discussion with a crucial distinction: 'It is necessary to keep the question of the meaning of an art form separate from the question of the meaning of a work of art' (Schutz, ed. Wagner, 1982, 180). He immediately distinguishes between the objectification of meaning achieved by artists in their creations, based on inter-personal communication, and the meanings which are independently imposed by institutionalized structures of communication. To put this in different language, Schutz is suggesting that individual works of art should be understood to be socially constructed, whereas the art forms through which individual intentions are expressed possess intrinsic meaning. Schutz confesses that he is uncertain whether these 'intrinsic' art forms are themselves constructs. As he puts it: 'It is difficult to decide whether a sharply articulated art form receives its meaning only from the content with which it is filled and from the specifically given idea which it concretely presents' (Schutz, ed. Wagner, 1982, 181). For Schutz, the uncertainty arises from an equivocal use of the term 'meaning'. He offers the following alternative meanings of meaning: 'On the one hand, the term signifies the reversal of attention from the posited symbol to the symbol to be interpreted; on the other hand, it is used as expression of the inherent necessity (*eigene Gesetzlichkeit*) of anything spiritual (*geistig*)' (Schutz, ed. Wagner, 1982, 181). In the second instance, Schutz elaborates, 'the art form is taken to be something which persists in objective unchangeability; it is not accessible to the subjective positing of meaning. While it can be filled with most different contents, it remains invariable and constant in itself' (Schutz, ed. Wagner, 1982, 181).

Schutz's important general observations introduce his detailed discussion of opera and drama as art forms. Schutz argues that the key instrument of dramatic communication is language, but the use of language in drama is radically different from its use in poetry.

In distinction from the novel form, the dramatic form represents speaking *agents* on stage without authorial intervention. On the basis of this initial discussion of drama, Schutz proceeds to an examination of the distinctive characteristics of opera. By reference to the work of Schoenberg, Stravinsky, Berg and Wagner, Schutz reflects on the nature of the addition to drama provided by music which, according to Schopenhauer 'is will, not idea' (Schutz, ed. Wagner, 1982, 190). He has recourse to the work of Bergson, who cited 'melody' as an example of 'inner duration'. Melody belongs to primary experience whereas music belongs publicly 'to outer time through rhythm' (Schutz, ed. Wagner, 1982, 193). 'Programme' music is a false attempt to impose the meaning of external events on to the originary musical impulses of melody. Within the opera form, the overture is an attempt to establish the primacy of music before the advent on stage of actors communicating extraneous meanings through their music.

The sequentially second article of Part II, 'Spracharbeit' [language work], dated 1925, is offered by Wagner as the opening piece with the title: 'Meaning Structures of Language'. It is already evident that Schutz's prior interest was in the nature of I–Thou relations, in social relations as inter-personal relations, and that the contexts in which he examined these relations derived from his initiation into, and reflection on, German art and culture. What gradually emerges from his musicological and literary studies (in the third component of Part II on Goethe) is a transference of interest in I–Thou relations from the field of cultural production to that of social construction.

Schutz begins 'Meaning Structures of Language' by distinguishing between two epistemological procedures. Empiricism has led to the formulation of propositions leading to the construction of sciences and 'up to recent times' (Schutz, ed. Wagner, 1982, 125) this same orientation has been adopted in the *Geisteswissenschaften* [sciences of mind]. Alternatively, however, there is an approach which recognizes the primacy of experience prior to conceptual formulations. Tacitly paraphrasing Bergson, Schutz claims that experience exists in 'pure duration'. It is organized by memory rather than concepts. It remains internal experience without any reference to external being until 'knowledge of the world outside of my duration' is executed by the 'acting I' through a process of symbolization. Such symbolization effects objectification. The novelty of this manuscript lies in Schutz's discussion of the function of language in effecting a transition from experiential solipsism to an understanding of objects. Although Schutz began by positing two forms of understanding, one involving empirical science and the other durational experience, the progression of his argument seems to imply that the former only becomes possible on the basis of the priority of the latter. Language mediates this developmental transition. As Schutz puts it, 'The world ... changes with name-giving and, further, with verbal communication' (Schutz, ed. Wagner, 1982, 128), or, again, 'the word governs the world by schematizing and re-forming it in a manner which is inaccessible to all other life forms' (Schutz, ed. Wagner, 1982, 129). The advent of language abolishes authenticity: 'From now on, I do no longer live in a world of *my* experiences but in the language world which is filled with plain experiences, with the experiences of everybody' (Schutz, ed. Wagner, 1982, 129). Although the word separates man from experience, it does nevertheless create 'a new world out of the ruins of experience' (Schutz, ed. Wagner, 1982, 130). Schutz argues that the main concern of philosophy 'for 2000 years' (Schutz, ed. Wagner, 1982, 130) has been to understand the relationship of words to things, and that modern philosophy is in this tradition in no longer having 'anything to do with *experience*' (Schutz, ed. Wagner, 1982, 130). Schutz suggests that modern philosophy supposes that cognition is possible 'in spite of the world of words' (Schutz, ed. Wagner, 1982, 130) but necessarily through it, without seeking to understand the nature of language as itself a life form. As Schutz puts it, the medium of words is a precondition which 'is definitely necessary but not at all self-understood' (Schutz, ed. Wagner, 1982, 131). Schutz does not want to question the value of the scientific superstructure, but, instead, he does seek to explore the process by which experience is translated into words.

The important point is that Schutz does not consider language as a vehicle which constitutes meaning but, rather, as itself a life form with its own meaning structure. He commends Cassirer's recent 'beautiful book' (the first volume on language of his *Philosophy of Symbolic Forms*, published in 1921), but insists that he is not attempting a comparable philosophy of language. Similarly, he insists that he is not attempting to establish a 'general grammar' in the way in which he supposes, in his first mention of Husserl, this had been attempted in his early *Logische Untersuchungen* [*Logical Investigations*]. Schutz claims that 'The principle of the theory of life forms states that real man necessarily lives in all life forms simultaneously' (Schutz, ed. Wagner, 1982, 131) and that it is only the development of symbolization that makes possible an analysis of the connectedness of 'life forms' and 'grammar'. In other words, Schutz is conscious that he is proposing to analyse language as an originary life form by using language in a way which is only possible in an advanced stage of its development. Schutz is attempting an analysis which is Bergsonian in that he is trying 'to imagine language in memory-endowed duration' where 'there are only perceptual images and memory images of qualitative experiences' (Schutz, ed. Wagner, 1982, 131). This undertaking aims at an understanding of the development of language prior to the language usages analysed phenomenologically by Husserl. For Schutz, the 'acting I' generates a 'temporal-spatial' world which is independent of my duration and the three main elements of every language – noun, adjective, verb – all relate to this 'acting I'.

Schutz seems clear that he is not concerned with logic, but less clear that it is as possible as he would wish to separate conceptual and experiential worlds. Indeed, he implies that language might constitute an autonomous sphere, neither constrained absolutely by experience nor concepts. Such a sphere might be the world of literary language, and it is therefore understandable that he next reflected on aspects of Goethe's creative production.

'Goethe: Novelle' is dated as 1925–26. Wagner gives 'Meaning Structures of Literary Art Forms' as his title for the piece because in fact it never reaches a discussion of Goethe's use of the novella, the story inserted into a novel. In the first sub-section of the manuscript Schutz reintroduces the theme mentioned at the end of his discussion of language. His comments on Goethe's work can only be tentative because criticism in respect of all literary work endeavours to use language to interpret one particular form of linguistic expression: 'Language analysis itself has to use the linguistic symbol system. Thereby, it begs the question' (Schutz, ed. Wagner, 1982, 159). The use of critical language is a barrier which prevents the reduction of meanings conveyed in literature ('the meaning of the spiritual world – as given in a literary work of art') to the 'original facts of experience'. There is the sense that the analytic use of language obstructs the encounter between Geist and experience. Schutz tacitly supposes that artistic expression is an expression *sui generis*. Works of art present themselves as intrinsically objective meanings to be interpreted by respondents rather than as objectifications constructed by subjective creators. In spite of the fact that literary works all deploy words, their objective presentations are differentiated according to genre. Schutz discusses the discrete characteristics of lyrical poetry, drama and narrative prose. Time is an important factor in distinguishing between literary forms. In Schutz's view, poetry 'transcends all time' (Schutz, ed. Wagner, 1982, 166), whereas drama operates in the present in direct encounter with the audience and narration always deploys the past tense. Additionally, Schutz suggests that the three literary forms of poetry, drama and the novel can be differentiated by their respective concentrations on 'expression', 'communication' and 'representation'. As representation, the novel is proximate to all other kinds of representative discourse, such as science. What distinguishes novelistic literary representation from other forms, therefore, is that it is offered within the 'symbol system of the work of art' rather than that of 'knowledge' (Schutz, ed. Wagner, 1982, 168). Schutz describes laws which have been prescribed historically for the production of art. He labels some of these 'style-immanent laws' (such as the unities of time and place in classical French drama) and some 'formal craft-rules' (such as perspective in post-fifteenth-century painting). These are historically contingent but he insists that 'In contrast to them, a group of essential laws of every species of art exist which can be demonstrated to be valid for any work of art beyond all limitations of period and area' (Schutz, ed. Wagner, 1982, 168).

Schutz calls these the 'meaning laws of the arts'. To qualify as such there needs to be a conjunction between the meanings of writers and listeners/readers. They are not reducible either to the intentions of writers or to the interpretations of readers. As Schutz states: 'The laws of meaning of literary creations transcend these two subjective and thereby real durations. They belong neither solely to the consciousness of the writer nor exclusively to that of the listener but to the objective context of language' (Schutz, ed. Wagner, 1982, 170).

Schutz seems uncertain whether his 'basic experience' is transcendentally and universally 'human' or whether it is constantly constituted and reconstituted in social engagement. Schutz advances his considerations in the context of German cultural history, discussing, in particular, the work of Goethe, Schiller and Lessing, but it is clear from his thinking about 'realism' that his analyses in terms of aesthetic theory have implications for his view of the relationship between the symbol system of everyday social life and that of the symbol system of the scientific knowledge of that life. The question is whether Schutz is able to transfer his geistlich [spiritual] assumptions about art derived from the German tradition of Geisteswissenschaft [science of the mind] and Kulturgeschichte [cultural history] to the sphere of the social sciences, whether there are there meaning laws which transcend the subordinate laws of 'immanent-style' and 'craft form'.

Wagner gives prime position in his edited volume as well as its overall title to the longest piece of the collection, which was also the latest to be written, dating it between 1925 and 1927. 'Lebensformen und Sinnstruktur' [life forms and meaning structure] moves away from aesthetic discussion to tackle the underlying philosophy of inter-personal relations. Schutz overtly expounds his position by reference to the thought of Bergson. He announces his fundamental orientation in his opening paragraph: 'My experiencing I is placed into the cosmos' (Schutz, ed. Wagner, 1982, 31). He embarks on an exploration of the 'basic experience' underlying all symbol systems. For Schutz, the 'I–Thou' relation is crucial because it is the existence of the 'Thou', other persons, in space and time, which forces the 'I' to relinquish its self-absorption in duration. Schutz is concerned with the unification of what might be called the subjective and the objective, the I and the Thou, and, additionally, he is intent on exploring how this unification can itself be the object of scientific understanding as opposed to experience. Schutz first discusses the passage from 'duration' to 'space-time'. He proposes 'to retrace the path from the inner experience of pure duration to the concept of space' by using Bergson's work.[4] This is a necessary exercise because it leads towards Schutz's goal – 'the grounding of the social sciences in the Thou experience' (Schutz, ed. Wagner, 1982, 34). Schutz emphasizes the primacy of experience in constituting science but he struggles with the problem of how to deploy conceptualization in his analysis of the relationship between experience and science without diminishing the experiential base. As he puts this: 'We will ask which method such a science would have to use in order to lift the irrational fundamental experience of the thou out of its own specific sphere and to transfer it into the rational realm of science without abandoning the circle of "symbols", to wit, the language-directed concepts of experience' (Schutz, ed. Wagner, 1982, 34).

Schutz's analytic practice formally reflects the process which he endeavours to explain. Understandably, therefore, the accounts of duration and memory which follow are representations of experience which do not engage explicitly

with competing scientific theories. These accounts 'follow the genial investigations of Bergson' (Schutz, ed. Wagner, 1982, 40), but Schutz contends that
they do not confront the problem of cognition and he explicitly states that
'Bergson tried to ignore the solution of the epistemological problem, in its
usual form' (Schutz, ed. Wagner, 1982, 41). By contrast, Schutz bypasses this
'usual form' so as to analyse the process which leads from experience to conceptualization: 'We are most of all interested in how and whereby the "appre-
hending" ... I or the I as such partakes in the outer world by creating or
acquiring concepts and language' (Schutz, ed. Wagner, 1982, 41–2).

If Bergson ignores the epistemological problem altogether, Schutz claims
that the work of Weber operates unsatisfactorily within an unexamined conceptual framework. In a section of recapitulation, Schutz suddenly announces
that the aim of his study is to investigate 'the methods of the sociology of
understanding' but to do so in a way, unlike that of Weber, which does not
presuppose the legitimacy of sociological enquiry. Weber 'had made this sociology into a science' but 'he did not find it necessary to say much about the
preconditions of his scientific undertaking' (Schutz, ed. Wagner, 1982, 42). In
brief, therefore, Schutz recognizes the shortcomings of the work of Bergson
and Weber without yet articulating that it is the work of Husserl which will
enable him to make connections between the phenomena which, respectively,
they interpret experientially and cognitively. Schutz states clearly that his study
'places a deliberately "pre-scientific" investigation of the experience of duration
and of meaning before the scientific-conceptual analysis of these contents as
objects of experience' (Schutz, ed. Wagner, 1982, 43).

Schutz argues that memory endows a range of meanings and these supplant
the apperceptive images of pure duration. The 'memory-endowed I' adds 'life
form' to its pure duration. He is then able to offer a table to convey 'the
bipolarity of the life forms'. The 'I in pure duration', for instance, is opposed
to the 'conceptual, logical I' and, 'free of meaning in itself prior to birth of
symbol', is opposed to 'complicated construction of meaning systems and dis-
solving of meaning systems in pure logic' (Schutz, ed. Wagner, 1982, 53). The
implication of this framework is that 'life forms' of all kinds are separations
from the primary experience of pure duration. These life forms all have their
particular meaning structures. Concept formation and logic are particular life
forms just as are drama, music, opera or poetry but, in other words, these
latter forms are not mediated by intellectuality. Schutz argues that we live 'in
all life forms simultaneously' (Schutz, ed. Wagner, 1982, 53) and that their
separation is only a heuristic device. One indication of the consequences of
this position is 'our inability to gain access to extended spiritual realms through
rational thinking as long as we bow to the primacy of conceptual thinking'
(Schutz, ed. Wagner, 1982, 53). There is an affinity between Schutz's position and Cassirer's philosophy of symbolic forms, but the crucial difference,
therefore, is that Schutz's life forms are all discrete divergences from pure

experience, whereas Cassirer's symbolic forms are socially constructed equivalents of Kantian categories of cognition.

Pursuing the notion of the role of action, Schutz distinguishes between the view of the world which it induces and the view induced by memory-endowed duration which had been the object of his enquiry to this point. He argues that 'in memory-endowed duration we can in no way assert that the quality experience "my hand" is particularly privileged in comparison to the quality experience "paper" or "pen"'. To recognize the distinctive awareness of 'my hand' we have to focus on the 'sphere of the acting I' (Schutz, ed. Wagner, 1982, 76). There is an 'I-consciousness of the body' which Schutz calls 'the somatic feeling of life'. '*This essence of feeling (esse) does not result in knowledge (cogito)*' (Schutz, ed. Wagner, 1982, 77). By exploring what happens when I 'lift my finger', Schutz, explicitly following Schopenhauer,[5] considers the extent to which this is an 'act of will' which implies correlation between physical impulse and consciousness. He later differentiates between involuntary and voluntary action and restricts his consideration of the acting I to reflection on intended action. Schutz wants to propose a distinction between the acting I and the I of ongoing experience but also to suppose the unity of the I. This means that he has to demonstrate that the I in action is a life form 'sui generis' which is not a function of consciousness but that, nevertheless, 'the unitary I, which exists, acts, and lives simultaneously in all these forms, becomes accessible to analysis only when we attempt a total synthesis of the living (*Lebendiges*)' (Schutz, ed. Wagner, 1982, 83).

The manuscript which Wagner edited breaks off shortly after this discussion. What we have of Schutz's reflections terminate *in medias res*. In general, however, it is possible to comment that the text assembled by Wagner as a book manifests a sequence of reflections. Initially, Schutz offered these reflections within the traditional discourse of aesthetic philosophy. However, in approaching a critique of Weber's sociology of understanding in the long text just discussed, Schutz appears to have recognized that he needed to consider questions related to the distinctive characteristics of different cultural forms in a manner which posed the problems pre-scientifically or, in other words, in a way which problematized the inherited conceptual traditions within which he was operating. As a consequence, the style of the 'Life Forms and Meaning Structure' text is radically exploratory. Schutz's discussion attempts to avoid discursive preconceptions. He advances his argument in a process of systematic introspection. Schutz's whole orientation, predicated on the detachment of conceptualization from experiential duration, derives from Bergson's *Matière et Mémoire*, but he does not often articulate his own position by engaging critically and intellectually with Bergson's philosophy. There are occasional references to other authors, such as Cassirer, Lask and Schopenhauer, but these are only incidental and subordinate to the main drift of the enquiry. Schutz does not want his 'pre-scientific' enquiry to be contaminated by existing discourses, either philosophical or scientific. Introversion is the basis of Schutz's project rather than engagement with other thinkers or with the findings of empirical social science. On the one occasion when Schutz refers to criticism of his thoughts which have been made 'from many quarters' (Schutz, ed. Wagner, 1982, 99), Wagner provides an editorial note to suggest that the statement hints at private discussions within the Geistkreis or Mises seminar circles. On several occasions Schutz illustrates his argument by allusion to personal experience, such as to his experience of anaesthesia as a child and his subsequent recollection of that experience in memory (Schutz, ed. Wagner, 1982, 62–3). There is, however, an underlying confidence that what he discloses in private and through self-absorption is revelatory of the universal human condition. The publication of his notes after his death endorses that confidence. By contrast, I suggest that we are able to use the publication of the notes to understand that they are evidence of Schutz's solipsistic mode of research. He advances a position which emphasizes the centrality of the I–Thou relationship but does so without allowing a Thou context external to his speculation to engage dialogically with his thinking. The Thou in his thinking is a projection of his I. The actual social context within which his thinking develops is eliminated. That thinking, therefore, is exposed as the product of the alienation of the milieu in which it was articulated. The question to be explored is how far Schutz's critique of Weberian sociology and his presentation of his ideas for the first time as a book to an extended public together contributed to a transformation of the solipsism of his preparatory notes.

'Toward a Viable Sociology'

Of the four lectures of 1928–29 given this general title in 1996 by the editors of Volume IV of Schutz's *Collected Papers*, only the first was given a title by Schutz himself. This was: 'Pragmatism and Sociology, better, the Social Sciences: On Scheler's Cognition and Work'.[6] Schutz's actual title suggests that he was pursuing his interest in the relation between everyday acting and the cognition belonging to the scientific attitude in respect of the sciences of social relations rather than yet in respect of the newly established discipline of 'sociology', and that he was doing this in response to Scheler's philosophical discussion of science and society rather than, yet, in response to Weber's sociological essays. The notes of the lecture show that Schutz was aware that Scheler distinguished between 'knowledge for the sake of knowing and knowledge for the sake of domination' (Schutz, ed. Wagner, Psathas and Kersten, 1996, 76), and he deduced that, for sociology, this corresponded respectively with a distinction between the scientific, 'value-free' orientation of the sociologist and the pragmatic, instrumentalist intentions of social actors. Schutz asks himself 'What is the relationship between social conduct (acting in the larger sense) to the knowledge of the actor?' (Schutz, ed. Wagner, Psathas and Kersten, 1996, 76), which means that he juxtaposes action, scientific knowledge and instrumental knowledge to ask what kind of knowledge is necessary to regulate behaviour. He comments that 'Understanding sociologists', among whom Weber would be counted, define social conduct as conduct oriented towards another person and therefore imply that we only have knowledge about others which is *relevant* for our own conduct. Their disposition is conducive to pragmatism. Schutz suggests that the 'problem of *relevance* is the fundamental problem of sociology' (Schutz, ed. Wagner, Psathas and Kersten, 1996, 76) because it raises the question whether the theoretical understanding of social behaviour in general is superfluous in relation to the practical understandings of actors of their own actions. In the notes for the three other lectures assembled as 'Toward a Viable Sociology' Schutz discusses the work of Leopold von Wiese[7] and considers the nature of mass, collective or group behaviour in relation to the individualistic emphasis of pragmatism. All that remains are fragments of thoughts, but Schutz appears to reject notions of collective consciousness. He resolutely insists that 'In contrast to the natural sciences, laws in the social and humanistic sciences are laws of meaning' because 'they occur in consciousness but not in <objective>[8] time' (Schutz, ed. Wagner, Psathas and Kersten, 1996, 79) and this rules out collective consciousness because 'mostly the behaviour of the mass is not related to meaning' (Schutz, ed. Wagner, Psathas and Kersten, 1996, 79). For Schutz, law formation in respect of social behaviour is integrally related to individual action rather than to objective law. He elaborates on the temporal dimension of projected action by reference to Husserl's work on inner time, but he still gives this a Bergsonian flavour by suggesting that 'perhaps all phenomena of understanding are of a pre-phenomenological nature because they belong to the pre-phenomenological consciousness of inner time (which alone conditions all seeing of essences)' (Schutz, ed. Wagner, Psathas and Kersten, 1996, 80).

It is apparent from these salvaged jottings of lectures given in the Mises seminar at the end of the 1920s that Schutz was preparing for a discussion of the meaning of the social world which would pursue his consideration of the relation between the life-world of primary experience and the meaning structure of art forms that he had examined earlier in the decade. The notes suggest that he did not accept the possibility that there could exist in societies a collective consciousness which would both represent individual meanings and also stand over and against them objectively. In *Der sinnhafte Aufbau der sozialen Welt* [the meaningful construction of the social world] Schutz turned his attention to Weber's solution of the problem which had been to regard 'ideal-types' as mediating concepts offering a bridge between the understanding of their own actions possessed by actors and the value-free analysis of those actions developed in detachment by social scientists. In a further piece published by the editors of Volume IV of Schutz's *Collected Works* – guidelines entitled 'Verstehen und Handeln' [understanding and acting] which Schutz had prepared for fellow members of the Mises seminar to stimulate discussion in June 1930 of a lecture he had given in May 1930 – Schutz's first paragraph indicates that his intention was to compare the nature of explanation in the social sciences with that in political economy. He had been making his argument within a context where members would be familiar with the debate about economic theory between classical economists and those associated with the rival German Historical and Austrian schools. Schutz's summary of the situation reflects his awareness of the contending positions. 'Like understanding sociology, history, and other social sciences', he begins, 'political economy claims that its subject matter is meaningful human action in the social world' (Schutz, ed. Wagner, Psathas and Kersten, 1996, 84). This is the contention of the Austrian school. 'Among these sciences', he continues, 'only political economy postulates "universally valid propositions"' (Schutz, ed. Wagner, Psathas and Kersten, 1996, 84). The purpose of his lecture had been to examine how this should be the case, whether or not the scientificities of sociology and political economy are analogous, and, he argues, this requires assessment of whether the 'intended meaning' in the social context predicated by Weber and 'understanding sociology' has the same character as the intended meaning posited by Austrian political economists. Quite specifically, Schutz was outlining the far-reaching significance of the attempt which he would shortly be making to examine the validity of the tenets of 'understanding sociology'. Schutz seems to accept that intended meanings correlate with meaning structures for economic agents in relation to economic behaviour in the same way as he had suggested they do for creative artists in relation to pre-existing art 'forms', but the question is whether that correlation is of the same kind when intended meanings and meaning structures are both identically *social*. In as much as Weber had in his career sought to transfer the methodology which he had acquired in economic research to the study of social relations, Schutz asks whether this was a legitimate intellectual move.

Der sinnhafte Aufbau der sozialen Welt

In his preface to *Der sinnhafte Aufbau der sozialen Welt*, dated March 1932, Schutz states that his study 'is based on an intensive concern of many years' duration with the theoretical writings of Max Weber' (Schutz, 1967, xxvii) and, in particular, on scrutiny of 'Weber's central concept of subjective meaning' (Schutz, 1967, xxvii) underpinning his 'understanding sociology'. Schutz's intention is to deploy the work of Bergson and Husserl on time to criticize Weber because 'only when we have grasped the nature of the internal time-consciousness can we attack the complicated structure of the concepts of the human sciences' (Schutz, 1967, xxvii).

In his first chapter Schutz explains that he is making a contribution to 'the controversy over the scientific character of sociology' (Schutz, 1967, 3) that had raged in Germany during the previous half century. As in his lectures to the Mises Circle, Schutz describes the controversy in part by referring somewhat ambivalently to the relative status of economic and sociological explanation: 'Can the history of man and his culture be reduced to laws such as those of economics?' followed by: 'Or, on the contrary, can we not say that so-called economic and sociological "laws" merely express the historical perspectives of the age in which they were formulated?' (Schutz, 1967, 4). Questions of this sort are the prelude to Schutz's initial representation of Weber's achievement. For Schutz, Weber was one of the first people to 'proclaim that the social sciences must abstain from value judgments' (Schutz, 1967, 5), must generate a science of society uncontaminated by political and moral ideologies. Weber attempted to carry out this scientification by 'reducing' (Schutz, 1967, 6) the objective world to the behaviour of individuals and by deploying theoretical constructs – 'ideal-types' – to disclose the ways in which the structure of the world is the product of the intended meanings of individuals. Schutz contends, however, that Weber's orientation was practical more than philosophical, with the result that he did not confront the epistemological difficulties of his methodology. Notably, Weber's insistence on scientific objectivity caused him to fail to recognize that scientists are themselves producers of intended meanings. As Schutz puts it, 'The structure of the social world is meaningful, not only for those living in that world, but for its scientific interpreters as well' (Schutz, 1967, 9). Social science is a constituting element in general social construction. The social scientist's contribution to social construction is based on 'systematizing scrutiny rather than that of living experience' (Schutz, 1967, 10) but the data on which systematizations are based derive ultimately from living experience. The consequence has been that levels of meaning or interpretation have developed such that scientists take these levels as their investigative starting-points without acknowledging the priority of their experiential origins: 'the problem of tracing back all the meaning-structures in question to a single basic element has hardly been acknowledged' (Schutz, 1967, 11). In other words, and in terms reminiscent of those already considered by Schutz in *Life World and Meaning Structures* in respect of art forms, social science has already constituted an autonomous meaning structure which is alienated from the life-world which itself possesses an intrinsic meaning structure which needs to be recovered. The question which Schutz poses, therefore, is an extension of the one asked – and unanswered –in the earlier work. Does the meaning structure of the social world have a priori status shaping the constructions of individuals in the same way as individual creativity is shaped by the rules of genres or forms of art (symbolic forms), or are those rules themselves contingently constructed, either only in the particular case of social meaning or in the case of all meaning structures?

The corollary of Schutz's interest was, of course, that he should attempt to explicate the character of social exchanges through precise observation of them rather than through engagement with current or past theoretical or empirical studies. The attraction of the works of Bergson and Husserl in guiding Schutz was that they differently sought to eliminate the intrusion of prior intellection on the observation of experience. The difference between the two was that Bergson emphasized the priority in experience of a non-human, biological, evolutionary force whereas Husserl proposed an anti-psychologistic scrutiny of the intentional engagement of transcendental egos with the phenomenal world as it presented itself to them. The shift which is apparent in *Der sinnhafte Aufbau der sozialen Welt* from the dominant influence of Bergson to that of Husserl reflects Schutz's inclination to retain commitment to an understanding of the life-world as a sphere of human agency. Schutz's book was not an attempt to produce a philosophical text but, rather, to produce a critique of the foundations of Weber's interpretative sociology which would enable better interpretative work to be undertaken. In his opening chapter Schutz outlines the steps to be taken in the following chapters to develop his argument. Without reference to 'science', chapter 2 is devoted to 'the way meaning is constituted in the individual experience of the solitary Ego' (Schutz, 1967, 13) of every and any person. Schutz announces that he will show how 'experience' is itself a construct, how 'the Ego constructs, out of its already lived-through stream of consciousness, a complex world of experience' (Schutz, 1967, 13). As it materializes, this chapter discusses Bergson's notion of duration rather than, as the wording of the English translation might suggest, the thinking of William James,[9] but the essential point is that Schutz argues that an external object 'is constituted out of appearances as we encounter them in our stream of consciousness. ... As they follow one another in regular sequence, our experience of the object is built up' (Schutz, 1967, 78–79). Schutz adheres to an associationist position which supposes that individual egos construct objectivities by aggregating atomistic appearances. This means that different people can fabricate different levels of meaning on the basis of the appearances which they encounter, whereas the Gestaltist position which he was to encounter in the work of Gurwitsch insisted that there are networks of meaning inherent in appearances such that individual meaning constructions are all modified by a pre-existing structure of meaning. The consequence of the position espoused by Schutz is that 'multiple realities' can be held by people as a consequence of their variable everyday need for levels of knowledge, whereas Gurwitsch insists that all knowledge is dependent on relations to prior 'fields' of knowledge which are potentially accessible to all. Schutz proposes that different levels of meaning are adopted by deploying different 'schemes' of understanding, but these are pragmatic rather than intrinsic schemes.

In summarizing his whole argument in his first chapter, Schutz next indicates that chapter 3 will 'make the transition from self-understanding to the understanding of others' (Schutz, 1967, 14) and that chapter 4 'will give an analysis of our knowledge of other persons and, on this basis, will present a general theory of the structure of the social world and thus of the proper subject matter of the social sciences' (Schutz, 1967, 14). Schutz announces that he will draw a 'radical contrast' between 'the understanding of one's associates and contemporaries ... and the construction of ideal types out of these', with the result that he will throw light on 'the difference between meaningful life in the social world and meaningful interpretation of that life through the social sciences' (Schutz, 1967, 14). What is left unannounced is whether these different meanings are of equal value. Schutz indicates that his final chapter (chapter 5) will analyse the basic concepts of interpretative sociology and show 'the mutually confirmatory character of Weber's categories' (Schutz, 1967, 15), but, without examining Schutz's detailed scrutiny of Weber, my purpose is to consider the implicit foundation of Schutz's critique.

Schutz begins chapter 3 by reaffirming what he had specified in a methodological appendix at the end of chapter 1 – that although he will carry out his study of internal time-consciousness 'within the "phenomenological reduction"' (Schutz, 1967, 43) the purpose of his work is to 'analyze the phenomenon of meaning to ordinary (*mundanen*) social life' (Schutz, 1967, 44) and this does not require recourse to phenomenological reduction. Schutz claims that the insights of eidetic reduction can be applied 'without risk of error' (Schutz, 1967, 44) to the phenomena of the natural attitude. Although he confines his analyses to the world of the natural attitude, Schutz specifies, as a proviso, that he is not presenting findings of empirical social psychology but, as a phenomenological psychologist, is seeking to find 'the invariant, unique, a priori structure of the mind, in particular of a society composed of living minds' (Schutz, 1967, 44). Schutz is suggesting a demarcation between the practice of philosophical phenomenology and the use of phenomenology to produce a more refined justification of interpretative sociology. In making this suggestion, Schutz tacitly accepts that meanings acquired at one level (the philosophical/ideational) have jurisdiction over meanings constructed in observation within the social world of the natural attitude (everyday knowledge) because they possess universal validity which is inaccessible for empirical enquiry. Schutz posits a hierarchy of structured meanings which is apparent socially within multiple varieties of operative 'realities'. He himself deploys philosophical access to a layer of meaning supposedly disclosing 'essences' and 'universals' to improve the methodology of sociology in its empirical attempt to understand the intentional behaviour of social agents. Schutz's thinking reflects the ambivalence of his position in Austria as both intellectual and banker and, as we shall see, additionally, in the United States, the ambivalence of his attempts to acquire intellectual authority in the fields of philosophy and social science. Schutz's reaffirmation of the position outlined in the appendix to chapter 1 at the beginning of the discussion of 'intersubjective understanding' in chapter 3 is very explicit:

> We are not going to be asking, therefore, how the Thou is constituted in an Ego, whether the concept 'human being' presupposes a transcendental ego in which the transcendental alter ego is already constituted, or how universally valid inter-subjective knowledge is possible. As important as these questions may be for epistemology and, therefore, for the social sciences, we may safely leave them aside in the present work. (Schutz, 1967, 98)[10]

There is a sense in which the intellectual dialogue which was to be pursued in the United States from 1939–59 between Schutz and Gurwitsch kept alive the debate between the philosophical and the sociological, and also a sense in which the position adopted by Gurwitsch fundamentally challenged Schutz's view that he could safely leave the important questions aside.

Schutz's Austrian texts of the late 1930s

In the late 1930s Schutz produced four manuscripts making a set entitled 'The Problem of Personality in the Social World'. A revised version of these was published as an article in the United States in 1945 as 'On Multiple Realities', and this version will be considered in the context of its publication, while keeping in mind the earlier date of its production, because it then became the subject of discussion between Schutz and Gurwitsch. As indicated above, Schutz only published a few articles or reviews in the period between the publication of *Der sinnhafte Aufbau der sozialen Welt* and his emigration to the United States. These require some brief comments because they shed further light on Schutz's reflections on the relative status of economics, sociology and philosophy.

In 1934, Schutz reviewed von Mises's *Grundprobleme der Nationalökonomie* [basic problems of political economy], published in Jena in 1933, which assembled a collection of articles. Schutz summarizes Mises' intention, which had been both to offer a liberal critique of Marxist theories of society and to develop a theory of rational action which was opposed to theories of social and economic behaviour associated with the German tradition of Geisteswissenschaften [cultural sciences] as well as those which embraced the naturalist tendency to treat the social sciences as natural sciences. According to Mises we do not understand the relationship, for instance, between means and ends in choosing our economic or social actions on the basis of our experience, but by recognizing a priori truths analogous to those of mathematics or logic. Schutz argues that Mises was correct in agreeing with Weber in rejecting the hermeneuticism of the cultural science tradition and the scientism of the naturalist tradition, but wrong in supposing that Weber was mistaken in challenging the primacy of purposive economic action in dictating social behaviour. For Mises, causal sociological explanations are subordinate to a priori economic laws, whereas Schutz was disposed to agree with the implication of Weber's work which recognized the relative autonomy of the sociological as a consequence of its recognition of non-rational influences on social behaviour. Although he recognizes the lucidity of Mises's discussions, Schutz defends Weber and, by implication, asserts the validity of his own refinement of Weber's 'understanding sociology' when he comments that 'one must warn against the misunderstanding that the sociology of understanding, as established by Max Weber, renounces genuine sociological comprehension and therefore is not a theoretical science' (Schutz, ed. Wagner, Psathas and Kersten, 1996, 92).

In an essay of 1936, Schutz responded to a lecture given that year in Vienna by von Hayek on '*Wesen und Wirtschaft*' [knowledge and economics]. Entitled *Nationalökonomie. Verhalten des Menschen im sozialen Leben* [political economy. Human conduct in social life], Schutz's essay was circulated between friends, including Mises, Machlup and Kaufmann, but it was not published in spite of the fact that Hayek invited Schutz to submit it in translation for his journal, *Economica*. Schutz again took the opportunity to examine the relationship between abstract concepts of economic theory such as 'equilibrium' and the social economy of exchange, between 'objective' and 'subjective' explanations of economic behaviour, suggesting that the emphasis of the subjective implied a recognition of the explanatory primacy of the social over reference to abstract economistic laws. Schutz argues that Austrian economics escaped 'the sad fate which ... befell the theory of pure law' (Schutz, ed. Wagner, Psathas and Kersten, 1996, 96) by insisting that economic theory relates to individual actions, but he discusses attitudes to 'data' to make his point that, nevertheless, Austrian economics was wrong to suppose that theoretical economic explanation operates on a 'higher' level than ordinary experience. Rather, for Schutz, it offers one response to phenomena among a plurality of possible responses. He insists that 'neither I nor you nor anyone in the fullness of his existence is identical with those subjects of economic life of which economists speak' and that, to that extent, in economic theory 'a fictive world comes into existence alongside the actual world' (Schutz, ed. Wagner, Psathas and Kersten, 1996, 99). The complication for social scientists is that in some circumstances they find themselves constructing objective data 'with those phenomena that are given as "data" to actors whom they observe in the social world' (Schutz, ed. Wagner, Psathas and Kersten, 1996, 97) with the result that the fictive and actual worlds are indistinguishable. Schutz insists, following Weber, that in this situation 'the social scientist is and remains *observer* of the social world' (Schutz, ed. Wagner, Psathas and Kersten, 1996, 101) and must advance his interpretation of it in terms of the logic of his fictive typification without modifying it in reaction to his engagement with it. There are no a prioristic laws of social behaviour but functional typifications which, like the principle of marginal utility in economic theory, maintain internal coherence. Schutz concludes by asking whether this means 'that what economists do is nothing but a figment of their imagination and that it is thus without any connection with the realities of daily life?' (Schutz, ed. Wagner, Psathas and Kersten, 1996, 105). His assertion about economic theory would also represent his view of objective sociology. He asserts that 'adequately modified, the propositions of political economy are valid in economic reality' (Schutz, ed. Wagner, Psathas and Kersten, 1996, 105) and, therefore, are pragmatically effective for securing 'the comprehension and control of economic life' (Schutz, ed. Wagner, Psathas and Kersten, 1996, 105).

In this discussion paper stimulated by Hayek's lecture, Schutz makes only brief, passing reference to the relevance of the work of Husserl for his understanding of the everyday world of social experience. Schutz's 1937 review of Otaka's *Grundlegung der Lehre vom sozialen Verband* [foundation of the theory of social organization], which amalgamated the influence of Kelsen and Husserl, enabled him to escape from defining his position primarily in reaction to his mentors in the field of Austrian economic theory. As represented by Schutz, Otaka derived from Kelsen the view that social organization is a product of the mind and from Husserl the inclination to examine how, in general, ideal objects become actualized, or, to put this in the terminology used by Schutz in response to Hayek, how subjective, fictive constructs become actualized as objective facts. Schutz criticizes Otaka for having considered only Husserl's early work rather than the more recently apparent 'constitutive thematic of phenomenology' (Schutz, ed. Wagner, Psathas and Kersten, 1996, 211). The consequence is that Otaka emphasized the noematic aspect of the noetic–noematic correlation. Schutz summarizes Otaka as arguing that 'as long as sociology only has its eye on the multiplicity of actualities founding the ideal object, "Social Organization", it must as a consequence be led to deny the identically existing social organization' (Schutz, ed. Wagner, Psathas and Kersten, 1996, 212–13). Schutz quotes Otaka's view that turning attention away from 'the founding multiplicities to the founded unity and identity of the ideal object' (Otaka, 1932, 92, quoted in Schutz, ed. Wagner, Psathas and Kersten, 1996, 213) gives access to the true and actual nature of social organization. Schutz agrees here with Otaka that a sociology of the natural attitude cannot clarify empirically the nature of the state or of social organization, but he contests Otaka's recourse to a phenomenological analysis which retains elements of idealism. Instead, Schutz suggests that what Otaka 'calls "material" mental formation as well as "social mental formation" have their founding actuality in previous social actions' (Schutz, ed. Wagner, Psathas and Kersten, 1996, 214). Schutz accuses Otaka of explicitly approaching Spann's 'universalistic conception of society' (Schutz, ed. Wagner, Psathas and Kersten, 1996, 217) and, therefore, of supporting his contention that the universal 'stands over against the particular in a relationship of domination' entailing 'government and administration, coercion and enforcement' (Schutz, ed. Wagner, Psathas and Kersten, 1996, 217).

Published a year before the Anschluss and Schutz's enforced flight from Austria, Schutz's defence in this review of a phenomenologically constitutive understanding of the multiplicity of actualities involved in the process of defining state authority is an implicit critique of the theories of the state underpinning the power of Hitler. It is the first suggestion that his phenomenological critique of 'understanding sociology' implies a democratic political philosophy. On settling in the United States, Schutz used his association with the phenomenological movement as an entrée into American academic circles. As we shall see, he gradually used the position which he acquired philosophically to pursue his critique of sociology of the natural attitude and to advance the acceptance of sociological analysis as one discourse among many discourses of social understanding within a democratic society. His engagement with the thinking of Aron Gurwitsch enabled him to pursue the noetic/noematic debate and its political consequences which he articulated in reply to Otaka.

Summary

Schutz's early thinking was influenced by the disruption of the hierarchical social order of the Hapsburg Empire and its replacement by an Austrian Republic; by the influence of the Austrian school of economics; by his alienation as a Jew; by his schooling at a 'Gymnasium' with a classical curriculum; by his membership of several private circles of liberal intellectuals (although not 'the' Vienna Circle of Carnap and Neurath and the logical positivists); and by the fact that he was a 'part-time' intellectual. As a banker in his day job, he was part of 'everyday' Vienna except for his evening participation in the coffee-house circles. Schorske's account of the fin-de-siècle phenomenon explains the surge in creativity in terms of the disaffection of a new, young generation from the liberal values of their parents (see Schorske, 1979). Freud's notion of the Oedipus complex articulated the grounds for this disaffection at the time and offers endorsement of Schorske's post hoc social psychological interpretation. Schorske's concern, however, was mainly with the generation which had reached maturity by the date of Schutz's birth in 1899. Wagner seems closer to the mark when he describes Schutz's 'estrangement' on his return from serving in the war, but this retains a sense of psychological maladjustment. I prefer to suggest that, as a second-generation young Viennese person, Schutz was alienated from his social and political environment. That alienation manifested itself in an intellectual detachment which was made operationally possible as a consequence of his non-academic employment. These were the conditions which enabled Schutz to develop a refinement of Weber's 'verstehende' sociology (which attempts to understand social actions from the point of view of the actors), analysing social relations without himself engaging with political contexts of social action. Gustav Mahler (1860–1911) once said: 'I am thrice homeless. As a Bohemian among Austrians, as an Austrian among Germans, as a Jew throughout the world. Everywhere an intruder, never welcomed' (Mahler-Werfel, 1946, 89–90, quoted in Field, 1967, 8). I suggest that Schutz's focus on the analysis of inter-personal relations was a refuge from a confrontation with the challenge social democratically to establish a new kind of state organization.

One of the mentors acknowledged by Schutz – Hans Kelsen – thought that any recourse to state authority as guarantor of legality was analogous with recourse to metaphysical or religious moral imperatives as a basis for guiding behaviour. State and legal authority are unified and both are established through mutually supporting procedures of party politics and political representation. The state is not above the law but, equally, the law enshrines positivist values which are immanent rather than transcendent. Kelsen's theory emphasized the importance of constitutions and his theoretical work had direct implications for the development of the state within which he was working. It was logical that he should be invited to be a member of the committee which drew up the constitution of the new Austrian Republic in 1920. Kelsen's was a social democratic position and he was increasingly in conflict with the German proponent of a contrary, authoritarian position – Carl Schmitt. Through the 1920s, Kelsen published more than six major texts, all concerned with the nature of democracy and the relations between society, law and the state. In 1929/30, he moved to Cologne and, in that time, opposed Schmitt's theoretical justification of the modifications introduced to the original constitutions of both the Austrian and the German republics.

Schmitt's *Der Begriff des Politischen* [the concept of the political], published in Munich in 1932,[11] opened with the statement that 'The concept of the state presupposes the concept of the political' (Schmitt, 2007, 19 [1932]), that is to say that there are essential characteristics of politics which transcend the constitutive actions of state members. We have seen that, in his earliest work, Schutz grappled with the problem whether the meanings of works of art derive essentially from the characteristics of distinct art forms or are constituted by individual creators. He proceeded to transpose this question to ask whether social relations are regulated by discrete laws. Influenced by the economists of the 'Austrian school', Schutz resisted the notion that there might be abstract laws of social behaviour analogous with those supposed by some to be in operation in economic behaviour. Like them, Schutz emphasized the primacy of individual *action* but this emphasis was predicated on a taken-for-granted view of the identities of selves and others as universal rather than as relationally or dialogically constituted socially. Schutz's *Der sinnhafte Aufbau der sozialen Welt* [the meaningful construction of the social world], published in 1932 while he was still in Austria, was an attempt to understand how individuals themselves construct meanings in opposition to Weber's methodological imposition of sociologically explanatory 'ideal-types', but Schutz did not entertain the possibility that these meaning-constructing selves might be socially constituted. In short, Schutz contrived to analyse the 'self' in 'society' while retaining both the idea of a transcendent self and the idea of an autonomous, a-political, social sphere.

Notes

1 Early in his life Schutz dropped the umlaut in his surname and I have followed this throughout.
2 1929 according to Wagner, but 1927 according to Barber.
3 See pp. 20–8.
4 Schutz specifies that he is using Bergson's ideas 'especially as formulated in his later writings', which presumably means *L'Évolution créatrice* [creative evolution] (1907) rather than the publications of the 1890s.
5 Schopenhauer, *Die Welt als Wille und Vorstellung*, 1818.
6 'Pragmatismus und Soziologie, besser Sozialwissenschaften: Zu Scheler, Erkenntnis und Arbeit'. The full title of Scheler's essay was: 'Erkenntnis und Arbeit. Eine Studie über Wert und Grenzen des pragmatischen Motivs in der Erkenntnis der Welt' [cognition and work. A study of value and limits of the pragmatic motive in cognition of the world], first published in his *Die Wissensformen und die Gesellschaft* [forms of knowledge and society] in 1926.
7 Leopold von Wiese (1876–1969).
8 The markings indicate that this word was interpolated by Wagner.
9 As we shall see in chapter 3, Schutz consciously related his thinking to that of James when he was seeking to assimilate his 'continental' phenomenological thinking to the American tradition in the early 1940s.
10 It should be noted that this passage attracts the comment from the editors of the English translation that 'This paragraph is an adaptation'.
11 This was originally published in 1927 in *Archiv für Sozialwissenschaft und Sozialpolitik*, 58, 1, 1–33.

2

Gurwitsch in Germany and France, 1901–38

This chapter offers a brief outline of Gurwitsch's career in the first half of his life and then considers in detail the texts, published and unpublished at the time, which he produced in this period. It concludes with a summary of the correlations between these social and intellectual trajectories, both in relation to the early period in Germany and to the 1930s in France.

The career

Aron Gurwitsch was born in Vilnius in Lithuania in January 1901. There were rabbis in the background on both sides of his family. After the pogroms of 1905–6, the family moved to Danzig. Gurwitsch attended the Städtliches Gymnasium there from 1907 until 1919, where 'he studied mathematics and history, as well as English, German, French, Greek and Latin' (Gurwitsch, ed. Huertas-Jourda, 2002, 14). In 1919 he began to study Philosophy and German Literature at the University of Berlin. He was admitted to a seminar of Carl Stumpf, who then supervised his work in philosophy and psychology. Gurwitsch studied physics with Max Planck and philosophy with Alois Riehl as well as Stumpf. It was Stumpf who suggested that Gurwitsch should go to Freiburg to hear Husserl, and he attended Husserl's course there on 'Natur und Geist' [nature and spirit].[1] Stumpf also sent Gurwitsch to Frankfurt to work with two of his students – Kurt Goldstein and Adhémar Gelb – in the Institut zur Erforschung der Folgeerscheinungen von Hirnverletzungen [Institute for Research into the Consequences of Brain Injuries] which they had founded in 1916. Goldstein had been appointed Professor of Neurology at Frankfurt in 1923. He moved to a Chair in Neurology at the University of Berlin in 1930. The work which he undertook with Gelb was to lead to the publication of *Der Aufbau des Organismus. Einführung in die Biologie unter besonderer Berück-sichtigung der Erfahrungen am kranken Menschen* [*The Organism: A Holistic Approach to Biology Derived from Pathological Data in Man*] which Goldstein wrote in Amsterdam in 1934 after he had been forced to leave Germany. It was Gold-stein who, in 1928, invited Gurwitsch to attend the conference at Davos which became famous for the debate which occurred there between Cassirer and Heidegger. At Davos, Gurwitsch also heard Piaget and met Nikolai Hartmann and Lucien Lévy-Bruhl.

In a curriculum vitae which he supplied to Schutz in 1948 with a view to gaining employment in the New School for Social Research in New York, Gurwitsch recalled that he passed his doctoral examination at Göttingen, where he had been supervised by Moritz Geiger, with a thesis on philosophy which 'concerned relations between phenomenology and Gestalt theory' (Grathoff, ed., 1989, 104–5). He added that he had also been examined in mathematics and physics. According to Grathoff, Gurwitsch had wanted to be supervised by Scheler for his doctoral dissertation but had been prevented by Scheler's death (in May 1928) (Grathoff, ed., 1989, xx). Gurwitsch received his doctorate on 1 August 1928 (see Gurwitsch, ed. Métraux, 1979, ix). The precise title of the dissertation was: 'Phänomenologie der Thematik und des reinen Ich. Studien über Beziehungen von Gestalttheorie und Phänomenologie' [phenomenology of thematics and of the pure ego. Studies of the relation between Gestalt theory and phenomenology].[2] He embarked on a project for a Habilitation thesis which pursued a problem he had identified in Part IV of his doctoral dissertation. In April 1929 Gurwitsch married Alice Stern after, according to Embree, she had returned from Palestine, 'where she participated in the kibbutz movement' (Gurwitsch, ed. Huertas-Jourda, 2002, 18). According to Grathoff, she 'was engaged in Zionist youth work ... in Frankfurt, where she met Aron' (Grathoff, ed., 1989, xxxv). While in Frankfurt, Gurwitsch con-tributed regularly to the 'Frankfurter Israelitische Gemeindeblatt' [the Frankfurt Israeli community news-sheet].

In the spring of 1929, Gurwitsch, with the support of Husserl and Hart-mann, gained a research grant from the Prussian Ministry of Education and he and his wife moved to Berlin. There Gurwitsch wrote his Habilitation thesis, entitled *Die mitmenschlichen Begegnungen in der Milieuwelt* [Human Encounters in the Social World]. The thesis was not published in Gurwitsch's lifetime,[3] but Embree mentions four articles published in German journals from 1930 to 1933 which suggest the diversity of his interests at this time.[4] In these years, Gurwitsch importantly published, in 1932, a review in the *Deutsche Literaturzei-tung* of Husserl's 1930 'epilogue' to his *Ideen zu einer reinen Phänomenologie und phänomenologischer Philosophie*, vol. I [ideas of a pure phenomenology and phe-nomenological philosophy, vol. I] of 1913 (Gurwitsch, 1932). In December 1931, Gurwitsch enclosed an almost complete copy of the thesis in a letter to Max Dessoir.[5] He had already much earlier sent a copy to Husserl, who began to read it at the very end of 1929.[6] Gurwitsch and Husserl were in occasional correspondence between 1930 and 1932. By 1932, Gurwitsch was already exploring the idea of leaving Germany because of the political situation. He tried to obtain a grant from the Rockefeller Foundation and Husserl drafted a letter of support[7] in November/December, 1932, but the application did not materialize or was unsuccessful. Instead, Gurwitsch applied for a French visa. He arrived in Paris in April 1933, without having achieved his Habilitation as a consequence of the collapse of the jury with the arrival to power of National Socialism on 30 January 1933.

With the intellectual support of Alexandre Koyré, Lucien Lévy-Bruhl[8] and Léon Brunschvicg,[9] and with financial assistance from America, Gurwitsch was appointed as a lecturer at the Institut d'Histoire des Sciences et des Techniques, which was affiliated with the Sorbonne. Although Gurwitsch only previously knew Koyré and Lévy-Bruhl, Embree comments that the centralization of the French intellectual world in Paris meant that he quickly became acquainted with relevant people in this field (Gurwitsch, ed. Huertas-Jourda, 2002, 23).

Gurwitsch's first series of lectures was entitled 'Le développement historique de la Gestaltpsychologie' [the historical development of Gestalt psychology]. These six lectures, given in 1933–34, led to his first published article in French (Gurwitsch, 1934) and to two subsequent articles of 1936 (Gurwitsch, 1936b and 1936c). Gurwitsch gave his second course at the Sorbonne in 1934–35 on 'intentionalist psychology'[10] and, the following year (1935–36), the third on the work of Goldstein and Gelb. His interest in the psychology of language led to his second French publication – a review of *Psychologie du langage* published in 1935 (Gurwitsch, 1935). This was followed by an article in which Gurwitsch discussed Delacroix's views on the acquisition of language (Gurwitsch, 1936a). The outcomes from his lectures on Goldstein and Gelb were slightly delayed. They led to two articles specifically discussing the work of Goldstein (Gurwitsch, 1939 and 1940a).[11] Lester Embree has retrieved an article entitled 'Quelques principes fondamentaux de la phénoménologie constitutive' [some fundamental principles of constitutive phenomenology] which Gurwitsch wrote in 1937 for publication in *Recherches philosophiques*, a journal which folded before the article could appear (Gurwitsch, ed. Huertas-Jourda, 2002, Appendix III), and also the text of the last lecture which Gurwitsch gave in Paris, entitled 'Phénoménologie des signaux et des significations' [phenomenology of signs and meanings] (Gurwitsch, ed. Huertas-Jourda, 2002, Appendix IV). These are significant additions to the retrieval (derived from 233 pages of typescript) undertaken by José Huertas-Jourda and Lester Embree of the text of the course of lectures given by Gurwitsch between February and April 1937 to which they have given the title *Esquisse de la phénoménologie constitutive* (Gurwitsch, ed. Huertas-Jourda, 2002).

Gurwitsch's last intellectual activity in Paris was the writing of what was to be published in English in 1940 as 'On the Intentionality of Consciousness' (in Farber, ed., 1940, 65–83). The German attack on Belgium and Holland began on 10 May 1940. The Gurwitsches fled on 19 May 1940 as German troops approached Paris. They managed to get a crossing from Le Havre to New York, securing berths on the strength of an invitation for a one-year lectureship at the Johns Hopkins University.

Gurwitsch's early thought

The account which David Hume gave in his *Enquiry Concerning Human Understanding* (1748) of our belief that the sun will rise tomorrow was an important moment in the history of Western European philosophy. He contended that our belief is the consequence of accumulated experience ('custom' or 'habit') rather than of rationality. This contention was not restricted to phenomena of temporal change, nor was it subjectivist. In the last sentence of Section V, Hume generalized his position and suggested that there might be some unknown correlation between objective phenomena and our perceptions of them.

Lester Embree relates the story of how Gurwitsch came to the attention of Carl Stumpf while he was a student at the University of Berlin: '[Gurwitsch] asked how Hume could know that an idea was fainter than the corresponding impression unless the impression was preserved or reactivated for the comparison. Stumpf remarked that this was indeed a genuine problem and thereafter took a special interest in Gurwitsch' (Gurwitsch, ed. Embree, 1972, xvii–xviii).

It is possible to suggest, therefore, that Gurwitsch's reflections from that early date were shaped by the problem highlighted by Hume and imported to the German tradition by Kant in his scrutiny of the relation between empirical and a priori knowledge: how to account for and recognize the persistence of knowledge beyond the immediate effects of sense impressions. Gurwitsch's exploration of this problem was pursued at first philosophically in a mode of thinking derived from Stumpf and developed under the influence of Husserl, but subsequently he drew upon his observations of the practice of Gelb and Goldstein in experimental physiology.

Doctoral dissertation, 1929

From the outset, Gurwitsch indicates that the discussion in his dissertation is defined by the prior work of Husserl. Gurwitsch's essay 'will be phenomenology in the sense established by the *Ideen*' (Gurwitsch, 1966a, 175), or, again, 'as far as the orientation and problems of this essay are concerned, we shall not go beyond the *Ideen*' (Gurwitsch, 1966a, 175). The 'orientation' of the essay is in accord with phenomenological 'reduction', and the main 'problem' is concerned with the question of 'intentionality' on the grounds that this is 'the general theme of phenomenology and psychology' because it is 'intentionality' which 'grants to consciousness its specific sense, denoting the fundamental component of the essence, "consciousness-at-large"' (Gurwitsch, 1966a, 175). In other words, Gurwitsch follows Husserl in wanting to carry out a rigorously scientific analysis of consciousness in itself, neither as an expression of individual psychological dispositions nor as a reflection of an external reality. This involved an intermediary position which accepts that inherent in consciousness is the defining element which is that all consciousness is consciousness *of* something ('intentionality'). In simpler language, Gurwitsch proceeded to specify the questions which concerned him:

> As does the *Ideen*, so the present essay begins with pure consciousness in the form of the cogito; something is given to me; I am presented with, or confronted by, something objective. The inquiry is dedicated to the cogito and its noematic correlates. What does it mean that something objective is given? What is, in every case, the given? And what do changes in the cogito signify? (Gurwitsch, 1966a, 176)

Gurwitsch's intention was to remain faithful to Husserl's work while seeking to develop it and, in some respects, modify it. He considered that he was able to carry out this intention by introducing lines of thought derived from Gestalt theory. Gurwitsch calls the 'something' with which consciousness is always concerned its 'theme'. He then summarizes Husserl's view that '*cogitationes*' are 'specific acts of the ego' but that, in spite of this variation in modes of ego correlative with different forms of cogitation, it is 'always one and the same identical pure ego which lives in respectively varying modes' (Gurwitsch, 1966a, 178). Gurwitsch quotes from Husserl: 'The noematic content remains identically the same over against "mere alterations in the distribution of attention and its modes"' (Gurwitsch, 1966a, 180). In short, Gurwitsch's dissertation gives detailed consideration of Husserl's understanding of the place of the ego in the relationship between 'noesis' and 'noema', where the former is the meaning-giving element of the act and the latter is the meaning given in the act. As Gurwitsch concluded his introductory remarks, his essay was concerned above all 'with the egological interpretation of the cogito and the attentional, as well as with the conception which sees a "primal source of generations" in the pure ego, emphasizing its spontaneity' (Gurwitsch, 1966a, 180).

The dissertation is divided into four sections. Section I is concerned with the structure of the 'theme'. It asks what it means 'to say of something given that it forms our theme' (Gurwitsch, 1966a, 181). Importantly, this is a phenomenological question. 'Theme' and 'object' are not synonymous. Gurwitsch is concerned with the theme 'only *so far as* it is presented to consciousness' (Gurwitsch, 1966a, 183).

Gurwitsch's early formulation of his position has to be examined further precisely because what is at issue, here in relation to psychology but later in relation to other human and social sciences as well as natural sciences, is the nature of the distinctively different explanatory endeavour of phenomenological analysis as compared with the analyses of the sciences of the 'natural attitude'.

Having clarified the status of his examination of themes rather than objects, in Section II Gurwitsch argues that themes are always presented in a privileged domain in association with 'co-given' themes which are always 'also there'. Gurwitsch illustrates his argument with easy examples. Our attention may be primarily focused on an inkwell on our desk but, co-given, might also be the view out of the window beyond the desk. Equally, we may have co-given memories of previous occasions when we sat at a desk. 'The domain of the co-given comprises an enormous variety and heterogeneity' (Gurwitsch, 1966a, 197) and Gurwitsch sets himself the task of differentiating between characteristics of the domain. He first considers the temporal and then the spatial impacts of the co-given. Although Gurwitsch does not yet use the term, the important point is that co-givens are 'constitutive'.

Questions then arise about the influence of co-givens in relation to the dominant theme and also about the relative influence of different co-givens. Gurwitsch concludes that 'the fundamental distinction must be drawn between that which "belongs to my theme" and determines my attitude and that which does not belong to it' (Gurwitsch, 1966a, 201). Gurwitsch calls the former the 'thematic field' and insists that 'The relation of theme to thematic field is reciprocal; it is a correlation' (Gurwitsch, 1966a, 206). Hence 'the inkwell looks differently on the desk than when I put it on the piano' (Gurwitsch, 1966a, 206). This is because it 'is not found in its authentic milieu' (Gurwitsch, 1966a, 206), to which Gurwitsch adds the footnote that 'the concept of the "authentic milieu" of a thing is to be distinguished from that of its "natural surroundings"' (Gurwitsch, 1966a, 206). This remark, made in passing, is important because, in his subsequent writing, the distinction forms the basis for a differentiation between 'communities' and 'societies'. For the moment, Gurwitsch emphasizes that, in spite of the reciprocity between theme and thematic field, 'the theme – understood as always in the noematic sense – remains *the same in strict identity*' (Gurwitsch, 1966a, 207). He designates this peculiar nature of the theme as its 'consistency'. Gurwitsch argues that cogivens have an intrinsic coherence which he calls their 'inner bearing'. They are not random aggregates of elements. They have a 'Gestalt connection'. Nevertheless, he distinguishes between two forms. Some constituents of a theme are 'formed', by which he means that they have no independence, being wholly defined by the Gestalt within which they are located, whereas others are 'formative' or, perhaps, created. The main issue is that of the consistency of the theme. As Gurwitsch states, 'The independence of the theme from the field is not absolute' (Gurwitsch, 1966a, 210). If it were, the field would just be superadded and not at all integral. The consequence, as Gurwitsch elaborates, is that 'A given theme does not fit into just any thematic field; the thematic field belonging to an artistic object appropriately contains artistic objects; to a mathematical proposition belongs a mathematical horizon, and not just any set of mathematical objects can suitably function as horizon of a certain theorem' (Gurwitsch, 1966a, 211).

In making the point here that 'themes' are not limitlessly transferable between 'thematic fields', Gurwitsch suggests that the limitations relate to the fact that there are 'material' (sachlich) bonds between fields and themes. The limitations relate to the sense of things and not to any 'horizon of originarity'. It was this latter notion which led Husserl to suppose that in some way the transcendent ego defines the scope of possible cognitive combinations. In the introductory summary of his dissertation Gurwitsch had quoted passages from both Husserl's *Ideas* and his *Logical Investigations* which suggested that 'attentional modifications' to intentionality could be considered to have 'the *character of subjectivity*' (Gurwitsch, 1966a, 179). Gurwitsch returns to this question in detail towards the end of Section II. He summarizes Husserl's view that the cogito is a distinctive 'mode of performance'. Although Gurwitsch has been discussing the notions of 'theme' and 'thematic field' in relation to cognition as a convenience for his presentation while acknowledging that intention occurs similarly in perception generally, he now confronts an interpretation of Husserl which indicates that cognition is distinctively different as a form of specifically attentional intentionality. Here Gurwitsch explicitly takes issue with Husserl's view or, rather, he aligns himself with the position that he takes Husserl to have advanced in the first edition of *Logical Investigations*, in opposition to the one he takes Husserl to have adopted later in *Ideas*. He identifies Husserl's position in *Logical Investigations* as having been a polemical stance against 'Natorp and the Kantian Ego of the "pure apperception"' (Gurwitsch, 1966a, 215) but he finds it convincing because it corresponds 'more adequately to the phenomenological findings than do the descriptions in the *Ideen* where each act is presented as an act of the ego' (Gurwitsch, 1966a, 215). Gurwitsch suggests that Natorp 'was not without influence as to Husserl's position in the *Ideen*' (Gurwitsch, 1966a, 215) and hence it is possible to suggest that Husserl's *Ideas* bears the marks of some contamination by Marburg Neo-Kantianism.

In short, Gurwitsch was driven to the conclusion that, in *Ideas*, Husserl had reneged on the disposition expressed in the *Logical Investigations*, to subject everything, including the 'pure ego', to phenomenological scrutiny. In Section III, therefore, Gurwitsch set himself the task of analysing 'attentional modifications' in an exclusively phenomenological manner, exactly as he had already endeavoured to consider 'thematic modifications'. In Gurwitsch's view, Husserl considered synthesized consciousness to be a step change at the end of a process of synthetic addition, whereas Gurwitsch wants to deploy Gestalt thinking to argue that synthesized consciousness is categorally different. Gurwitsch deploys Gestalt thinking to counter what he takes to be the vestiges of traditional associationist psychology in Husserl's phenomenology. He summarizes his view clearly in an important passage:

> Every act of consciousness as a real psychological event is a noesis to which corresponds a noema as its intentional correlate. The concept of intentionality refers to this relation between noesis and noema. It designates the peculiar nature of the noesis, which is to be in correspondence with a noema, in such a way that one and the same noema can belong to a plurality of noeses. Indeed, the noema is ideal, atemporal and reiterable, while the mental states as events of consciousness are temporal and, on that account, can never recur, once they have passed. (Gurwitsch, 1966a, 257)

In section IV of the dissertation, Gurwitsch finally offers his outline of a 'phenomenology of the pure ego'. He first suggests that there is a category of the co-given in consciousness in addition to what he has already called the 'thematic field'. He calls this category 'marginal consciousness' and he particularly explores the status of 'marginal memories'. He gives a simple example: 'I go to a city in which I have already been before; standing in front of a building, I remember having already seen it, and the remembrance of my previous seeing is the co-given potential theme' (Gurwitsch, 1966a, 273).

As this example suggests, Gurwitsch is able to conclude that 'To every past experience, however remote, belongs a chain of mental states terminating in the Now and comprising the former as a member' (Gurwitsch, 1966a, 274). The importance of this temporal dimension of the marginal consciousness for Gurwitsch becomes clear when he asserts that 'The phenomenologically reduced pure ego is nothing but the chain along which all experiences are ordered and which terminates in the present Now continuously gliding forward' (Gurwitsch, 1966a, 278).

He insists that this conception of the pure ego as within a temporal chain accounts satisfactorily for everything which has previously been ascribed to 'hypostatized' conceptions such as of the pure ego as the 'subject of the act'. Because mental states, for Gurwitsch, are not extrapolated from the temporal chain of consciousnesses, 'Their belonging to the context of consciousness makes them my experiences in contradistinction to those of other conscious beings' (Gurwitsch, 1966a, 280). It is this orientation which makes phenomenological analysis 'subjective', not any reference to supposed a-historical concepts of subjectivity. This refusal to acquiesce in any universal or transcendental notion of the pure ego immediately raises, of course, the problem of how we can relate to other minds if we are not able to presuppose that all humans have an abstractly definable pure ego in common. The resolution of this problem became the project towards which Gurwitsch turned in preparing his Habilitation thesis.

Habilitation thesis, 1929–32

The thesis which was submitted but never accepted was finally published in German in 1976 (Gurwitsch, ed. Métraux, 1976) and in English translation as *Human Encounters in the Social World* in 1979 (Gurwitsch, ed. Métraux, 1979). The purpose of my discussion is to re-situate the content of the argument within the moment of its production and, therefore, to contribute to an understanding of the historical development of Gurwitsch's thought in its socio-political context.

Using the conceptual framework developed by Gurwitsch in his doctoral thesis, we can say that the 'thematic field' of that dissertation usurps its 'theme' in the Habilitation thesis. The doctoral dissertation focused, as theme, on Husserl's representation of the pure ego. The Habilitation thesis begins with a definition of the problem to be addressed which is presented (in Part I: 'The Traditional Problem') in terms of the nature of the relationship between my understanding of *my* mental state (which, as we have seen, Gurwitsch believes to be temporally or historically contingent) and my understanding of the mental states of *others*. The process is one of 'mitmenschlich' encounter, that is to say, of encounter between fellow human beings. The translation as 'human' (which would be 'menschlich') should not cause us to suppose that understanding of others is the consequence of the shared introspective awareness of common humanity. Gurwitsch's Habilitation thesis extends his understanding that individual states of consciousness are the products of the individual absorption of individual, temporal chains of consciousness to explore the implications for our communication with and relatedness to others.

Gurwitsch's approach remains rigorously phenomenological but he is now concerned with the identified problem rather than with his position vis-à-vis the thought of Husserl. He is determined to analyse 'what is it that is given to us when we perceive our fellow human beings?' (Gurwitsch, ed. Métraux, 1979, 2). Gurwitsch acknowledges that in everyday life we assume that the minds of others operate in the same ways as our own and he contends that existing attempts to explain this, either epistemologically or psychologically, are fallacious because both deploy the traditionally formulated assumptions of those discourses. Instead, 'the problem is grounded in a definite formulation of the phenomenology of consciousness from which the epistemological as well as the psychological modes of inquiry are derived because they are founded upon it' (Gurwitsch, ed. Métraux, 1979, 3).

Gurwitsch first argues against existing theories. The consequence of Gurwitsch's introductory consideration of 'the traditional problem' is that he concludes that it must be completely reformulated. Consistent with the view taken in his doctoral dissertation, Gurwitsch argues that current work in the field had all been ego-centric whereas he proposes to subject the relationship of encounter to phenomenological analysis without reference to egological presuppositions.

Part II of the thesis examines the 'problem of the concept of the natural surrounding world'. Gurwitsch suggests that fellow human beings encounter each other 'originarily' in the world of 'natural living'. We do not encounter each other primarily as 'cognizing subjects' over against other people as objects to be cognized. Importantly, he also suggests that these 'originary encounters' are not between isolated or 'mere' individuals. We continuously encounter fellow human beings, he says, 'in a determined horizon, namely, in that of the relevant concrete sector of our "natural living"' (Gurwitsch, ed. Métraux, 1979, 36). In other words, we encounter others within socially preconditioned contexts. Our encounters with others, therefore, are not facilitated by transcendental notions of common selfhood but by contingently constructed affinities.

It becomes clear that Gurwitsch's phenomenological analysis of fellow human being tends towards a sociological analysis of the conditions of human encounter, but, crucially, towards sociological analysis which does not privilege itself within encounters but regards itself as an instrument for examining the preconditions of all encounters, including those within which it is itself engaged. The purpose of Part II of the thesis is to try to define what the phrase 'natural surrounding world' signifies, and to ask how 'we comport ourselves in it and how is this comportment[12] to be described?' (Gurwitsch, ed. Métraux, 1979, 37). Gurwitsch begins by acknowledging that Husserl recognized the 'world of the natural attitude' in *Ideas I*,[13] but he also comments that Heidegger radicalized this recognition by positing *Dasein* as 'being-in-the-world'.[14] He proceeds to explore Husserl's meaning without embarking on detailed consideration of the work of Heidegger. Nevertheless, Gurwitsch finds a shortcoming in Husserl's work in that he conceptualized the 'natural concept of the world' within the Western European tradition of philosophical thought. Gurwitsch provides a detailed footnote and an addendum to paragraph 10 in which he outlines an analysis of the '*historical roots*' (Gurwitsch, ed. Métraux, 1979, 47) of the concept of 'natural world' in the work of Descartes. As in his doctoral dissertation, Gurwitsch is intent on seeking to be more rigorously phenomenological than even his master. Gurwitsch labels Husserl's doctrine 'one-sided' and claims that he will 'examine the ground of that one-sided setting of the problem which can only be overcome by an essentially different formulation of world and of being-in-the-world' (Gurwitsch, ed. Métraux, 1979, 39).

Drawing perhaps on his observations of the practice of Gelb and Goldstein, Gurwitsch accepts that we can, as, for example, physicians, objectivize others cognitively, but he contests the assumption that this is the normal or ideal form of interaction. He asks:

> is the clinical attitude toward the patient, interpreted in this context in the sense of a paradigm for the distancing attitude of the cognizing subject toward his object, really representative for the way in which we encounter fellow human beings in our daily living when we encounter them precisely not as observers and investigators with the intention of cognizing them? (Gurwitsch, ed. Métraux, 1979, 57)

Next Gurwitsch devotes a section to consideration of Scheler's contribution to thinking about the 'natural world', concluding, however, that Scheler barely recognized important problems whereas Heidegger 'seized upon them' (Gurwitsch, ed. Métraux, 1979, 66), with the result that Gurwitsch now gives detailed attention to Heidegger's thinking. In section 13 of the thesis, Gurwitsch expounds Heidegger's notion of 'being at hand' as developed in his *Sein und Zeit* (first published in 1927). In an addendum to this section, Gurwitsch summarizes Heidegger's distinction between modes of knowing: 'The explication of the "natural world" as a surrounding world of utensils is oriented around the contrast of "living in …" as "standing in a situation" to "*cogitare*" as "standing over against and freely contemplating"' (Gurwitsch, ed. Métraux, 1979, 73).

Gurwitsch indicates that the consequence of Heidegger's distinction is that cognition is not an intrinsic orientation but, instead, one which depends on a deliberate withdrawal or distancing from living in an originary surrounding world. However, Gurwitsch contends that 'withdrawal' as the precondition for cognition does not signify that cognition is deficient or deprived in respect of its origin. Cognition has 'structures which constitute its self-sufficiency' (Gurwitsch, ed. Métraux, 1979, 81), and these relate to the processes of intentionality. The important advance over the work of Husserl made by Gurwitsch with the help of Heidegger is to suppose that the phenomenology of intentionality is not predicated on a prior preconception of consciousness but, rather, is based on a recognition that consciousness is a contingent extrapolation from our natural world relationships. Gurwitsch expressed this in the following way: ' the problem of the constitution of cognition … must seek its bearings on the basis of "being-in-the-world"' (Gurwitsch, ed. Métraux, 1979, 81).

The title of Part III is 'Consociate Being Together', and Gurwitsch examines the implications of his view of consciousness as derivative for the main question of the thesis which is concerned with our relations to the world of our fellow human beings. It is in the milieu of the surrounding world 'that we also encounter our fellow human beings' (Gurwitsch, ed. Métraux, 1979, 95). The focus of Part III is to 'present the different dimensions in which this being-together can take place, to clarify the particular sense of being-together according to the dimension involved, as well as to describe the corresponding knowledge about fellow human beings' (Gurwitsch, ed. Métraux, 1979, 95).

Just as Gurwitsch argued in his doctoral dissertation that in our perception every 'theme' is surrounded by a 'thematic field' which is 'co-given', so he now suggests that every direct reference to other beings in the world is surrounded by a 'horizon' which is 'co-included'. We do not relate to the world of fellow human beings 'as human beings'. Rather, they exist 'concretely in the "co-included" situation' (Gurwitsch, ed. Métraux, 1979, 97). The co-included situations which define the nature of the specificities of the human beings encountered are diverse: 'situations become visible in the horizons in which sellers, anonymous buyers, purveyors, employers, listeners, readers, masters, servants, etc., act out their roles' (Gurwitsch, ed. Métraux, 1979, 97). It is the sense of co-inclusion which generates the human conviction of fellow human being, but the different dimensions of co-inclusion define that human fellow being differently. Gurwitsch therefore turns to an analysis of these different horizonal determinants.

He first considers the 'being-together of partners in a common situation' (Gurwitsch, ed. Métraux, 1979, 104), which he exemplifies in terms of the relationship of fellow workers. In this context we reciprocally constitute ourselves in relation to others. How we do so relates to the roles we adopt: 'the situation prescribes a *role* to us which we take over as long as we are in the situation in question' (Gurwitsch, ed. Métraux, 1979, 107–108). In the workplace, as an example, our identities are defined by that context, but this is just one of many contexts within which we are defined.[15] Gurwitsch acknowledges the value here of Karl Löwith's *Das Individuum in der Rolle des Mitmenschen* [The Individual in the Role of Fellow Human Being], published in 1928, but he insists that he differs from Löwith in emphasizing the pluridimensionality of being-together and in subjecting different dimensions to phenomenological analysis.

Gurwitsch suggests that the kind of being-together in partnership which he has discussed in relation to workplace partnerships is to be distinguished by virtue of the fact that it always has a beginning and an end. Identities which are operative within situations cease outside those situations. The partner can be 'dismissed' and 'This "dismissal" of the partner has the meaning that he can withdraw into the realm of his freedom' (Gurwitsch, ed. Métraux, 1979, 117). Gurwitsch proceeds to follow both Tönnies,[16] in his *Gemeinschaft und Gesellschaft* [community and society] of 1926 (first published in 1887), and Vierkandt,[17] in his *Gesellschaftslehre*[theory of society] of 1923, in suggesting that encounters within 'society' are analogous with those in the workplace. He quotes Tönnies to the effect that 'In the concept of society, the original or natural relations of human beings to each other must be excluded' (Tönnies, 1926, 51, quoted in Gurwitsch, ed. Métraux, 1979, 117). In this view, societal relations are contractual ones. By contrast, Gurwitsch explores the contention that 'community' (Gemeinschaft) is different in kind from 'society'. As Gurwitsch elaborates:

> The example of the peasant family shows that a more comprehensive life-context is essential for a community. This life-context, which makes up the community as community, does not, so to speak, float in mid-air. Rather the life-context itself possesses a basis on which community is grounded and in which it is rooted. This basis is the *communal possession*. (Gurwitsch, ed. Métraux, 1979, 122)

By 'communal possession' Gurwitsch means that there are communal bonds which precede the contractual relations of society. He specifies that 'Along with the common land, the national language, the past of the people, their state, their culture, etc., function as the foundation of their community' (Gurwitsch, ed. Métraux, 1979, 123).

Gurwitsch proceeds to single out the historical dimension of communal possession. Unlike 'partnership-relationships', 'community-relationships' cannot be avoided. We are born into a historical community. He resists the notion that this is a 'blood relationship'. Just as the ego was seen as a historical construct in the doctoral dissertation, so Gurwitsch extends the same orientation to community living: 'We therefore determine ourselves as *essentially historical beings. The communalization of people always already signifies its historicalization (Vergeschichtlichung)*' (Gurwitsch, ed. Métraux, 1979, 126).

Nevertheless, Gurwitsch is anxious to be sure that this process should not be 'absolutized'. There are limits of societal or communal membership. We do not choose the community into which we are born but, according to Gurwitsch, 'In spite of the extent of membership, there remains to the member of the community a private sphere' (Gurwitsch, ed. Métraux, 1979, 131). As a result, it is up to individuals whether they emphasize their personal freedom or adhere to superimposed restrictions. The availability of this choice engenders tension. Gurwitsch argues, in a familiarly Gestaltist fashion, that the community-relationship has priority over partnership-relationships just as wholes have priority over parts. This implies that there is a radical difference between partnership-relationships which grow naturally out of primary, community-relationships, and those which appear to be artificially constructed by free agents. There are always tensions, Gurwitsch supposes, between 'outsiders' and 'insiders' or between those who, like Luther, try to reassert original values against those which have become institutionalized historically in communal practices. Significantly, Gurwitsch notes that this is a problem for 'science'. He refers in a footnote to Lévy-Bruhl's 'critique of animism' as an example of a failure to understand primitive cultures as a result of a 'delimitation of understanding by its own historical communalization' (Gurwitsch, ed. Métraux, 1979, 135).

Gurwitsch recognizes that this disposition towards historical interpretation of the essence of community-partnership runs the risk of denying the capacity of individuals to construct meanings in their concrete, everyday situations without explicit reference to historical precedents. As a consequence he examines a 'third foundational sociological category' (Gurwitsch, ed. Métraux, 1979, 137), namely 'groups' in addition to communities and societies. 'Whenever people are seized by a new "idea", a new feeling of life, a god, a hero, etc., and find themselves together as seized by them, then a new social formation arises among them' (Gurwitsch, ed. Métraux, 1979, 137). These new formations disrupt existing communities. Gurwitsch uses Weber's notion of 'charisma' to illustrate how such groups come into existence. The essential difference between communities and groups is that common feeling is pre-existent in communities whereas it is constitutive of groups.

Having suggested the tripartite typology of encounter situations, Gurwitsch moves towards a conclusion by emphasizing that, unlike, for instance, Scheler, he does not seek to recommend any type as prescriptive. His phenomenological account is descriptive. He mentions en passant that, for him, 'cognition is to be acquired *exclusively* on the road that leads to science' (Gurwitsch, ed. Métraux, 1979, 146) and not as a blueprint for action. In the framework of his essay, he says, he cannot embark on a critique of Scheler's theory of science and, as a result, the dissertation tantalizingly leaves undiscussed the question whether or how 'science' escapes the pitfalls of historical communalization. Gurwitsch's descriptive account enables him to observe that

> the manifestation of the charismatic and the flaring up of groups are particularly favourable to those epochs in which, because of some need or other, communal bonds are loosened. Those people whose bonds to what has been handed down and transmitted have weakened, and for whom the traditional, hence the taken-for-granted, has become problematic in a determinate way, are to a conspicuous extent directly predestined for the impression of the new that the manifestation of the charismatic signifies: that against which the new power prevails is, in these cases, already weak. (Gurwitsch, ed. Métraux, 1979, 147–8)

In as much as Gurwitsch would seem to have been finally led to sociological analysis, he formulates, in conclusion, an anticipatory self-defence. The last section considers 'the fundamental sociological categories as structures of "living in"'. He argues that his analyses were of the phenomena of fellow human being in terms of partnership, membership, and fusion, and that these are not to be identified with the concrete social consociations of society, community and group to which they seem to correspond. The relationship has to be understood phenomenologically. That is to say, for Gurwitsch, the analytical categories and their objective correlates are forms of givenness relative to our perceptual intentions. There is no provision of any representation of objective reality. The 'objectivities' of sociological classification are functions of the forms of social encounter which have been articulated. The conceptual framework which the thesis has articulated (its 'modal categories') has to be understood as an evanescent product of itself rather than an independently valid representation of reality. In this respect, Gurwitsch concludes, our knowledges of the world of fellow human beings and the world of material things are 'in every case abstract moments in our universal "consciousness of the world"' and 'are articulated in precisely the same way' (Gurwitsch, ed. Métraux, 1979, 156).

Lectures and articles of the 1930s

The productions of the 1930s show that Gurwitsch was intent on defining 'constitutive' phenomenology in relation to the mainstream phenomenological tradition descending from Husserl and on engaging with the issues broached by the social sciences without succumbing to their 'natural attitude' assumptions. This section follows these intentions by reference both to those of his publications subsequently collected in translation in *Studies in Phenomenology and Psychology* (Gurwitsch, 1966a) and to those productions retrieved and published in French in *Esquisse de la phénoménologie constitutive* [outline of constitutive phenomenology] (Gurwitsch, ed. Huertas-Jourda, 2002).

One of Gurwitsch's last publications in German in Germany was a review of Husserl's *Nachwort* [postface] to his *Ideen* which was stimulated by Boyce Gibson's translation of the original text into English (Husserl, trans. Gibson, 1931). At the end of the 1920s, Husserl began to go on the offensive in defence of his view of phenomenology against the distortions introduced by Heidegger in *Being and Time* (Heidegger, 1927). The lectures which Husserl gave in Paris in February 1929 were parts of this counter-attack, as was the *Nachwort*, which was published independently in German in 1930 (Husserl, 1930). We have seen that Gurwitsch oscillated in his doctoral dissertation in his preference for the Husserl of the *Logical Investigations* or the Husserl of *Ideen*. He took the opportunity of his review of the *Nachwort* to clarify his position with respect to Husserl's two major texts and to comment on the relationship between Gestalt psychology and phenomenological philosophy. This is written in the manner of a Husserlian disciple as in the doctoral dissertation. The review makes no reference to the orientation generated by Heidegger which was apparent in the Habilitation thesis. Gurwitsch's review of Husserl's *Nachwort* implicitly established the main tasks for his intellectual effort in the following decade. He was to continue to define his personal position relative to the work of Husserl, but he was also to pursue the implications of affinities between Gestalt psychology and phenomenology. He would explore the consequences of adopting a phenomenological attitude towards 'science' but the tentative insights of the Habilitation thesis which seemed to lead towards a sociological analysis of the phenomena of 'scientific' or 'intellectual' role-playing fell into unpublished abeyance. Indeed, Gurwitsch ended his review by asserting that Husserl's defence against the charge of 'intellectualism' was superfluous 'because the reproach itself is pointless'. As Gurwitsch elaborates this point in the final sentence of the review: 'Philosophy as clarification of the world and, more particularly, as clarification in a radical sense – in which alone the clarification deserves to be called philosophical – can by its very nature be nothing else than "intellectualistic" because clarity and clarification are precisely matters of intellect' (Gurwitsch, 1966a, 114–15).

In spite of the logic of the discussion in his Habilitation thesis, it was as a philosophical intellectual that Gurwitsch would present himself to his fellow human beings in Paris.

Gurwitsch's first French publication, entitled 'La place de la psychologie dans l'ensemble des sciences' [the place of psychology in the totality of the

sciences] (Gurwitsch, 1934), reflects the first course on the historical development of Gestalt psychology which he gave in 1933–34. Gurwitsch argues that
psychology has, from the outset in Western European philosophy, been mod-
elled on the sciences of the natural world. He suggests that this has remained
the case through to the theory of 'psychophysical parallelism, which is almost
generally accepted in contemporary psychology' (Gurwitsch, 1966a, 57). 'Associationism is not only inspired by Newtonian physics; it applies and extends
it to the realm of psychology' (Gurwitsch, 1966a, 59). The dominance of the
physical model enabled the development of Herbartian psychology which was
'dominant for several decades in Germany and, still more, in Austria' (Gurwitsch, 1966a, 60). This in turn enabled the development of Freud's thought,
for whom 'man resembles a closed physical system endowed with a certain
quantity of energy' (Gurwitsch, 1966a, 61).

Gurwitsch believed that phenomenological psychology becomes liberated
from this model by rejecting the 'constancy hypothesis'. The consequence,
Gurwitsch suggests, of the subservience of psychology to physical models,
whether of mechanics or quantum physics, is that psychology 'does not seem
to deepen or enrich our scientific knowledge of reality to a considerable
extent' (Gurwitsch, 1966a, 64). Fortunately, however, we can overcome this
limitation by adopting a 'historical, or genetic, orientation' in respect of all
sciences. There is space for a psychology which concentrates on our subjective
impressions, precisely those things which are excluded from the attention of
the sciences confronting the world of neutral objects. Modern physics broke
with 'the ambient world as it is known to the common man, and each of us
is, in his daily life, such a common man' (Gurwitsch, 1966a, 65). Deliberately
situating his argument in relation to the influential thought of Léon Brunschvicg, Gurwitsch argues that, in spite of Brunschvicg's contention that 'reality is
not as it presents itself but as it is constructed by science' (Gurwitsch, 1966a,
65), our everyday, inter-subjective experiences are not modified by science
and retain their independent validity. However, Gurwitsch is not acquiescing
in a scientific/experiential dualism. On the contrary, the task of psychology
is to bridge the gap, an endeavour which cannot be undertaken by a priori
adopting the models of science to understand experience. Gurwitsch spells
this out clearly:

> The true structure of reality may be as science reveals it. However, not only must
> scientific theories be verified in terms of 'subjective' phenomena and our experi-
> ences of them, but, what is more, it is only by starting from the ambient world
> in which we never cease to exist that the scientific conquest of reality can be
> undertaken. This conquest, realized by constructions of the mind, is a creation of
> the mind. It is not a creation made once and forever at a certain moment in time.
> Instead, it is accomplished in the course of a continuous progress throughout
> history. (Gurwitsch, 1966a, 66)

This attitude to science is an extension of the attitude Gurwitsch adopted towards the constantly contingent historical development of the ego in his doctoral dissertation. Whereas the Habilitation thesis seemed to be pursuing the possibility that the 'ambient world' is the natural community of fellow human beings while the world of science is that of 'constructed' societies or groups, Gurwitsch here considers that the spheres of experience are themselves differentiated. Whereas, in other words, the Habilitation thesis reflected the German discourse about Gemeinschaft and Gesellschaft which had immediate implications for contemporary thinking about the relationship between the Volk and the State, Gurwitsch here adapts to concerns articulated in a French tradition that can be traced back, perhaps, to Rousseau. Gurwitsch raises the point that the transition from experience to scientific rationality may be observed in child development, effected by the acquisition of language, and also observed in the transition from 'primitive' to 'civilized' mentality.

The function of psychology, as understood by Gurwitsch, is that it should not be an empirical science among others. In his own words, 'It is not one science among the others; instead, it is their foundation' (Gurwitsch, 1966a, 68). He concludes that 'in this manner psychology approaches philosophy' (Gurwitsch, 1966a, 68). Without mentioning phenomenology at all, Gurwitsch here posits for psychology the function which he had hitherto advanced for phenomenology.

It is clear that Gurwitsch's oscillation between advancing the analytical claims of psychology or phenomenology was a matter of emphasis dictated by context. His position was consistent. He wanted to propose a role for psychology which was functionally similar to the role for a phenomenology informed by Gestalt psychology to which he was committed philosophically. In his second course of lectures in Paris in 1934–35, Gurwitsch did seek overtly to expound Husserl's notion of 'intentionality'. We only have available one lecture in this course, to which Embree gave the title 'Thème et attitude' [theme and attitude]. The title of the course was 'Psychologie intentionnaliste' [intentionalist psychology]. Judging only by the one lecture that we can study and by the course title, it would seem that, again, Gurwitsch was transposing the emphasis of 'intentionality' in Husserl's phenomenology to advance a new orientation in psychology. The 'Thème et attitude' text is of interest because Gurwitsch reiterates the views expressed in both his doctoral and Habilitation theses and takes the opportunity to attempt to establish connections between the emphases separately developed in those two theses. The reiteration of the doctoral thesis is more emphatically Gestaltist in that Gurwitsch insists that our perceptions relate to thematic fields which are intrinsically coherent. In other words, he is more clear than in his doctoral thesis that the determinant of our knowledge is the structure of the noemata which remains identical irrespective of our particular noetic activities. There is a correspondence between the noematic and the noetic, but the former is the determinant. Although we

constitute our knowledge, we do so in relation to a network of prior meanings, both actual and possible, which remains unchanged by our various perceptions. There are always further possible meanings beyond those which we
perceive. Gurwitsch also reiterates those parts of his Habilitation thesis which
deployed Heidegger's insights and terminology, but he now suggests that our
orientation towards objects is of two categorally different kinds. He differentiates between perceptual and functional dispositions. Gurwitsch illustrates his
point by reference to different experiences of a lamp on a table. In order to
use the lamp for a purpose 'I don't need to know how it is constructed, nor
to know the mechanism which makes it function' (Gurwitsch, ed. Huertas-
Jourda, 2002, 323). For the former, Gurwitsch uses 'savoir' and for the latter
he uses 'connaître' but, importantly, both kinds of knowledge are discrete in
relation to what Heidegger called 'knowledge-to-hand' or practical knowledge.
Gurwitsch concludes his exemplary comments on the lamp by remarking that
they 'show the difference which exists between the horizon of the physicist
and that of the worker, neither of these horizons being substitutable for or
integrated with the other' (Gurwitsch, ed. Huertas-Jourda, 2002, 323). There
is a sense in which Gurwitsch is suggesting that practical knowledge provides
access to 'choses réiformes' [reified or, literally, reformed, things] which are
defined only by 'their qualities and objective properties which are visual,
tactile, thermic, etc.' (Gurwitsch, ed. Huertas-Jourda, 2002, 326). Thinking in
terms of a mind/body dualism, therefore, Gurwitsch implies that practical
knowledge is not to be denigrated as 'primitive' but to be regarded as the
means of access to extended bodies, the concomitant of systematic doubt about
accumulated accretions of consciousness. Gurwitsch recognizes the claims of
intellectualism and idealism and considers such thinking in predefined thematic
categories to be superior to practical knowledge, but he also seems to be suggesting that the constructions of consciousness should always be rooted in
practical engagement with things in their thinghood. He rejects the notion
that we might be talking about 'levels' of knowledge. He insists that practical
and conscious actions constantly co-exist in ways which are not absolute or
predefined. These forms of cooperation 'are susceptible to minute study and
in this way a vast field is opened up for future research' (Gurwitsch, ed.
Huertas-Jourda, 2002, 329).

With this concluding remark, Gurwitsch appears to announce the future
direction of his work. The doctoral thesis considered intentionality and consciousness within the parameters established by Husserl, seeking to refine some
of his mentor's views by juxtaposing them with Gestalt psychology. In considering the 'surrounding natural world' for fellow human beings, the Habilitation thesis moved away from close adherence to Husserl and sought to
accommodate Heidegger's ontological position and aspects of contemporary
German philosophical sociology. Gurwitsch remained confident, however, that
his phenomenological approach to the issue of inter-subjective knowledge was

superior to those of epistemology and psychology, both operating with 'natural attitude' assumptions. Gurwitsch's review of Husserl's *Nachwort*, his last German publication, remained an internal text of a disciple. There are signs that, in the early 1930s in France, Gurwitsch adapted the presentation of his arguments to suit the prevailing mood of his new context. He appears disinclined to disparage transcendental idealism and also disinclined to embrace the emergent Heideggerian critique of Husserl. Without relinquishing his phenomenological orientation, Gurwitsch seems to have tacitly accepted that this orientation could be best advanced in his new context by representing it as a new mode of psychological enquiry – one which would allow him to subject to scrutiny the cooperation between phenomena traditionally understood epistemologically and ontologically. He would seek to deploy a phenomenological psychology to transcend the opposition between epistemology and ontology which had been clearly revealed in the debate at Davos in 1930 between Cassirer and Heidegger.

It was only in the last few years of the 1930s that Gurwitsch seems explicitly to have given the name of 'constitutive phenomenology' to the approach which he was developing. In 1937, he wrote an article entitled 'Quelques principes fondamentaux de la phénoménologie constitutive' [some fundamental principles of constitutive phenomenology] which was never published and, in the same year, he delivered, between February and April, the lectures which have been assembled posthumously by Embree and Huertas-Jourda and published under the title *Esquisse de la phénoménologie constitutive* [outline of constitutive phenomenology]. Taken together, these two texts are important for understanding the development of Gurwitsch's thought, but it must be remembered that neither was publicly known during his lifetime.

Embree considers 'Quelques principes fondamentaux de la phénoménologie constitutive' indisputably to be Gurwitsch's 'best exposition … of the principles of philosophy which he had devoted himself to developing beyond Husserl' (Gurwitsch, ed. Huertas-Jourda, 2002, 331). While Gurwitsch was still engaged in clarifying his view of the relationship between Gestalt psychology and phenomenology, he also embarked on an attempt to communicate that view as philosophy. Nevertheless, as he insists at the outset, the proposed philosophy does not attempt to be systematic but, rather, is an invitation to ongoing observation. The fundamental contention, for Gurwitsch, is that all 'objects', whether things, valuables, works of art, historical facts, social institutions, 'only become accessible to us thanks to certain acts of consciousness which are, or can be, lived' (Gurwitsch, ed. Huertas-Jourda, 2002, 332). Hence the title 'constitutive phenomenology' because we should not be concerned to discover any fantasy knowledge of 'things-in-themselves' but only to record 'objects' as they are constituted by consciousness. Importantly, consciousnesses are 'lived'. Gurwitsch is not seeking to define objects in relation to consciousness as such but as they are constituted by multiple consciousnesses. The unified identities of objects are constituted out of the multiple and diverse individual consciousnesses of them without which they have no existence. For Gurwitsch, this process has nothing to do with 'subjectivism'. Unified identities cohere across time and space even though they depend for their existence on individual consciousnesses which are constrained by these dimensions. The living acts of consciousness are the performances of psychic beings but the constitution of objects is the consequence of a synthesis at the level of consciousnesses without reference to their psychic provenance. The notion of selfhood underlying subjectivity is itself a constituted object and therefore cannot be the motor for generating objectivity. What is at issue is not the traditional epistemological problem of the relationship between 'real' objects and sense impressions. Instead, the issue is the nature of the correlation between objects and their enabling consciousnesses. The consequence of this position is that research about objects entails research into the acts of consciousness which made them possible but, also, it involves research into the reciprocal nature of the correlation.

In Gurwitsch's account, the transcendentalism of objects is constituted. He removes any vestige of idealism attaching to transcendental phenomenology. The effect is that objectified identities which have been constituted by consciousnesses living at different times and places prescribe any new consciousness of them enacted by any new living person. There is a genuine reciprocity, however, because Gurwitsch emphasizes equally that 'each object stimulates acts of a type which is correlative to the category to which the object belongs' (Gurwitsch, ed. Huertas-Jourda, 2002, 337). The consequence is that 'the category of objects and the categories of acts correspond with each other reciprocally' (Gurwitsch, ed. Huertas-Jourda, 2002, 337) and that, therefore, the challenge for a 'constitutive phenomenology' is to analyse all the manifestations of correlations. Gurwitsch emphasizes that the understanding which he takes from Husserl is that sensorial perception is a special case of experience in general, namely the perception of 'reformed things' whose reiformity has already been constituted by a prior process of act/object correlation. It is necessary to labour this point because it was to become the basis of Gurwitsch's objection to Merleau-Ponty's *Phénoménologie de la perception*. Gurwitsch clarifies in a footnote that 'although we must guard against assimilating experience in general to perceptual experience, it is useful to start from perception in considering it as a paradigmatic example of experience in the wider sense' (Gurwitsch, ed. Huertas-Jourda, 2002, 340).

Objects depend on consciousness for their constitution, but acts of consciousness are first of all relative to themselves, with the result that they can be said to have an absolute character. In a section on 'the phenomenological reduction', Gurwitsch issues the reminder that he is not talking here about everyday consciousness or the consciousness as identified by scientific psychology with the physical organism. He is talking about consciousness 'exclusively as a medium or, if you like, as a theatre of the constitution of all sorts of objects' (Gurwitsch, ed. Huertas-Jourda, 2002, 347), including psychic human realities such as 'the soul, the mind, the self, the personality, social and historical being, etc.' (Gurwitsch, ed. Huertas-Jourda, 2002, 347). This separation of an absolute conception of consciousness from 'natural' consciousness is achieved by phenomenological reduction which 'places the existential character of the whole world between brackets' (Gurwitsch, ed. Huertas-Jourda, 2002, 347). The reductive perspective does not deny natural phenomena. It is not a form of scepticism. It seeks to ensure that all objects, the world and all 'realities', including human 'realities', are understood to be constituted phenomena rather than intrinsic realities. Gurwitsch's essay is a clarion call for investigations of consciousness undertaken in a way which, as he concludes, ensures that they possess 'philosophical value' and which enables them 'to avoid anthropological paralogisms' (Gurwitsch, ed. Huertas-Jourda, 2002, 350).

The piece named by editors as *Esquisse de la phénoménologie constitutive* [outline of constitutive phenomenology] repeats in more detail many of the points sketched succinctly in 'Quelques principes'. Gurwitsch's discussion leads him to reaffirm the necessity for a phenomenological reduction which, he insists, is much more than 'a radical modification of the *natural attitude*' (Gurwitsch, ed. Huertas-Jourda, 2002, 72). In order to demonstrate that the phenomenological reduction is not just a negation of the natural attitude, Gurwitsch devotes a chapter to the relationship between the two. There is a new tone in Gurwitsch's presentation. Without any specific reference to Heidegger, the chapter resurrects some of the orientation of the Habilitation thesis by starting discussion from the everyday experience of ordinary people. We all find ourselves in a world which we take to be 'really existent' and are conscious of our selves as placed in a world which is our 'ambiance' (a rendering of the German 'Umwelt'). In what appears to be an existentialist presentation of our situation, Gurwitsch says that 'the subject' is placed in the presence of many different objects, but 'one' does not always relate to these objects as a 'pure spectator' (Gurwitsch, ed. Huertas-Jourda, 2002, 73). On the contrary, a contemplative attitude is rare and cannot be wholly sustained even by a subject who is habitually disposed to do so ('such as a scientist' (Gurwitsch, ed. Huertas-Jourda, 2002, 73)). The normal attitude to our ambiance is practical. We relate to objects primarily as tools for our use. In a significant third section of the chapter, Gurwitsch explores the implications of his differentiation between practical and scientific acts of consciousness for the 'human sciences'. He takes the view that in these sciences an attempt is made to understand ambiances by analysing the origins and development of social institutions. This is the basis for the constitution of 'historical, archaeological, philological, economic, sociological sciences, and others' (Gurwitsch, ed. Huertas-Jourda, 2002, 81), and Gurwitsch concludes: 'in the human sciences, objects remain functional objects' (Gurwitsch, ed. Huertas-Jourda, 2002, 81). These sciences, in other words, are all practical. The contrast with the physical sciences, however, is not simple. Gurwitsch argues that the error of the physical sciences, to which both Descartes and Locke contributed, was to differentiate the contemplative attitude from the practical in terms of a differentiation between the mental and the material. By suppressing any acknowledgement that objects derive their meanings from their functionality, the physical sciences cultivated abstract concepts which were all predicated on a mental detachment from physical objects, denying that these are 'reiformed things'. Correct physical science, however, operates with notions such as 'atoms, ions, electrons, energy, etc.' (Gurwitsch, ed. Huertas-Jourda, 2002, 82) which can only be characterized mathematically rather than perceptibly. The consequence is that with the universe as it is constructed by physics, we are before 'the *scientific truth of the world*' [la *vérité scientifique du monde*] (Gurwitsch, ed. Huertas-Jourda, 2002, 83). Physicists base their work on perception only so as to translate data into physical terminology and, to that extent, 'the physical universe must be regarded as superior to the perceptible world' (Gurwitsch, ed. Huertas-Jourda, 2002, 83). However, this is not to say that physical science offers a 'superior' understanding of physical reality but rather, simply, that it gives an account of the world which is derived from, but abstracted from, perception and exists as a function of a mathematic-physical category of thinking without direct reference to reality. The assumption that the abstract discourse of physics is empirically verifiable in a direct way has led to the view that mathematized nature is a correct substitution for nature as it is given to us. Recognition that physical science is the product of a specific operation of consciousness rather than a substitute account of reality means, for Gurwitsch, that this process of constitution is as susceptible to analysis as any other in terms of historical and social generation. Gurwitsch points to the development of the tradition of geometric thought as a way of understanding physical science.

Gurwitsch reiterates that all consciousnesses, whether everyday, practical, or abstracted, scientific, are grounded in existence or existential, and, as such, operate implicitly without any reflection on their relative validity. The exception is the conscious act of practising philosophy by undertaking a phenomenological reduction. Its discrete raison d'être is to make explicit those things which remain implicit in all other acts. To undertake its task, the existential base of its activity is, exceptionally, 'put in brackets' or 'inhibited', but not suppressed. Some functional denial of its own existential base is a *sine qua non* for the performance of its task. In effect, the phenomenological reduction does not 'reduce' or negate all constituted act/object constitutions but practises a self-denying methodological suppression of its own existentiality for the purpose of subjecting all others to scrutiny. In practising phenomenological reduction, subjects still conceive themselves as social and historical individuals in their ambiances, but the practice imposes an inhibition of these self-conceptions such that the 'concrete human self [Moi] becomes … a phenomenon' (Gurwitsch, ed. Huertas-Jourda, 2002, 90). Crucially, Gurwitsch emphasizes that 'every anthropological element must therefore strictly be kept apart from phenomenological considerations' (Gurwitsch, ed. Huertas-Jourda, 2002, 91), and, equally, he clarifies that although there is a special relationship between psychology and phenomenology, an 'intimate' connection, there must be no doubt that there is a great difference in principle between the ways in which they treat consciousness. Phenomenology is concerned with 'reduced consciousness' rather than with the actual consciousness which is the concern of the human sciences.

Gurwitsch concludes with a section entitled 'Methodological Remarks', where he specifies that 'the attitude that the phenomenologist adopts in his researches is therefore that of reflexion' (Gurwitsch, ed. Huertas-Jourda, 2002, 241). Depending on whether the research focus is on the act or the object in the act/object correlation, this reflexion will be either noetic or noematic. Reflexion does not generate anything in itself. It is not a process of subjective introspection (a phrase which Gurwitsch would not even recognize as mean-ingful). 'Reflexion does not create anything new' (Gurwitsch, ed. Huertas-Jourda, 2002, 242). It is simply a means towards the analysis of correlations or constitutions.

In spite of Gurwitsch's continuing engagement with psychological theories, the *Esquisse* and 'Quelques principes' mark a significant shift in that they defend a specific function for phenomenological philosophy in terms of the general argument about the status of practical and contemplative acts of consciousness. They suggest a demarcation of philosophical endeavour from the natural sciences while refusing to accept the kind of idealist philosophy that had gained authority in France between the wars. It was this separation which Gurwitsch attempted to sustain when he experienced a forced change of ambiance on migrating from France to the United States at the end of the 1930s.

Summary

Born in Lithuania, Gurwitsch was a nomadic intellectual within the Weimar Republic. Like Schutz, he was educated at a 'Gymnasium' and, like Schutz, again, he was a Jew. He studied under Stumpf in Berlin, which meant that he was influenced by his tutor's hostility to Mach's positivism which was dominant in Vienna. With Stumpf's encouragement, Gurwitsch worked along-side the physiologists Goldstein and Gelb in Frankfurt and audited some of Husserl's courses at Freiburg. Unlike Schutz, Gurwitsch regarded himself as a disciple of Husserl and dedicated his career to refining Husserl's early work by seeking to import evidence derived from Gestalt psychology (itself a movement which, partly through the influence of Stumpf, imported the legacy of German idealist philosophy into empirical physiology by emphasizing the corporeal self-regulating powers of the mind in opposition to the views of materialist behaviourists). I have considered Gurwitsch's doctoral and Habilitation theses in the contexts of their production. The first proposed a modification of Husserl's notion of the Ego and was published (in a specialist journal of psychological research) but, in the second, which was only published in translation posthumously, Gurwitsch was clearly influenced by his reading of Heidegger towards understanding social encounters in terms of interactions in the 'life-world' between mutually constituting selves rather than in terms of any a priori shared identity.

Gurwitsch insisted in his doctoral thesis that the ego is socially constituted, and, in his Habilitation thesis, that consciousness, which has transcendental status, nevertheless emerges out of primary, communal experience. Events in Germany at the time, however, may have caused him to want to have reservations about the tendency of the arguments of the Habilitation thesis in favour of the pre-rational origins of rationality. In France, where he influenced Merleau-Ponty, who was only slightly his junior, Gurwitsch began in the 1930s to develop a 'constitutive phenomenology', analysing phenomenologically the process by which objective structures are constituted out of subjective experience, but his publications were mainly concerned with the exposition of Gestalt psychology and were not primarily contributions to 'philosophy'. Gurwitsch insisted on the primacy of consciousness but was prepared to acknowledge that 'fields' of consciousness have their origins in primary experience. In opposition both to the tradition of German idealism and to the subjectivism of the Romantic critics of Kant, he appears to have become committed ideologically to the rationalist tradition of French thought which he considered to have been actualized politically in the events of the French Revolution.

Notes

1 For a discussion of Husserl's courses, see Staiti, 2014, chapter 5. It seems probable that Gurwitsch attended the course of 1927.
2 This was published, Gurwitsch, 1929, and published in English translation in Gurwitsch, 1966a.
3 It was published posthumously as Gurwitsch, ed. Métraux, 1976, and, in translation into English as Gurwitsch, ed. Métraux, 1979.
4 Gurwitsch, 1930; Gurwitsch, 1931; Gurwitsch, 1933a; and Gurwitsch, 1933b.
5 See Gurwitsch, ed. Métraux, 1979, ix.
6 See Gurwitsch, ed. Huertas-Jourda, 2002, 20.
7 See Gurwitsch, ed. Métraux, 1979, x.
8 See Gurwitsch, ed. Huertas-Jourda, 2002, 23.
9 See Gurwitsch, ed. Métraux, 1979, xi.
10 One of these lectures is presented as Appendix II of Gurwitsch, ed. Huertas-Jourda, 2002.
11 This article is presented as Appendix V of Gurwitsch, ed. Huertas-Jourda, 2002.
12 Notice the use of 'comportment'. We shall see that Merleau-Ponty's first book was *La structure du comportement*.

13 He cites paragraphs 27ff.
14 Gurwitsch refers to Heidegger, 1927, Part I, Chapters 2ff.
15 Notice the clear difference from the position of Sartre. For Gurwitsch, roles are constitutive whereas, for Sartre, role-playing is an act of 'bad faith' because it is indicative of a failure to use freedom to define one's own essence.
16 Ferdinand Tönnies (1855–1936) was Emeritus Professor of Sociology at the University of Kiel from 1921 until 1933, when he was ousted from his post.
17 Alfred Vierkandt (1867–1953) was Professor of Sociology at the University of Berlin from 1913 until 1934, when he was made to retire.

3

Schutz and Gurwitsch in America, 1940–80

This chapter considers the social and intellectual adjustments made by Schutz and Gurwitsch as a consequence of their migrations to the United States. It does so by examining elements of their correspondence in the 1940s and by considering the development of their original views in the new cultural context.

The careers

Alfred Schutz was working in Paris when the Germans invaded Austria on 13 March 1938. He remained in Paris for over a year but, on 14 July 1939, he realized his intention of emigrating to the United States, sailing for New York on that date. Following the German invasion of Poland and the consequent declarations of war against Germany by Britain and France in September 1939, the Gurwitsch family moved to a Paris suburb for six months before securing a passage on a boat from Le Havre to New York on 19 May 1940.

Apart from *Der sinnhafte Aufbau der sozialen Welt* of 1932, which remained untranslated, Schutz had published only three reviews in German journals during the 1930s. As a result of his employment with an international banking company, he was exceptional among immigrants in already having a secure position on arrival in New York. Schutz was able to continue the practice which he had established in Austria of being 'a bank executive by day and a phenomenologist by night' (Gurwitsch, ed. Embree, 1972, xxiii). He initially came into contact with staff in the New School for Social Research in New York through his attempts to find funding to facilitate the emigration to the United States of friends and colleagues such as Gurwitsch. Schutz was invited to be a Visiting Professor at the Graduate Faculty for the academic year 1943–44. He became a full Professor after the death of Felix Kaufmann in December 1949. He finally gave up his 'day job' in banking in 1953 (Grathoff, ed., 1978, 112). He subsequently became Chairman of the Department of Sociology, 'simultaneously building up the Philosophy Department and ruining his health with his professional double life' (Grathoff, ed., 1989, xxvi). He died in May 1959.

During this period of twenty years, Schutz published nearly forty articles or reviews. Many of these appeared in the journal *Philosophy and Phenomenological Research* which was founded in 1940 and edited by Marvin Farber. Most of these publications were given a 'second life' as they were assembled after Schutz's death in four volumes of *Collected Papers*. Attention will be given to a selection of these in the context of their original production. The titles of the most important of Schutz's articles in this period are indicative of his interests.[1]

Throughout this period, especially in the early years, Schutz was active in supporting many of his fellow immigrants, including Gurwitsch, in seeking employment. Schutz and Gurwitsch had first met, at Husserl's instigation, in Paris in 1935. They began a correspondence in 1939 which continued until Schutz's death. The text of this correspondence will be used to contextualize the publications of both men in the period from 1940 to 1960, but its formal significance needs to be highlighted. The first point to emphasize is that the correspondence was conducted in German throughout the period. The second point is that the exchange contains very little information about the attitudes and feelings of the correspondents in relation to American society and politics. They both constantly ask each other for news about their situations. It is evident that they reacted differently to how their lives were developing, but there is a strong sense that for both their exchange was a substitute for social and intellectual engagement within a real community. Formally, they used their correspondence as a partial compensation for their sense that they were not integrated within their host community, neither as German-speakers nor as Jews. The different ways in which the two men expressed this formal significance have an important correlation with the substance of their discussions. In spite of his day job as an international banker, Schutz felt the lack of social integration and scope for social action whereas Gurwitsch longed for inclusion within a community which would also offer a field of intellectual participation. A few comments expressed during the war years when both were new immigrants are indicative. As early as March 1941, Gurwitsch wrote to Schutz identifying that a common 'tréfonds' [subsoil] secured their relationship:

> In the few years of our acquaintance you have given me such magnificent proofs of your friendship, and that primal ground of our commonality and our concord has manifested itself so often: that primal ground, on the basis of which we then agree or disagree, and are unhappy when we disagree, and yet never completely unhappy, since we have just this *tréfonds*. (Grathoff, ed., 1989, 34–5)

Typically, Gurwitsch suggests that the possibility of intellectual difference within a field of consciousness is predicated on a fundamental, experiential affinity. In response, Schutz gives a slightly different gloss: 'we have to try to create in *our* world that order which we have to do without in our *world*. The whole conflict – including that between our different approaches – lies hidden in the shift of emphasis' (Grathoff, ed., 1989, 37).

For Schutz, the challenge is to construct a world of inter-personal, social relations out of despair at the nature of socio-political reality. The meaningful construction of the social world is aggressively a-political and, equally, independent of any prior experiential harmony. Gurwitsch was predisposed to want to argue that fields of consciousness are grounded in an experiential and communal real world whereas Schutz was inclined to acquiesce in the process by which, as autonomous individuals, we pragmatically inhabit our own constructed, alternative realities.

For his first decade in America, Gurwitsch struggled to find satisfactory employment. He and his wife felt very alone. He wrote in August 1940 that they were 'still rooted in another world' (Grathoff, ed., 1989, 18), but he found some solace in living in a Jewish community. He secured a position as Lecturer in Philosophy for two years (1940–42) at Johns Hopkins University, Baltimore. In 1942–43, he was in receipt of a grant from the American Philosophical Society and he was made a fellow 'by courtesy' at Harvard. He found the situation more congenial: 'There are many Europeans here, clustered around Harvard. There is a nice tone and solidarity among them. One is accepted with the matter-of-factness of those who belong' (Grathoff, ed., 1989, 63–4). He began working on James and, as early as December 1942, mentioned that this work might lead to a book which would be an outline of a field theory of consciousness. This context in which Gurwitsch experienced some relief from his previous feeling of alienation was the one in which he reacted to Schutz's article entitled 'The Stranger'.[2] From 1943 to 1946 he received a temporary position as an instructor teaching physics at Harvard. When this three-year contract ended, Gurwitsch received another grant for 1946–47 from the American Philosophical Society and a further grant from the American Council for Émigrés in the Professions. Nevertheless, he became determined to go to France. Koyré and Berger were instrumental in arranging a post and salary for him. Schutz wrote from Amsterdam in October 1946 to try to dissuade Gurwitsch from making this move. He listed reasons why the proposal was unwise, mentioning finally 'The absolute unclarity of the internal political situation (Communism, anti-Semitism)' (Grathoff, ed., 1989, 84), and suggested that the philosophical ethos would be uncongenial: 'Philosophy must be "engagé": see Sartre. Politics smothers philosophy too' (Grathoff, ed., 1989, 86). Gurwitsch was initially not convinced. He was reading Merleau-Ponty's *La structure du comportement* at this time and was dismayed that it communicated many of his thoughts while his own work was not becoming known in the

United States. In December, 1946, he expressed the view to Schutz that 'regardless of what I have the opportunity to say here, it will be scattered in the winds and cast on a sterile stony ground' (Grathoff, ed., 1989, 88). Schutz persisted, pointing out, in June 1947, that Koyré, Wahl and Aron all had arrangements or contingency plans to leave France to go to the United States. In August 1947, Gurwitsch reported to Schutz that he had been offered a post at Wheaton College, Norton, Massachusetts but was still intent on going to France. Schutz's advice seems to have prevailed, however, and for 1947–48 Gurwitsch was a Visiting Lecturer in mathematics at Wheaton. In 1948, he was appointed Assistant Professor of mathematics at the newly established Brandeis University, near Boston, Massachusetts (founded by members of the American Jewish community as a private, coeducational, nonsectarian institution of higher learning). Towards the end of 1948, Schutz encouraged Gurwitsch to apply for a post in the New School for Social Research, but Löwith was appointed. After three years at Brandeis Gurwitsch was appointed Associate Professor of Philosophy at the same institution. He retained this position until 1959. He appears to have found stability at last at Brandeis within a Jewish university but his intellectual affinities remained European. He made the first of several visits to Europe in the summer of 1949 and he spent the year 1958–59 as Fulbright Exchange Professor of Philosophy at the University of Cologne, where he heard of Schutz's death. On returning to the United States in 1959, Gurwitsch was appointed Professor of Philosophy in the Graduate Faculty of Political and Social Science in the New School for Social Research, succeeding Schutz. He remained in this post until 1971, and he died in 1973.

Gurwitsch's first publication in America was his contribution to the collection of essays edited by Farber entitled *Philosophical Essays in Memory of Edmund Husserl* (Gurwitsch, 1940b) to which Schutz also contributed. Gurwitsch's essay, which had been commissioned while he was still in France, was entitled 'On the Intentionality of Consciousness'. Like Schutz, Gurwitsch contributed frequently to the *Journal of Philosophy and Phenomenological Research.*[3] 'On Contemporary Nihilism' was published in the *Review of Politics* (Gurwitsch, 1945) and was Gurwitsch's only direct attempt to correlate his philosophical position with his understanding of the political events which had shaped the previous decade of his life. New light was shed on this dimension of Gurwitsch's thought by Embree's publication in 1991 of a correspondence between Gurwitsch and Cairns of 1941 which he entitled 'Two Husserlians discuss Nazism' (Embree, 1991). Succeeding publications all appeared in the *Journal of Philosophy and Phenomenological Research*. According to Embree, Gurwitsch 'began to write his systematic work while at Harvard' (Gurwitsch, ed. Embree, 1972, xxvii) between 1943 and 1946. It is clear from some other publications of these years[4] that Gurwitsch retained his contacts in Paris, and the work to which Embree refers was first published in a French translation by Michel Butor as *Théorie du champ de la conscience* [theory of the field of consciousness] (Gurwitsch, 1957b) before it was subsequently published in the United States as *The Field of Consciousness* in 1964 (Gurwitsch, 1964a). Gurwitsch announced to Schutz in October 1950 that *The Field of Consciousness* was finished (Grathoff, ed., 1989, 120), but he also added that it is 'actually four books in one' (Grathoff, ed., 1989, 120), and that he had taken out what was really a fifth book which he intended to publish separately under the title of *Les trois domaines du Réel* [The Three Domains of Reality] which Schutz had commented on 'some years ago'(Grathoff, ed., 1989, 160). In a later letter to Schutz of 17 February 1952, Gurwitsch explains that he had written the putative *Les trois domaines du Réel* during the war when the works of Sartre and Merleau-Ponty were not accessible but that his intention was now to incorporate comment on French phenomenology. Embree clarifies that this fifth book was the fourth and last chapter of the first draft of *A Field Theory of Consciousness*, written during the Second World War, and that what was published in 1957/1964 was an elaboration into six parts of the first three chapters of the original draft. Embree was responsible for retrieving the fourth chapter and publishing it as *Marginal Consciousness* in 1984 (Gurwitsch, ed. Embree, 1984) and for juxtaposing the whole of the four original chapters in Volume III of Gurwitsch's *Collected Works* (Gurwitsch, ed. Zaner, 2010). In his editorial introduction to *Marginal Consciousness* in Volume III of Gurwitsch's *Collected Works*, Embree suggests that the seven-page Conclusion of *The Field of Consciousness* was a substitute for the excised 150 pages on the marginal consciousness which Gurwitsch had drafted a decade earlier, and he comments that the proposed critiques of Sartre and Merleau-Ponty never materialized (except for the section devoted to Merleau-Ponty in *Théorie du champ de la conscience* and its English translation).

Perhaps as a result of his year in Cologne and of his established status at the New School of Social Research, Gurwitsch's philosophical presence was restored in Western Europe at the end of the 1950s while, in the United States, his publications appeared to be less totally associated with the development of the phenomenological movement. In German, he published a contribution to the phenomenological theory of perception (Gurwitsch, 1959a) and an essay on the concept of consciousness in Kant and Husserl (Gurwitsch, 1964b). This latter had first appeared in French (Gurwitsch, 1960), a year after another French publication on conceptual thinking (Gurwitsch, 1959b). Some of these publications appeared in English translation relatively quickly, either in the collection of his own work which was published as *Studies in Phenomenology and Psychology* under his own editorship and with his own introduction (Gurwitsch, 1966a), or in other collections such as Sayre and Crosson, eds, 1963. The diversification of outlets is indicated by the appearance of one article in the *Journal of Philosophy* (Gurwitsch, 1961) and by the publication of his discourse on Schutz – which he subsequently used in 1966 as his introduction to Volume III of the *Collected Papers* of Schutz (Schutz, ed. Schutz, 1966)

– and an article on Leibniz, originally published in Hebrew in 1963, both in *Social Research* (Gurwitsch, 1962, and Gurwitsch, 1966b).

In the last years of his life, Gurwitsch maintained his reputation in both American and European contexts. He consistently advanced positions which he had developed early in his career, either in new discussions or by issuing previously unpublished work. He continued to expound his conception of phenomenological psychology by reference to the work of Husserl (Gurwitsch, 1966c), but he became markedly more involved in seeking to provide a phenomenological understanding of both the natural and the social sciences (Gurwitsch, 1967b; 1969) while retaining his adherence to the work of Goldstein (Gurwitsch, 1971) and interest in that of Leibniz (Gurwitsch, 1972b). He contributed to discussions of phenomenology in collections such as *Phenomenology and Social Reality:Essays in Memory of Alfred Schutz* (Gurwitsch, 1970), and in a collection in honour of Dorion Cairns (Gurwitsch, 1973).

The American thought of Schutz and Gurwitsch

Writing in 1977, before the publication of the correspondence, Lester Embree outlined his perception of the differences between the positions of Schutz and Gurwitsch and presented his view of the ways in which they were complementary. Embree introduces his discussion by quoting an example of a knowledge problem offered by William James in his *The Principles of Psychology* (1890). James describes the different reactions of four men taking a tour of Europe. One talks about picturesque views, another about distances and prices, a third about theatres and restaurants, and a fourth barely remembers the names of the places through which he had passed. The question arises, as Embree puts it, 'how it was that things of different sorts *stood out* in the fields of consciousness of the different travellers' or 'how it was that the different egos *were interested in* things of different sorts' (Embree, 1977, 45). Succinctly, Embree comments that Gurwitsch approached the problem of selectivity in the first way and Schutz in the second way. Embree identifies three particular 'surface differences' between the positions of Gurwitsch and Schutz. The third 'surface difference' identified by Embree is between their two views of the status of the 'ego'. As Embree puts it: 'Gurwitsch denied that egos qua subjects of mental lives exist, while Schutz accepted such egos in explicit opposition to Gurwitsch's position' (Embree, 1977, 48).

In the early period of their adaptation to the American context, the initial question is how Schutz and Gurwitsch attempted to present themselves in relation to the socio-intellectual and socio-political fields of the host community. Schutz became involved in an exchange with Talcott Parsons in relation to the development of a philosophy of social science while Gurwitsch, still before the entry of the United States into the war, was in correspondence with another phenomenologist, Dorion Cairns, about the threat of Nazism to

Western values. These two short encounters provide some background to the attitudes shared and developed between Schutz and Gurwitsch in their prolonged correspondence.

Preamble 1: Schutz–Parsons, 1940–41

While Schutz's contribution to the memorial volume ('Phenomenology and the Social Sciences') must have been in press, he embarked upon a brief correspondence with Talcott Parsons. Parsons invited Schutz to read a paper on 'Rationality and the Structure of the Social World' in April 1940 as part of a seminar series on Rationality organized by Parsons and Joseph Schumpeter at Harvard in 1939–40. Parsons had already given a paper in the series in the Winter term of 1939–40. Entitled 'An Approach to the Analysis of the Role of Rationality in Social Action', it summarized the position given by Parsons in detail in his two-volume *The Structure of Social Action*, first published in 1937. Early in 1940, Parsons sent Schutz a copy of this paper. He wrote to Schutz in October to elicit a response and under the misapprehension that Schutz had written a critique of the paper. In fact, Schutz had only completed a draft review of Parsons's *The Structure of Social Action* which he sent to Parsons on 15 November 1940.

Schutz seems to have focused in his draft review on the concluding chapters of Parsons's two volumes. Schutz was not disposed to challenge Parsons in terms of interpretation and counter-interpretation of Weber. Schutz's draft review was blunt in its criticism. He carefully paraphrased the development of the structure of social action theory proposed by Parsons, but the dismissiveness of his attitude is well represented by a summary comment in which Schutz remarks that Parsons's analyses

> only answer the question of how a theoretical scheme can be established which is capable of explaining what may happen or what may be considered as happening in the mind of the actor. And so Parsons is not concerned with finding out the truly subjective categories, but seeks only objective categories for the interpretation of subjective points of view. (Grathoff, ed., 1978, 36)

Schutz considered that the Parsonian position was indicative of a more general tendency. He considered that the kind of sociology proposed by Parsons could be likened to behaviourism in psychology. For Schutz, the fallacy of the theory of behaviourists consisted in 'the substitution of a fictional world for social reality by the promulgation of methodological principles represented as being appropriate to the social sciences which, though proved successful in other fields, prove a failure in the realm of intersubjectivity' (Grathoff, ed., 1978, 46). Schutz argued that social scientists were in the process of carving out a sphere of social activity which they might analyse autonomously without reference to the meanings of their actions held by actors. Schutz comments that these social scientists contend that they 'may and should restrict themselves to describing what this world means to them, neglecting what it means to the actors within this social world' (Grathoff, ed., 1978, 46–7). This attitude is instrumental in constructing a profession but its effects are pernicious in social science just as they are in 'modern economics'. Parsons fails to recognize that his theory of the relation between norms and actions imposes itself as a dominant norm in relation to the a-theoretical dispositions of actors.

A short correspondence between Schutz and Parsons followed. Parsons could not relate to Schutz's concern with the prior problem of all conceptualization. He commented that 'I am afraid I must confess to being skeptical of phenomenological analysis' (Grathoff, ed., 1978, 88), and he elaborated that he emphasized the subjective point of view 'but in the form of subjective categories in a conceptual scheme and not in the form of an account of what the subjective social world "really" is' (Grathoff, ed., 1978, 90). Schutz resisted being marginalized on the grounds that his concerns were 'ontological'. Schutz asserted vehemently that he was 'not an ontological dogmatist' (Grathoff, ed., 1978, 103) but, instead, always sought to understand the ontological basis of conceptualizations adopted in changing situations of social scientific empiricism.

Underlying the disagreement between Schutz and Parsons, therefore, was a tension in respect of their views of the proper relationship between philosophy and social science and, more particularly, of the relationships between ontology, epistemology and methodology. It is clear that in the period between 1939 and 1941 Schutz was adjusting to his new situation by arguing on two fronts. On the one hand, he was intent on defining his position in relation to the work of Husserl, using the movement which was seeking to introduce phenomenology into North America to articulate some of his reservations about Husserl's legacy. The correspondence with Gurwitsch helped in this endeavour. On the other hand, he was eager to use his phenomenological interest in the foundations of social relations to challenge the increasing domination of a social scientific understanding of those relations. The correspondence with Parsons helped him to clarify his position in relation to sociology.

Preamble 2: Cairns–Gurwitsch, 1941

An exchange between Cairns and Gurwitsch was given stimulus by a letter which Cairns wrote to *The Nation* in response to a letter from one Betty Barzin. Ms. Barzin had compared favourably the treatment of Bergson by the Vichy government with the treatment of Husserl by the Nazis, concluding that the difference illustrated 'the gulf which divides, always will divide, Latin civilization and German Kultur' (Embree, 1991, 84). She suggested that the behaviour of the French government indicated that 'the love of the spirit for the spirit's sake, will live there forever' in spite of the fact that it was 'at the same time ousting Jews from places of learning' (Embree, 1991, 84). Cairns responded vigorously in a letter published in *The Nation* on 29 March 1941. He was primarily intent on challenging the supposed duality between 'Latin' and 'German' culture. While condemning the Nazis, Cairns argued that National Socialist ideology should not be identified with German culture. Gurwitsch wrote to Cairns a fortnight later enclosing a draft letter which he was proposing to send to *The Nation*.[5] He focused on the division between cultures proposed by Ms. Barzin and on Cairns's scepticism about the persistence of the liberalism of the French tradition. Gurwitsch insisted that the Dreyfus affair had shown the French tradition was fundamentally opposed to anti-Semitism and was characterized by a continuing 'soif de Justice' [thirst for justice]. He shared the optimism of Ms. Barzin that the French love of the spirit for spirit's sake would survive but felt unable to accept Cairns's optimism that a comparable spirit among 'good', anti-Nazi Germans, might be saved. He thought that Cairns was indulging 'in an illusion' because he failed to acknowledge that Hitler had been brought into power by the German people. Cairns responded to Gurwitsch by contesting the basic idea that whole national cultures can be characterized. Gurwitsch defended his position in an important letter of response of 27 April 1941. He elaborates on what he means by 'Latinity':

> What I mean is an idea: the idea of a universal civilization, which has universal human significance. This is the idea that there is but one truth valid for everybody and for all mankind regardless of what might differentiate several groups within mankind, so that, in the light of this idea, these differences turn out to be without any deeper importance. (Embree, 1991, 95)

Gurwitsch goes on to stress that it was this idea which, mainly as a result of the work of Descartes, infused the French intellectual tradition. It was present in past German civilization, but 'it was in Germany that the counter-movement against this idea was started' (Embree, 1991, 96). The first culprit was Fichte, and the second was Hegel. Importantly, Gurwitsch blames Fichte for the rise of subjectivism, and, in relation to Hegel, he emphasizes that his own belief in the absoluteness of universal spirit is clearly differentiated from Hegel's idealism. In response to Cairns, therefore, Gurwitsch argues that Nazism is not the 'accidental' (Embree, 1991, 98) product of German culture such that the accident can be eliminated. On the contrary, Nazism is the direct consequence of the corruption of the 'Latin' ideal effected by the post-Kantian generation of German philosophers, a corruption which has now contaminated the whole of German culture so that it is now 'incorrigible' (Embree, 1991, 97). Cairns's response of 26 June 1941 appears to have ended the exchange. Cairns reiterates his view that 'The ideal of *universal* civilization should not be called "Latin"' (Embree, 1991, 102) and he opposes the apparent implication of Gurwitsch's position, that 'mankind must destroy German culture root and branch' (Embree, 1991, 102).

What was a private correspondence between Gurwitsch and Cairns in the year 1941 provided evidence in 1991 when it was published that Gurwitsch held passionate views about the ideological context of his past life experiences and that he attempted to integrate these political views with his fundamental philosophical objections to subjectivist reduction. We have to keep this dimension in mind when we consider what appears to have been Gurwitsch's fear of the diminution of the status of the objective noema that he sensed in the work of both Schutz and Merleau-Ponty.

Schutz–Gurwitsch: the preliminary exchanges, 1939

Gurwitsch sent an advance copy of what was to be published as 'On the Intentionality of Consciousness' in a letter of 5 August 1939, which began the correspondence. In reply, Schutz sent a detailed critique a few weeks later. He also indicated in this letter that his contribution (in German) would be finished shortly and that he would at once send Gurwitsch a copy. This was what would be published as 'Phenomenology and the Social Sciences'. The two essays were published in the same Husserl memorial volume in 1940. This is the context underlying the first, private Schutz/Gurwitsch intellectual exchange.

Gurwitsch's essay is offered within the field of philosophy. He begins by detailing how Husserl came to think that there is a class of mental facts (designated as 'acts') which 'have the peculiarity of presenting an object to the subject' (Gurwitsch, 1966a, 124). Gurwitsch argues that Husserl supposed that in experiencing such 'acts' subjects acquire consciousness of objects. He focuses on Husserl's *Formale und transzendentale Logik* [formal and transcendental logic] of 1929 concentrating on the '*noesis-noema doctrine*' (Gurwitsch, 1966a, 131–2) and indicating the respects in which he would like to go beyond Husserl's position. To illustrate his distinctions, Gurwitsch talks about a tree as an exemplary 'perceived thing'. The combination of these words is crucial. The tree as a 'real object' is different from the ways in which it might present itself to perception, either, for instance, as giving shade or as a recollection in the memory of another tree. These modes of possible presentation of the tree to perception are the *noema* of the tree. The received perception in any particular case is determined by the *noesis* of the perceiving subject. The physical phenomenon of the tree is separate from the psychic phenomenon which has a dual construction, comprising a combination of multiply potential structures of presentation with individual agents of reception. The important point to emphasize is that the noema is as distinct from the act of perception as it is from the real object. Gurwitsch specifies that it is 'an irreal or ideal entity which belongs to the same sphere as meanings or significations' (Gurwitsch, 1966a, 133) which is 'the sphere of sense (*Sinn*)' (Gurwitsch, 1966a, 133). This sphere of irreality or ideality is a-temporal. It is not dependent on temporal actualizations.

Schutz's critique is extremely technical but, in essence, he questioned Gurwitsch's concentration on consciousness. He first made a highly important introductory remark, reminding his correspondent that 'As you know, for me the question concerning the "correct", namely orthodox, Husserl interpretation is always secondary to the question concerning the true states of affairs' (Grathoff, ed., 1989, 6).

Although Schutz was anxious to make it clear that he could indulge in scholarly debate about the interpretation of Husserl's work if required, his implication is that he was more interested in phenomenology as a methodology than as a philosophy. There is the sense that Schutz feared that Gurwitsch was engaged in debate that used a discourse which presupposed in its attitude to consciousness precisely what needed to be subjected to scrutiny. As Schutz puts it, the 'double-sidedness of consciousness' (the noetic–noematic correlation) 'is not a demonstrable finding of phenomenological analysis, but rather the linguistic expression for a two-fold possibility of interpreting "the same" phenomena' (Grathoff, ed., 1989, 6). Just as Schutz was arguing that Parsons's theorizing failed to work from the preconceptual, so he considered that Gurwitsch was excessively trapped within Husserlian exegetical debate, operating in relation to constituted phenomena rather than by interrogating their origins. Pursuing Gurwitsch's illustration of the basis of the identity of a tree, Schutz presents himself as primarily interested, therefore, in talking of 'the tree-*thing* of the natural attitude, not of the tree-*noema* or the tree-*noematis*' (Grathoff, ed., 1989, 7). Schutz broadens his criticism to suggest that 'with that hubris which phenomenology shares with all transcendental systems' it cannot cope with 'this world, our *life*-world' which 'is after all there' (Grathoff, ed., 1989, 7). Phenomenological discourse is in danger of obliterating natural attitudes of the life-world when it should be offering a procedure to clarify those primordial experiences. Schutz was trying to secure the support of Gurwitsch to challenge the academicization of a scholastic phenomenology, but the important question is whether their trans-cultural migration forced them to subscribe for survival to a detached intellectualism precisely because they were both divorced from their originary social contexts.

Schutz and 'Sartre–Gurwitsch': exchange 1, 1941–43

On 19 December 1940, Gurwitsch sent Schutz a copy of a paper which he had started in September. This was subsequently published as 'A Non-Egological Conception of Consciousness' (Gurwitsch, 1941). In his covering letter, Gurwitsch prepares Schutz for his reading of the article on Sartre. He refers to the fact that he and Schutz had often discussed the problem addressed by the article and that both had known for some time that 'something is wrong with the transcendental ego' (Grathoff, ed., 1978, 31) but that he and Schutz were attempting to deal with this issue from opposite points of view: 'Something must be dropped: in you transcendental, in myself and Sartre ego is the drop-out' (Grathoff, ed., 1978, 31). Gurwitsch admired Sartre's work at this time on the basis of his reading of *La transcendence de l'ego* and *L'imagination*, both of which were published in 1936. Gurwitsch's willingness to align himself with Sartre against Schutz is based on his reading of texts produced by Sartre before *L'Être et le Néant* (1943) and before Sartre's post-war articulation of an existentialist position.

Gurwitsch begins 'A Non-Egological Conception of Consciousness' by repeating his recognition that Husserl's position in respect of the ego changed from that formulated in the first edition of his *Logische Untersuchungen* (1900) to that advanced in his *Ideen* (1913). In the former, Husserl rejected any suggestion that acts of consciousness derive from a centre of consciousness, whereas in the latter he accepted that there might be a 'pure ego' which is exempt from phenomenological reduction. Crudely, the former was a non-egological theory whereas the latter had become egological. Gurwitsch endorses Sartre's vindication of Husserl's former view. They are in agreement that 'on the level of non-reflection there is no ego at all' (Gurwitsch, 1966a, 292) by which they mean that the ego is constituted by consciousness rather than being the source of consciousness, but Gurwitsch hints at a difference of opinion with Sartre which suggests that Schutz was wrong in identifying a 'Sartre–Gurwitsch' position. Gurwitsch references his doctoral thesis to show that he had already developed a non-egological view of consciousness before the publication of Sartre's texts[6] and it becomes clear that the Gestaltist element in Gurwitsch's thinking differentiates it from that of Sartre. Sartre's view is that the fact that there is no source of the ego in consciousness means that there is no ego except the empirical, psychical or psychophysical ego, which means that it has to be understood to be an object in the physical world, to be a 'transcendent existent' (Gurwitsch, 1966a, 293). By contrast, Gurwitsch is not satisfied with this solution because, for him, it begs the question of how we become conscious of this object and how it is constituted for consciousness. For Gurwitsch, it is through reflection and the dialogical correlation between noesis and noema that the transcendent existent is constituted. Because this is an ongoing process, there can be no recourse to a hypostatized notion of a transcendent existent. As Gurwitsch puts it, 'as in regard to material things, thinking in terms of substantiality gave way to thinking in terms of functions and relations' (Gurwitsch, 1966a, 299). The consequence is that, for Gurwitsch, unlike for Sartre, the ego has no self-evident status. 'The ego's being carries with it a certain character of provisionalness' (Gurwitsch, 1966a, 300), a historical contingency. There is no absolute, a-historical, ontic entity. Anachronistically speaking, there are signs here which show the grounds on which Gurwitsch disliked phenomenological ontology and existentialism in that the notion that existence

precedes essence is predicated on a commitment to the absoluteness of existence independent of constituting consciousness.

Farber invited Schutz to write a reply to Gurwitsch's article. Instead of
doing so, Schutz incorporated his critical comments into an article which he
was writing on Max Scheler. Schutz's 'Scheler's Theory of Intersubjectivity
and the General Thesis of the Alter Ego' was published in 1942 in the second
number of the journal *Philosophy and Phenomenological Research*. Schutz begins
his article by summarizing Scheler's 'concept of man' as advanced in his *Die
Stellung des Menschen im Kosmos* [The Place of Man in the Cosmos], published
in 1928. Scheler posited five levels of psychical existence. Behaviour of plants
and animals in the first four levels is susceptible to zoological, biological,
physiological or psychological analysis. These modes of analysis are also applicable to human behaviour but the principle which distinguishes the behaviour
of man in the fifth level is that it is governed by 'Geist' [mind] belonging to
'Persons'. By reference to Scheler's earlier books, Schutz clarifies this concept
of 'Person'. The 'experienced I' [Erlebnis-ich] is objectifiable whereas the
'Person' cannot be objectified because 'The Person manifests himself exclusively by performing the acts in which he lives' (Schutz, ed. Natanson, 1962,
153). The distinction made by Scheler between the Person as unanalysable
originator of action and the 'I' as empirically analysable subject influenced the
theory of inter-personal relations or inter-subjectivity which he developed in
his book on 'sympathy'.[7] The logic of Scheler's position is that relations with
'alter egos' [other egos] are not dependent on cognition. As persons, however,
people relate instinctively to each other within communities. This is the
essence of what Scheler called his 'perceptional theory of the alter ego'. Schutz
proceeds to offer critical observations on Scheler's theory. Schutz argues,
against Scheler, that the sense of prior belonging to a community which constitutes all persons as persons does not really give priority to the communal
'we' because this sense is always 'my' sense. In the 'natural attitude' people
can always turn their attention, by reflection, from the objects of their thinking
to the fact of their thinking. From this reflection, without the need for any
'transcendental reduction', my 'self' emerges. Schutz claims that this 'self' 'does
not merely enter the field of my consciousness in order to appear on its
horizon or at its center' (Schutz, ed. Natanson, 1962, 169), and he adds that
'the whole stream of consciousness is through and through the stream of my
personal life' (Schutz, ed. Natanson, 1962, 169).

The former comment is clearly a critique of Gurwitsch while the latter
criticizes James. It is at this point that Schutz inserts, as a footnote, his response
to Gurwitsch's 'A Non-Egological Conception of Consciousness'. He introduces it by saying that, in discussing a theory of Sartre, Gurwitsch was dealing
with the same problem in relation to the provenance of the 'self'. Schutz refers
to the chief Sartre–Gurwitsch argument 'against the egological theory maintained in the present paper' (Schutz, ed. Natanson, 1962, 169, fn. 43). Schutz

does not acknowledge the distinction which Gurwitsch tried to make between his position and that of Sartre. To clarify, Gurwitsch realized that the position Sartre adopted in *La transcendence de l'ego* was covertly dependent on the commitment to the existence of a 'pre-reflective cogito' which he articulated in the introduction to *L'Être et le Néant*. Sartre's opposition to Husserl's view of a transcendental ego was fundamentally an opposition to its transcendence or essentialism in favour of a view that egos are constituted existentially by a process of cognition which is more basic than ratiocination. Gurwitsch wanted to avoid such conceptual dependence on a notion of universal, human physical existence as the originator of selfhood. Instead, his conception was that individuals define themselves as subjects in correlation with historically cumulative objectivities (later to be called 'fields'), such that self-identity is never a-historically absolute. Sartre's critique of Husserl's transcendental view of the ego was itself clandestinely egotistical on different grounds. Schutz was resolutely egotistical by emphasizing personal acts of reflection within the natural attitude of everyday living without seeing any need for a specialist form of reflection, named reduction, which, in his view, was a device to retain unnecessarily a metaphysical dimension. Without quite appreciating that Gurwitsch was arguing for a continuous correlation between subjective/objective or noesis/noema which denied any abstract egological position, Schutz tended to consider that the views of Sartre and Gurwitsch were similarly impregnated with Cartesian intellectualism and that both should be opposed in favour of analysing the self-constituting effects of people's ordinary activities.

Schutz's phenomenological orientation was distinctly positivist. He attributed what he regarded as inconsistencies in Scheler's notion of the Person to its origin 'in his philosophy of religion and ethics' (Schutz, ed. Natanson, 1962, 171). The footnote on 'Sartre–Gurwitsch' was only a minor intrusion on Schutz's discussion of Scheler but the fact that Schutz thought it to be an appropriate opportunity to publish his critique suggests that he considered the Sartre–Gurwitsch position to be weighed down by unnecessary intellectualism just as much as that of Scheler. To that extent, Schutz's critique of Scheler in the rest of the article is addressed in part to Sartre–Gurwitsch. The substance of that critique is that Schutz objects to Scheler's elevation of the 'Person' above the 'self', or, as he puts this himself, 'the artificial distinction between mere "functions" belonging to the Self and "acts" belonging to the Person' (Schutz, ed. Natanson, 1962, 172). By undertaking mundane analyses of intersubjective encounters, Schutz argues that his general thesis of the alter ego deduced from what he calls his 'phenomenological psychology' provides 'a sufficient frame of reference for the foundation of empirical psychology and the social sciences' (Schutz, ed. Natanson, 1962, 175), and he points to the fact that this was the basis of the position which he had adopted in his *Der sinnhafte Aufbau der sozialen Welt* (not at this time available in English translation).

In the private exchange between Schutz and Gurwitsch which followed from Schutz's pre-publication release to Gurwitsch of his critique of 'Sartre–Gurwitsch', Gurwitsch attempts to differentiate his position from that of Sartre. In Schutz's response, he apologizes for not appreciating these differences, admitting that he hadn't read Sartre's work, but he continues to dispute the substance of the position which Gurwitsch had identified as his own. Tellingly, Schutz concludes these last comments with a statement of his objection to the 'whole non-egological conception' which, in his view, 'leads to the result that I can only advert to my thinking, but not to my acting' (Grathoff, ed., 1978, 53).

Succinctly, we can say that this early exchange between Schutz and Gurwitsch shows the main outline of where the lines were drawn between them. Gurwitsch insisted that reflection requires thought which unavoidably draws upon conceptual instruments developed independently (marginally) whereas, for Schutz, reflection is primarily the outcome of personal introspection or inter-personal encounter without any extraneous conceptual mediation.

Schutz–Gurwitsch and 'On Multiple Realities', 1942–45

In a letter to Gurwitsch of 9 November 1942, Schutz announced that he had finished the 'Stranger' and was planning to 'rewrite for American readers' (Grathoff, ed., 1989, 65) the papers which he had written during his last summer vacation in Europe in 1938. The re-written version of the 1938 papers was published in 1945 as 'On Multiple Realities' (Schutz, 1945c). There was an unexplained gap in the correspondence between the two men for almost a full year between mid-1944 and mid-1945, such that Schutz resumed the exchange in June 1945 with a formal rather than cordial greeting. The resumption of dialogue was the consequence of Schutz's receipt from Gurwitsch of an off-print of his essay entitled 'On Contemporary Nihilism' (Gurwitsch, 1945). Schutz offered some comments on this essay and their relations were fully restored by September when Gurwitsch sent Schutz a detailed critique of 'On Multiple Realities'.

Gurwitsch's 'On Contemporary Nihilism' was his most overt attack on the depreciation of rationalism in contemporary intellectual circles. He considered that the psychological and sociological sciences were both instrumental in effecting this depreciation. The consequence was that the distinction maintained by the ancients between 'episteme' [knowledge] and 'doxa' [opinion] no longer exists. A tolerance of different opinions has developed which in fact is an indifference to truth. Gurwitsch proceeds to attack the attempts of pragmatic philosophers to develop a theory of truth on the basis of effect. This denies what Gurwitsch insists which is that 'Truth is a rational system, the system of reason, however the nature thereof be conceived; it depends upon no human desires and has no connection with the need for compensation'

(Gurwitsch, 1945, 174). This denial is indicative of contemporary 'nihilism' which Gurwitsch defines as 'the substitution of "concrete" things for "abstractions"'. It leads to a relativism the effects of which have been all too horribly evident in regard to political morality in recent German history. By contrast, rationalists know that 'right, like all other "abstractions", is an idea of reason, and that an idea, by virtue of its essential nature, is abstract and universal' (Gurwitsch, 1945, 175). Gurwitsch identifies nihilism with both naturalism and vitalism. All give primacy to corporeal behaviour. Gurwitsch argues that the dominant contemporary ethos is to conceive of human behaviour exclusively in sociological or psychological terms on the assumption that these are practical versions of fundamental nihilism. He provides an account of seventeenth-century rationalism, however, to suggest that this current equation of the human and social sciences with the naturalistic attitude is erroneous. The article makes a plea for the recognition that, following the tradition of European rationalism, naturalist explanations of human behaviour are the products of conscious acts of cognition, exemplified particularly in mathematical reason.

'On Contemporary Nihilism' shows clearly how much Gurwitsch thought was at stake in his philosophical reflections. He was writing at a time when the totalitarianism[8] which he regarded as the corollary of the collapse of the criterion of truth seemed certain to be defeated militarily but he warned that the greater challenge was now to defeat the false principles which had generated it and to revive well-founded substitutes. Gurwitsch celebrates the principles of the French Revolution, founded, in his view, on Cartesian rationalism. He ends by countering the argument that he is recommending recourse to principles which only obtained in the historical past. He contends that we have drifted into nihilism 'by our own consent', with the result that 'if we were free to drift into this pitiful condition, we are still free to redress our condition' (Gurwitsch, 1945, 198). Gurwitsch thought, therefore, that there was all to play for in contemporary philosophy and politics. Hence the urgency of his suspicion of Merleau-Ponty's apparent acceptance of naturalism in emphasizing the pre-eminence of corporeal perception, and, hence, equally, his anxiety that his friend Schutz was courting naturalism by recognizing the equal validity of multiple realities by offering a social psychology which was unregulated by any adherence to absolutes.

In response, Schutz admitted that 'On Contemporary Nihilism' had given him a better understanding of the basis of Gurwitsch's critique of sociology. Schutz thought that Gurwitsch had thrown the baby out with the bath water 'in attributing to all sociology the nihilistic tendencies which, e.g., are without doubt exhibited by the currently so modern sociology of knowledge' (Grathoff, ed., 1989, 74). Schutz thought that there was still scope for his unpretentious accounts of social phenomena. The first of these to be published was 'The Stranger'. Schutz takes the term 'stranger' to mean 'an adult individual of our times and civilization who tries to be permanently accepted or at least tolerated by the group which he approaches' (Schutz, ed. Brodersen, 1964, 91). This refers primarily, but not exclusively, to immigrants, such as himself. As such, Schutz analyses his own experiences. He refers to sociological analyses of the same topic but his investigation concentrates on how 'the cultural pattern of group life presents itself to the common sense of a man who lives his everyday life within the group among his fellow-men' (Schutz, ed. Brodersen, 1964, 91). In other words, Schutz focuses on primary experiences within society. Schutz differentiates his intention from that of the sociologist who '(as sociologist, not as a man among fellow-men which he remains in his private life) is the disinterested scientific onlooker of the social world' (Schutz, ed. Brodersen, 1964, 91). Sociological analysis is differentiated from common-sense analysis by virtue of the sociologist adopting a role or a distinct persona. Schutz's discussion enables him to consider how a stranger adjusts the common-sense assumptions of his original everyday life to those of the host community, but the article does not enquire further into the status of these insights relative to detached analyses provided by social science, and neither does it raise the question whether the rules of social scientific analysis might themselves be similarly susceptible to cross-cultural adaptation. 'The Homecomer' (Schutz, ed. Brodersen, 1964) follows the same methodological procedure, concentrating on a different kind of estrangement, that of the returning war veteran. In 'The Well-Informed Citizen' Schutz posits three different kinds of knowledge held by participants in civil society, those of 'the expert, the man on the street, and the well-informed citizen' (Schutz, ed. Brodersen, 1964, 122) without confronting the implications of his understanding of the 'social distribution of knowledge' for the operations of democracy except in concluding that there is a danger that public opinion polls are tending to give social approval and authority to public opinion instead of to either expert or well-informed knowledge, such that 'it is the duty and the privilege ... of the well-informed citizen in a democratic society to make his private opinion prevail over the public opinion of the man on the street' (Schutz, ed. Brodersen, 1964, 134).

It is in the resurrection in 1945 of his 1938 papers that Schutz confronts the question, unresolved in 'The Stranger' and 'The Homecomer', or, subsequently, in 'The Well-informed Citizen' (1946) of the relative status of common sense and scientific analyses. Schutz's intention is to 'clarify the relationship between the reality of the world of daily life and that of theoretical, scientific contemplation' (Schutz, ed. Natanson, 1962, 208). Resurrected, the papers constitute a post hoc expression of the preliminary separation of everyday from scientific realities which Schutz had proposed before putting it into practice in articles such as 'The Stranger' and 'The Homecomer'. Schutz first discusses in detail the reality of the world of daily life. Our knowledge in this world is practical or pragmatic. Schutz suggests that within this world we suspend belief in the same sort of way as phenomenological reduction suspends belief in the outer world. The difference is that in our daily life we suspend doubt about the existence of that outer world. There is, as Schutz states, an *'epoché of the natural attitude'* (Schutz, ed. Natanson, 1962, 229). Schutz next considers 'the many realities and their constitution'. Schutz speaks of 'provinces of *meaning*' because 'it is the meaning of our experiences and not the ontological structure of the objects which constitutes reality' (Schutz, ed. Natanson, 1962, 230). Schutz asserts that the fundamental province of meaning is the world of working and that all other provinces of meaning are modifications of this. He repeats the view which he had articulated towards the end of 'Life Forms and Meaning Structure'[9] that the intellectual challenge now was to define the characteristics of different provinces of meaning. In 'On Multiple Realities' he tries to move towards a consideration of the province of meaning of the social sciences by examining the nature of the constitution of imaginary worlds and the world of dreams. Schutz suggests that the world of scientific theory is one which is contemplative and without direct practical intent. Contemplation can have a practical outcome, as when politicians meditate on public opinion (Schutz, ed. Natanson, 1962, 245), but the aim of scientific theorizing 'is not to master the world but to observe and possibly to understand it' (Schutz, ed. Natanson, 1962, 245). This means that theoretical discourse is 'subject to permanent revision ... without creating any change in the outer world' (Schutz, ed. Natanson, 1962, 247). Although all provinces of meaning are subjectively constructed, the hallmark of social scientific meaning is that it involves an epoché, a bracketing or suspension, of 'the subjectivity of the thinker as a man among fellow-men' (Schutz, ed. Natanson, 1962, 249). Schutz elaborates in a footnote that 'theoretical thinking has to be characterized as belonging to the "natural attitude" so that, in other words, social science entails an instrumental bracketing *within* the natural attitude which is not to be confused with the phenomenological reduction which attempts to bracket the natural attitude absolutely'. Schutz states that a defining characteristic of the theorizing self is that it is solitary: 'it has no social environment; it stands outside social relationships' (Schutz, ed. Natanson, 1962, 253). Schutz tries to overcome this apparent inadequacy of theoretical social science by reiterating that all provinces of meaning are subjective constructs including the province which functionally excludes subjectivity. By reiterating this point, Schutz concludes that abstract social science can be vindicated by reinserting it within the inter-subjectivity of the world of everyday life and by refusing to assume that it offers access to a province of meaning which has paramount reality.

One would have expected Gurwitsch to see in Schutz's argument a direct contradiction of his own conviction that meaning should not be stripped of its universal, objective dimension. Surprisingly, Gurwitsch is emollient in response. He affirms that 'You have my complete agreement with your exposition of the "daily life world" as world of work' (Grathoff, ed., 1989, 75). This had always been the case, as his Habilitation thesis showed. What concerns Gurwitsch is the process of constitution of the sciences. He rejects Schutz's view that science is one province of meaning among multiple, equally valid, realities. He argues, first, that the constitution of the sciences has to be understood historically by carrying out a positivist analysis of the sedimentations of meaning, and, secondly, that the question of the existence of the sciences 'must be posed as a question of the transition from the order of the "life-world" to the "Pythagorean" order' (Grathoff, ed., 1989, 75). Gurwitsch calls 'orders of being' what Schutz calls 'multiple realities'. He refers to the chapter of his book which he had started in 1943. 'Orders of being' was to become 'orders of existence' when that book was finally published in French in 1957. I turn now to Gurwitsch's position as advanced in that book as the culmination of his post-war thinking where he attends again to Schutz's notion of 'multiple realities'.

Gurwitsch: Théorie du champ de la conscience, *1957* [The Field of Consciousness, *1964*]

Théorie du champ de la conscience is Gurwitsch's summative statement of the views whose development I have tried to trace contextually. Gurwitsch repeats many of the ideas which he had gradually formed in earlier unpublished and published work. Rather than repeat much of what I have tried to explicate in relation to the milieu of its production, I concentrate on the new impact of Gurwitsch's statement of the 1950s and 1960s, especially so as to allow for an appreciation (in chapter 4) of Merleau-Ponty's late critique of the views of the person who had earlier been his mentor.

Gurwitsch's 'Introduction' to *Théorie du champ de la conscience* is an 'exposé of the problems' to be discussed. Gurwitsch states these immediately in terms of everyday experience, but the apparently simple presentation contains the essence of his complex thought. 'Experience', he begins, 'always presents us objects, things, events, etc., in terms of fixed contexts and textures, never of givens nor of dispersed and isolated facts' (Gurwitsch, 1957b, 9). Our experience, in other words, is never of the immediately given but is always contextually mediated by factors which themselves are not detachedly arbitrary. He illustrates with an example taken from perceptual experience. We are interested in a building. We walk around it to get a variety of views of it and we accumulate a number of perceptions all related to the building but, at the same time, we are conscious of other linked factors which might be differently connected to it, such as a shop behind the building on the other side of the road, or a sore foot as we walk along the footpaths, or our memory of a similar building we saw many years ago. To formulate his problem, Gurwitsch defines the field of consciousness as 'the totality of co-present givens' (Gurwitsch, 1957b, 10), and, consequently, to develop a 'theory of the field of consciousness' is 'to embark on an analysis of the phenomenon of context in general as well as on the elucidation of different types of context, that is to say of types which differ from each other by virtue of differences related to principles of organization' (Gurwitsch, 1957b, 10–11). This general statement enables Gurwitsch to indicate that his intention is to establish the thesis that 'each total field of consciousness is made up of three domains which possess specific kinds of organization' (Gurwitsch, 1957b, 12). These domains are the 'theme', which is the focus of the interest (such as the building in the example); the 'thematic field', which is the background or 'horizon' which is intrinsically related to the theme (such as the memory of similar buildings); and the 'margin', which is co-present with the other two domains but has no intrinsic relation to them (such as the shop). Using his own categorization of domains, Gurwitsch implies that Gestalt psychology constitutes a thematic field in relation to his dominant phenomenological theme. I concentrate on Gurwitsch's discussion of Merleau-Ponty and then on the novel elements of Part 6 and the conclusion.

Part 4, devoted to the 'phenomenological theory of perception', has four chapters which consider 'the perceptual process', 'analysis of the perceptual noema', 'the noetic analysis of perception' and 'intentional analysis' before turning to Merleau-Ponty's account of 'the organization of perceptual life'. Gurwitsch emphasizes in the third chapter that every act of perception is mixed up with anticipations of other perceptions and that these other perceptions amount to an 'interior horizon' which impinges upon immediate sense impressions. These anticipations help to constitute the potential meanings of perceptive acts. For Gurwitsch, there is no 'pure' sense impression. All our perceptions are modified by our accumulated consciousness of contextually potential meaning. In this way there is an internal noematic dimension to our noetic experiences.

This is the framework within which Gurwitsch discusses Merleau-Ponty.[10] He comments that Merleau-Ponty's book developed a theory of perceptual organization with which he is in essential agreement, but he highlights two differences of position. He detects, first, an element of realism in the distinction he thinks that Merleau-Ponty makes between things themselves and the series of appearances corresponding with them. Secondly, he shows that Merleau-Ponty 'links the constitution of real things and of the perceptual world in general to corporeal existence rather than to consciousness' (Gurwitsch, 1957b, 244). In short, Gurwitsch suspects that, in spite of apparent agreement, Merleau-Ponty does not accept his fundamental contention that real objects and our own corporeal identities are the constructs of our consciousnesses. Gurwitsch already suspects that Merleau-Ponty's position tends towards an emphasis on the primacy of existence. As a result of his suspicion that this is the tendency of French phenomenology, based on a Heideggerian reading of Husserl, Gurwitsch explicitly devotes Part 6 to consideration of 'Ontological problems'.

Gurwitsch adopts the term 'order of existence' to indicate the infinity of contexts within which any theme may be situated. Differences between orders of existence can be defined in terms of different principles of relevance which regulate them. In a sub-section entitled 'the order of reality and its sub-orders', Gurwitsch explains that 'the perceptual world is the fundamental stratum' of reality in general and that by 'perceptual world' he means 'that order of existence which, in the pre-theoretical or a-theoretical attitude of everyday experience, unquestionably counts for every one of us as external reality' (Gurwitsch, 1957b, 302; 1964a, 382). This unreflecting perceptual world is primary and prior to all scientific and theoretical explanations. For the first time, Gurwitsch publicly articulates the position which he had advanced in the closing part of his unpublished Habilitation thesis. The perceptual world comprises different spheres of activity such as those of work, the family and the political system in which we participate as citizens. Modern life has contributed to the autonomization of these spheres and each has its own rules of relevance, but they all must be considered as 'sub-orders of the encompassing and all-embracing order of existence which is reality in general' (Gurwitsch, 1957b, 307; 1964a, 387), embracing temporally and geographically distant manifestations. For Gurwitsch, this is the 'life-world' of all our existences, deliberately connoting the work of Husserl. In the following sub-section, Gurwitsch concentrates on 'autonomous orders of existence'. There are, first, 'imaginary worlds' which are detached from reality and each other, and he instances novels, plays and epic poems as examples of autonomous imaginary worlds which are distinct genres. These correspond with the 'symbolic forms' discussed by Schutz in relation to the life-world. Secondly, Gurwitsch argues that 'ideation' constitutes an order of existence which is detached from reality in a way which is different from the detachment of imaginary worlds. 'Eide' [ideas] do not present themselves in isolation but belong to a network of 'eidetic domains' and they are essentially a-temporal. The world of Platonic ideas is upheld 'without, however, being interpreted in the sense of metaphysical realism' (Gurwitsch, 1957b, 309; 1964a, 390). This means that Gurwitsch preserves the autonomy of an order of existence within which other orders of existence may be examined while still insisting that this order is constituted and is not metaphysically real. Tantalizingly, he concludes that in this present investigation he 'must abstain from further penetration into the problem of ideation' (Gurwitsch, 1957b, 310; 1964a, 391). He does, however, clarify his position a little by differentiating it from that adopted by Schutz and by showing why a sphere transcending the 'natural attitude' to which Schutz restricts himself, is necessary. He summarizes the account which Schutz gives in 'On Multiple Realities' of the different 'finite provinces of meaning', each of which has a distinctive cognitive style. Gurwitsch regards these as equivalent to his 'orders of existence'. For Schutz, Gurwitsch argues, 'among the different "provinces of meaning" the "world of working" enjoys a privileged status' (Gurwitsch, 1957b, 316; 1964a, 397). In order to think our lives in ways other than at this primary level, we have to take a leap into a different province of meaning. Schutz is thus led 'to advance the idea of a typology of the different finite provinces of meaning in terms of the epoché peculiar to each' (Gurwitsch, 1957b, 316; 1964a, 398). In Gurwitsch's view, the inadequacy of Schutz's account of 'multiple realities' is that they are presented as co-existing entirely within the world of the 'natural attitude'. We can choose to move out of the world of pragmatic, everyday existence into worlds of fantasy or science and, in doing so, we adopt the rules of those provinces of meaning. On this view, according to Gurwitsch, 'no philosophical problems concerning existence arise' (Gurwitsch, 1957b, 319; 1964a, 401). Schutz offers simply a 'phenomenological psychology' which describes the roles people may choose to adopt by selecting different provinces of meaning without providing grounds for assessing the relative validity of those provinces, without, that is, subjecting his own province of meaning to philosophical scrutiny. 'In contradistinction to Schutz's approach' (Gurwitsch, 1957b, 319; 1964a, 401), Gurwitsch argues that he is concerned to analyse the nature of the provinces of existence themselves as systems of meaning which cohere in terms of relevance to each other rather than, as was the case in Schutz's position, in terms of relevance to individual agents.

In short, Gurwitsch forcibly reaffirmed his primary philosophical commitment to transcendental reduction even though his recognition of orders of existence enabled him to recognize differences among personal and cultural world-views. He explains these differences by deploying the concept of 'marginal consciousness', to which he devotes the concluding chapter of *Théorie du champ de la conscience*. He clarifies that contingent elements, such as 'an awareness [conscience] of our embodied existence' (Gurwitsch, 1957b, 334; 1964a, 417), are co-present when we focus our attention on 'themes'. When we are focused on solving a mathematical problem, for instance, we are conscious of sitting uncomfortably in a chair. When we undertake a phenomenological reduction we suspend existential dimensions such as that of bodily sensation, but Gurwitsch insists that 'Suspension of the existential belief … in no way purports its suppression, not to speak of the elimination of those phenomena to which, in the "natural attitude", the existential belief is attached' (Gurwitsch, 1957b, 336; 1964a, 419–20). In other words, Gurwitsch does not dismiss the level of analysis undertaken by Schutz but argues that it falls short of providing sufficient explanation. Equally, Gurwitsch does not dismiss the emphasis of the corporeal developed by Merleau-Ponty but argues that it should not acquire the central importance which he assigns to it. Rather, it should be regarded as marginal and contingent in relation to the essentially ideational process of transcendental reduction.

Summary

Schutz and Gurwitsch found themselves together in the United States in 1940, having met briefly in Paris in the 1930s. Presenting themselves as phenomenologists gave them both an entrée into American intellectual life. They assimilated themselves as intellectuals although Gurwitsch in particular always oriented himself towards continental Europe. They both associated themselves with the developing 'phenomenological movement' in American philosophy. Schutz used this stance to sustain, in his critique of Parsons, his original refinement of Weber, and gradually to establish himself, still part-time, as a philosopher of social science. Partly forced by his difficulty in securing stable employment, Gurwitsch found himself teaching mathematics and the sciences and, in this context, elaborated a philosophy of the sciences which saw them as socially constituted 'fields' of consciousness. Schutz and Gurwitsch, particularly Gurwitsch, were prepared to express their political views in relation to Nazi Germany but they seem not to have engaged in internal American politics. Both sought to reconcile the philosophical position of Husserl with that of William James as a means of assimilating themselves intellectually but they showed no interest in the socio-political consequences of pragmatism as argued by John Dewey or as articulated in respect of universities by C. Wright Mills. In their correspondence with each other between 1939 and 1959, both consciously cultivated an exchange which almost replicated the ethos of the Viennese circles to which Schutz had belonged in cultivating a refuge for intellectual detachment. Schutz's text of 1932 was not published in English until 1967 with a title which distorted its original meaning. The text which was the culmination of Gurwitsch's early career was first published in French in 1957 and then in English in 1964. Schutz died in 1959 and Gurwitsch in 1973, by which time an American philosophical universalism had supplanted the instrumentalism of Dewey and the cultural relativism of Boas and Mead. Academic and publishing 'industries' developed to consolidate the philosophical achievements of the two men. For different reasons, the main editor of Gurwitsch, Lester Embree, and the main editor of Schutz, Helmut Wagner, were disinclined to historicize the texts which they retrieved from archives so as to concentrate on their absolute value within philosophical discourse. My endeavour has been to re-situate these texts within the contexts of their production. My purpose was to show that the original European meanings of the texts were neutralized by absorption into a consciously a-political tradition. The paradox is that Gurwitsch wanted to emphasize the primacy of consciousness in regulating our current behaviour while equally arguing that neither this consciousness nor our selves are absolutes but are both the products of historical construction from communal origins. The concept of 'field' was an attempt to steer a middle way between idealist universalism and sociological reduction. The debate between Gurwitsch and Schutz in relation to the work of Sartre shows that neither sympathized with existentialism, but from different points of view. Schutz sought to retain the notion of autonomous acting selves, behaving inter-personally and unimpeded by inherited cognitive dispositions, whereas Gurwitsch thought that although existence precedes essence, such existence is already impregnated with historical meanings which deny the possibility that individuals might have the freedom to constitute themselves. Schutz condemned Parsons as well as Weber for superimposing their intellectual explanations on the behaviour of social agents, but, in doing so, he denied the extent to which *all* agency is immanently motivated by intellectual conceptions, the agency of those observed as much as that of those observing as scientists. Gurwitsch thought that he recognized in the French tradition a culture which reconciled a rationalism with individual creativity in conformity with his theoretical position. He was not an indigenous inheritor of that cultural tradition, but was mentor to someone who was. Merleau-Ponty was in a position to try to operationalize some of the socio-political consequences of Gurwitsch's intellectual balancing-act.

Notes

1 See References.
2 See the discussion of this reaction in the next chapter.
3 For a chronology of Gurwitsch's publications, see References.
4 See, for instance, Gurwitsch, 1951 and Gurwitsch, 1953, this latter clearly as a consequence of his attendance at the 11th International Congress of Philosophy, held on the philosophy of religion, Brussels, August 1953.
5 The letter was never published. Embree provides the text.
6 See Gurwitsch, 1966a, 292, fn. 11.
7 First published in 1913 as *Phänomenologie der Sympathiegefühle* [The phenomenology of feelings of sympathy].
8 It is significant that 'On Contemporary Nihilism' was translated from the French at the instigation of Hannah Arendt (see Grathoff, ed., 1989, 74).
9 See pp. 20–8.
10 As a consequence of the long gestation of Gurwitsch's book, notice that the 1957 book only considers Merleau-Ponty's position in relation to his *Phénoménologie de la perception*, without reference to his subsequent publications (see the comments to this effect in chapter 4).

4

Maurice Merleau-Ponty, 1908–61

This chapter focuses on the career and work of Merleau-Ponty. He remained in France for the whole of his life, enduringly initiated into the French intellectual tradition. During the 1930s he worked with Gurwitsch and was also responsible for publicizing some of the late work of Husserl which, during the war, was held in archives in Louvain. He was involved, with Sartre, in attempting to conceptualize post-war social construction. He tried to integrate his phenomenological thinking with political engagement in a way which had not been done by either Schutz or Gurwitsch but, finally, commitment to philosophy prevailed. Consideration of the work of Merleau-Ponty provides a link between the a-political orientation of the productions in America of Schutz and Gurwitsch and Bourdieu's transposition of Merleau-Ponty's thinking from the field of philosophy to that of sociology.

The career

Maurice Merleau-Ponty was born in 1908 in Rochefort-sur-Mer in the Charente-Maritime in south-west France. After studying at provincial lycées, he prepared for entry to the École Normale Supérieure at the lycée Louis-le-Grand, Paris for two years before admission to the École in 1926. He studied for a licence in philosophy, obtaining a Diplôme d'études supérieures in 1929 under the supervision of Émile Bréhier for a thesis on 'La notion du multiple intelligible chez Plotin' [Plotinus's[1] notion of the intelligible many]. Although no copy of this thesis has survived, the subject indicates that Merleau-Ponty was early aware of a 'neo-Platonist view of knowledge', one which was in opposition to the legacy of the pre-Socratic philosophers. Although, according to T.F. Geraets, he respected his teachers, 'especially Léon Brunschvicg',

Merleau-Ponty could not agree with them that 'man and nature are the objects of universal concepts'.[2] Rather, Merleau-Ponty was attracted in the late 1920s by the philosophy of Bergson, especially admiring the first chapter of Bergson's *Matière et mémoire* in which, in respect of time, he distinguished between lived experience ('durée') and objectified conceptualization. Merleau-Ponty's Bergsonian orientation influenced his selective reading of Husserl, to whose work he had been introduced through the lectures delivered at the Sorbonne between 1928 and 1930 on contemporary German philosophy by Georges Gurvitch.[3] He also attended Husserl's 'Paris Lectures', given in German in February 1929. These were published in French translation in 1931 as *Méditations cartésiennes. Introduction à la phénoménologie* [Cartesian meditations. Introduction to Phenomenology]. In spite of these initial contacts with the work of Husserl, Geraets concludes that the influence of Husserl's thought was limited until 1933.

Merleau-Ponty gained his agrégation in philosophy in July 1930 before carrying out compulsory military service from mid-October 1930 until mid-October 1931, after which he commenced work as Professor of Philosophy in a lycée at Beauvais. It was only after the completion of his military service that Merleau-Ponty began to study systematically the new schools of psychology which seemed to be supplanting associationism. On 8 April 1933, he submitted an application for a project on the nature of perception in which he specifically mentioned experimental research undertaken in Germany by the Gestalt school which seemed to be suggesting that form is not constructed from sensations but is inherent in sensible knowledge. He concluded by arguing that 'in the present state of philosophy, there should be a place for attempting to synthesize the results of experimental psychology and neurology in relation to the problem of perception' (Geraets, 1971, 10).[4]

In February and June 1934, Merleau-Ponty officially inscribed his two doctoral thesis topics, respectively 'La nature de la perception' [the nature of perception] and 'Le problème de la perception dans la phénoménologie et dans la "Gestaltpsychologie"' [the problem of perception in phenomenology and in Gestalt psychology]. In April he applied for a renewal of his research grant.[5] His application makes it clear that he had become aware of the potential value of Husserl's phenomenology in facilitating a dialogue between philosophy and Gestalt psychology.

Merleau-Ponty's application was denied, but he was appointed Professor at the lycée in Chartres and, in 1935, he moved to Paris, where he taught at the École Normale Supérieure until 1939 when he was mobilized for military service. According to Embree, Merleau-Ponty first met Aron Gurwitsch in the Autumn of 1933 (Embree in Toadvine, ed., 2002, x). During the second half of the 1930s, Merleau-Ponty attended Gurwitsch's lectures and they had prolonged discussions together. Gurwitsch acknowledges Merleau-Ponty's help in correcting the French text of 'Quelques aspects et quelques développements de la psychologie de la forme' [some aspects and some developments in the psychology of form] (Gurwitsch, 1936b) and Merleau-Ponty also corrected the French of Gurwitsch's critical study of the papers of the 11th International Congress of Psychology (Gurwitsch, 1938). According again to Embree (in Toadvine, ed., 2002, x), Merleau-Ponty told Father van Breda, curator of the Husserl archives at Louvain, about Gurwitsch's *Esquisse* course when he visited Louvain in April 1939. Merleau-Ponty's engagement with Gurwitsch's attempt to reconcile phenomenology with Gestalt psychology was significant for his work for his two doctoral theses, the first of which (*La structure du comportement* [the structure of behaviour]) was completed by the end of 1938, although its publication was delayed until 1942. Before the war, Merleau-Ponty published one article (Merleau-Ponty, 1935) which was influenced by his reading of Max Scheler's *L'homme du ressentiment* [the man of 'ressentiment'] (1919), and reviews (Merleau-Ponty, 1936a and 1936b) of Gabriel Marcel's *Etre et Avoir* (1935) and Sartre's *L'Imagination* (1936).[6] Merleau-Ponty used his reviews to advance the view that Christian belief in a new society created by love should not be conceived as 'a negation of the earth, as a reversal of terrestrial life'[7] but as an immanent transcendence distinguishing it from 'humanitarianism'.[8] He made common cause with Marcel in agreeing that what was wrong with philosophers was that they had adopted what Marcel called an 'attitude spec-taculaire'[9] [attitude as of a spectacle] which deprived their objects of their 'human aspect', but, nevertheless, Merleau-Ponty was not disposed to follow Marcel in emphasizing the primacy of the personal. In respect of this engage-ment with two Christian apologists, Merleau-Ponty first articulated his emerg-ing commitment to dialectical knowledge without privileging either the 'subjective' or the 'objective'.

On returning to Paris, Merleau-Ponty attended Kojève's lectures on Hegel's *Phenomenology of Spirit*[10] which provided an introduction, with a Marxist ten-dency, to the reading of Hegel and a critique of Christianity. He also began serious study of the work of Karl Marx. Sartre recollected that, before 1939, Merleau-Ponty had become 'closer to Marxism than he ever was again' (Sartre, 1961, 315). Nevertheless, he resisted adherence to Marxist dogma and did not join the Communist Party.

Geraets quotes from an interview with Merleau-Ponty, published in 1960, in which he commented that he knew that 'it was philosophy that I wanted to do' (Chapsal, ed., 1960, 148, quoted in Geraets, 1971, 4) from the day in which he entered the philosophy class as a lycée student (in the mid-1920s). Merleau-Ponty early turned his attention to developments in psychological thought after he had completed his formal philosophical study and his obliga-tory military service. Indication of these studies of psychology and of his association with Gurwitsch are apparent in his first thesis, completed in 1938 and published in 1942 as *La structure du comportement* (Merleau-Ponty, 1942). Indication of the influence of 'late' Husserl in the period between the completion and publication of this thesis is apparent in the second thesis, published in 1945 as *Phénoménologie de la perception* (Merleau-Ponty, 1945a). This short account of the two theses together will seek to provide an account of Merleau-Ponty's thought as it became established before his period of political engagement immediately after the Liberation in 1945.

Texts

La structure du comportement

La structure du comportement constituted a representation of Merleau-Ponty's accumulated knowledge in the field of psychology, assembled so as to consider the possibility of a philosophical resolution of the apparent impasse between opposing positions in contemporary French thought, that between a 'philosophy which makes all nature an objective unity constituted before consciousness, and the sciences which treat the organism and consciousness as two orders of reality' affecting each other like causes and effects (Merleau-Ponty, 1942, 3). In his introduction, Merleau-Ponty asked whether the solution lay in a 'return' to the kind of criticist philosophy, derived from Kant and most associated at the time with Brunschvicg, which supposed that things-in-themselves (noumena) are unknowable and that we should remain satisfied with how they are presented to us (phenomena) – without, however, taking the phenomenological line that such phenomena alone constitute what there is to know. Merleau-Ponty was searching for a bridge between psychic or mentalist and physiological or materialist understandings of nature, and he chose to test these rival positions in relation to 'comportement' [behaviour], both animal and human, on the grounds that, in his view, the 'notion' of comportment in these contexts was 'neutral'. In other words, Merleau-Ponty did not suppose that the French word 'comportement' in the title would, in English translation as 'behaviour', seem to imply a work predicated on sympathy for 'behaviourism' which stood for one of the positions in contention.

   La structure du comportement was essentially a critical review of contemporary physiological and psychological researches in respect of the coherence of their theoretical formulations. Merleau-Ponty did not himself engage in any empirical practice. The first chapter considers reflex behaviour in terms of physical and chemical stimuli alone while the second chapter considers in detail Pavlov's attempt to explain how organisms relate to their environments in more complex ways than just in terms of sensorial reaction. Merleau-Ponty rejects Pavlov's notion of 'conditioned reflex'. Instead, he makes explicit his agreement with, and indebtedness to, Goldstein (and Gelb) in their opposition to the old, atomistic physiology. Consideration of perception figures prominently in Merleau-Ponty's attempt to move from the negative critique of old views to a positive new understanding of behaviour. Instead of classifying behaviours as either elementary or complex, Merleau-Ponty outlines three orders of inter-relation between body and mind and insists that explanations should be offered neither, 'comme on dit' [as one says], of the superior by the inferior nor of the inferior by the superior. Traditionally, 'inferior' explanations relate to mechanical actions which, like physical events, operate in objective space and time, while 'superior' explanations relate to interior motivation which is always intentional. Merleau-Ponty argues, however, that behaviour does not operate exclusively in either. At decisive moments in experience, which Merleau-Ponty discusses as 'apprenticeship', habits become constituted which fix trial-and-error physical actions to become mentally regulative for future behaviour.[11] Representing exteriority as 'en soi' [in itself] and interiority as 'pour soi' [for itself] in terminology not yet fully developed by Sartre,[12] Merleau-Ponty sug-gests that it is at these decisive moments that 'behaviour detaches itself from the order of in-itself and becomes the projection beyond the organism of a *possibility* which is interior to it' (Merleau-Ponty, 1942, 190–1), or, in other words, that future-oriented behaviour escapes from automatic determinism. A corollary of Merleau-Ponty's argument, based on literature largely concerned with animal behaviour, is that it is a mistake to consider that animals who do not possess 'consciousness in the sense of pure consciousness, *cogitatio*' are 'automatons without interiority'. Equally, it is a mistake to suppose that humans are differentiated from other animals by virtue of possessing a pure conscious-ness. To varying degrees, behaviour is 'thought and not in itself'; it is 'not a thing, but no more is it an idea, not the envelope of a pure consciousness' (Merleau-Ponty, 1942, 193). Merleau-Ponty offers 'form' as the notion which enables him to avoid these antithetical positions and he spends the rest of *La structure du comportement* attempting to apply this notion specifically to human behaviour.

The third chapter is entitled 'L'ordre physique, l'ordre vital, l'ordre humain' [the physical order, the vital order, the human order]. Merleau-Ponty's discus-sion of the third, human order involves consideration of 'the life of conscious-ness'. He insists that he is not constructing 'a metaphysic of nature' (Merleau-Ponty, 1942, 244) but, rather, describing a third kind of dialectic particular to the third order – one whereby human behaviour responds to physico-chemical stimuli through the mediation of constructed objects. For the first time in *La structure du comportement* Merleau-Ponty reinforces his argu-ment by reference to the work of Husserl, deriving his terminology of 'objects of use', such as clothing or the garden, and 'cultural objects', such as books, music or language, respectively from Husserl's *Ideen* and his *Méditations cartési-ennes* (Merleau-Ponty, 1942, 245). Merleau-Ponty refers to this process of construction as one of 'labour'[13] rather than of 'action' because, again, he considers that, as used by Bergson, action implies the operation of a mystical force rather than the intended performance of individuals.[14] Merleau-Ponty hints here at the enquiry to be undertaken in his main thesis where he was to seek to analyse perception as a phenomenon in itself, rejecting prior assumptions about its sensorial origins.

Not only does Merleau-Ponty emphasize the distinctively productive labour of perception in the human order, but he also suggests that what additionally defines man is the capacity 'to go beyond created structures to create others from them' (Merleau-Ponty, 1942, 265). This capacity in part explains how the three orders of form – physical, of the organism and psychic – must not be regarded as substantively different but, rather, as the consequence of a process of 'new structuration', meaning that the superior form is liberated from the inferior while remaining founded in it ((Merleau-Ponty, 1942, 278). By taking this view of the psychic or mental order as a result of his philosophical consideration of psychological and physiological research, Merleau-Ponty finds himself forced to ask, finally, how his notion of achieved consciousness relates to the history of thinking about consciousness in the Western philosophical tradition, or, as he puts it, 'What therefore is the relation between consciousness as universal milieu and consciousness rooted in subordinate dialectics? Must the point of view of the "foreign spectator" ["spectateur étranger"] be abandoned as illegitimate in favour of unconditioned reflexion?' (Merleau-Ponty, 1942, 279).

Merleau-Ponty was prepared to recognize that his philosophical conceptualization was the product of his personal engagement, through his education, with a tradition of philosophical 'cultural objects'. The question was whether this stance in respect of experience should be renounced so as to observe phenomena without presupposition. Implicitly, the question was whether phenomenological research should be thought to be denying accumulated wisdom in order to generate a new kind of rigorous science. Although Merleau-Ponty poses this question, which potentially challenges the whole tradition of Western philosophical thought and also his personal initiation into its language, he responds, in *La structure du comportement*, with a final chapter which exploits his formation to examine in detail the legacy of that tradition in respect to the discourse about the mind and body. His summary of philosophical thought leads him to the same conclusion as his earlier inspection of research findings in psychology and physiology. He shows sympathy with Descartes's achievement in retaining a sense of internal autonomy for the mind in opposition to the challenge of the empiricist convictions underlying the scientific revolution, but he insists that the opposing mentalist and materialist views were both fatally flawed in assuming a dualism. The mind must not be conceived as an artisan who uses the body as a tool: 'the mind does not use the body, but constitutes itself through it by transporting it from physical space' (Merleau-Ponty, 1942, 316). Classical discussions of perception make the mistake of 'confronting the constituted world with the perceptive experience of that world', whereas what is needed is an 'inversion of the natural movement of consciousness which we impose' so as, instead, to observe perception 'as a type of originary experience'

(Merleau-Ponty, 1942, 332) which, therefore, does not self-fulfillingly reflect the world but shapes it.

After completing *La structure du comportement*, Merleau-Ponty was influenced by a special number of the *Revue internationale de philosophie*, published in January 1939, devoted to the work of Husserl, who had died on 27 April 1938. This collection introduced him to Husserl's last works and, in March 1939, he wrote to ask permission to consult Husserl's unpublished works which had been deposited at Louvain. In one week at the beginning of April he read parts of Husserl's unpublished works and had conversations with Eugen Fink. As Geraets concludes, 'the year 1939 is of capital importance' (Geraets, 1971, 30) in defining Merleau-Ponty's interpretation of the work of Husserl.

The war interrupted Merleau-Ponty's research. He was mobilized in August 1939 and served until September 1940, when he was demobilized following the French defeat. He returned to Paris and resumed teaching, now at the lycée Carnot. He began to work in a resistance group called 'Sous la botte'. When Sartre returned to Paris in the Spring of 1941 after his period of captivity, he and Merleau-Ponty picked up an association which had only been slight while they were contemporaries in the École Normale Supérieure in the late 1920s. They founded a resistance group called 'Socialism and Liberty'. Stewart comments that 'During this time, Merleau-Ponty was a convinced Marxist, whereas Sartre remained rather noncommitted' (Stewart, ed., 1998, xix). 'Socialism and Liberty' only lasted one year but it 'served the function of bringing Sartre and Merleau-Ponty together again and of showing them their common philosophical interests and social concerns' (Stewart, ed., 1998, xx). This bore fruit after the end of the war when, as co-editors, they launched *Les temps modernes* in October 1945. The intention was that the journal would sustain the purpose of 'Socialism and Liberty' which had been to advance a political programme recommending a socialist middle way between communism and Gaullism. Merleau-Ponty's 'magnum opus', *Phénoménologie de la perception* [phenomenology of perception] (Merleau-Ponty, 1945a), was published in 1945. The product of his academic research of the previous few years was published, therefore, at almost the same time as he was becoming active, as the editor of *Les temps modernes* responsible for political articles, in articulating his political ideology.

Phénoménologie de la perception

Towards the end of *La structure du comportement*, Merleau-Ponty cited 'late Husserl' [la dernière philosophie de Husserl] (Merleau-Ponty, 1942, 332, fn. 1) and also an article of Eugen Fink (Fink, 1930), who was associated with the late turn in Husserl's thinking. It seems likely, therefore, that the transition from *La structure du comportement* to *Phénoménologie de la perception*, was away from Gurwitsch's emphasis of consciousness towards the adoption of the view expressed in Husserl's late and posthumous works which concentrated on the originating 'life-world'. While Gurwitsch and Merleau-Ponty agreed that the constitution of the physical universe is accomplished on the basis of the perceptual world, Embree's interpretation is that Merleau-Ponty 'did not recognize the problem of the constitution of that very perceptual world, including, ... the phenomenal body. Gurwitsch did' (Embree, 1981, 159). For Gurwitsch, according to Embree, 'Everything transcendent is transcendentally constituted' and to be investigated by noetic–noematic reflection, whereas 'Merleau-Ponty' had embraced the 'existentialist' notion, as announced by Sartre, that 'existence precedes essence' (Sartre, 1996, 26 [1946]). It could also be that Gurwitsch's main allegiance to 'early' Husserl was tinged with an acceptance of the dominant identification of Hegel's phenomenology, as expressed in his *Phenomenology of Mind*, with philosophical idealism. By contrast, Merleau-Ponty's position may well have been influenced by the interpretation of Hegel offered in Kojève's lectures where, in the course of 1938–39, he insisted that 'Knowledge can never *transcend* sensible reality. For the Mind is itself a sensible being, and non-sensible or "supra-sensible" being is only a vain fantasy' (Kojève, ed. Queneau, 1947, 496–7).

In *La structure du comportement*, Merleau-Ponty had been prepared to agree with the critique of Freud articulated by Sartre in *La transcendance de l'ego*, but the new emphasis in his thinking in *Phénoménologie de la perception* leads him to regard Sartre's phenomenology as essentially Hegelian rather than Husserlian or, certainly, as indebted more to 'early' than 'late' Husserl. Right from the preface to *Phénoménologie de la perception*, Merleau-Ponty is explicit that his new book pursues the argument of the old in a new way by exploring the implications of 'late' Husserl. There was a tension in Husserl's legacy. On the one hand, 'phenomenology is the study of essences' but, on the other, it is also 'a philosophy which puts essences back into existence' (Merleau-Ponty, 1962, vii; 1945a, 7). Merleau-Ponty had become convinced that transcendental/idealist interpreters of Husserl emphasized the former dimension which they found in 'early' Husserl, while existentialist interpreters were in danger of emphasizing the latter to the exclusion of consideration of the characteristics of essences. Merleau-Ponty insists that both emphases are contained in Husserl's thought and that there is no distinction to be made between the phenomenologies of Husserl and Heidegger, as if between transcendentalism and existentialism. For Merleau-Ponty, 'the whole of *Sein und Zeit* springs from an indication given by Husserl' (Merleau-Ponty, 1962, vii; 1945a, 7–8) which came to the foreground of Husserl's thought late in life in his account of the 'life-world'. It was false to suggest that Husserlian phenomenology initiated a dichotomy between essence and existence, and Merleau-Ponty's intention is to follow his understanding of the development of Husserl's thought whereby his initial essentialism became grounded in existence without losing the characteristics of its apparent autonomy. 'Late' Husserl was a progression from 'early' without negation. The thrust of *Phénoménologie de la perception* is to give expression to Husserl's 'late' thought without supposing that it contradicts the early. In general terms, Merleau-Ponty's introduction repeats the position which he had advanced in *La structure du comportement*, only adopting a slightly different terminology, that of epistemology rather more than of psychology/physiology. His starting-point is the adoption of 'late' Husserl on the basis of his access to the Louvain archives rather than the response to the psychology literature which he had absorbed earlier in the 1930s. His account of perception is to be derived from direct experience more than from exegesis of existing theories. In this way, the intention of the manner in which the account is given reflects the substance of that account. Merleau-Ponty devotes space to exposing the shortcomings of both empiricism and intellectualism, considered as emphasizing the independent influence of either material sensation or mental consciousness, but he is aware that in writing in this way he is involved procedurally in juxtaposing his experience and his knowledge of traditions of thought. The new factor in *Phéménologie de la perception* is that Merleau-Ponty extends the observation with which he concluded the earlier work so as to explore the implications of trying to treat science as immanent within the conditions which it endeavours to explain. This dilemma is stated most clearly in relation to psychoanalysis, but, importantly, Merleau-Ponty broadens his enquiry. Part I is devoted to discussion of 'The Body'. The problem is to consider the relation between 'experience and objective thought', to understand the noema without reducing it to being the product of different noeses or, as Merleau-Ponty states this, 'to understand how vision can be brought into being from somewhere without being enclosed in its perspective' (Merleau-Ponty, 1962, 67; 1945a, 95). In the fifth chapter ('The body in its Sexual Being'), Merleau-Ponty refuses to countenance the isolation of sexual drives, arguing that 'There is interfusion between sexuality and existence, which means that existence permeates sexuality and *vice versa*, so that it is impossible to determine, in a given decision or action, the proportion of sexual to other motivations, impossible to label a decision or act "sexual" or "non-sexual"' (Merleau-Ponty, 1962, 169; 1945a, 7–8). He insists that behaviour must be understood in totality rather than by attempting to distinguish between mental and physical elements. In an amazing conclusion to this chapter, Merleau-Ponty broadens this point to argue that

> Man is a historical idea and not a natural species. In other words, there is in human existence no unconditioned possession, and yet no fortuitous attribute. Human existence will force us to revise our usual notion of necessity and contingency, because it is the transformation of contingency into necessity by the act of taking in hand. (Merleau-Ponty, 1962, 170; 1945a, 209)

In a lengthy footnote at the end of the chapter, Merleau-Ponty spells out the consequences of this view for an understanding of historical materialism which should not reduce history to materially determined events any more than should psychoanalysis regard the mind as acting in accordance with determined physiological laws. 'Historical materialism', he states, 'is not a causality exclusive to economics' (Merleau-Ponty, 1962, 171; 1945a, 210). Almost casually, Merleau-Ponty's footnote points to the relevance of his discussion of epistemological and ontological issues for the development of a position in respect of history and politics. Part II of *Phénoménologie de la perception* is devoted to consideration of 'The World as Perceived', focusing on 'Sense Experience', 'Space', 'The Thing and the Natural World' and 'Other Selves and the Human World', and Part III examines 'Being-for-itself and Being-in the world', focusing on 'The Cogito', 'Temporality' and 'Freedom'. It is in this last chapter that Merleau-Ponty indirectly confronts the position adopted by Sartre in *L'être et le néant*. He begins by reiterating his constant contention that 'no causal relationship is conceivable between the subject and his body, his world or his society' (Merleau-Ponty, 1962, 434; 1945a, 497) because this would suppose the pre-existence of separately autonomous elements. By the same token, 'motivation' is ruled out. Merleau-Ponty rejects the primacy assigned by Sartre to the notion of 'for-self' in favour of an insistence on a continually constitutive encounter between Sartre's triad of 'for-self', 'for-others' and 'in-itself': 'Everything that I "am" in virtue of nature or history – hunchbacked, handsome or Jewish – I never am completely for myself, ... and I may well be these things for other people, nevertheless I remain free to posit another person as a consciousness whose views strike through to my very being, or on the other hand merely as an object' (Merleau-Ponty, 1962, 435; 1945a, 498). Deploying Gurwitsch's notion of 'field',[15] Merleau-Ponty elaborates further his view that freedom is not absolute: 'If freedom is to have *room* in which to move, if it is to be describable as freedom, there must be something to hold it away from its objectives, it must have a *field*, which means that there must be for it special possibilities, or realities which tend to cling to being' (Merleau-Ponty, 1962, 438; 1945a, 501).

In Merleau-Ponty's thinking, the rationalist's dilemma – 'either the free act is possible, or it is not – either the event originates in me or is imposed on me from outside' (Merleau-Ponty, 1962, 442; 1945a, 506) – does not apply because it falsely assumes a separation of interior from exterior: 'our freedom does not destroy our situation, but gears itself to it' (Merleau-Ponty, 1962, 442; 1945a, 506). Merleau-Ponty elaborates this position in relation to our self-consciousness in history: 'Taking myself in my absolute concreteness, as I am presented to myself in reflection, I find that I am an anonymous and pre-human flux, as yet unqualified as, for instance, "a working-man" or "middle class"' (Merleau-Ponty, 1962, 442; 1945a, 506). People are simply intrinsically human. Their identities are the products of second-order construction: 'I am never in my heart of hearts a worker or a bourgeois, but a consciousness which freely evaluates itself as a middle class or proletarian consciousness'

(Merleau-Ponty, 1962, 442; 1945a, 506). These examples taken from 'class' terminology are important in relation to Merleau-Ponty's latent political philosophy. He does not deny the discourse of class struggle but it remains an 'abstract' discourse 'until it is worked out in the dealings men have with each other, and in the relations of the man to his job' (Merleau-Ponty, 1962, 446; 1945a, 509). In conclusion, Merleau-Ponty asks where his argument leaves 'freedom' since he does not accept the absence of constraint or, as he puts it in clear opposition to Sartre, since 'I can no longer pretend to be a nihilation (*néant*) and to choose myself continually out of nothing at all' (Merleau-Ponty, 1962, 452; 1945a, 516). Merleau-Ponty's answer is to assert that 'To be born is both to be born of the world and to be born into the world. The world is already constituted, but also never completely constituted; in the first case we are acted upon, in the second we are open to an infinite number of possibilities' (Merleau-Ponty, 1962, 453; 1945a, 517).

To illustrate this last point, Merleau-Ponty tries to analyse the situation of a man who is 'tortured so as to make him talk' (Merleau-Ponty, 1962, 453; 1945a, 518), suggesting that there is, for such a man, a compulsion to resist which is dictated by his awareness of the attitudes of those comrades with whom he has become associated. He is free to betray them but constrained by their expectations (by which his dispositions were inter-subjectively constituted in reciprocal relation with theirs). J.-P. Cléro (2001) has taken this passage to be an oblique reference to the situation of resistants subjected to torture during the Nazi Occupation. He highlights it as one of the very few moments in the text where contemporary political events impinge on its content. He grants that *Phénoménologie de la perception* was written under circumstances which imposed indirectness, but he proceeds to ask whether it can be said that Merleau-Ponty's philosophical consideration of perception was a form of sublimation of his political inclinations.

'La guerre a eu lieu', 1945

Merleau-Ponty published a series of articles in *Les temps modernes* in 1946 and 1947, some of which were collected in *Humanisme et terreur* [Humanism and terror] (Merleau-Ponty, 1947c) and others of which were collected in *Sens et non-sens* [sense and non-sense] (Merleau-Ponty, 1948). Notably, these included 'La guerre a eu lieu' [the war has taken place] (Merleau-Ponty, 1945b), which was his contribution to the first number of *Les temps modernes*. At the same time, Merleau-Ponty maintained his 'professional' philosophical interests. He gave a paper in November 1946 before the Société française de philosophie, entitled 'Le primat de la perception et ses conséquences philosophiques' [the primacy of perception and its philosophical consequences].[16] In the summary of his argument, Merleau-Ponty made it clear that he was becoming less concerned to produce a phenomenological critique of Gestalt psychology and, instead, more concerned to argue phenomenologically that perception is the foundation of rational activity, including philosophical thought. He was teaching philosophy in Lyon between 1945 and 1948, and his 1946 paper reflects the interest which he was developing in his courses there and, in particular, in a course which he gave at L'École Normale Supérieure in 1947/48 entitled *L'union de l'âme et corps chez Malebranche, Maine de Biran,et Bergson* [the union of soul and body in the work of Malebranche, Maine de Biran and Bergson].[17] Merleau-Ponty's old supervisor, Émile Bréhier, argued in response to the paper that Merleau-Ponty was 'changing, inverting the ordinary meaning of what we call philosophy' (Merleau-Ponty, ed. Prunair, 1996, 73). Merleau-Ponty was appointed to the Chair of Psychology and Pedagogy at the Sorbonne in 1949.

'La guerre a eu lieu' [the war has taken place] is an important article because it becomes apparent that implicitly Merleau-Ponty took the opportunity to reflect on the consequences of the formal detachment of the text within which he had developed a critique of that detachment. The text is written in the first-person plural, but it is a personal confession or admission of guilt. Before the war, 'we', formed in a context where 'generations of socialist professors had been formed'[18] (Merleau-Ponty, 1996 [1948], 169), were complacent about developments in Germany which belonged to the 'universe of thought' (Merleau-Ponty, 1996 [1948], 170) rather than experience. 'We' thought that our comfortable existence was the 'natural lot of men' and we did not realize that this was a condition to be achieved and defended. The universe of thought which 'we' inhabited was not rooted in our particular social circumstances. 'We' lived as close to Plato as to Heidegger and didn't internalize that 'we' were actually living in France. Even as soldiers in the Winter of 1939–40, 'we' still felt able to regard the enemy as human individuals but, after June 1940, it was no longer possible to treat Germans humanely. To attempt to retain any notion of common humanity suddenly became an act of betrayal, an acquiescence in German victory. In 1939, 'we' didn't think in terms of Jews or Germans, but 'only of men or even of consciousnesses' and that at any time each of us could choose 'to be and to do what we wanted in a constantly new liberty' (Merleau-Ponty, 1996 [1948], 175). Merleau-Ponty characterizes the culture of the inter-war years during which he had matured as fundamentally a-political. Before the war, 'politics seemed unthinkable to us because it is a statistical treatment of men' which was a substitute for understanding 'singular beings each of whom is a world for self' (Merleau-Ponty, 1996 [1948], 176). The Occupation taught us to consider all our actions contextually, as much in terms of their consequences as their intentions, with the result that our decisions whether or where, for instance, to publish our work became pragmatic rather than principled. We acquired a kind of 'popular immoralism' (Merleau-Ponty, 1996 [1948], 179). A 'pure morality' was only possible for those with leisure and privilege. For the rest of us, 'we are in the world, mixed up with it, compromised with it' (Merleau-Ponty, 1996 [1948], 179).

It was precisely this experience of the Occupation which seemed to point to the truth of Marxism, but Merleau-Ponty is quick to indicate that Marxism was in danger of reconfirming pre-war prejudices by supposing that history is determined transcendentally rather than as a consequence of human interventions. Already he advances a defence of proper, as opposed to routinized, Marxism. Specifically, Merleau-Ponty argues that being a Marxist should not involve embracing an international formula for social change, should not involve subsuming individual difference under a global proletariat. It involves a quest for the universal 'without giving up on what we are' (Merleau-Ponty, 1996 [1948], 182). 'La guerre a eu lieu' is mainly a philosophical reflection on French society before and during the war. Bravely, Merleau-Ponty was willing to warn that the camaraderie generated within the resistance movement was, paradoxically, comparable with the inter-personal complacency of the pre-war period. It could not survive the particular conditions of its production and should not be the blueprint for future social reorganization. The important lesson of the war and the Occupation, for Merleau-Ponty, is that 'values remain nominal, even without value, without the economic and political infrastructure which allows them to come into existence' (Merleau-Ponty, 1996 [1948], 185). He insists that the challenge, post-war, is to embed the complacent pre-war values of 1939 in everyday practice without renouncing them. This involves becoming immanently involved in the network of social relations without having recourse to any sphere of transcendent values: 'In the coexistence of men, ... morals, doctrines, thoughts and customs, laws, work, words, express themselves to each other, everything signifies everything. There is nothing beyond this unique flash [fulguration] of existence' (Merleau-Ponty, 1996 [1948], 185).

Sartre had not yet promoted the label of 'existentialism' for his version of ontological phenomenology. It is clear from 'La guerre a eu lieu' that Merleau-Ponty was in the process of applying the descriptive phenomenology which, influenced by 'late' Husserl, he had developed through his examinations of perception and Gestalt psychology, to a consideration of the nature of his engagement with contemporary political and social affairs. The fundamental difference of position from that of Sartre was initially concealed in their joint venture with *Les temps modernes*, but it is clear from this first article that Merleau-Ponty's approach was conducive to a form of sociological enquiry, acknowledging pluralism, whereas Sartre's orientation was psychoanalytic and dualist.

Humanisme et terreur, *1947*

In articles which appeared in *Les temps modernes* subsequently in the late 1940s, Merleau-Ponty continued the detailed investigation of the ethical dilemma involved in reconciling ideological or principled commitments to objectively formulated movements with attachment to personal liberal and humanist values which he had highlighted in relation to the example of torture in *Phénomé-nologie de la perception* and had pursued in respect of resistance in 'La guerre a eu lieu'. Just as this latter article related to the legal judgements in process in France during the post-war period of 'épuration', so the articles which were collected as *Humanisme et terreur* in 1947 (Merleau-Ponty, 1947c [1969]) were provoked in the first instance by reflection on the Moscow Trials of 1936–38[19] (especially the Bukharin–Rykov trial of 1938) and, more directly, as a response to the fictional version of those trials produced by Arthur Koestler in *Darkness at Noon* (Koestler, 1940), published in French translation as *Le Zéro et l'Infini* (Koestler, 1945).[20]

Merleau-Ponty's three articles on this topic were published in *Les temps modernes* in 1946 and 1947 (Merleau-Ponty, 1946d, 1946a and 1947a). They were collected in *Humanisme et terreur*, for which Merleau-Ponty wrote a preface. The first article indicates that Merleau-Ponty's source for information about the events was the account published by the People's Commisariat of Justice of the USSR in 1938,[21] and his preface refers in a footnote to his use of a 'recent remark of Stalin' (Merleau-Ponty, 1947c, 28; 1969, xxxiii). However, the main thrust of Merleau-Ponty's discussions is to evaluate Koes-tler's secondary account rather than interpret directly the proceedings released from Moscow. (Koestler's fictional 'Rubashov' is taken to be his representation of Bukharin.) According to Merleau-Ponty, the basic premise of Koestler's representation of Rubashov's dilemma is that he thought there are only two conceptions of human ethics, either one which believes that the individual is sacrosanct or one which subordinates the individual to the needs of the com-munity. The substance of Merleau-Ponty's argument in his three articles is that Koestler, in his representation of Rubashov, operated with a false duality between the individual and the communal. Merleau-Ponty was intent on defending Marx against Marxist misunderstanding. Merleau-Ponty identifies the non-dialectical view of the existence of objective laws of history with 'a sort of sociological scientism', but Merleau-Ponty's *practice* was becoming soci-ological in a different way. In the preface to *Humanisme et terreur*, Merleau-Ponty spends time representing and responding to the critical reviews of his original three articles. He states that his purpose in doing so is that 'they have something to teach us about the Communist problem' (Merleau-Ponty, 1947c, xxvi; 1969, xxx), and he also insists that he is not interested in ad hominem debate. On the contrary, the names of his critics 'are unimportant, for our purpose is entirely sociological' (Merleau-Ponty, 1947c, xxxviii; 1969, xlii). The corollary of the belief expressed at the end of *Phéménologie de la perception* that 'we are open to an infinite number of possibilities' and at the end of 'La guerre a eu lieu' that we should immerse ourselves in 'the co-existence of men' is that Merleau-Ponty offers a phenomenology of responses to texts. He considers this to be a sociological endeavour which actualizes the conclusion of his philosophical work, but he makes no attempt to analyse the social conditions generating alternative responses to texts, nor does he allow himself to develop the thought that his own philosophy should itself be subject to sociological scrutiny. As a consequence, Merleau-Ponty failed to realize the integrity of thought and experience in respect to socio-political action that he had adumbrated. The desired integrity belonged to a sphere of intellectual consciousness which, therefore, betrayed itself, reinforcing the mentalist detachment from experience which, conceptually, it opposed.

Sens et non-sens, *1948*

In assembling many of his articles of the immediate post-war period in 1948 in *Sens et non-sens* (Merleau-Ponty, 1996 [1948]), Merleau-Ponty grouped them under three headings – 'works', 'ideas' and 'politics' – and, in a short preface, tried to explain the meaning of the whole text in relation to these categories. The general character of thought from the beginning of the twentieth century, he argues, is that many books have expressed 'the revolt of immediate life against reason' (Merleau-Ponty, 1996 [1948], 7) and have been sceptical about rationality in morals, politics and art. This scepticism has been unsustainable, with the result that revolutionary thinkers of this sort have taken refuge in unconditioned acceptance of dogma, either communist or religious, for part of their lives while remaining conservative in their everyday existence. Merleau-Ponty argues that this dual living is untenable. Having personally rejected his earlier Catholicism, Merleau-Ponty tacitly confirms his disengagement from doctrinaire communism exposed in *Humanisme et terreur*. There is no escaping reason. 'We are born to reason just as to language' (Merleau-Ponty, 1996 [1948], 7) but this 'reason' cannot be the disembodied Reason of the Western philosophical tradition. 'We need to form a new idea of reason' (Merleau-Ponty, 1996 [1948], 7). Merleau-Ponty seeks a rationale for his philosophic practice which does not impose a dissociated sensibility, one which attempts to assimilate thought and experience without exclusively privileging one or the other. He turns first to consideration of the status of art (the section of articles on 'works') to clarify his position. The meanings [sens] of works of art reside neither in the intentions of artists nor in the appreciations of respondents. 'Meaning is inseparable from signification [signe]' (Merleau-Ponty, 1996 [1948], 7), by which Merleau-Ponty suggests that meaning is dependent on a pre-existing network of signs such that 'self'-expression is never achievable and both reason and unreason are similarly derivative, without autonomy. Similarly, when we consider morals (the section of articles on 'ideas') Merleau-Ponty argues that there is no recourse to absolute principles but only to 'the spontaneous movement which links us to others for good or bad, both egotistically and altruistically' (Merleau-Ponty, 1996 [1948], 8). Finally, in relation to politics (the third set of articles), Merleau-Ponty looks back at his own misplaced optimism that the proletariat might arise self-expressively as a collective and transform human history. This hope has been dashed by the dominant dualism in political affairs, characterized by American anti-communism and the military ambition of the Soviet Union.

The tone of the preface to *Sens et non-sens*, therefore, is one of grim despondency which is only alleviated by Merleau-Ponty's concluding assertion and challenge to the effect that the apparent impossibility of realizing a 'human world' can be averted provided humans 'measure the risk and the task'. It is clear that Merleau-Ponty was turning away from commitment to dogmatic communism. This was beginning to happen before the moment when Sartre overtly embraced it. Rather than adopt a dogmatic position about the role of the proletariat in world history, Merleau-Ponty was intent on encouraging an amelioration of the human condition by promoting the exchange of plural values on the assumption that these are merely objectifications of different social experiences. It was this intention that caused him to explore the importance of the study of language and of social science in relation to his phenomenological philosophy.

In a letter of 18 September 1949, Merleau-Ponty insisted that the important achievement of Husserl was that he had sought 'to give a new foundation to reason without ignoring what experience teaches' (Van Breda, 1962, 429–30). This was the prelude to Merleau-Ponty's sustained exploration of the relationship between phenomenology and the human and social sciences, and the relationship of both to the practice of philosophy and to political engagement. In April 1951, he gave a paper entitled 'Sur la phénoménologie du langage' and in July 1951 the *Cahiers internationaux de sociologie* published his 'Le philosophe et la sociologie'. The paper which Merleau-Ponty wrote in 1952 for his candidature for appointment to a Chair at the Collège de France[22] indicates clearly the direction of his thinking in its summary of the progression from his earlier work to the research which he was then planning. The inaugural lecture which he gave at the Collège de France in January 1953, and published the same year as *Éloge de la philosophie* (Merleau-Ponty, 1953), confirms that his interest in the social sciences was subordinate to his overriding dedication to the pursuit of a new kind of philosophizing.

In 'Sur la phénoménologie du langage [on the phenomenology of language], Merleau-Ponty made explicit the important distinction between 'early' and 'late' Husserl to which he had briefly referred at the end of *La structure du comportement*. He suggested that in the former period Husserl had regarded 'empirical languages as "muddled" realizations of essential language' (Merleau-Ponty, 1960, 137), whereas in the late period, the use of language was represented by Husserl 'as the operation by which thoughts which, without it, would remain private phenomena, acquire intersubjective value and, finally, ideal existence' (Merleau-Ponty, 1960, 137). In other words, Merleau-Ponty considered that late Husserl had come to regard language as constitutive of objectivity rather than a reflection of a prior form, or, to put this in terms developed by Saussure, as 'parole' [spoken language] rather than 'langue' [essential linguistic form]. Adopting the position of the late Husserl, Merleau-Ponty was driven to reflect on the status of the language traditionally deployed in philosophy. Husserl had tended to see his phenomenological analyses as 'preparatory' to a philosophical position which would 'crown' them, but Merleau-Ponty concluded, in a section on the consequences of his discussion of language in relation to phenomenological philosophy, that this separation was not possible. It is because philosophy is constructed from the totality of experiences articulated in language, both historically and contemporaneously, that Merleau-Ponty finds it possible to understand Husserl's 'enigmatic proposition' that 'Transcendental subjectivity is inter-subjectivity' (Merleau-Ponty, 1960, 157). Philosophy is constructed inter-subjectively in language exchange, but Merleau-Ponty's discussion of the relationship between philosophy and sociology did not allow him to consider that intersubjectivity might be synonymous with social construction and that sociology might usurp the function which he was recommending for philosophy. In 'Le philosophe et la sociologie' [the philosopher and sociology] he had recourse to the Husserlian notion of 'intentionality' to justify the separate discourse domains. Merleau-Ponty proceeds to argue that the opposition between philosophy and sociology is based on a false characterization of each. He argues that dialogue between the discourses becomes possible as soon as both are defined phenomenologically. Philosophy is not a discourse which competes with social science for legitimacy. Rather it is a discourse which appropriates the explanatory discourses of the sciences so as to identify the underlying assumptions on which those sciences are founded. Philosophy absorbs or 'envelopes' the meanings of scientific discourses as articulated in the present, absorbing, in other words, all historical meanings which remain current in the present. All knowledge is our knowledge within the world which we ground in shared experience within communities. For Merleau-Ponty, science and sociology objectivize the way in which such participatory communication occurs, but he calls 'philosophy' 'the consciousness which we must retain of the open and continuing community [communauté ouverte] of living speaking, and thinking *alter egos*, each present to the other and all in relation to nature' (Merleau-Ponty, 1960, 178–9). Following Husserl, Merleau-Ponty dismisses the autonomous discourse of traditional philosophy but retains the impulse not just to found transcendentalism on inter-subjectivity but also to retain philosophy as a necessary form of consciousness in relation to subjective experience.

The intention was that inter-subjectivity should operate trans-historically and trans-culturally, but Merleau-Ponty proceeds to presuppose the content of the desired exchanges, or pre-judge the concerns of inter-subjective dialogue. Where might the 'open community' be actualized? In spite of the desired social openness of conceptual exchange, Merleau-Ponty operated within an institutional context which formally embodied the idealist intellectual separation of which he disapproved.

It was in these early years of the 1950s that a rift developed with Sartre which was the consequence of their differences of opinion in regard to the relation between philosophy and political action. The turning point for Merleau-Ponty's position was the outbreak of the Korean war. For the first time he saw the Soviet Union as an imperialist power whereas, by contrast, Sartre still considered that the conflict was provoked by American interests. Not wanting to display the difference of view publicly in *Les temps modernes*, Merleau-Ponty resigned from his post as political editor (staying on as editor-in-chief). Sartre 'converted' to communism in June 1952, and proceeded to write a series of articles for *Les temps modernes* between 1952 and 1954 entitled 'Les Communistes et la paix' [the Communists and peace] in which he defended the Communist Party. Merleau-Ponty resigned completely from the journal in 1953 and his *Les aventures de la dialectique* [Adventures of the Dialectic] (Merleau-Ponty, 1955) was a response to these articles.

Although Merleau-Ponty no longer published in *Les temps modernes* after the end of 1952, he continued to write 'political' articles for the newspaper *L'Express* between 1954 and his premature death in May 1961. Many of these articles were published in *Signes* [Signs] (Merleau-Ponty, 1960). The development of his thinking in this period can be charted by reference to the courses of lectures which he gave at the Collège de France.[23] In 1959/60, he lectured on Husserl and also on 'Nature and Logos' while the subjects for his last year were 'Cartesian ontology and ontology today' and 'Philosophy and non-philosophy since Hegel'.[24] These final courses indicate a shift of position which Merleau-Ponty effected in part in distinction from the work of Gurwitsch. Stéphanie Ménasé insists that there is no mention of Gurwitsch's *Théorie du champ de la conscience*, published in 1957, in Merleau-Ponty's manuscripts of 1958, but indicates that Merleau-Ponty refers to the book in a note of June 1959 in a way which suggests that he was already aware of its content. In general terms, Ménasé suggests that references to Gurwitsch's text appear often during the period when Merleau-Ponty was modifying his project on 'Être et Monde' [being and world] which he was developing during 1959. The suggestion is that the notes which Merleau-Ponty made in response to the publication of Gurwitsch's *Théorie du champ de la conscience*, posthumously published as 'Notes de lecture et commentaires sur *Théorie du champ de la conscience* de Aron Gurwitsch' [Reading Notes and Comments on Aron Gurwitsch's the Field of Consciousness] (Merleau-Ponty, ed. Ménasé, 1997; 2001), contributed to Merleau-Ponty's articulation of a new notion of an 'indirect ontology'. These incipient modifications were probably contemporary with the writing of a passage which he abandoned but which was published by Claude Lefort as an annexe in *Le visible et l'invisible* (Merleau-Ponty, ed. Lefort, 1964a, 205–13).[25] During this period when Merleau-Ponty was referring to his notes on Gurwitsch (between Spring/Summer 1959 and Autumn 1960), he wrote *L'oeil et l'esprit* [the eye and the mind] (Merleau-Ponty, ed. Lefort, 1964b),[26] reviewed old articles for collection in *Signes* [Signs] (Merleau-Ponty, 1960), wrote a preface for that collection, and gave lectures on Bergson and Husserl in addition to his Collège de France lectures.

Ménasé considers that Merleau-Ponty's new criticism of eidetic reduction in these last works was linked to his reading of Gurwitsch's book in part because its presentation of Merleau-Ponty's thought as found in *Phénoménologie de la perception* enabled Merleau-Ponty to revise what he had written in that text. Taken with Gurwitsch's critique of Merleau-Ponty already mentioned, Merleau-Ponty's notes on Gurwitsch, combined with his other work of the period, help to clarify the distinction between the positions of the two men. The orientation which gives coherence to the work which Merleau-Ponty produced in the last few years of his life can be expressed as one of opposition to dualistic detachment. Within his philosophical thinking he had come to realize that it was not enough to give phenomenological primacy to perception, seen as a corporeal or existential impulse, in opposition to the tradition, derived from early Husserl and sustained by Gurwitsch, which gave primacy to consciousness. Within his philosophical thinking he articulated his sense that however much phenomenological research might try to restrict its attention only to phenomenal presentations, the effect of the strategy of 'eidetic reduction' was to perpetuate a division between either perception or consciousness on the one hand and, on the other, a reality which still retained an ideal status. Merleau-Ponty agrees with some of Gurwitsch's objections to his existentialist tendency, but he agrees from a point of view which completely rejects the insistence on the primacy of consciousness which was the basis of Gurwitsch's critique. Referring specifically to Gurwitsch's treatment of 'the perceptual process',[27] Merleau-Ponty notes that 'Gurwitsch, like all the analytic-rationalists, analyses the *Gestalthafte* as "noematic structures"' and adds that 'the eidetic method is responsible for the intellectualism of H[usserl]' (Merleau-Ponty, ed. Ménasé, 1997, 328). In a handwritten digression in his notes, Merleau-Ponty comments specifically that he reproaches Husserl for 'his dualism (dualism noema-existing thing)' (Merleau-Ponty, ed. Ménasé, 1997, 330, fn. 31). Merleau-Ponty considers that Gurwitsch wrongly consolidates Husserl's covert intellectualism in developing his theory of the 'field' of consciousness. Whereas Merleau-Ponty had considered perception to be a corporeal activity in *Phénoménologie de la perception* and had thereby incurred Gurwitsch's opposition, he now treats it as an action of the whole body, simultaneously material and mental. In particular, Merleau-Ponty rejects Gurwitsch's 'orders of existence'. He rejects Gurwitsch's view that 'the products of the imagination are excluded from reality' (Gurwitsch, 1957b, 307, quoted in Merleau-Ponty, ed. Ménasé, 1997, 338). In response to Gurwitsch's view that systems of colours or musical sounds are autonomous, a-temporal 'worlds', dissociated from 'reality', Merleau-Ponty insists that the sound system is a cultural product and that there is no ideational autonomy or a-temporality but, rather, 'another temporality'. He concludes, therefore, that what philosophy must recover is 'not an eidetic-reflexive system, but the cradle of every system: the amorphous sound, containing all the possibilities of culture, existential eternity, active nature, not as a destiny or as a limit to our initiatives, but on the contrary as the most real entity, the sound of openness, taking into itself the infinity of Cartesian being'[28] (Merleau-Ponty, ed. Ménasé, 1997, 339). Merleau-Ponty had come to realize that in distancing himself from transcendental phenomenology he was not wanting to develop a philosophy *about* the life-world, as, perhaps, was the case with 'late' Husserl, nor was he wanting to elaborate a discourse *about* Being-in-the-world, as was the case with Heidegger. Instead, he was wanting to situate his philosophizing immanently within the life-world as his enactment of his being in the world.

Merleau-Ponty advanced contemporaneously this substantive philosophical position in the aptly entitled *L'oeil et l'esprit* [the eye and the mind], where he celebrated Cézanne's life work as exemplifying the kind of monist engagement in the world that he was now recommending, but there was still the problem of how now to reconcile this new view with his earlier intellectual involvement with political affairs.

Signes, *1960*

The collection of earlier articles entitled *Signes* [Signs], published in 1960, gave Merleau-Ponty the opportunity to try to tackle this problem. The introduction to *Signes* is dated February and September 1960, and was written, therefore, before and after writing *L'oeil et l'esprit*. The collection is divided into two Parts, assembling articles which can, respectively, be said to be 'philosophical' and 'political'. In the first sentence of his introduction, Merleau-Ponty makes the immediate observation: 'How different – how downright incongruous – the philosophical essays and the ad hoc, primarily political observations which make up this volume seem!' (Merleau-Ponty, 1960, 9; 1964, 3). He devotes his introduction to a consideration of the two kinds of activity. In the part written in February 1960, Merleau-Ponty examines philosophically the relationship between philosophy and politics by specific reference to their relations in the period between 1930 and the present as his career developed. Merleau-Ponty insists that philosophy and politics have to be reintegrated by eschewing detachment by means of taking 'philosophy and history as they are being made' (Merleau-Ponty, 1960, 9–10; 1964, 3). In rejecting the possibility of a detached, 'philosophical' perspective on politics, however, Merleau-Ponty does not relinquish an a-political function for philosophy. 'Is it not an incredible misunderstanding', he asks, 'that all, or almost all, philosophers have felt obliged to have a politics, whereas politics arises from the "practices of life" and escapes understanding? The politics of philosophers is what no one *practices*. Then is it politics? Are there not many other things philosophers can talk about with greater assurance?' (Merleau-Ponty, 1960, 13; 1964, 5). Merleau-Ponty takes the opportunity offered by assembling a collection of his earlier texts to review the relationship between philosophy and political comment in those texts. In discussing the plight of those 'who are or used to be Marxists' (Merleau-Ponty, 1960, 13; 1964, 6) Merleau-Ponty is indirectly reflecting, in the style of analysis he had already adopted in 'La guerre a eu lieu', on his own intellectual trajectory from the late 1930s until the time of writing. He contends that 'the Marxist identity of thought and action' (Merleau-Ponty, 1960, 17; 1964, 8) has become a postponed ambition and that Marxism has become a '*secondary truth*' retaining 'a real heuristic value' (Merleau-Ponty, 1960, 19; 1964, 9) without offering a valid basis for historical explanation. The Marxist supposition that its philosophy could provide a systematic, explanatory correlation between 'thought' and events was wrong and, Merleau-Ponty argues, we now have to learn the proper relationship which enables philosophy to function politically without commitment to a prior political agenda. This has to be a philosophy which 'discloses exactly the Being we inhabit' (Merleau-Ponty, 1960, 26; 1964, 13). This philosophy rests 'upon the insurpassable richness, the miraculous multiplication of perceptible being ['du sensible']' (Merleau-Ponty, 1960, 30; 1964, 16). It is 'the exact opposite of a philosophy of God-like survey. It plunges into the perceptible, into time and history' (Merleau-Ponty, 1960, 39; 1964, 21). In short, Merleau-Ponty argues that he has come to recognize that the practice of philosophizing is an immanent activity *sui generis* which has social and political impact without predicating the kind of systematic theory of the relationship between 'philosophy' and 'politics' which had motivated his writing in the immediate post-war period.

Merleau-Ponty resumed writing his introduction to *Signes* in September 1960, primarily in response to the preface, dated March 1960, which Sartre wrote to a new edition of Nizan's *Aden Arabie* (Nizan, 1960), first published in 1931. Merleau-Ponty takes the opportunity here to reflect more specifically about the relationship between being a philosopher and taking political action rather than between philosophy and ideological commitment. Sartre's preface offers a brief psychological analysis of Nizan's class and family background to seek an explanation of his aggressive activism: 'Nizan, this city man, conserved a sort of rustic naturalism out of fidelity to his childhood' (Nizan 1960, 37). Sartre's account is tinged with regret, remorse at the contrast between Nizan's anger and his own contemporary passive acquiescence in unacceptable social and political developments. Sartre argues that Nizan now speaks to the generation of 'angry young men',[29] whereas those, like himself, who have spent years protesting and petitioning have only learnt one thing – their 'radical impotence' (Nizan, 1960, 14).

In reflecting on his own political engagement in the same historical period, Merleau-Ponty refuses to acquiesce in Sartre's self-immolation. Although Merleau-Ponty recognizes the intensity of the self-deprecation of his former friend, it is important to note that he considered Sartre's reflections to be fundamentally misguided for reasons which further underline the differences which caused the disruption of their collaboration in 1953. Merleau-Ponty suggests that, in his preface to *Aden Arabie*, Sartre is offering his present self as judge of his former self and he opines that this is a fraudulent presentation which is a logical consequence of Sartre's persistent inability to acknowledge that changing selves are the consequences of changing constitutive social conditions. Merleau-Ponty posits that 'there are two ways of being young' (Merleau-Ponty, 1960, 45; 1964, 25). Some 'are fascinated by their childhood' while others 'believe that they have no past and are equally near to all possibilities'. 'Sartre was one of the second type', and, tacitly, Merleau-Ponty of the former. Merleau-Ponty elaborates the consequences of this difference. Sartre conserved a controlling transcendent ego whereas Merleau-Ponty accepted that his identity was a constantly modifying adjustment to alterations in its milieu. For this reason, Merleau-Ponty argued that Sartre's interpretation of Nizan's career was flawed in concentrating excessively on the psychology of paternal influence. Merleau-Ponty acknowledges that Nizan was affected by the fact that his father was a 'transfuge', someone who had betrayed his working-class origins, but he insists that the flight to Aden which was an attempt to come to terms with this inheritance 'would have been no more than a diversion if Nizan had not found in the colonial regime ... the clear image of our dependence in respect of the external world' (Merleau-Ponty, 1960, 49; 1964, 27–8).[30] It is because Merleau-Ponty emphasizes that we are constituted by external circumstances that he is able to advise young readers not to believe 'too hastily that Sartre's life is a failure because he failed to rebel' (Merleau-Ponty, 1960, 42; 1964, 23) and to formulate some tentative optimism for the future on the grounds that ongoing changes in social conditions will generate adaptive responses among young people who may no longer be obsessed by the issues which concerned his generation.[31]

There is a poignancy about Merleau-Ponty's cautious optimism, expressed such a short time before his unexpected death. The same conviction underlies both the hope that future change may be possible and also, unlike Sartre, his lack of regret that he had not followed Nizan's example. For all the political commitment expressed in publications in the post-war years, the final message given by Merleau-Ponty is that his social trajectory caused him to philosophize rather than to be an activist. He believes that the way that he philosophizes has a socio-political impact in spite of being a-political. He does not express regret at his lack of active political engagement but, instead, a slightly weary recognition of limits of possible achievement. Effecting the transition between the two parts of the introduction to *Signes*, Merleau-Ponty recognizes the conflicting demands of politics and philosophy and, tacitly accepting his career concentration on philosophy, concludes that 'Perhaps the truth is that one would need many lives to enter each realm of experience with the total abandon it demands' (Merleau-Ponty, 1960, 41; 1964, 22).

Summary

Trained academically as a philosopher, Merleau-Ponty's doctoral theses, both published during the Second World War, established his reputation as a phenomenological philosopher. His exploration of 'perception' enabled him to articulate a corporeal or materialist critique of the assumptions of intellectualism. He recognized, instead, an ongoing dialectic between perception and consciousness. The consequences of his military service early in the Second World War and of his experience of the Nazi Occupation were that his commitment to an epistemological dialectic within philosophy transposed to the field of politics where he became involved in advancing a dialectic between thought and action which he differentiated from what he regarded as the reified, formulaic dialectic of Marxist dialectical materialism and which he also differentiated from what he thought to be the covertly Hegelian nature of Sartre's existential engagement. Merleau-Ponty was aware that his political engagement was intellectual rather than active but he did not agree with Sartre's regret that he had not followed the active course taken by their contemporary at the École Normale Supérieure, Paul Nizan. After his rift with Sartre and his appointment to the Chair of Philosophy at the Collège de France, Merleau-Ponty developed his commitment to a phenomenology of inter-subjectivity within the field of philosophy, many of the outcomes of which were only apparent in publications issued posthumously in the early 1960s. Merleau-Ponty tried to reconcile a theory of corporeal perception with one which emphasized the primacy of consciousness and to relate this reconciled position to the field of political action. Having initially argued that he would be practising a new kind of philosophy, he eventually, with some element of resignation, resorted to advancing his position within instituted Philosophy.

Notes

1 Plotinus, 204–70 CE.
2 This is the view of Sartre, expressed in his 'Merleau-Ponty vivant', Sartre, 1961, 306 (translated in Stewart, ed., 1998, 565–626), quoted in Geraets, 1971, 6.
3 Geraets notes that it is 'probable' that Merleau-Ponty attended these courses on Husserl, Heidegger and Lask (Geraets, 1971, 7, fn. 17).

4 'Projet de travail sur la nature de la perception' [project on the nature of perception], 1933. Geraets provides the full text of the application (Geraets, 1971, 9–10), and it was subsequently published in Merleau-Ponty, ed. Prunair, 1996, 9–13.
5 'La nature de la perception' [the nature of perception], 1934, in Merleau-Ponty, ed. Prunair, 1996, 15–38.
6 This article and these reviews have been collected in Merleau-Ponty, ed. Prunair, 1997.
7 Merleau-Ponty, 1935, 297, quoted in Geraets, 1971, 17.
8 Merleau-Ponty, 1935, 299, quoted in Geraets, 1971, 17.
9 Marcel, 1935, 25 quoted in Merleau-Ponty, 1936a, 100, all quoted in Geraets, 1971, 19.
10 These were published in 1947, see Kojève, ed. Quéneau, 1947.
11 I dwell on this exposition of Merleau-Ponty's argument in *La structure du comportement* because of the resonance of his thoughts with positions advanced by Bourdieu and discussed in subsequent chapters – see, in particular, chapter 6.
12 Merleau-Ponty's distinction is reminiscent of the underlying philosophy contained in Sartre's *La Nausée* (Sartre, 1938).
13 Merleau-Ponty explicitly chooses here a 'Hegelian term' (Merleau-Ponty, 1942, 246).
14 Merleau-Ponty refers generally to Bergson's *Évolution créatrice* when making this point (Merleau-Ponty, 1942, 246).
15 In the course of development in Gurwitsch's thinking but not yet published.
16 Published in Merleau-Ponty, ed. Prunair, 1996, 39–104.
17 An edition of this course of lectures was published in 1968 and an augmented edition based on further notes was published as Merleau-Ponty, ed. Deprun, 1997.
18 L'École Normale Supérieure.
19 These were the show trials instigated by Stalin to eradicate dissident groups and opponents of his economic policies, aimed at backsliding revolutionaries as well as counter-revolutionaries. They highlighted the tension between adherence to humane, extra-historical values and commitment to the progressive domination of the proletariat.
20 Originally written in German between 1938 and 1940 and translated into English for publication.
21 See the footnote in Merleau-Ponty, 1947c, 28 (Merleau-Ponty, 1969, 26).
22 Published posthumously by Martial Guéroult as Merleau-Ponty, ed. Guéroult, 1962, and collected in Merleau-Ponty, ed., Prunair, 2000, 36–48.
23 Résumés of many of these courses were published in 1968, with a preface by Claude Lefort (Merleau-Ponty, ed. Lefort, 1968, translated as Merleau-Ponty, ed. O'Neill, 1970).
24 The notes of the courses of 1959–61 were published in 1996 (Merleau-Ponty, ed., Ménasé).
25 Lefort is explicit that Merleau-Ponty replaced the text of this annex with the chapter of the book entitled 'Interrogation et intuition' and that, therefore, he was rescuing a text which Merleau-Ponty discarded.
26 This was written during a stay of two or three months near Aix during the Summer of 1960 where Merleau-Ponty 'every day enjoyed the landscape which for ever bears the imprint of the eye of Cézanne', enabling him to 'reinterrogate the nature of vision as well as of painting' (Merleau-Ponty, ed. Lefort, 1964b, I–II).
27 Part IV, Chapter 1 of *Théorie du champ de la conscience*.
28 'Ce que la philosophie doit retrouver, ce n'est pas un système eidético-réflexif, c'est le berceau de tout système: le son amorphe, contenant toutes les possibilités de *Bildung*, l'éternité existentielle, le *wesen* actif, non pas comme un destin ou une

limite à nos initiatives, mais au contraire comme l'*ens realissimum*, le son d'*Offenheit*, recueillant en lui l'*Unendlichkeit* de l'être cartésien'.

29 In English in the original.

30 It should be clear that my rendering of Merleau-Ponty's critique of Sartre on Nizan deliberately suggests a similarity between the ways in which the careers of Nizan and Bourdieu can be conceptualized.

31 See the passage quoted at the head of the postscript of this book.

II

Pierre Bourdieu. Evolution of an intellectual social project

Anyone already familiar with the work of Bourdieu will have noticed the affinities between his thinking and that of Merleau-Ponty, itself expressed in language derived from the phenomenological movement as represented, in part, in the work of Schutz and Gurwitsch. Some instances are indicative. Merleau-Ponty's discussion of the nature of 'habits' as forms of 'apprenticeship' resonates with Bourdieu's use of the concept of 'habitus' and its function in 'pedagogic work'. His argument that an emphasis on perception requires an 'inversion of the movement of consciousness' neatly articulates in anticipation what was to become Bourdieu's insistence that intellectual endeavour has to be understood as grounded in practice. His view that we have to change our usual notion of necessity and contingency because human existence is 'the transformation of contingency into necessity' is one that was fundamental to Bourdieu's attitude towards history and social change. Bourdieu shared Merleau-Ponty's opposition to Sartre as expressed by the phrase: 'the world is already constituted, but also never completely constituted', which he constantly endorsed in what is known as his 'soft determinism'. Similarly, Merleau-Ponty's statement that Marxism has become a 'secondary truth' accurately expresses the view which Bourdieu adopted when analysing the relationship between social 'conditions' and 'positions'. Merleau-Ponty's interpretation of the transformative influence on Paul Nizan of his experience of colonialism is uncannily prescient in respect of Bourdieu, and, finally, Merleau-Ponty's philosophical resistance to what he regarded as Gurwitsch's 'intellectualist' concept of the 'field' of consciousness points the way towards Bourdieu's attempt to deploy it to understand the processes by which fields become 'embodied' in societies.

I do not try to argue in any detail that Bourdieu was specifically 'influenced' by the thought of Schutz, Gurwitsch or Merleau-Ponty. It was not a matter of influence so much as that Bourdieu embodied the tensions that are apparent in the thinking of the three antecedents. The purpose of this Part is to examine the way in which Bourdieu assimilated the philosophy which he was taught, integrating it with his primary experiences, in such a way as to reconcile intellect and experience in a form of social science pursued as a mode of action rather than in a philosophical position held in detachment.

5

The 1950s

Early career

In this chapter I explore the beginnings of Bourdieu's career. It was, perhaps, his enforced period of military service in Algeria which extinguished any aspiration to become a philosopher which may have lingered after his time at the École Normale Supérieure. What he saw in Algeria and how he saw it crystallized the awareness of the tension between familial and scholarly experience which he had already sensed in his youth. His time in Algeria enabled him to recognize the abyss between the way in which indigenous culture operated intrinsically and the way in which this was interpreted in terms of their own rational criteria by observing anthropologists.

Pierre Bourdieu was born on 1 August 1930 in Denguin in the Béarn region of the French Pyrénées-Atlantiques, not far from the Spanish border. He went to the local elementary school before passing to the lycée Louis Barthou in Pau, which he attended as a boarder from 1941 to 1947. He passed an entrance examination to attend the lycée Louis-Le-Grand in Paris which was one of the principal schools for students aspiring to enter the École Normale Supérieure. He passed the concours for the École and entered in 1951. He completed there a Diplôme d'études supérieures [diploma of higher study] under the supervision of Henri Gouhier. He secured his agrégation at the first attempt (Lescourret, 2008, 62). He graduated at the end of 1953. Deciding not to remain at the École for a further year of research, he took up a post as Professor of Philosophy at the lycée Théodore-de-Bainville in Moulins in the Bourbonnais. During this period he registered to undertake doctoral research under the supervision of Georges Canguilhem but, after only a year and a month teaching in Moulins, he was called up for military service in Algeria and was never able to pursue his doctoral project.

Pierre Bourdieu was twenty-five years old when he set foot in Algeria, in October 1955 (Bourdieu, ed. Yacine, 2013). He was posted to an air force unit of the military staff of the French administration, based in the Chéliff valley, 150 kilometres west of Algiers. In the Spring of 1956, he was drafted into the 'cabinet' of the Resident Minister in Algeria, Robert Lacoste. This enabled him to work with the Service de Documentation et d'Information of the Gouvernement Général, in Algiers. It was here that Bourdieu participated in the preparation of two reports which were published in 1959 in a publication of the Secrétariat social entitled *Le sous-développement en Algérie* [underdevelopment in Algeria] (collected in Bourdieu, ed. Yacine, 2013, 72–82 and 39–51). It was here also that he was charged with the task of undertaking enquiries[1] for ARDES (Association pour la recherche démographique économique et sociale) [the Association for Demographic, Economic and Social Research], supplementing sociologically the work of statisticians from INSEE (Institut national de la statistique et des études économiques) [National Institute of Statistics and Economic Studies]. He was demobilized at the end of 1957 after thirty months of military service (Lescourret, 2008, 73). He then secured a post teaching sociology in the Faculty of Letters of the University of Algiers, which he held from 1958 to 1960. On the eve of the 'putsch of the colonels' (22 April 1960), Raymond Aron enabled Bourdieu to leave Algeria and come to Paris to become secretary to the research group which he had recently established as the Centre européenne d'histoire sociologique [the European Centre for Sociological History]. It seems that Bourdieu carried out further fieldwork research in Algeria between June and September 1960, before taking up his post in Aron's Centre. Jean-Claude Passeron was called to Paris by Aron at the same time to be his assistant. Bourdieu renewed the slight acquaintance which he had had with Passeron when both were students at the École Normale Supérieure. Thrown together by Aron's patronage, they made a 'contract of objectives' to be fulfilled together.[2] Bourdieu taught the sociology of religion at the Sorbonne (Lescourret, 2008, 155) before, retaining his role in Aron's research Centre, he was appointed maître de conférences at the University of Lille in 1961. At Lille he taught the social history of sociological theories (Lescourret, 2008, 167) and, in the second year, the sociology of religion, which included consideration of Weber on religion (Lescourret, 2008, 168). During the first few years of the 1960s, Bourdieu published books and articles which followed from his work in Algeria and he also managed projects within Aron's Centre for which he partly secured collaboration with staff and students at Lille. These were projects on students, photography, museums/art galleries and language, which were reflected in collaborative publications. In 1964 he accepted a position in the VIth section of the École Pratique des Hautes Études, which was to become the École des Hautes Études en Sciences Sociales (EHESS) in 1975. In 1964 he also became Co-director of Aron's Centre, which was now called the Centre de Sociologie Européenne (CSE).

Bourdieu gave an account of his studies at the École in response to Axel Honneth's questions in an interview of April 1985. There are three key passages. These are Bourdieu's words. First: 'When I was a student in the fifties, phenomenology, in its existentialist variety, was at its peak, and I had read *Being and Nothingness* very early on, and then Merleau-Ponty and Husserl' (Bourdieu, 1990c, 3). Secondly, Bourdieu stated that he followed the classes outside the École of Éric Weill, Alexandre Koyré and Martial Guéroult, and he commented that it was 'pretty much thanks to them and to what they represented – a tradition of the history of the sciences and of rigorous philosophy (and thanks also to my reading of Husserl, who was still little translated in those days) – that I tried, together with those people who, like me, were a little tired of existentialism, to go beyond merely reading the classical authors and to give some meaning to philosophy' (Bourdieu, 1990c, 4). Bourdieu mentioned next that he had regarded Georges Canguilhem and Jules Vuillemin as 'real "exemplary prophets" in Weber's sense', but the third passage I want to emphasize is the response Bourdieu gave when Honneth pushed him as to whether he had ever been interested in existentialism. Bourdieu replied:

> I read Heidegger, I read him a lot and with a certain fascination, especially the analyses in *Sein und Zeit* of public time, history and so on, which, together with Husserl's analyses in *Ideen II*, helped me a great deal – as was later the case with Schütz – in my efforts to analyse the ordinary experience of the social. But I never really got into the existentialist mood. Merleau-Ponty was something different, at least in my view. (Bourdieu, 1990c, 5)

These passages are richly suggestive. Bourdieu was making explicit that he was influenced by the socio-historical orientation of contemporary French philosophers of science and, equally, was familiar with phenomenological discussions of time without adhering to an existentialist position. For the purposes of this book, Bourdieu's brief allusion to the distinctive feature of Merleau-Ponty's work is significant.

Texts

Diplôme d'études supérieures and proposed thèse d'état

We know precisely from Bourdieu's comment in his interview very late in life with Yvette Delsaut that he submitted for his Diplôme d'études supérieures in 1954 a 'translation, prefaced and with notes and comments' (Delsaut and Rivière eds, 2002, 192) of Leibniz's *Animadversiones in partem generalem Principiorum Cartesianorum* [Critical remarks Concerning the general part of Descartes' Principles] under the supervision of Henri Gouhier.

Studying the response of one key Western European rationalist to another in relation to epistemological issues, Bourdieu must have appreciated in general terms that 'Leibniz stood on the interface between the holistic and vitalist world-view of the Renaissance, and the atomistic and mechanistic materialism that was to dominate the eighteenth and nineteenth centuries' (Ross, 1984, 1–2), or between scholastic a priorism and scientific empiricism. He would have known of Leibniz's inclination to search for a universal language or logic and to suppose that mathematics might constitute the basis for these universals.

Concentration on Leibniz's *Animadversiones* would have been influential in more specific ways. I highlight five main points.

First, Descartes's first proposition in the first part, 'On the Principles of Human Knowledge', of his *Principia*, was the famous emphasis of methodological doubt: 'In the search after truth, one must, once in a lifetime and as far as possible, doubt everything' (Schrecker and Schrecker, eds, 1965, 22). Leibniz argued, in opposition, that this supposed a distinction between truth and falsehood which is too absolute and wrongly dependent on 'doubt' rather than ratiocination: 'The degree of assent or dissent which any proposition deserves must be considered; or still more simply, for every proposition the reasons must be examined' (Schrecker and Schrecker, eds, 1965, 22). Bourdieu was to be sympathetic to this response when, later, he recommended to sociologists that they should follow Bachelard's injunction that hypotheses should be subjected to rigorous scrutiny. Secondly, Descartes's sixth proposition was 'That we have free will, hence we are able to refuse our assent to doubtful things, and thus to avoid error' (Schrecker and Schrecker, eds, 1965, 25). Leibniz exposed here what he took to be Descartes's confusion between perception and action. 'We have free will', he argued, 'not when we perceive, but when we act'. There are objective facts which are not dependent on our decision, such as whether honey is bitter or sweet, or whether a proposed theorem appears to be true or false. In a proto-phenomenological phrase, Leibniz continued that 'Consciousness need only examine what appears to it' (Schrecker and Schrecker, eds, 1965, 25). Intrinsic to this argument, thirdly, is the position which Leibniz adopted in response to Descartes's seventh proposition, that 'We are unable to doubt that we exist while we doubt; and this is the first certainty we can get in philosophy'. Leibniz acknowledged that Descartes's *cogito ergo sum* thesis is 'excellent', but, he added, 'it would have been only fair not to neglect other truths of the same kind. In general it can be said that all truths are either truths of fact or truths of reason'[3] (Schrecker and Schrecker, eds, 1965, 25). This tension between two spheres of truth and the nature of the relations between them was to be central to Bourdieu's work. In his thirteenth proposition, fourthly, Descartes considered 'In what sense the knowledge of all things depends upon the knowledge of God'. Leibniz thought that God was not 'aptly introduced here' but he insisted that he did believe in the appropriateness of reference to God on other grounds: 'For God is the first cause of all things no less than their ultimate reason; and a thing cannot be known better than by its causes and reasons' (Schrecker and Schrecker, eds, 1965, 27). This introduces, fifthly, the notions of mechanism or finalism but the comment is not exactly equatable with a distinction between efficient and final 'causes' because Leibniz maintains the separation of the spheres of reason and fact.

Leibniz's *Animadversiones* responded to Descartes's 'principles of human knowledge' and also to his second Part, 'On the Principles of Material Things'. Describing the motivation for writing the *Animadversiones*, E.J. Aiton has commented that 'Owing to the close connection between his metaphysics and dynamics ... it was natural that Leibniz should wish to clarify and disseminate his ideas in philosophy at the same time as those in his new science of dynamics' (Aiton, 1985, 196–7). Leibniz's response to the simple question posed by Descartes as proposition 25 of Part II of his *Principles* has generated much debate in the philosophy of science and has implications for social science. Descartes asked: 'What is motion, properly speaking?' Leibniz answered that if motion is thought to be relative, 'there is no natural reason why motion should be ascribed to one object rather than to others. Hence there would be no real motion at all. To be able to say that an object is moving, we will require, therefore, not only that it change its position with respect to others, but also that this body contain in itself the cause of change, a force, an action' (Schrecker and Schrecker, eds, 1965, 45). S. Puryear has argued that in his 'middle years', in the 1680s and 1690s, 'Leibniz appears to endorse two incompatible approaches to motion, one a realist approach, the other a phenomenalist approach' (Puryear, 2012, abstract). The truth of reason (phenomenal and metaphysical) might be that motion is relational while the truth of fact (real and empirical) might be that it is a 'force'.[4]

In summary, we can say with confidence that work for his Diplôme d'études supérieures would have familiarized Bourdieu with debates in Western European Enlightenment thinking revolving round a set of related polarities – between real and phenomenal, efficient and final, body and mind, subjective and objective, empirical and metaphysical – as well as with Leibniz's particular disposition to resolve these dualistic problems by uncertainly or ambivalently embracing a form of pluralism. Nothing can be said with equal confidence about the project for a 'thèse d'État' which Bourdieu proposed in 1956.[5] The proposal seems to have been for a philosophical study to be supervised by Canguilhem but it was never pursued, perhaps because of the call-up to military service. The consequence, therefore, is that Bourdieu arrived in Algeria aware of epistemological disputes within the philosophical canon and with an unrealized desire to pursue a philosophical enquiry. Accounts of Bourdieu's teaching style at Moulins suggest that he was committed to communicating the practical value of philosophical thought, and events in Algeria encouraged this disposition.

Sociologie de l'algérie

Bourdieu's philosophical awareness of the tensions between rational analysis and primary experience corresponded with his life experience in that he had seen the disjunction between everyday and academic discourse, accentuated by the disparity between the domestic use of the Béarn dialect and the scholarly deployment of French. He sensed the same tensions acutely in Algeria when he was employed to carry out research on the indigenous population, using the conceptual tools developed in Western European social science. His first book – *Sociologie de l'algérie* (Bourdieu, 1958) – shows these tensions operating on several levels. First, there is the nature of the publication itself. It was written for the Que Sais-je series of the Presses Universitaires de France. These were innovative in format in that they were paperback introductions of a prescribed length (128 pages) on a wide range of topics, all selling at the same price, constituting a systematic, encyclopaedic popularization of specialist subjects.[6] As the title indicates, it was intended as a scientific sociology of Algeria to be read by the French-speaking reading public at a time when the French state was engaged in military suppression of the movement for independence in a region which it regarded constitutionally as a component of its metropolitan territory. The very notion that 'Algeria' could be analysed as a 'state' was, therefore, contentious and it was only with great difficulty that any account could be thought to be a-political. The task was a double challenge because the sociological method of analysis was necessarily in question and because there was doubt whether the object of the analysis possessed legitimate identity.

Bourdieu addressed both of these issues in a very brief introduction. In the first sentence he states that 'It is obvious that Algeria, when considered in isolation from the rest of the Maghreb, does not constitute a true cultural unit' (Bourdieu, 1962d, xi).[7] He avoids confronting this as a problem, however, and, more to the point, also avoids considering the relationship between any supposed 'cultural' identity and independent nationhood, by suggesting that his study has methodological unity because, in effect, its object constitutes a case-study of encounter between indigenous ('autochtone') and European civilizations such that 'the unity of the object is a function of the unity of the problematic' (Bourdieu, 1958, 5). The truth of reason determines the exploration of truths of fact. In the second paragraph, Bourdieu insists that his account is not partisan. He invokes the objectivity of science to suggest that he is therefore able to offer a representation of the real for the attention of readers:

> Any intention other than that of bringing to light the process which has led to the current situation will not contribute at all to the disinterest and impartiality which must inspire these researches. Sober and objective statement is neither stealthy nor resigned when it provokes people to become conscious of facts which, because they are human, conceal within themselves their meaning and value. (Bourdieu, 1958, 5)[8]

Bourdieu's account is an attempt to disclose the inherent meanings of actions rather than to impose interpretative meaning.

Even though Bourdieu was familiar with some regions of Algeria as a result of his military service, *Sociologie de l'algérie* was clearly the product mainly of library research. The second level of tension, therefore, relates to the sources of information at Bourdieu's disposal. The published text includes a selected bibliography amounting to references to forty-three books or articles and to six reviews. These fall roughly into three categories. There are recently published French texts (in other words, of the 1950s) which sought to analyse the situation in North Africa, either as historical or geographical accounts. There are French texts about North Africa of the late nineteenth century or early twentieth century. These older texts constitute elements of the anthropological record and were source books for Bourdieu's account of the *status quo ante* of the Algerian tribes. These two categories indicate what Bourdieu had read in order to offer his account of the 'culture' of four tribal groups – the Kabyles (chapter II), the Shawia (chapter III), the Mozabites (chapter IV) and the Arabic-Speaking Peoples (chapter V). Lastly, Bourdieu's bibliography includes several texts which had clearly guided him in establishing his methodology and his analytical approach. In writing his book, Bourdieu was confronted with two kinds of methodological problem. As we have seen, he was disposed to regard the phenomenon of encounter between indigenous and colonial cultures as the object of his study. This means that from the outset he approached his study with the mindset implicit in his proposed doctoral research – to study the temporal dimension of encounter and also, I submit, to do so phenomenologically without seeking to identify 'real' causes. Max Weber's *Gesammelte Aufsätze zur Religionssoziologie* is included, but there are no other references to founding fathers of sociological thinking.[9] Rather, he lists texts by recent American authors. These books all belong to a period of transition in the nature and influence of cultural anthropology in the United States. They embody a tension between the inclination to study 'societies' holistically and, therefore, in terms of internal relativisms of culture, politics, economics and religions, and the inclination to suppose that 'technological change', as it was occurring in the United States, was the necessary model and driving force for global social change transcending all local particularisms. Quite apart from this polarity, the relativist, acculturalist orientation had become side-lined in as much as it tended to autonomize the study of 'culture' independent of politics. As someone who had no training as a 'sociologist', it is clear that Bourdieu was particularly influenced by the methodology advanced by Herskovits in his *Acculturation* (1938). Herskovits argued, for instance, that it was important to establish a cultural base-line so as to attempt to measure processes of cultural adaptation.[10] Methodologically, Bourdieu's *Sociologie de l'algérie* constituted the 'base-line description' which, for Herskovits, was a pre-requisite for acculturation analysis. In his first paragraph, Bourdieu made it clear that the book was not intended as an end in itself but as the pre-requisite for future empirical studies:

> This study, which is a conceptual outline of more extensive analyses, includes a description of the *original* social and economic structures ... which, although not the main purpose of the book, is indispensable for an understanding of the breakdown of the social structures caused by the colonial situation and the influx of European civilization. (Bourdieu, 1962d, xi)[11]

Bourdieu's intention was to analyse the social dynamics of French colonial intervention, but this involved offering a putative 'static' account of the social *status quo ante*. The acculturalist project could not evade the methodological challenge which was that of the sociologist of how to describe or represent the structure of any society. If we take Bourdieu's representation of just one Algerian tribe – the Kabyles – as an example, we find that he chose to emphasize that it was what he called a 'gentilitial democracy' – one that cohered socially on the basis of familial relationships rather than by reference to an objectively formulated political constitution or legal system. Bourdieu began his account with a summary of the topography and climate of Kabylia, suggesting the implications of these for its economic condition, but his emphasis, in sub-sections, was on its 'social structures', its 'judicial system' and its 'domestic organization', before concluding with a sub-section which tendentiously made a distinction between types of 'lived' or 'constituted' democracy, suggesting that the 'gentilitial family provided the *pattern* according to which the political structure was conceived' (Bourdieu, 1958, 27). Bourdieu used the English word 'pattern' in his French text and this, therefore, connotes the title of the text by Margaret Mead cited in the bibliography.[12]

It is important to note, finally, of *Sociologie de l'Algérie*, that Bourdieu was attracted by the character of Kabyle society which he represented. As a corollary of the methodological tension between objective and subjective analyses, the question arises in relation to Bourdieu's first book, how far the 'objective' account offered of Kabyle social organization reflects, first, the perceptions of the nineteenth-century anthropological record used by Bourdieu which incorporated the values of the early French military and administrative officials in the region, and, secondly, the affinity which he felt between the constituted social system which he represented and that which he had experienced in rural Béarn.

Reports and articles, 1959–62

'La logique interne de la civilisation algérienne traditionnelle' [the internal logic of original Algerian society] and 'Le choc des civilisations' [the clash of civilizations] were successive chapters in the report on under-development in Algeria published by the Secrétariat social in 1959. In the first, Bourdieu tried to analyse 'the internal logic' of Algerian society 'rather than by reference to a normative ideal – which could only be Western society taken as a model' (Bourdieu, ed. Yacine, 2013, 72). In these terms, he suggests, traditional Algerian society 'appears as a systematic and integrated totality' (Bourdieu, ed. Yacine, 2013, 72). The objective reality corresponds with his disposition to interpret societies holistically. He recommends, and quotes from, the work of Xavier Yacono on the history of the Bureaux Arabes from early colonial days. The officers of the Bureaux Arabes recognized that the traditional, integrated system possessed a coherence which was adapted to its physical environment and which might be adversely affected by imported 'improvements'.[13] In general, therefore, Bourdieu ponders 'whether such a coherent totality does not have to be replaced by another totality, to avoid simply destroying the existing order without any guarantee that a better order can be established' (Bourdieu, ed. Yacine, 2013, 73). In response to his own question, Bourdieu posits a general formula whereby 'any cultural system requires, on the one hand, a minimum of adaptation to the world, and, on the other hand, a minimum of coherence between its different elements' (Bourdieu, ed. Yacine, 2013, 74). He does not pursue this idea, however, but instead characterizes constituent elements of Algerian society which, in his view, are held together by 'the same "spirit", the same "intention", characteristic of a "style of life" that we shall call traditionalist, for want of a better term' (Bourdieu, ed. Yacine, 2013, 75). These elements cohere through 'the logic of honour and prestige, and certainly not in terms of the logic of self-interest, which everything inclines us to do' (Bourdieu, ed. Yacine, 2013, 75). Bourdieu considers mutual aid; *khammessat* (a form of sharecropping in which the tenant receives a fifth of the crop); work; the future; saving; and credit. He exemplifies that these elements form an integrated system which retains cohesion as a result of shared values. In a short final section Bourdieu explores the gulf between the self-perception of this traditional society and the 'under-developed' label attached to it by Western criteria. Objectively, it would take a 'social revolution' to introduce the benefits which technological development might procure. At the same time, even precarious self-sufficiency is associated, subjectively, with a degree of self-satisfaction. The improbability of change or the unavailability of future expectation suppress aspiration and induce brave acquiescence in the status quo. Without judgement, Bourdieu concludes:

> it is no cause for surprise that a society that is poor only in relation to a wealth external to it that it cannot know, and moreover a wealth that it cannot discover internally, does not recognize itself as such, and is stubbornly, sometimes desperately, attached to a social order and a system of values in which a lived philosophy of existence is expressed. (Bourdieu, ed. Yacine, 2013, 82)

Having discussed the logic of traditional Algerian society in his first chapter, Bourdieu turned his attention in the following chapter to the consequences for it of the 'incursion of European civilization' (Bourdieu, ed. Yacine, 2013,

39). Before making some 'methodological remarks', Bourdieu announced the general proposition that 'any cultural change takes place in a particular situation, in conformity with universal laws' (Bourdieu, ed. Yacine, 2013, 39). He defers to the definition of acculturation given by Redfield, Linton and Herskovits,[14] distinguishing between 'culture-change', 'assimilation' and 'diffusion' but he is preoccupied with the specificity of the Algerian situation as opposed to their attention to the acculturation within the United States of black Africans and American Indians and, importantly, he insists that the phenomenon of colonization introduces a political dimension which intrudes on theories of cultural change. To reinforce this latter point, Bourdieu considers Germaine Tillion's analysis of Chaouïa society, published in 1957 as *L'Algérie en 1957*. She had studied the Aurès – 'an isolated territory relatively closed in on itself' (Bourdieu, ed. Yacine, 2013, 41) – with the result that she concluded that the dysfunctions of traditional society 'are simply the result of the laws of acculturation' (Bourdieu, ed. Yacine, 2013, 41) such as the disaffection caused by schooling and by gender differentiation in schooling opportunities. Disinclined to allow such cultural autonomy, Bourdieu insists that 'In reality, other causes have also played a part' (Bourdieu, ed. Yacine, 2013, 41) and he proceeds to emphasize the effects of colonial land management. Following François Perroux, Bourdieu calls this 'the domination effect'. Nevertheless, Bourdieu is anxious not to counter the autonomization of the 'cultural' with an emphasis of the dominance of economic or political effects. On the contrary, he insists that the clash of civilizations is a clash of opposing totalities. As he puts it: 'The European, in fact, brings his universe with him; … he offers in each element of his behaviour, each one of his words, a whole system of values' (Bourdieu, ed. Yacine, 2013, 44). In doing so, the European transforms a condition experienced traditionally as one of necessity into one of contingency, making 'what had seemed "natural" appear as an object of choice' (Bourdieu, ed. Yacine, 2013, 44). Bourdieu argues that colonial interventions lacked sociological sophistication. He does not present himself as an opponent of intervention as such but, instead, argues that the function of political intervention should have been to regulate acculturation processes rather than to exploit them for the economic advantage of the colonial power. He concludes that sociological analysis of the colonized society is an essential pre-requisite for the development of economic practices suited to indigenous needs: 'Sociological analysis of underdeveloped countries suggests the need to develop a non-Keynesian economic theory that would be to Keynesian economics, valid for the case of the West, what non-Euclidean geometries are to Euclidean geometry' (Bourdieu, ed. Yacine, 2013, 44). Bourdieu's conclusion, therefore, articulates the rationale for the whole of his Algerian research project.

Just as there is always a logic of discovery governing the operation of research projects, so there is always a rhetoric of communication governing the reporting of findings. Bourdieu was not only a novice in social science methodology in 1958. He was also uninitiated into a field of discourse. *Sociologie de l'algérie* was an introduction to Algerian society commissioned in mainland France for a general mainland readership. It was not primarily a book for sociologists. The two chapters just discussed belong to a report prepared under the auspices of the Governor General. In the period between 1959 and 1963, Bourdieu was in search of ways to communicate his views and findings which would inform readers but also safeguard his commitment to practise research which would enable the self-expression and self-determination of the people he was studying. His publications were of several kinds. While still in Algeria, he wrote an article entitled 'Guerre et mutation sociale en Algérie' [war and social mutation in Algeria] (Bourdieu, 1960; Bourdieu, ed. Yacine, 2013, 104–14), which was published in the review founded in association with the Centre d'études des sociétés méditerranéennes established in 1955 at Aix by Georges Duby. Back in France, Bourdieu published two articles of reflection on the Algerian War of Independence, the first in the journal *Esprit* (Bourdieu, 1961; Bourdieu, ed. Yacine, 2013, 92–103) and the second in a collection on the future of Algeria edited by Perroux (Bourdieu, 1962a; Bourdieu, ed. Yacine, 2013, 85–91). Additionally, in 1962–63 Bourdieu published articles which focused on some of the key points in his argument concerning the deculturation effected by colonialism on traditionally integrated values – in relation to work and unemployment (Bourdieu, 1962c; Bourdieu, ed. Yacine, 2013, 162–79) and in relation to time and economic behaviour (Bourdieu, 1963; Bourdieu, ed. Yacine, 2013, 52–71) – and also highlighted consideration of the applicability of Marxist conceptualization to the Algerian situation (Bourdieu, 1962e; Bourdieu, ed. Yacine, 2013, 146–61). The first two of these were published in a new journal devoted to the sociology of work, and the third was a contribution to *Les temps modernes*. There is a sense in which Bourdieu extracted from his coherent perception of Algerian society topics which were in part dictated by the concerns of the journals. This process continued through to 1965 after the publication in France of the books detailing the findings of his Algerian fieldwork: *Travail et travailleurs en Algérie* [work and workers in Algeria] (Bourdieu, Darbel, Rivet and Seibel, 1963) and *Le déracinement, la crise de l'agriculture traditionnelle en Algérie* [the uprooting: the crisis of traditional agriculture in Algeria] Bourdieu and Sayad, 1964a). Two of these atomized articles appeared in English-language collections which were advancing work in the field of 'mediterranean anthropology' and therefore helped to establish Bourdieu's reputation outside France in that autonomized intellectual context (Bourdieu, 1964 and Bourdieu, 1965), while a third was a contribution on 'uprooted peasants' derived from *Le déracinement* written for the relatively new journal of research on rural issues, *Études rurales*.[15]

These articles deserve attention[16] but I focus on the two large texts which Bourdieu must have been seeing through the press in the early 1960s at the same time that he was organizing the series of CSE research projects which were to be the basis of publications, mainly in the second half of the 1960s, which will be discussed in the next chapter. I concentrate first on the personal analysis which he produced in 1962 of the peasant condition in his home region of the Béarn, published in *Études rurales*.

'Célibat et condition paysanne', 1962

This article is a substantial monograph of a hundred pages. Bourdieu indicates in a footnote on the first page that the study was based on research undertaken in 1959 and 1960 in a village in the Béarn that he calls Lesquire. It is clear from photographs which embellish the article that Lesquire is Lasseube, the village to which his parents moved when he was a child. Bourdieu's study of his home village was undertaken, therefore, in parallel with his fieldwork in Algeria, presumably during periods of vacation from his job in the University of Algiers. The products of these researches reveal the same methodological tensions and need to be considered closely together. The first point to be made is that, aged about thirty, Bourdieu interviewed some people with whom he had grown up. The ages of all the interviewees are scrupulously given, with the result that the correlation with the age of the interviewer is explicit. In a late republication of the article, Bourdieu also recalls that his father helped him to interview people of the older generation.[17] Bourdieu was testing comparatively the validity of his experiential knowledge of the situation and the findings of his objective analyses, and deliberately inserting the temporal dimension, raising the possibility that the experiential/objective dichotomy is false in as much as the shift between the two modes of knowing occurred in his personal, developmental trajectory. Similarly, Bourdieu's deployment of his father was indicative of his methodological assumption that interviews are what he was later to call 'maieutic' encounters which require some tangible degree of socio-cultural affinity between interlocutors. Secondly, the article addresses a *problem* rather more than a *situation*, just as, in *Sociologie de l'Algérie*, Bourdieu emphasized that his study was of the clash of civilizations more than of Algerian society. In his recollection, Bourdieu states that he was alerted to the problem of the celibacy of many of his contemporaries by the reaction of one of his former fellow pupils to an old class photograph, pointing out that 'almost half' of those in the photo were 'unmarriageable' (Bourdieu, 2008, 3). In the article itself, significantly, Bourdieu introduces the problem differently. He draws attention to the 'paradox' that their 'failure to marry' was regarded by the 'men themselves' as the most striking symptom of the crisis of their society, even though, 'traditionally', younger sons had always been condemned 'to emigration or bachelorhood' (Bourdieu, 2002, 17; 2008, 9). What had been accommodated as normal was now perceived by social agents as anomic.[18] The problem to be studied was, therefore, inherent in the self-perceptions of their situations of those interviewed. The second basis for identifying the problem, however, lay, for Bourdieu, in the anomaly that the statistics of marriage demonstrated that there was a low decrease in marriage in the region between 1940 and 1959 relative to the annual average marriage numbers in earlier years, especially given that the overall population was itself diminishing. The second source of the problem was that there was an apparent mismatch between the perceptions of actors and the relevant objective statistics. Bourdieu set himself the task of investigating what might be thought to be the delusions of people in respect of their actual social situations and in respect of the numerical measurement of those situations to be found in statistical data (on the assumption, that is, that Bourdieu alone was aware of all sources of information).

To try to deal with the identified problem Bourdieu first gave an account of the system of matrimonial exchanges as it existed prior to 1914. Marriage transactions operated according to strict rules in order to safeguard 'the continuity of the lineage without compromising the integrity of the heritage' (Bourdieu, 2008, 12). The role of the eldest son was crucial in this system. Younger children received a share of the inheritance but this was only a compensation rather than an equal share. Matrimonial negotiations were family affairs rather than the consequences of the wishes of individuals. At the same time, negotiations were not exclusively economic. Rather, the economic dimension was integrally related to issues concerning honour and status. In spite of these general regulations, Bourdieu suggested that there were opportunities to mitigate or modify them, and he also reflected in any case on the nature and influence of 'rules' which were largely uncodified. Arguing mainly through interpretation of the spoken words of interviewees, Bourdieu indicated that the traditional, regulative system disadvantaged younger sons, who responded either by remaining dedicated in an unmarried state to the interests of their family homestead or by leaving the country for the town or to emigrate. Following his historical account of the *status quo ante* in the Béarn, Bourdieu devotes a section to analysing the factors which had upset the traditional system.

The bibliography of the article cites thirty-nine texts concerned with the history and customs of the Béarnais region. Quite apart from the dimension of Bourdieu's personal involvement in the research phenomenon, 'Célibat et condition paysanne' was, on the analytical level, a study of internal acculturation to match the acculturation observed in Algeria as a consequence of colonial imposition. The decline of the regulatory system allowed for the possibility of marriage based on individual choice, a possibility actualized differentially by men and women as well as one which increasingly benefited younger sons. Bourdieu emphasized that the increased individuation was reflected in a spatial differentiation between practices among peasants in rural hamlets and those now living in villages or towns. These interpretations are supported by detailed statistical tables. The nature of Bourdieu's ratiocination is illustrated by the opening of the third section of the article in which he elaborates the opposition between the 'bourgs' [conurbations] and the 'hameaux' [hamlets]. Bourdieu posits that the restructuring of matrimonial exchanges might correlate with 'a restructuring of the overall society' (Bourdieu, 2008, 63). Before pursuing this possibility by 'analysing the role played by this opposition in the experience of the inhabitants of Lesquire', however, 'we must describe its genesis and form on the basis of the objective data' (Bourdieu, 2008, 63). Methodologically, Bourdieu triangulates historical conceptual inspiration, lived experience and statistical data. He concludes that what he analyses as a statistician is, in experience, a social construct in as much as 'The peasant perceives himself as a peasant only in the presence of the *citadin*; but the *citadin* himself only exists as such by opposition to the peasant' (Bourdieu, 2008, 80).

There are three further dimensions to Bourdieu's article. First, the last section examines 'the peasant and his body'. Having established correlations between general social divisions and those enacted in matrimonial exchanges, Bourdieu explores whether the identified social conditions contributing to the phenomenon of celibacy are 'necessitating' or 'permissive' (Bourdieu, 2008, 81), that is to say, whether they are determining or only admitting of possibility. The corporeal dimension of the distinction between the behaviours of town and country dwellers is graphically recounted in relation to modes of behaviour at traditional small country balls which, echoing language used in respect of Algeria, are 'the scene of a real clash of civilizations' (Bourdieu, 2008, 83). Secondly, the article was published with extensive appendices. These itemize sources of bibliographic information and conceptual inspiration (which, among other things, demonstrate indebtedness to the work of Le Play[19]), but also provide brief specifications about the twelve interviewees as well as some transcripts of their conversations. There is also a final appendix which, by reference to statistical information about Brittany, endeavours to reflect on the generalizability of the findings from the Béarn across French regions. Thirdly, some of Bourdieu's own photographs of the neighbourhood of his home village are interspersed within the text. They are not explicitly assigned a function in the communicative process but they are indicative of Bourdieu's attempt to recognize the utility of visual evidence in both creating and transmitting a message.

Travail et travailleurs en algérie, *1963*

Many of the features of 'Célibat et condition paysanne' are found in *Travail et travailleurs en algérie*. Before considering these in more detail, it needs to be said that a second edition of *Sociologie de l'algérie*, 'entirely revised and corrected', was published in 1961 and that an English translation was published as *The Algerians* (Bourdieu, 1962d) in the United States in the year, 1962, in which, in July, Algerian independence was formally agreed. The second French edition was still constrained by the length prescription of the series, but the English edition allowed for elaboration. At the same time, it shows signs of what Bourdieu was later to call the 'censure' operated by two main influences – Claude Lévi-Strauss and Raymond Aron. The English text added nineteen maps and graphs. Bourdieu's mode of presentation is reminiscent of Lévi-Strauss's general practice of codifying kinship relations in the same way as logical statements. At the time when Bourdieu was revising his *Sociologie de l'algérie*, Lévi-Strauss's structural anthropology was in the ascendant. This is not to say that Bourdieu was accepting the universalist implications of Lévi-Strauss's structuralism, but it suggests that, on returning to Paris from Algeria in 1960, Bourdieu was partly disposed to regard his work as a contribution to the discourse of anthropology in general and to Lévi-Strauss's descriptive style in particular.

The censure exercised by Aron must have been more inescapable. It was Aron who had given Bourdieu a job back in France. In his theoretical work of the late 1950s Aron had made it clear that he was hostile to the influence both of Marx and of Durkheim, and his contributions to political debate about the future of Algeria showed that he had little sympathy for social movements through which indigenous peoples might give voice to their feelings and their desires for self-determination. Bourdieu's *The Algerians* was published with a preface written by Aron. This ends with restrained optimism for the future. However, this is not based on any hope for future cultural assimilation or accommodation, but rather for a rational acceptance of negotiated political separation. Aron's summary is redolent both of his developing theory of war and peace, which insisted that conflicts never deliver 'winners', and also of his confident assumption that the ended armed struggle had beneficially introduced the indigenous peoples to 'modern civilization'.

Bourdieu would certainly have rejected the condescending tone of Aron's preface, but it was only in the delayed publication of his Algerian fieldwork that he was able to escape methodological and ideological censures to retrieve the original meanings of his earlier interventions.[20] *Travail et travailleurs en algérie* is presented in two parts. The first of these offers statistical data compiled by three INSEE colleagues. Chapters in a first section provide information about 'the Algerians': the family; the internal migrations of the population; workers in metropolitan France; the distribution of the population according to various categories; employment and unemployment, both individually and in families; working time in non-agricultural and agricultural occupations; individual and family incomes; the proportion of family income earned by the head of family; the qualifications of the population according to age and gender; and, finally, the evolution of the family. A second section provides 'matching' figures about 'the Europeans'. Part I is introduced by a chapter, signed by Bourdieu, entitled 'Statistiques et sociologie' [statistics and sociology] and concludes with a 'methodological note' which itemizes the plan of the survey, reproduces the questionnaires, details the budget and explains the mathematical calculations employed, all on the express understanding that the 'study constitutes a contribution to the practice of surveys in Algeria' (Bourdieu, Darbel, Rivet and Seibel, 1963, 229). In his introduction, Bourdieu articulates some of the same problems encountered in undertaking the 'Célibat et condition paysanne' project, although the argument is advanced rather more as a contribution towards a defence of empirical practice than as a philosophical disquisition relating to the possibility of inter-personal knowledge. Bourdieu insists that research practice involves a dialectical relationship between statistical categorization and ethnographic observation – predicated on a recognition of the phenomenological equality of both modes of perceiving reality. He concludes with a sub-section which emphasizes that the enquiries were conducted by teams of researchers who were mainly Algerian ('en majorité algériens' (Bourdieu, Darbel, Rivet and Seibel, 1963, 13), thereby indicating both his recognition that this was practically necessary and his intention that the process of enquiry should encourage the kind of self-determination which he thought to be necessary for Algeria to achieve an independence which would not be conditioned by prior dependence.[21]

Bourdieu perceived that the terminology of 'independence' concealed the difficulties inherent in securing self-identity or autonomy. He perceived this for the Algerians, arguing for the need for a 'revolution within the revolution' to ensure a self-determination uncontaminated by the imposed values of the defeated colonizers, but he was also profoundly aware of the difficulty of his attempting to secure an equally uncontaminated social scientific independence. Part II of *Travail et travailleurs en algérie* is entitled 'Étude sociologique' [sociological study] and is entirely written by Bourdieu. This Part consists of a foreword,[22] followed by interpretative chapters, and then by detailed appendices. The foreword considers the status of the colonial ethnographer by reference to an article by Michel Leiris which appeared in *Les temps modernes* in 1950. Leiris suggested that 'colonial' ethnographers undertaking research within colonies are unavoidably tarnished with responsibility for the social situations which they analyse. Bourdieu thought that this was redolent of a 'desperate effort to salvage responsibility in a necessary situation with the aim of extricating freedom from the hold of the system and hence of restoring good conscience in its integrity by supposing that there is a place for free will in such a universe' (Bourdieu, Darbel, Rivet and Seibel, 1963, 258–9). By contrast, Bourdieu adopted a different stance. For him, the choice was 'between the language of necessity or fate and the language of liberty and responsibility' (Bourdieu, Darbel, Rivet and Seibel, 1963, 258), and he chose the former. There is no refuge in a free zone. On the contrary, ethnographers and the societies they study are both trapped within social conditions not of their own making. The function of the scientist is rigorously to explore the character of both preconditioned situations. This rejection of detachment causes Bourdieu to articulate a rationale for the activity of the ethnographer which entails the enablement of indigenous self-expression and self-determination:

> he strives to restore to other men the meaning of their behaviour which the colonial system, among other things, has removed from them. Refusing to find a refuge and recourse against his own anxieties in the dramas and anguish of others, he can admit at the same time that his witness is of no use for anything or to anyone and feel bound by the imperative duty to proclaim what men have said to him because they had it to say to him and not in order that he should say it. (Bourdieu, Darbel, Rivet and Seibel, 1963, 259)

In other words, Bourdieu was determined that his 'science' should not be narcissistic. It should possess a functional objectivity which entailed recognizing that it does not possess validity independent of the social conditions within which it is produced and disseminated.[23] Nevertheless, the bulk of Part II, sub-titled a 'sociological study', consists of Bourdieu's unreflexive thoughts on the relationship between facts and interpretation as evidenced in the encounter between statistical findings and ethnographic enquiry. The first chapter, 'Nécessité économique et modèles culturels' (economic necessity and cultural models), starts from an anomaly which is similar to that which was the starting point for 'Célibat et condition paysanne'. Bourdieu discusses the disparity between levels of unemployment experienced by people (high) and suggested statistically (relatively low), and concludes that it arises in part from different definitions of work. Although people could be said to be 'wrong' about their employment situation, Bourdieu chooses to explore the consequences of their misperception, to explore their consciousnesses as phenomena in themselves[24] without reference to exogenous explanation. In doing this, Bourdieu explores the potential for revolutionary change in the attitudes of the Algerians. He questions the validity of Franz Fanon's suggestion that the colonial proletariat is too implicated in the economic system of the privileged to become active revolutionaries. Instead, Bourdieu takes the view that it is only when the indigenous population internalizes the rational assumptions of the dominant system that it acquires the capacity to make forward projections and plan future revolution. The challenge is to effect that process of adaptation so that self-determination has a real chance.

It follows that Bourdieu devoted the second chapter to a consideration of the process of change from 'traditionalism' to 'rationalization of behaviour'. Although Bourdieu was attracted by the integrity of traditional society, he was fully aware that *realpolitik* dictated that it could not survive unmodified. His commitment was to enabling modifications to occur through a process of cultural encounter which honoured the wishes of those in transition. Bourdieu's discussion is initially framed by theoretical consideration of the relationship of capitalism to both culture and the economy. He begins by presenting Weber's view that capitalist organization constitutes 'an immense cosmos which pre-exists individuals' (Bourdieu, Darbel, Rivet and Seibel, 1963, 313), but he argues that the colonial situation is different and he prefers Sombart's view that 'capitalist organizations ... were, for the most part, created by men who were not capitalists at all' (Bourdieu, Darbel, Rivet and Seibel, 1963, 313).[25] Indigenous Algerians, therefore, were in a situation analogous with that described by Sombart and were in a forced encounter with colonizers for whom the Weberian view was apt. For Bourdieu, the process of self-determination involved a restitution of the pre-capitalist capacity to construct an adapted economic system and resistance to the assumed universality of the socio-economic system incorporated in the practices of the colonizers. The process of adaptation in Algeria highlights what the Western tradition has forgotten, namely 'that the functioning of every economic system is linked to a system of determinate attitudes with regard to the world and, more precisely, with regard to time' (Bourdieu, Darbel, Rivet and Seibel, 1963, 315). Bourdieu's observation of the Algerian process is, at the same time, an expression of his inclination to challenge the validity of the 'immense cosmos' determining Western behaviour. Bourdieu presents a section on 'the spirit of calculation' which ' precedes calculation' in which he argues, supported by charts and statistical data, that, for the Algerians, 'everything seems to happen as if material conditions of existence exercised their influence over attitudes, particularly over the attitude towards time, that is to say toward the economic attitude, mediated through the perception that the subjects have of it' (Bourdieu, Darbel, Rivet and Seibel, 1963, 346). Importantly, Bourdieu argues that the correlation between material condition and future life-chances is not direct but is mediated by the consciousness of the people concerned. This leads naturally to a discussion of the utility of imposed, Marxist categorizations of the social condition of people. There is a continuum of life-chances. The poorest are 'condemned to project impossible possibilities' (Bourdieu, Darbel, Rivet and Seibel, 1963, 346–7), whereas those with higher incomes have the capacity to project real possibilities. This operates inter-generationally: a higher proportion of the children of lower-income fathers remain in the same kind of employment as do the children of higher-income fathers.[26] Bourdieu describes conditions of existence through the continuum, outlining the full implications for mobility of precarious and secure employment. He suggests that varieties of future expectation correlate with varieties of family size.[27] He outlines the position-dependent differences between 'the pressure of necessity' and the 'contagion of needs', highlighting housing and furnishings.[28]

Bourdieu concludes with a brief 'sketch for a table of the social classes', settling on a distinction between four categories – sub-proletarians, proletarians, small bourgeoisie and modern bourgeoisie. He claims that his adoption of this categorization is re-aligned in relation to the concepts normally used and actually used in the statistical data (socio-professional categories based on kind of employment) 'which would suggest superficial analogies'. His categorization is designed so that it should 'appear clearly that each of the social classes derives its specificity from its encounter with a particular situation and from its insertion in an original historico-cultural totality' (Bourdieu, Darbel, Rivet and Seibel, 1963, 384). Again, Bourdieu's intention is that the classification adopted in the work should emerge from the observed phenomena rather than through the 'superficial' imposition of the a priori models embedded within colonial data-gathering. Bourdieu's brief commentary here is a caution-ary introduction to the statistical appendices which follow, beginning with an account of 'the sample and its representativeness', including, as Appendix III, a 'statistical verification' of the social stratification which repeats the insistence that the categories used were 'constructed *a posteriori*' (Bourdieu, Darbel, Rivet and Seibel, 1963, 438), and ending (Appendix XI) with a reproduction of the survey questionnaire.

Bourdieu demonstrates his commitment to giving voice to the Algerians by offering a series of appendices (IV to IX), amounting to seventy pages, which contain transcripts of narratives. These are all attributed ('Worker. Oran' or 'Taxi-driver, Algiers') and they are assembled in different appendices in accordance with themes which are editorially superimposed ('Bakchich and exploitation', Appendix V, or 'work at all costs', Appendix VI). As such, the narratives are framed to constitute supporting evidence for the conceptual interpretation which Bourdieu had articulated in the main body of Part II of the book. Appendix IX is the main exception. It reproduces, in twelve pages, the narrative, autobiographical and reflective, of a cook working in Algiers, originally from Michelet, born in 1915. Some interpretative sub-titles are added but, these apart, the appendix is the uncontrolled account of a person whom Bourdieu calls 'a spontaneous sociologist'. An Algerian speaks. Taken alongside the occasional photographs, mainly taken by Bourdieu, which are interspersed throughout the text, the narrative of the spontaneous sociologist contributes to the totality of *Travail et travailleurs en Algérie* which offers a counterpoint of multi-formal components suggesting a social reality of multiple complexity.

Summary

In as much as *Travail et travailleurs en Algérie* can be taken as the summit of Bourdieu's production following his researches in Algeria and published early after his return to mainland France, a few comments need to be made in anticipation of the discussion in the next chapter of Bourdieu's work within the CSE. It is clear, first, that Bourdieu refused to compartmentalize the social reality which he observed. His observations and interpretations were distin-guished by their appreciation of complex interrelationships between phenom-ena. Some of the articles which he published in France artificially deconstructed the totality which he recognized. Articles on time, honour and shame seemed to consign his interpretations to a field of anthropological theoretical problematic, obscuring Bourdieu's crucial understanding of how these were seminal elements in the process of socio-economic transition from traditional to modern organization. There was a similar danger that the reproduction of his 'political' articles might conceal his conviction that the political dimension of change in Algeria was inseparable from cultural change.

It is also clear, secondly, that Bourdieu's sensitivity to the epistemological problems associated with undertaking anthropological research as a colonizer within a colonial situation took a particular form. It was not just that he was conscious that he might be complicit in importing modern, Western concepts to understand a traditional social organization which possessed its own logic and integrity. More acutely, he was aware, as he often said, of an affinity between the traditionalisms of the Algerian tribes and of his own native Béarn. Again, this was not just a perceived affinity between the objective realities of two spatially separated societies. Importantly, Bourdieu knew that he was a product of Béarn society and that, therefore, the trajectory which had led him to the intellectual stance which he was adopting towards Algerians was itself a case-study for the kind of acculturation or adaptation which he had observed. Bourdieu's work in Algeria was objectively analytical in respect of the process of acculturation but it was also implicitly subjectively self-regarding as an instance of the same process. This converging dual concern persisted in Bourdieu's work in France.

Notes

1 In Kabylia between 1957 and 1960. For a detailed timetable of Bourdieu's research activities in Algeria derived from his various publications, see chapter 2 of Robbins, 1991, and footnotes 1–3 in Robbins, 1991, 202.
2 See Lescourret, 2008, 145. Passeron refers to this contract in his obituary of Bourdieu – Passeron, 2003, 81.
3 'Veritates esse vel facti vel rationis' (Leibniz, ed. Schrecker, 2001 [1959], 38).
4 To pursue this debate, see Adams, 1994; Hartz, 2007; Lodge, 2003; and Plaisted, 2002.
5 Yvette Delsaut cross-examined Bourdieu about this in the late interview (November, 2001) included in the *Bibliographie des travaux* (Delsaut and Rivière, eds, 2002, 191). Bourdieu was not very forthcoming about what had happened. All we know from this is his recollection of the proposed title: 'Les structures temporelles de la vie affective' [the temporal structures of affective life] and the fact that Canguilhem was the proposed supervisor. The archives of Canguilhem at the École Normale Supérieure has a record of the theses supervised by Canguilhem in the period which gives the following title for Bourdieu's proposed thesis: 'L'émotion comme structure temporelle: essai d'interprétation des données physiologiques' [emotion as temporal structure: an interpretative essay on physiological data] (I am grateful to Nathalie Queyroux for this information). Canguilhem was trained medically as well as philosophically and was forcibly influenced by Kurt Goldstein's *The Structure of the Organism*. The recollected title and the official title suggest that Bourdieu might have

been wanting to carry out research which would explore physiological phenomena philosophically, perhaps using the non-rational orientation of Bergson's *Les données immédiates de la conscience* as well as the work on Time of Husserl and Heidegger to provide an alternative interpretation of emotions to that offered by Sartre in his *Esquisse d'une théorie des émotions*. This proposed research would have continued the interest generated by the work of Leibniz in that it might have examined self-consciously the deployment of both empirical and philosophical procedures to analyse phenomena of behaviour – emotions – which are themselves amalgamations of feeling and reason. But this is all speculative.

6 The series was founded in 1941 by the editor of the Presses Universitaires de France. Bourdieu's *Sociologie de l'Algérie* was no. 802 in the series.

7 I quote from the English translation of Bourdieu's text. Here the introductory paragraph of the original French text was relegated to a footnote.

8 This passage was omitted from the equivalent passage in Bourdieu, 1962d, xi.

9 I have speculated elsewhere (Robbins, 2014a) about the way in which Bourdieu used Weber's analysis of Christian Puritanism and the spirit of capitalism to describe the social behaviour of the Mozabite tribe which adhered to a fundamentalist Islamist position.

10 Herskovits (1895–1963) carried out fieldwork in West and East Africa and, in 1941, published *The Myth of the Negro Past* which examined the cultural adaptations of American Africans.

11 This is the translation of Bourdieu, 1958, 5 offered as a footnote on the first page of the English translation (Bourdieu, 1962d). The French of the original text has: 'comporte une description … des structures économiques et sociales *originelles* qui n'a pas en elle-même sa fin' [which is not an end in itself], which is not quite adequately captured by 'although not the main purpose of the book'.

12 The text of Mead cited in Bourdieu's bibliography is: *Cultural Patterns and Technical Change*, 1955, a work which itself shows Mead's allegiance to the thinking advanced by Ruth Benedict in her *Patterns of Culture*, 1934.

13 For more detail, see Collot, 1987, 86.

14 Specifically to their 'A memorandum on acculturation', *American anthropologist*, 38 (1936), 52–64. Redfield went on to publish *The Primitive World and its Transformation* (1953) and *Peasant Society and Culture* (1956) based on cultural anthropology fieldwork in Mexico. Ralph Linton (1893–1953) succeeded Franz Boas as the head of the Anthropology department at Columbia in 1937, although he was not sympathetic to Boas's diffusionist approach to culture change. In 1945 he published *The Science of Man in the World Crisis* and his *The Tree of Culture* was published posthumously in 1955. For Herskovits, see footnote 10 above.

15 Bourdieu and Sayad, 1964b. Translated in Bourdieu, ed. Yacine, 2013, 117–45.

16 The edition assembled by Tassadit Yacine has now made this readily possible. I am grateful for this although I have reservations about the structure of the re-presentation of Bourdieu's Algerian work which I expressed in a review for *Sociologica* (Robbins, 2015a).

17 See Bourdieu, 2008, 3. This introduction gives graphic detail of the familiarity of the situation which Bourdieu was seeking to analyse objectively.

18 It is important to note that although Bourdieu uses the word 'anomie' to describe the condition of the bachelors, he makes no explicit allusion to Durkheim's theory in his account of their malaise. It is also perhaps worth noting that Bourdieu married in 1962.

19 Frédéric Le Play (1806–82) is regarded historically as a counter-revolutionary social reformer and thinker. In his note, Bourdieu comments that it was in the mountains of the Béarn that Le Play situated a family organization which he considered to be

ideal and which was eliminated by the standardizing imposition of the Napoleonic Code.

20 The political break with Aron was not made until 1968 while the conceptual break with Lévi-Strauss was made explicit in 1972.

21 I translated 'Statistiques et sociologie' with a commentary in 1994 with Bourdieu's approval and republished it internally in the University of East London in 1999 (see Bourdieu/Robbins archive, University of East London). Subsequently, I collected just my commentary in Robbins, 2006, 119–25.

22 I co-translated this foreword and wrote a commentary. See Robbins, 2003.

23 Bourdieu was already consistently advancing a Leibnizian view in opposition to Cartesian dualism. Given that Leiris had come under the spell of Sartre at the time of writing his article, Bourdieu was also tacitly indicating his rejection of the libertarianism of Sartre's existentialism.

24 I use this phrase deliberately to suggest that Bourdieu's intention can be said to have been phenomenological.

25 This quote is from the French translation, as *Le Bourgeois*, 1926, Paris, Payot, p. 235 of *Der Bourgeois* (1913).

26 This discussion anticipates the formulation of the 1960s of the notion of 'reproduction'.

27 This anticipates Bourdieu, 1966a.

28 This not only anticipates Bourdieu, 1979a, but also Bourdieu, 2000b.

6

The 1960s

Introduction

The last chapter focused on Bourdieu's publications in the early 1960s which consolidated the research that he had undertaken in Algeria in the last few years of the previous decade. This established the pattern of activity which was to persist until 1980. Fieldwork or empirical research progressed in tandem with more generalized social and philosophical reflection. Bourdieu had not yet articulated a working philosophy of science, but he proceeded on the tacit assumption that he was offering intelligent responses to the phenomena which he observed without prior commitment to any instituted explanatory discourse. Without indicating any explicit allegiance to phenomenological method, his practice was, nevertheless, fundamentally phenomenological in that he showed little interest in defining his research problems by reference to the pre-existing analytical categories in vogue in the discourses of intellectual disciplines. When publishing his thoughts or findings in journals, he found himself constrained by the disciplinary expectations of those journals, but his conceptualizations were unrestrainedly creative and exploratory. Because he did not acknowledge the a priori validity of discipline-based problem formulations and did not accept a realist philosophy of science, it is never possible precisely to unravel the dialectic in his work between non-empirical thinking and empirical enquiry. He was committed to the view that research 'findings' are always a function of the questions originally posed and that, equally, such findings modify post hoc the nature of those questions and pose different questions for future exploration.

Maintaining this methodological position was difficult for Bourdieu during the early period when he was actively managing a series of research projects within the Centre de Sociologie Européenne, which, as the name suggests, was established for the purpose of carrying out *sociological* research. Bourdieu cultivated an ethos of 'collective research' but he directed the projects and was responsible for the co-authored publications. Alongside the empirical research and the preparation of publications communicating its findings, all undertaken collaboratively, Bourdieu also personally published several important articles in this period. (Some of these were also the result of close cooperation, particularly with Jean-Claude Passeron.) Some of these were clearly related to the issues raised in the research projects, but others were more speculative. They all suggest a constant interaction between theoretical and empirical work. I regard these texts as 'collateral' and a proportion of them will be considered in relation to the main published books of the period.

Texts

'Sociologues des mythologies et mythologies de sociologues', 1963

Behind the enquiry on students and their studies which Bourdieu directed in CSE in 1961–62 and 1962–63 would have been Aron's belief that the French educational system needed to adapt to participate in the modernization process. The first 'collateral' article which Bourdieu and Passeron published together indicates, however, that their concern was not primarily with the educational system as such, but with the function of that system at a time of confusion about claims which were being advanced that society was experiencing the emergence of a 'mass culture'.

'Sociologues des mythologies et mythologies de sociologues' [sociologists of mythologies and mythologies of sociologists] was published in December 1963 (Bourdieu and Passeron, 1963) before any presentation had yet been made of the findings emerging from the educational research project. Bourdieu and Passeron begin by characterizing the claims being made 'in the most diverse regions of the intellectual universe' that mankind is on the brink of a 'mutation' from which will emerge a new man, one determined by the visual rather than the verbal. They suggest that this is a mythology of the mass media advanced in a way which does not allow for the possibility of evidential challenge. Massmediology, Bourdieu and Passeron claim, 'is a metaphysic' (Bourdieu and Passeron, 1963, 1007). It is not a sociology because 'it retains a nostalgia for deducing *a priori* when it should only consult experience' (Bourdieu and Passeron, 1963, 1007). Given that there exists a system of compulsory schooling, Bourdieu and Passeron argue that the School, which is often seen as in opposition to the mass media, should pride itself on its true 'mass action' since alone it can 'repeat its message insistently and additionally can coerce and train' (Bourdieu and Passeron, 1963, 1005). It is clear that this article provides the impetus for the enquiry on student culture. The main issue is whether educational institutions encourage the development of the real culture of the masses or whether they communicate a consecrated culture which is as much an imposition as is the myth generated by the massmediologists. A sub-textual interest is in the process by which a new 'spirit of the times' is generated and disseminated.[1] Bourdieu would certainly have been encouraged to consider the role of language in this process and he would also have seen, first, that art galleries have power comparable to that of schools in prescribing exclusive values and, secondly, that a new technological cultural form, photography, had the potential to stimulate a genuinely mass action but was in danger of mimicking the aesthetic and social discriminations of established cultural institutions. In the first half of the 1960s, Bourdieu and Passeron seemed to be optimistic that their analyses would encourage schools or universities and art galleries to become responsive to the cultures immanent within the whole population in such a way as to counteract the adverse effects of contrived theories of the mass media. This optimism waned as the decade advanced.

Les étudiants et leurs études *and* Les héritiers, *1964*

These two texts were both published in 1964 and each refers to the other. The first was the first published 'Cahier' [report] of the CSE. The chapters of the paper give all the findings of the 1961–62 and 1962–63 researches in tabular form with commentary, while two appendices give statistical information about the samples and reproduce the questionnaires which had been used. The presentational practice of the paper is similar, therefore, to that adopted in *Travail et travailleurs en algérie* – data and interpretation are juxtaposed and information is offered to enable the reader to reach a judgement about the validity of both – but there were no interviews and no transcripts of student self-understandings. The project had concentrated solely on students following courses in philosophy and sociology. This reflected practical convenience but it suggests the clandestine presence of a self-regarding orientation similar to that, for Bourdieu, of 'Célibat et condition paysanne'. The project endeavoured to provide scientific analysis of the factors conditioning student choice between the two subjects of study and it was undertaken by two main researchers, both of whom could be said to be refashioning themselves as sociologists rather than the philosophers they were by training. There was an ongoing dialectic between the subjective dispositions of the researchers and the objective outcomes of their enquiry. The main intention of the project was to determine whether the French higher education system was fit for purpose in enabling students from culturally deprived regions to take advantage of new opportunities in a modernizing society. Bourdieu and Passeron recognized that it was already known statistically that 'the scholastic system continually eliminates a high proportion of children originating from the most disadvantaged classes' (Bourdieu and Passeron, 1964a, 13), but they contended that their findings showed there was an even more fundamental deficiency in the system, in that even those disadvantaged students who did gain entry failed as a consequence of the inappropriateness of the practices of the institutions. The capacity to benefit from higher education opportunity was not realized by simple admission but also required internally that pedagogic practice should acknowledge that it is a process of acculturation. Bourdieu and Passeron argued that evaluation of the social function of the higher education system could not be satisfied with generating a simple and static correlation of social background with success rates, but should aim to factor in an understanding of the more subtle dynamics of teaching and learning in a changing society (Bourdieu and Passeron, 1964a, 10).

The research was not designed to establish that cultural differences were the consequences of different social origins, reflecting a prior social reality. Instead, it was designed to show that social and cultural differences are inseparable and that, through time, the social which is synonymous with natural or indigenous culture is modified by degrees of initiation into artificial, acquired culture. *Les étudiants et leurs études* [students and their studies] posits a continuous dialectic between two types of culture. In highlighting educational processes as instruments of cultural differentiation, Bourdieu and Passeron were already indicating that the social situation is not intrinsically social if by that were meant socio-economically class determined, but instead a context of constant accultural affectivity, constant oscillation between natural and acquired cultures, within generations and inter-generationally, whereby one person's natural culture encounters another's acquired culture and vice versa. The important achievement of *Les étudiants et leurs études* was that it showed that social exclusion (to use this term anachronistically) is a continuous process. There is no one Culture with a capital C to be acquired by the socially deprived which will remedy their supposed deficiencies. Cultural capital does not possess absolute value which is quantifiable. It only possesses value in exchange and the exchange is a social struggle as much as a struggle of cultural value judgement.

Les Héritiers [The Inheritors] (Bourdieu and Passeron, 1964b) had a different function from that of the working paper. It has a short foreword which gives precise details of the surveys on which the book's argument is based and it offers a caution about generalizing beyond the particular facts cited. There are two appendices[2] which attempt to enable readers to consider the general validity of the findings derived from the particular enquiry described in the text. The first gives statistical information about students in France between 1900 and 1963, and the second provides 'some documents and survey results', some of which relate to findings from contemporary surveys of education in Poland and Hungary. In the main text, some of the tables of the working paper are reproduced, but the argument of the book is framed within three chapters which offer an interpretative framework. In the subsequent English translation these were called 'Selecting the Elect', 'Games Students Play' and 'Sorcerers' Apprentices'. The first of these was headed by a quotation from Margaret Mead's *Continuities in Cultural Evolution*, the second with a quotation from Durkheim, and the third with a quotation from Hegel. These are not merely decorative extracts. They fulfil a significant function in the total presentation. The quote from Mead, for instance, gives her interpretation of the function of 'vision behaviour' among North American Indians. The substantive interpretation contained in the passage from Mead has a symbolic[3] status and, additionally, the references alone to Mead, Durkheim and Hegel have the effect of inserting connotations and allusions which elevate the status of arguments derived from a circumscribed survey of student attitudes.[4]

The fact that this allusive discourse co-exists with the representation of the empirical findings of the research should not minimize the power of the arguments made in the book which are based on evidence. The text attempts precisely to articulate the meaning of statistical information. Five tables are embedded in the narrative account. The first, for instance, details 'educational opportunity and social origin, 1961–62'. It correlates the 'objective chances (probability of access)' of potential students and the 'conditional probabilities' of their entering Schools of Law, Science, Arts, Medicine and Pharmacy with the occupational categories of their parents. Inherent in this tabular presentation are several key arguments which relate back to Bourdieu's Algerian research. There is the assumption that statistical information measures objective career chances but there is also the counter-balancing assumption that it proscribes actual aspiration or expectation. There is, in other words, an awareness of a constant dialectical relationship between objective facts and experienced possibilities which is in place affecting the choice of possible futures made by potential students from different kinds of background imposed by the careers of their parents. The 'choice' of subjects of study is a refined aspect of the general nature of the process of 'selecting the elect' which suggests that 'subjects' possess actual or ascribed characteristics which condition choices. The tension which Bourdieu experienced methodologically in correlating statistical data with his interpretations of the qualitative responses to questionnaires – the correlation which he had explored in 'Statistics and Sociology' in *Travail et travailleurs en algérie* – became more acute the more clearly he sensed an affinity between his own situation and that of the students he was seeking to analyse. Experientially, the students under scrutiny were those who, like himself and Passeron, were choosing between the subjects of sociology and philosophy. Bourdieu's analysis of the phenomenal dialectic between the conditions motivating their agency and the structured alternatives presented to them was, for him, itself a comparable dialectic as he sought to reconcile quantitative and qualitative data or to reconcile abstracted mathematical formulae with personal perceptions. Given that he was asking whether students could be said to be determined by statistical probabilities of which they were unaware in making their life choices or in what ways those probabilities were socially internalized, it was inevitable that he should wonder how far his objectification of their choices itself constituted a model which might appropriate statistical information and offer a surrogate determinism. In short, latent in Bourdieu's methodology was an anxiety whether sociological explanation unjustifiably imposed its models on the life experiences of those it examined.

'Selecting the Elect' first offers an interpretation of official statistics, but tables which follow calibrate responses to the questionnaires which had been issued for the project. The exegesis of the specific responses is designed to construct a logic which leads to the general conclusions that 'everything that defines the relation of a group of students to their studies, expresses the fundamental relation of a social class to the whole social structure, to social success, and to culture' (Bourdieu and Passeron, 1979, 21) and that 'All teaching, and more especially the teaching of culture (even scientific culture), implicitly presupposes a body of knowledge, skills, and, above all, modes of expression which constitute the heritage of the cultivated classes' (Bourdieu and Passeron, 1979, 21). The first conclusion indicates that Bourdieu and Passeron were trying to reconstruct the ways in which student experience is *totally* conditioned in ways which are not captured by empirical enquiry which isolates particulars and 'fragments the object of analysis' (Bourdieu and Passeron, 1979, 153).[5] The second conclusion is expressed more succinctly in the original French. All teaching, they argue, presupposes bodies of 'savoirs', 'savoir-faire' and, above all, 'savoir-dire' (Bourdieu and Passeron, 1964b, 38). What was to be designated as 'cultural capital' emphasized practical and linguistic competences as much as prior cultural knowledge.

The second chapter of *Les héritiers* explores the 'games students play'. The argument is that 'Student and teacher, products of the system, express the logic of the system' (Bourdieu and Passeron, 1979, 42). The perception of the situation is similar to Bourdieu's representation of the 'internal logic' of traditional Algerian society. In both cases, individuals become unwittingly complicit in reinforcing arrangements by which they are constrained. In both cases, the socially dominant have the power to ensure that the system which sustains their power reproduces itself. In the case of Algeria, the internal logic of traditional society was destroyed as a result of the intervention of the dominant representatives of an alternative system. Tacitly, Bourdieu and Passeron suggest that a war of independence is necessary within French higher education to deconstruct the authority of professors so as to allow curriculum content to be negotiated between all participants in the system.

The concluding chapter does not directly argue for systemic change. Rather, it suggests that the logic of the existing system is sustained by a belief in the 'unequal giftedness' of people[6] and the assumption that the national competitive exam, the *concours*, provides a neutral mechanism for measuring degrees of giftedness. Although this 'contradicts real justice' (Bourdieu and Passeron, 1979, 69), which would be better served by an evaluation which might make allowance for 'social handicaps', nevertheless the educational system is constrained by society's requirement that it should supply qualified employees to its occupational system. They argue that a recognition of socially constructed differences of capacity could be accommodated equitably within the existing system if a 'rational pedagogy' (Bourdieu and Passeron, 1979, 76) were to be adopted which would ensure that communication in teaching and learning situations was systematically sensitive to cultural differences.

Un art moyen, essai sur les usages sociaux de la photographie, *1965*

One way to summarize the methodological problems which Bourdieu experienced in writing up the findings of his Algerian and educational researches is to say that he was always acutely aware of the reciprocal relationship between the logic of scientific discovery and the rhetoric of intellectual communication. There was a desire to clarify the scientific status of his findings as such by meticulously representing the procedures by which they were achieved and by articulating their limitations, while, at the same time, this representation was itself part of a rhetorical strategy to generalize more effectively, both philosophically and politically. There was a constant attention to the relationship between particular findings and general conclusions. Another way to summarize these same difficulties is to say that Bourdieu was sensitive to the tension between ordinary or everyday observation and the formulation of conclusions in accordance with recognized professional rules. Consideration of *Un art moyen* illustrates these difficulties, understood in both ways.

Un art moyen was published in March 1965. This French edition provides a chronology of the research projects on which it was based. It details twenty-one projects undertaken over three years by nearly twenty named researchers.[7] Even more than was the case with the educational research, the task of managing these projects and of producing findings was a challenge for Bourdieu both in respect of maintaining a common investigative purpose and, finally, of communicating a coherent meaning.

In his introduction, Bourdieu insists that in every society throughout history there has existed a 'hierarchy of legitimate objects of study' which has involved the exclusion, 'under the guise of objectivity' (Bourdieu, Boltanski, Castel, Chamboredon and Schnapper, 1990, 1), of some modes of experience. Bourdieu's research on photographic practice was, therefore, an attempt to demonstrate that sociological research need not endorse social exclusiveness by its choice of object. It was an attempt to advance the study of hitherto unconsecrated objects, the kinds of cultural form embraced by students as revealed in the questionnaires of the educational project but not recognized in university curricula. It constituted an attempt to retrieve everyday practice but, importantly, this did not involve forfeiting an understanding of the objective framework within which subjective actions occur.

As a new social phenomenon, photographic practice appeared to be uncontaminated by the legacy of consecrated rules of art. Technology had appeared to provide an instrument for the production of naive experience. As Bourdieu puts it: 'Nothing is more directly opposed to the ordinary image of artistic creation than the activity of the amateur photographer'. As such, therefore, it was amenable to analysis without the traditional accretions of aesthetic judgement associated with other forms of creative activity, and yet, he continues, 'even when the production of the picture is entirely delivered over to the automatism of the camera, the taking of the picture is still a choice involving aesthetic and ethical values' (Bourdieu, Boltanski, Castel, Chamboredon and Schnapper, 1990, 5–6).

Part I of *Un art moyen* is dominated by Bourdieu's personal concerns and his attempt to integrate analysis of photographic practice with his consideration of the transition from rural to urban society and from traditional to modern culture which he had explored, within the discourse of social anthropology, in respect of Algeria and the Béarn. Chapter 1 – 'The Cult of Unity and Cultivated Differences' – offers an interpretation of the findings of his two photographic enquiries. In Chapter 2 – 'The Social Definition of Photography' – Bourdieu again draws heavily on his fieldwork in Algeria/Béarn to rehearse the critique of Kantian aesthetics which he was to articulate further in *La Distinction* [distinction] (Bourdieu, 1979a; 1986a), contending that the way 'working-class' people appreciate photographs 'refers to a system of norms whose principle is always ethical' (Bourdieu, Boltanski, Castel, Chamboredon and Schnapper, 1990, 86) rather than to 'aesthetic' criteria.

It is only in the short introduction to Part II that Bourdieu tries to fit the findings of the other teams of researchers into a meaningful whole. The 'great mass of users of photography' 'realize the social function of photography in their behaviour without perceiving it as such' (Bourdieu, Boltanski, Castel, Chamboredon and Schnapper, 1990, 101). However, there are those who 'either by choice or by professional obligation, cease to give it this immediate and unquestioned attachment' (Bourdieu, Boltanski, Castel, Chamboredon and Schnapper, 1990, 101). These are the people whose attitudes and motives are recorded in Part II of *Un art moyen*. By implication, these are the people who distort traditional, inter-personal values and introduce artificial distinctions. There are collective norms which shape the primary attitudes of ordinary people, but these are different from the socially constructed norms by which 'professionals' reinforce a separation from primary experience in the interest of acquiring social privilege. 'Professional' photographers are instruments of the disenchantment of the Durkheimian collective consciousness. Bourdieu's dismay that photographic practice and appreciation might be defaulting from the sphere of everyday, ethical experience to that of reified, instituted judgements clearly cross-refers to the project on museums/art galleries which commenced in 1964, but it also is redolent of his personal insecurity as an amateur photographer[8] and as a professionally untrained sociologist directing research within a sociological research centre.[9]

L'amour de l'art, *1966*[10]

The first edition of *L'amour de l'art* was published in 1966. The book is the report of research on the public use of public museums/art galleries in France which had been commissioned by the Ministry of Cultural Affairs. Whereas for *Un art moyen* Bourdieu had edited and synthesized contributions from other researchers, the preface to *L'amour de l'art* specifies that Bourdieu 'wrote up the text of this book' (Bourdieu, Darbel and Schnapper, 1990, vii). Bourdieu's account of the research process, given at the beginning of the second chapter, admits that budgetary constraints dictated the scope of the enquiry such that 'the methodological choices put into operation were bound to be compromises between the ideal and the actual conditions of the enquiry' (Bourdieu and Darbel, 1966, 21). There was little possibility of recording the everyday experiences of ordinary people. By default, instead, the project was forced to draw upon previous research (unspecified) and to regard the project as one which enabled a 'process of verification' with the intention 'of abstracting general properties from the observed reality' which 'are indispensable for the construction of a model' (Bourdieu and Darbel, 1966, 21). The function of the project, for Bourdieu, was that it enabled an exploration of a situation in respect of consecrated art which was similar to that of unconsecrated photographic practice. Bourdieu was interested in the responses of visitors to art displayed in art galleries in the same way as he had been interested in the responses of uninitiated students to the course offerings in higher education, namely in the institutionalization of 'values' in relation to everyday practical experience.

Perhaps as a result of the practical constraints on the enquiry mentioned by Bourdieu and also as a result of his collaboration with a statistician, the text of *L'amour de l'art* is heavily mathematical. There is a balance in the text between interest, on the one hand, in the subjective process of art appreciation or the social conditions making visiting possible and, on the other, in the objective 'rules' of cultural diffusion governing its communication. Bourdieu's underlying argument is presented in the first chapter, 'Signs of the Times', which suggests that 'fundamentalists' and 'modernists' in 'the religion of art' are actually united in supposing that the capacity to appreciate art is a predestined gift. The fundamentalists assume that the capacity to appreciate is natural or innate while the modernists, among whom would be counted the mass mediologists, emphasize the distinctively non-cognitive nature of visual communication. In opposition, Bourdieu contends that art appreciation and the disposition to visit museums are learned or acquired and are dependent primarily on conditions which can be analysed sociologically in the same way as can access to schooling and to schooling success. Indeed, the degree of accessibility of schooling correlates precisely with the degree of attraction of art galleries. Continuing the analogy with religious belief, Bourdieu suggests that protectors of cultural values fear their depreciation if it should be accepted that they are accessible to the laity.

The second chapter of *L'amour de l'art* outlines the research process and defends the 'formalization' effected by mathematical modelling. The third chapter expands on the fundamental argument that 'museum visiting increases very strongly with increasing level of education' (Bourdieu, Darbel and Schnapper, 1990, 14), while the fourth chapter elaborates on the suggestion that 'In addition to visiting and its patterns, all visitors' behaviour, and all their attitudes to works on display, are directly and almost exclusively related to education, whether measured by qualifications obtained or by length of schooling' (Bourdieu, Darbel and Schnapper, 1990, 37). Based upon the views of respondents to the surveys whether they prefer to visit alone or in groups, or to have available, or not, detailed information boards, and other such practical questions, Bourdieu argues that 'it is the classes most equipped with personal aids to visiting such as guidebooks and catalogues ... who most often reject the institutional and collective aids' (Bourdieu, Darbel and Schnapper, 1990, 53). The less well educated visitors feel unworthy or incompetent, with the result that they tend to exclude themselves rather than be excluded. There is a direct relation between the disposition of individuals to be appreciative of art works and the degree of complexity of the classificatory system adopted in displaying works. As Bourdieu illustrates, 'Someone who only knows how to divide art into Romanesque and Gothic, puts all Gothic cathedrals, undifferentiated, into the same class, whereas someone with greater competence can discern stylistic differences' (Bourdieu, Darbel and Schnapper, 1990, 41). In effect, Bourdieu is arguing that all appreciation of art works depends upon a capacity to recognize the network of meaning inherent in their mode of presentation, but, equally, he acknowledges that this network is not an idealist Gestalt but, on the contrary, one which changes socio-historically.

It is clear that Bourdieu's interpretation of the problem of museum-visiting relates closely to the argument of *Les héritiers* that what was needed was the introduction of 'rational pedagogy' into teaching practice. When, he concludes, 'the school does not bother to work methodically and systematically ... to bring everyone in the school into direct contact with works of art ... it renounces the power ...of exercising the continued and prolonged action ...which ... is alone capable of *mass-producing* competent individuals endowed with the schemes of perception ...which are the condition for the appropriation of cultural goods' (Bourdieu, Darbel and Schnapper, 1990, 67). The school remains the crucial institution for generating a mass culture as a result of engagement with the possessors of all cultures. Bourdieu recognized the difficulty of 'breaking the circle which ensures that cultural capital reproduces cultural capital' (Bourdieu, Darbel and Schnapper, 1990, 70). The danger remained that 'the school only has to let the objective mechanisms of cultural diffusion run their course and refrain from working systematically to provide everyone, in and through the educational message itself, with the instruments necessary for an adequate reception of the academic message, for initial inequalities to be intensified and for the transmission of cultural capital to be legitimated by its sanction' (Bourdieu, Darbel and Schnapper, 1990, 70).

The following chapter tries to identify what these 'objective mechanisms of cultural diffusion' might be. They are not confined to museum-visiting. It simply 'obeys a logic recognized by communication theory' (Bourdieu, Darbel and Schnapper, 1990, 71). In general terms, 'each time a unique message is proposed to a differentiated society, it is subject to a quantitatively and qualitatively varied reception' (Bourdieu, Darbel and Schnapper, 1990, 76) and its effectiveness depends on the extent to which it meets the expectations of the receivers. The mode of presentation of museums tends to perpetuate exclusivity. When choosing between possible policy decisions whether to attract new or habitual visitors, 'curators nearly always choose the one which tends to increase the aristocratic character of the museum and its public' (Bourdieu, Darbel and Schnapper, 1990, 95). There is, in other words, a structural discrimination inherent in the ways in which museums present themselves and there is, therefore, a vicious collusion between the objective exclusiveness of the institutions and the respondent self-exclusion of educationally disadvantaged visitors.

Taken together, *Un art moyen* and *L'amour de l'art* complement *Les héritiers*. What remains unclear from the collection of texts is Bourdieu's attitude towards the competing cultural forms under consideration. *Un art moyen* seemed to suggest that photography was a new art form whereby technology was offering the whole population the opportunity to express itself intersubjectively without reference to established canons of aesthetic judgement, but, equally, it exposed the extent to which new forms of instituted judgement were emerging that were already constructing a separation of artificial from natural photographic practice.

'Collateral' texts

In the first half of the 1960s Bourdieu was preoccupied in communicating the work that he had undertaken personally in Algeria and in managing research projects of the CSE and supervising the publication of their findings. We have seen that all these ventures were characterized by Bourdieu's disposition both to import interpretation of data based upon his wider reflections and to make explicit in appendices the nature of the correlation between that interpretation and information acquired empirically, either through statistical data, questionnaire responses or interview transcripts. There was a sense in which his mode of presentation indicated that there was a tension between his tasks as a research manager and his personal preoccupation with philosophical issues. He published some articles which were 'spin-offs' from the main texts just discussed. At the same time, however, he began to publish articles which were less dependent on empirical findings and were more indicative of his pursuit of an independent intellectual perspective. In short, there was a constant counter-point in Bourdieu's work between theoretical reflection and empirical analysis, and there was a continuous process of cross-fertilization between these inclinations. I refer chronologically to 'Condition de classe et position de classe' [class condition and class position] (Bourdieu, 1966a); 'Une sociologie de l'action est-elle possible?' [is a sociology of action possible] (Bourdieu and Reynaud, 1966); 'Champ intellectuel et projet créateur' [intellectual field and creative project] (Bourdieu, 1966c); 'La comparabilité des systèmes d'enseignement' [the comparability of systems of education] (Bourdieu and Passeron, 1967a); 'Sociology and Philosophy in France since 1945. Death and Resurrection of a Philosophy without Subject' (Bourdieu and Passeron, 1967b); 'Systèmes d'enseignement et systèmes de pensée' [systems of education and systems of thought] (Bourdieu, 1967); 'Éléments d'une théorie sociologique de la perception artistique' [elements of a sociological theory of art perception] (Bourdieu, 1968a); and 'Structuralism and Theory of Sociological Knowledge' (Bourdieu, 1968b).

The significance of these texts has to be discussed in the context of Bourdieu's translation of Panofsky's *Gothic Architecture and Scholastic Thought*, with an afterword (Panofsky, ed. Bourdieu, 1967), the joint publication of *Le métier de sociologue* [the craft of the sociologist] (Bourdieu, Chamboredon and Passeron, 1968), and the publication, with Passeron, of *La reproduction. Éléments pour une théorie du système d'enseignement* [reproduction, elements for a theory of the system of education] (Bourdieu and Passerron, 1970). The challenge is to recognize the progression in Bourdieu's work of autonomous strands of thought which he synthesized intellectually while sustaining consciousness of their dialectical relation with empirical work and political contexts. Bourdieu's arguments were always densely formulated. I try to follow these in detail in respect of the first three articles mentioned above and point only in summary fashion to the ways in which his thinking seems to have developed in this period as expressed in the other texts. The common feature of these texts is that in all of them Bourdieu explores in different ways issues in regard to the epistemology of the social sciences. In particular, Bourdieu becomes involved in discussion of the nature of 'structuralist' explanation.

'Condition de classe et position de classe', 1966

Bourdieu's argument in 'Condition de classe et position de classe' continues reflection generated by his work in Algeria and is stimulated by literature specifically related to anthropological knowledge, but he broadens the debate to reflect on questions raised in the range of his empirical work, focusing a great deal on the nature of language. Bourdieu poses the basic question in his opening sentence when he asks what might sociologists *mean* by 'structure' when they talk about 'social structure'. Does 'structure' have one meaning [un sens]? The argument of 'Condition de classe et position de classe'[11] is very dense but it is important to examine it in detail because it retrospectively clarifies some of Bourdieu's views in his earlier work and anticipates future developments.

Bourdieu's first sentence indicates that he wants to assess the sociological *conceptualization* of society as a 'structure'. From the outset, he is sensitive to the tension articulated by Leibniz between truths of reason and truths of fact, and he tries to expound the relations between these orientations. He 'provisionally' offers a 'minimal definition' (Bourdieu, 1966a, 201) which is expressed in terms of reality, that is to say that the question is whether 'the constituent parts of a stratified society' are simply juxtaposed or have properties which are the consequence of their 'belonging to the totality or, more precisely, to their position in the complete system of relations which orders the meaning of each individual relation' (Bourdieu, 1966a, 201). To take seriously the 'notion' of social structure, Bourdieu contends that every social class is defined in relation to other social elements, and must be thought to have '*properties of position*, relatively independent of intrinsic properties such as a certain type of professional practice or material conditions of existence' (Bourdieu, 1966a, 201). Bourdieu points to a difference between conceptualizing society in terms of 'positions' rather than 'conditions' of class, but these remain meanings which are in the mind. In Bourdieu's terminology, we designate as 'conditions' those elements of structures which reflect physical realities, whereas by 'positions' we refer to parts of total structures which are relational, mutually generated without direct correspondence with reality. In spite of the apparent opposition between 'condition' and 'position' implied in the title of the article, Bourdieu tacitly uses a third term – 'situation' – to suggest natural facts. To clarify his meaning, Bourdieu illustrates by reference to the 'peasant condition'. We can, like Weber (according to Bourdieu), isolate in the peasant condition those things which relate to the 'situation and practice of working the soil' with which aspects of peasant religiosity are correlative, or we can identify the peasant condition as a position which is variable within different societies at different historical moments, although even here there is an identifiable principle of variability which revolves around the country/town dualism. The first approach implies an understanding of absolute, universal characteristics while the second recognizes the significance of relative adaptations within observed societies. Bourdieu comments that positional and conditional properties can only be dissociated 'by an operation of the mind', thus retaining a separation between reason and fact, and he also adds that class positions are not defined exclusively within the social structure but also within the system of relations of production. Tacitly, therefore, he accepts that class situations have a *real* economic dimension which defines the extent to which positional adaptability is possible, what he calls the '*margin of variation*' (Bourdieu, 1966a, 202). Reasserting his insistence that he is expounding interpretative distinctions, Bourdieu concludes his introductory outline of the problem by remarking that their value can only be gauged by 'testing their heuristic fecundity', admitting to a fundamental pragmatism.

Bourdieu proceeds to examine some of the implications of the condition/ position/situation schema which he has introduced. He restates the positional emphasis by citing an article of Max Wertheimer on Gestalt theory which Gurwitsch had used approvingly in *Théorie du champ de la conscience*.[12] In other words, Bourdieu's account of the interpretative framework which he describes is based on an absorption of the view that, as a framework, it is gestaltist or noematic even though, within, it posits constitutive positionality. The relativist, or positional, mode of understanding enables recognition that the 'same' class can be different between different societies and over time. It enables a refined comparative analysis which is denied by theories of universal condition. According to Bourdieu, both Marx and Weber were wrong in supposing that 'the question of the conditions of comparability of "parts" of different structures and of the validity of general laws in sociology' had been resolved (Bourdieu, 1966a, 202). Equally, however, there is a danger that the concentration on positionality might obliterate recognition of common characteristics and become simply the accumulation of narratives of difference, what Bourdieu calls 'idiography'. No 'trans-cultural and trans-historical general propositions' (Bourdieu, 1966a, 204) can be established by juxtaposing isolated case-studies. So saying, Bourdieu makes it clear that he is in sympathy with the sociological inclination to find such general propositions, and he proposes that these can only be ascertained comparatively by analysing structures themselves rather than either conditions or positions. Pursuing structural analysis in this sense discloses that there is a continuum of comparability such that some groups who possess relatively autonomous positionality in their societies manifest '*homologous positions*' across societies whereas others whose positionality is relatively limited by their dependence on their situations can be treated as identical. In short, the possibility of the perception of universal characteristics is a function of the situational dependency of some groups and, by the same token, the impossibility of perceiving anything more than homologous positions is a function of the situational independence of other groups such that they possess the relative freedom to construct themselves. Bourdieu seeks a comparison between social structures which is based upon analysis of how these structures are constituted rather than on the extrapolation of constituent elements.

Bourdieu proceeds to elaborate some of the benefits of the analysis of structures which he proposes. It focuses on the systematic analysis of case-studies and he suggests that it enables recognition that conditions/positions are dynamic within and between structures. It therefore enables the disclosure of *trajectories* which have trans-historical and trans-cultural characteristics, such as, for instance, the trajectory of the petite bourgeoisie which is a class that is in transition between what it once was and what it is not yet, to which, in Bourdieu's perhaps self-referential view, can be attributed its 'inclination to objectivism' (Bourdieu, 1966a, 207). He suggests other positional homologies which can be explained by the relative degrees of positionality or conditionality of social groups such as, retrospectively with respect to the research reported in *Les héritiers*, the differences of expectation from the schooling system of students originating in different class groups in society.

Bourdieu is not content to base his analysis on the differential positionality of groups without also taking into account what he calls their differential 'functional weight' (Bourdieu, 1966a, 210), by which he means the relative weight or power of elements which are in logical relation. Bourdieu's theory remains abstract and impersonal. It is analogous with mathematically based physics rather than with pure mathematical logic. Nevertheless, in the second half of the article, Bourdieu moves to a consideration of the behaviour of individuals more than groups. It is important to note that this analysis of 'personal' motivation is still the analysis of persons within abstract systems. It is as if he anthropomorphizes a system without recognizing the possibility of free choice for individual elements. It is at this point that the cultural dimension mitigates the austerity of the physical model. A number of the properties of a social class, Bourdieu suggests, can be attributed to the fact that 'the individuals who make it up enter deliberately or objectively into symbolic relations which ... tend to transmute them into *signifying distinctions [distinctions signifiantes]*' (Bourdieu, 1966a, 212). This transmutation occurs in accordance with its own logical necessity and Bourdieu seems to accept that understanding social structure involves recognizing a balance between constituent economic and symbolic systems. Bourdieu differentiates his position from that of Weber. He argues that Weber opposed classes and status groups as '*real* units' whereas Weberian analysis needs to be reinforced by recognizing them, instead, as '*nominal* units' such that the understanding of any society entails an interpretative choice whether to '*accentuate the economic or symbolic aspects*' (Bourdieu, 1966a, 212–13). Bourdieu does not pursue this crucial point (which, tacitly, recognizes interpretative choice as itself an act within the symbolic order) but, instead, embellishes Weber's representation of the relations between 'properly economic differences' and 'symbolic distinctions'. Anticipating the work of the 1970s leading to the publication of *Distinction*, Bourdieu discusses, for instance, clothing and language as examples of how signifying distinctions are constructed to render economic difference insignificant. He is conscious that relatively different situations give rise to different interpretations of the balance between economics and culture and, equally, that 'nominal' interpretations are components of these differently real situations.

In summary, what we see in 'Condition de classe et position de classe' is Bourdieu's *theoretical* attempt to accommodate real human agency within a system of relations which he is disposed to understand in a nominal, abstract or logical, way. Furthermore, he is aware that the notion of agency inherent in the abstract system extends to his own conceptual production of that system. He tries to reconcile individual noetic activity with structural noematic pre-determination. To overcome this dilemma, he needed to find a framework which would enable him to explain the mediating process between the real and the rational in a way which would be satisfactory in both realms. This can be said to be the essence of Bourdieu's endeavour in the second half of the 1960s.

'Une sociologie de l'action est-elle possible?', 1966

A review of Alain Touraine's *Sociologie de l'action* (Touraine, 1965) enabled Bourdieu specifically to articulate his view of social agency. He examines Touraine's 'basic postulates and propositions' (Bourdieu and Reynaud, 1966, 508) in such a way as to endeavour to clarify his own. Bourdieu summarizes Touraine's position by stating that Touraine espouses neither 'functionalism' nor structuralism but, instead, advances an 'actionalist' position, by which he means that he seeks to understand the *creation* of values through social action. So far so good for Bourdieu in that Touraine rejects 'naturalism', which tries to explain social action by natural forces, either psychological or historical, and also rejects 'idealism', which locates values in a non-temporal sphere. Bourdieu's agreement, however, is immediately followed by a reservation: 'To look for meaning in things or to pose it *a priori* is completely to betray sociology. It is to give up understanding the social genesis of social meanings, whilst on the contrary we must "reduce values to the movement of action itself"'[13] (Bourdieu and Reynaud, 1966, 510).

Bourdieu suggests that Touraine's solution undermines proper sociology in the same way as do naturalist and idealist orientations because it isolates individual action from the social nexus which generates it. Bourdieu offers en passant an important footnote. He points out a parallel between Touraine's rejection of both naturalism and idealism and Merleau-Ponty's critique of both empiricism and intellectualism which he takes to be the foundation of his analysis of perception in *Phénoménologie de la perception*, but he comments that Merleau-Ponty's conclusions, particularly as expressed in his 'Le métaphysique dans l'homme' [metaphysics in man] published in *Sens et non-sens* (Merleau-Ponty, 1948), are 'profoundly different' (Bourdieu and Reynaud, 1966, 510, fn. 5).[14] Bourdieu adds that Touraine does not cite Merleau-Ponty although he frequently cites Sartre. This brief remark is very revealing and underpins the way in which Bourdieu proceeds to criticize Touraine's theory. Bourdieu acknowledges that, for Touraine, the creator of social values cannot be the individual actor, but this recognition conceals the radical difference between the positions advanced by Bourdieu and Touraine. This radical difference coincides with that between Merleau-Ponty and Sartre. As in Sartre's *Critique de la raison dialectique* (Sartre, 1960), Touraine posits a 'historical subject' as social actor, an actor who enacts a historical social movement. Bourdieu argues that Touraine's view of a creative actor is not susceptible to empirical analysis but, rather, is the imposition of a metaphysical, Marxist, worldview which is as alien to sociology as idealism. Touraine elevates 'work' [travail] as the essence of the action of historical subjects but, in Bourdieu's view, reiterating his argument in 'Condition de classe et position de classe', the character of work is taken to be universal rather than a phenomenon which has different meanings in different contexts.[15] In opposition to Touraine and in language which echoes Merleau-Ponty, Bourdieu insists that 'social values are meanings. They have meaning for social actors since they orient their behaviour [comportement], motivate them through external sanctions as well as through the interiorisations of them which they make' (Bourdieu and Reynaud, 1966, 515). These individual meanings are the consequence of the insertion of actors within social contexts but they are not historically predetermined. In other words, Bourdieu insists that actors are not free agents, transcendent selves, somehow embodying a historical process. Actions need to be understood sociologically in respect of varying social contexts rather than with reference to a prescribed formula, but his critique of Touraine does not deal with the problem whether real social agents are as predetermined in his nominal system as are Touraine's historical subjects in their historical contexts. Bourdieu's discussion of Touraine makes it clear that his recognition that individuals generate signifying distinctions does not involve an acceptance of a-social individuality. He still needed to expound his view of the relation between the projects of individuals and the social system within which they are actualized.

'*Champ intellectuel et projet créateur*', 1966

Bourdieu's contribution to a special number of *Les temps modernes* devoted to the 'Problèmes du structuralisme' [problems of structuralism] which was published in November 1966, entitled 'Champ intellectuel et projet créateur' [intellectual field and creative project] (Bourdieu, 1966c), was a further attempt to clarify his thinking. The special number was edited by Jean Pouillon, who introduced it with 'un essai de définition' [an essay in definition]. The collection of articles offered a multi-disciplinary response which reflected the claims of structuralists to be providing a theory of general applicability. In his introductory presentation, Pouillon drew attention to the distinction in

French between 'structurel' and 'structural'. Succinctly, he concluded: '"structural" refers to structure as syntax, "structurel" refers to it as reality' (Pouillon, 1966, 780).

The tension in Bourdieu's work at this time can be expressed in the terms adumbrated by Pouillon. Bourdieu was interested in a 'structurel' reality which enacted processes of acculturation, but the explanatory discourse at his disposal was 'structural', predicated on the identification of universal patterns of human language and behaviour. The surprising aspect of Bourdieu's contribution to the special number of *Les temps modernes* is that he chose to explore this tension in relation to the problem of the contemporary analysis of cultural production in past history, rather than directly in respect of the analogous anthropological problem, with which he was familiar, of the Western European analysis of social behaviour within differently constituted societies.

Bourdieu's intention is to announce that his view of the nature of the creative process in history prescribes the parameters of explanatory discourse in the present about that past process. The underlying assumption is that, contrary to the view of the hermeneutic tradition associated with the work of Dilthey, present analysis must not proceed as if a bond exists between it and past creativity on the presumption that there exists some trans-historical or transcendent affinity which relates in origin to an essential human subjectivity. Bourdieu rejects the 'Romantic' ideology of the 'self'-expressive poet or thinker. Intellectual or artistic expression 'really' occurs within a social network. The 'syntactic' analysis of this network in part refers to the reality which is observed and in part itself has meaning within its own social network. The analysis of 'texts in their contexts' is a conceptual instrument for observers in defining their positions within their reality. The analysis of the 'fields' within which historical works were generated is an instrument of creative intellectuals in the present as they situate themselves within a present intellectual field. Hence, the notion of 'field' is deployed as a way of mediating between real/structurel and rational/structural interpretations.

Bourdieu illustrated his general position by reference to aspects of 'the history of Western intellectual and artistic life' (Bourdieu, 1966c; 1971f, 162). The first intellectual achievement in Western European history was the establishment of discourses and mechanisms for the advancement of intellectual activity *sui generis* rather than in deference to pre-established discipline. Within this achieved autonomy, there then developed a continuing struggle for cultural domination between discourses and between new institutions supporting their transmission, such as publishing houses and stage producers. In spite of this historical illustration from Western European society, Bourdieu resists the notion that this particular form of social organization is normative. The achievement of intellectual autonomy was a double-edged benefit. No sooner had a form of intellectual authority independent of external powers been achieved than the corollary materialized whereby independence became identified with 'indifference to the public' and intellectual exclusivity became the order of the day (as in the development of 'art for art's sake'). Separation from the 'public' became as much a defining characteristic of the new intellectualism as separation from ecclesiastical and class domination. This historically contingent construction of the intellectual as socially 'distinct' entered into subsequent consciousness. We must not, in other words, allow our contemporary perspective to be determined by its source in a historical contingency. Rather we must subject to scrutiny the whole situation that generated what we have extracted to constitute the legacy shaping our present practice.

In summary, Bourdieu's position, as stated in 1966, was that the attempt to relate texts to their contexts is based on a false antithesis. 'Contexts' of production and reception constitute textual meanings. 'Texts' are not the a-social expression of selves and, indeed, 'selves' are not essential but, rather, socially constructed. As biological entities, persons construct themselves by incorporating objectified discourses. There is no pre-existent personal identity regulating the appropriation of defining characteristics. Bourdieu was in sympathy with this 'existentialist' contention but disagreed with the view adopted by Sartre that we have the freedom to construct ourselves. In the absence of such freedom, individuals are automata which process thoughts as instruments of biological adaptation. The 'historical evolution' of intellectual fields is not one of 'progress' but one of continuous adaptation such that the re-emergence of total relations similar to those obtaining in Athenian society, for instance, is neither impossible nor inconceivable.

'Sociology and Philosophy in France since 1945. Death and Resurrection of a Philosophy without Subject', 1967

This article was an attempt to analyse historically the relative positions of the discourses of sociology and philosophy within the post-war French social system. Bourdieu announces that the article is not an attempt to write 'a philosophy of the history of philosophy or of the history of sociology, but a sociology of the main trends of sociology which, in order to restore their full meaning to works and doctrines, tries to relate them to their cultural context' (Bourdieu and Passeron, 1967b, 162). He footnotes a cross-reference to 'Champ intellectuel et projet créateur' to emphasize that it offers a comparison of the positions of disciplines in relation to each other and their contexts rather than on any assumption that they might possess a priori identity. Bourdieu was interested in the nexus connecting modes of thought in general, specific disciplines and institutions of education as illustrations of the adoption of cultural positions within social systems. This interest was pursued through structurel/ structural investigations, including the element of self-referentiality in 'Sociology and Philosophy in France since 1945. Death and Resurrection of a Philosophy without Subject'.

Bourdieu and Panofsky

Again in 1967, Bourdieu published in one volume a translation of two texts by Erwin Panofsky[16] – his *Gothic Architecture and Scholasticism* and his *Abbot Suger of Saint Denis*, with an afterword (Panofsky, ed. Bourdieu, 1967).[17] The main focus of Bourdieu's commentary is on the nature of the correlation suggested by Panofsky between the system of scholastic thought and its embodiment in the contemporary construction of Gothic cathedrals, but there are other hidden features. The important point for Bourdieu was that Panofsky was not content to observe a homology between thought and architectural style, to intuit an almost mystical connection, but, rather, undertook an analysis of the way in which the affinity was *enacted*.

The second chapter of Panofsky's *Gothic Architecture and Scholastic Thought* was devoted to 'the formative force of habits'. According to Panofsky, the connection was effected 'by diffusion rather than by direct contact' (Panofsky, ed. Bourdieu, 1967, 83), by the establishment of what he called 'mental habit' [habitude mentale], a notion which he derived from St. Thomas Aquinas's 'principle which regulates action'. Panofsky adopted a principle developed within scholastic thought to explain the correlation between thought and architecture, and suggested that diffusion was achieved through the mediation of *forms* of thinking inculcated in seats of learning, particularly in an area around Paris where scholasticism held a monopoly. In short, Panofsky insisted that the effect of pedagogy was based on the transmission of a 'modus operandi' and that content should be 'put in brackets' (Panofsky, ed. Bourdieu, 1967, 89), and that it should be recognized that the homology between thought and architectural style was dependent on the existence of a relatively closed epistemic community located in a specifically confined geographical space. In his afterword, Bourdieu celebrates Panofsky's *Gothic Architecture and Scholastic Thought* as 'one of the most beautiful challenges to positivism which has ever been launched' (Panofsky, ed. Bourdieu, 1967, 135). Bourdieu picks up Panofsky's emphasis on formal pedagogical transmission when he restates that 'by the very logic of its function, the school modifies or defines the content and the spirit of the culture which it transmits' (Panofsky, ed. Bourdieu, 1967, 148), pointing the way towards the analyses of *La reproduction. Éléments pour une théorie du système d'enseignement* (Bourdieu and Passeron, 1970). Most obviously, Bourdieu seizes on Panofsky's use of the notion of 'mental habit'. He begins to develop from this usage his own definition of the value of the 'habitus'. As Bourdieu summarizes:

> by using the scholastic concept of *habitus* to designate the culture inculcated by the school, Erwin Panofsky enables us to see that culture is not just a common code, nor even a common repertoire of responses to common problems ... but rather a collection of fundamental schemes, provisionally assimilated, on the basis of which are generated, according to an art of invention analogous with musical

composition, an infinity of particular schemas, directly applied to particular situations. (Panofsky, ed. Bourdieu, 1967, 151–2)

The mode of transmission of culture dictates the ways in which it can be modified. Habitus defines a process of formal transmission which enables substantive modifications. It does not transmit pre-existing collective culture but enables the construction of new cultures by the operation of a thought process (a modus operandi) which is a predetermined formula but one which allows for an art of invention within prescribed limits. Bourdieu notes that Panofsky opened the way to an extension of the use of the concept of habitus by suggesting that mental habits analogous to scholastic ones are at work in every civilization. Bourdieu pursues this to argue that schemes which function for cultivated people in societies with scholarly institutions fulfil the same function as those unconscious ones which 'the ethnologist discovers through the analysis of rites and myths in societies which do not have such institutions' (Panofsky, ed. Bourdieu, 1967, 151), referring to the 'primitive forms of classification' outlined by Mauss and Durkheim. In conclusion, Bourdieu comments that the virtuosity of Panofsky's analyses bring to his mind a phrase from another text by Panofsky in which he remarked that 'the historian of art differs from the "naïve" spectator in that he is conscious of what he is doing' (Panofsky, ed. Bourdieu, 1967, 167).[18] In summary, Bourdieu finds in Panofsky's work a conceptual tool for understanding phenomena associated, among others, with schools and pedagogy, language, epistemology of social science, art appreciation, ethnology. The range of fields to which Bourdieu applies Panofsky's perception about scholastic thought is symptomatic of Bourdieu's sense that this multivarious application is itself indicative of the extent to which his conceptual disposition is the effect of a habitus absorbed through his learning in a sequence of lycées and grandes écoles. Just as the objective homology between scholastic methods of disputation and the fabric of cathedrals was historically socially constructed rather than abstractly universal, so Bourdieu hints that his recognition of this homology and its transferability is a function of his own intellectual and institutional formation. Although the distinction between objective and subjective collapses by means of the operation of habitus both in history and in the interpretation of history, the thrust of Bourdieu's work at the end of the 1960s retained the Gestaltist emphasis which supposed that there are meaning structures independent of personal experience. He appears to have suppressed the latent reflexivity to which he drew attention in the conclusion to his afterword to Panofsky. We can briefly say that *Le métier de sociologue* was an attempt to outline a procedure, a system of thought, which would formally characterize or define social scientific explanation in terms of a 'modus operandi' [way of working] involving an 'ars inveniendi' [art of invention] rather than in terms of a cumulative canon of authoritative texts, hence as a guide to the 'craft' of a worker rather than to a corpus of prior knowledge. Following Bachelard's injunction that 'the scientific fact is won, constructed, and confirmed' (cited in Bourdieu, Chamboredon and Passeron, 1991, 10), *Le métier de sociologue* assembles passages which attempt to use this procedural formula to illustrate the commonality of research methodologies independent of the ideological assumptions or interpretations of individual researchers. Recognition of the rules governing the system of sociological explanation did not, for Bourdieu, involve accepting that such explanation adequately represents social reality. Sociological explanation is one system of thought which correlates with an institutional system and both these systems are shifting components of the total social system. Bourdieu pursued Panofsky's insight in a paper given in September 1966 and published a year later as 'Systèmes d'enseignement et systèmes de pensée' [systems of education and systems of thought] (Bourdieu, 1967). Subsequently, Bourdieu and Passeron collaborated to review their earlier empirical work on culture and education in *La reproduction* (Bourdieu and Passeron, 1970) which, significantly was sub-titled in French as 'éléments pour une théorie du système d'enseignement' [elements for a theory of the system of education]. This book adopted a scholastic mode of presentation, offering propositions and expositions, to suggest that the schooling system inculcates a mode of thinking which is peculiar to cultivated classes through the transmission of 'arbitrary' or historically contingent knowledge, exercising the authority of a dominant class to deny the equally valid mode of thinking operating within 'disadvantaged' or 'primitive' classes.

Summary

In the 1960s, Bourdieu published the findings of his Algerian fieldwork and directed a series of research projects on education and culture within the research group that Aron had founded. He transposed his perception that Algerian values had been arbitrarily reconceptualized in the process of colonial intervention to the metropolitan French situation where he demonstrated that 'equal opportunity' did not entail the recognition of multiple cultures but, rather, the selection of a minor proportion of the majority population to join a privileged elite, and that a supposedly neutral process of selection based on merit was skewed so as to reproduce the domination of that elite.

For Bourdieu, the validity of sociological discourse in a closed intellectual field and the validity of the education system as the exclusive vehicle for the inter-generational transmission of values and knowledge were both contingent characteristics of the French society in which he lived and worked. During the 'student revolt' of May 1968, Bourdieu attempted to highlight the extent to which the proposed reforms were advanced by those who were beneficiaries of the existing system. He called for the establishment of an Estates General to develop an educational policy which would meet the needs of the whole population, both cultivated and primitive. In other words, he tried to argue that the total social system needs to be accommodated in change. Adjustments to particular systems would not suffice. Perhaps the failure of the May 'events' caused Bourdieu to begin to emphasize that individuals can modify the structures or systems within which they operate rather than to seem to believe that systems are oppressive straitjackets. Until about 1970, there was always the sense that Bourdieu's thought accommodated objectively prescribed individual agency within his own objective conceptual framework. A new shift of emphasis developed whereby Bourdieu concentrated on the creativity of individuals within fields rather than on the fields as determinants of action.

Notes

1 One of the books challenged by Bourdieu and Passeron was Edgar Morin's (1962) *L'esprit du temps. Essai sur la culture de masse* [The spirit of the times. Essay on mass culture].

2 The English edition of 1979 (Bourdieu and Passeron, 1979) adds an epilogue which is a translation of Bourdieu's single-authored 'Classement, déclassement, reclassement' [classification, declassification, reclassification] (Bourdieu, 1978).

3 'Symbolic' in the sense articulated by Coleridge in distinction from 'allegorical': 'The symbol ... always partakes of the Reality which it renders intelligible' (Willinsky, ed., 1990, 58). See also Engell, 1989, 95.

4 This is a procedure which Bourdieu was later to denigrate as 'citology', that is, providing artificial authority for statements by association with canonical writers.

5 This is stated in a footnote to the first passage quoted.

6 A footnote spells out that Bourdieu and Passeron do not mean by this that they 'contest the natural inequality of human abilities' (Bourdieu and Passeron, 1979, 155).

7 Bourdieu was responsible, in 1961–62, with his wife, Marie-Claire, for an enquiry into 'photography in a rural milieu' (which was that of his native Béarn), and, in 1962–63, for an enquiry which took place in parallel in Paris and Lille on 'opinions and attitudes in relation to photography' which was also related to a survey, with a sample of 692 subjects, undertaken in Paris, Lille and a 'small provincial village' on 'photographic practice and attitudes in relation to photography' (see Bourdieu, Boltanski, Castel and Chamboredon, 1965, 333–4).

8 We now know, of course, from the posthumously published *Images d'Algérie* [images of Algeria] (Bourdieu, ed. Schultheis and Frisinghelli, 2003) that Bourdieu had himself been an enthusiastic photographer.

9 I have explored this issue in more detail in respect of the relationship between Bourdieu and Boltanski in Robbins, 2014b.

10 A second, augmented French edition was published in 1969 and it was this edition which is translated into English (Bourdieu, Darbel and Schnapper, 1990).

11 Unfortunately, the article has not been translated into English, although a German translation was included in the first major German collection of articles by Bourdieu in Bourdieu, 1970a.

12 Max Wertheimer (1880–1943) was, with Koffka and Köhler, one of the three founders of Gestalt psychology. Like Gurwitsch, he studied under Stumpf in Berlin. The article cited by Gurwitsch in Gurwitsch, 1957b, 100, and by Bourdieu is: 'Untersuchungen zur Lehre von der Gestalt' [investigations into Gestalt theory], *Psychologische Forschung*, I, 1921, 45–60.

13 Bourdieu is quoting here from Touraine, 1965, 12.
14 Merleau-Ponty's 'Le métaphysique dans l'homme' was first published in 1947 (Merleau-Ponty, 1947b). See chapter 4.
15 Bourdieu had argued for the non-universal characteristics of work in *Travail et travailleurs en Algérie* (Bourdieu, Darbel, Rivet and Seibel, 1963).
16 Erwin Panofsky (1892–1968).
17 Panofsky's 'L'Abbé Suger de Saint-Denis' was published in 1946. *Gothic Architecture and Scholasticism* was first given as a series of lectures in 1948 and then published in 1951.
18 The quote is from 'Iconography and Iconology' in Panofsky, 1955, 31.

7

The 1970s

Introduction

Jacques Rancière later criticized the work of Bourdieu and Passeron of the 1960s on the grounds that their analyses had reinforced the view that ordinary people live in 'méconnaissance' [ignorance] of the real conditions of their existence which can be identified by a 'Sociologist King' in a malign tradition going back to Plato's conception of the function of the 'Philosopher King'.[1] Perhaps himself sensing this deficiency in his earlier work, Bourdieu began in the 1970s to articulate an epistemological position which would protect the 'practical sense' of ordinary experience from the intrusions of the academic gaze. This did not mean that he was accepting the validity of a hierarchy of explanation but, instead, that it should be understood that everyone endeavours to reconcile their individual dispositions with their understanding of the constraints on their behaviour which have become historically objectified in social structures.

Bourdieu developed a theory of social scientific understanding which would allow him to reconcile his inclination to respect the self-understandings of social agents with his equally strong inclination to subject social behaviour to systematic explanation. This reconciliation led him to oscillate rather ambivalently between 'realist' and 'nominalist' accounts of social phenomena. He argued against the prevailing structuralism, most represented in the anthropological work of Lévi-Strauss, on the grounds that it imposed a detached, objectivist interpretation of the actions of others which was essentially an expression of the 'nominal' dispositions of the interpreters. On the other hand, he did not want to subscribe to a subjectivist interpretation of social actions, one which supposed that they emanate from free, transcendental selves. This kind of social psychological realism, epitomized in the work of Sartre, was, for Bourdieu, clandestinely as universalist as objectivist structuralism. Bourdieu tried to adopt the view that the real behaviour of individuals is always constrained by the objective structures within which they operate. The tasks of the sociologist are to understand the processes of constraint in any given situation and the immanent structures which exercise constraint. These tasks are *formal*. The name 'habitus' is given to the process of constraint, adaptation, assimilation between individuals and their structures which has a normal form but which is always socially contingent in reality. The 'habitus' itself can only be taken to 'exist' in each of the different situations in which it manifests itself. It is a static, conceptual, heuristic device for comprehending realities which are constantly dynamic. Similarly, the objective structures or champs [fields] have normal forms which are also socially contingent in reality. The analyses of different 'fields' again operate heuristically by presupposing categories such as the fields of religion, politics, law or religion. As such they appear to endorse the a priori categories of the philosophy of symbolic forms but, again, Bourdieu wants to insist that in reality fields are contingent, relational rather than absolute.

In this chapter, I first examine Bourdieu's articulation of his critique of structuralism. I then consider some of the texts in which he attempted to reconcile a constructivist orientation with its origins in structuralism, an attempt which was confused by the fact that he constantly sought to revisit and reinterpret the findings of projects which had been conducted prior to his change of theoretical position.

Texts

Esquisse d'une théorie de la pratique *1972*

Bourdieu published 'La maison kabyle ou le monde renversé' [the berber house or the world turned upside down] in a collection of essays offered to Claude Lévi-Strauss on the occasion of his sixtieth birthday (Bourdieu, 1970b). It was the product of work undertaken early in the 1960s. In 1972, Bourdieu published *Esquisse d'une théorie de la pratique, précédé de trois études d'ethnologie kabyle* [outline of a theory of practice, preceded by three ethnological studies of Kabylia] (Bourdieu, 1972a). Divided into two parts, it included, as the first part, three studies, the second of which was 'La maison kabyle ou le monde renversé'. Bourdieu reprinted the three studies in order to subject them to his critical evaluation in the second part of the book. The text was published in English in 1977 as *Outline of a Theory of Practice* (Bourdieu, 1977d), by which time Bourdieu had, first, in 1973, published an extract in English as 'The Three Forms of Theoretical Knowledge' (Bourdieu, 1973a), and, secondly, reorganized the original text in such a way that the three Kabyle studies and their critiques had become incorporated to constitute a manifesto for a 'post-structuralist' method. In this same period, Bourdieu published two articles on the work of Max Weber (Bourdieu, 1971b and c), the second of which was entitled 'Genèse et structure du champ religieux' [genesis and structure of the religious field], and gave two significant papers, the first in 1971 entitled 'L'opinion publique n'existe pas' [public opinion does not exist] (Bourdieu, 1971e) and the second in 1973 entitled 'Sur le pouvoir symbolique' [on symbolic power] (Bourdieu, 1977c). In these theoretical texts, the focus of Bourdieu's attention shifted towards offering accounts of the ways in which individuals constitute the structures within which they are constrained and away from primary concentration on the intrinsic character of those structures. This shift was also reflected in the interpretations which he offered of the findings of projects which he undertook within CSE. A project of 1972 on 'Le patronat' [leaders of business] gave rise to 'Les stratégies de reconversion. Les classes sociales et le système d'enseignement' [reconversion strategies. Social classes and the system of education] (Bourdieu, Boltanski and de Saint Martin, 1973) and to 'Le titre et le poste. Rapports entre le système de production et le système de reproduction' [title and post. Relations between the system of production and the system of reproduction] (Bourdieu and Boltanski, 1975a). As the titles of these works suggest, Bourdieu was deploying a terminology which focused on 'strategies' in respect of social behaviour and on 'genesis' with regard to structures. In his early career Bourdieu had attempted to incorporate the perspectives of those people whose behaviour he had observed within *his* understanding of their society as a social system. In order to legitimate his objective representations of the situations of observed people he had been meticulous in itemizing the procedures which he had adopted to make his interpretative transition from case-studies, interviews or survey responses. He was sensitive to the need for this legitimation because he was aware that otherwise his objectifications might be the consequences of his personal predispositions, that his research findings might simply be self-fulfilling confirmations of his research questions, or, as Pouillon expressed it, that his explanations might be 'structural' rather than 'structurel'. His critique of Touraine's 'actionism' enabled him to clarify that he wanted to disclose the meanings of the behaviour of individuals without imposing on them the predetermined framework of meaning supplied by historical materialism. At the same time, the influence of Panofsky enabled him to explain, by adopting the notion of habitus, the way in which observed individuals might themselves be seen to be generating their actions immanently within their prescribed contexts. Although Bourdieu avoided by this means imposing a direct imposition of extrinsic understanding on the self-understanding of individuals, he had not dealt with the possibility that he might be retaining an indirect imposition in as much as his concept of constituting structures had a status which was not dissimilar to the historical framing posited by Touraine. The challenge for

Bourdieu was to articulate a theory which allowed individuals to act in ways that would not be the outcomes of universal, free, 'self'-expression nor the consequences of their imprisonment within absolutely constraining intellectual and institutional systems.

'La maison kabyle ou le monde renversé' is dated in *Esquisse* as having been written in Paris in 1963–64, that is to say, at the time shortly after the publication of the second edition of *Sociologie de l'Algérie* in 1961, when Bourdieu added graphic representations of tribal genealogies to the original text in a manner which appeared to be influenced by the work of Lévi-Strauss. 'La maison kabyle ou le monde renversé' adopts the same style. It beautifully describes the spatial organization of the Kabyle house and indicates the homologies between the interior and exterior of the dwelling and also, by extension, those between the structures of the house, the village and the countryside. It describes the ways in which spatial divisions correlate with elements of the mythico-ritual system within Kabyle society. The existence of this system corroborates the suggestion in the afterword to Panofsky's book that in uncultivated societies there are coherent, non-intellectual systems of meaning which correspond with the intellectual systems in operation in cultivated societies, and also the suggestion in the review of Touraine's book that these systems tend towards proximity with 'natural' conditions in contrast with the positional artifice of cultural distinctions in more sophisticated societies. Bourdieu's purpose in commenting on these old articles is to reassert that he is not, through detached analysis, reducing symbolic exchanges to their economic function, nor celebrating the creative, mythopoeic achievement of individuals as autonomous selves, nor identifying universal structural characteristics of social organizations, but, instead, is indicating that individuals act within total systems in which myth, ritual and economic behaviour mutually reinforce each other and in which the values and behaviours of individuals are reciprocally reflected in and constituted by the network of systems which constitute the systemic totality of society.

Bourdieu's intention, therefore, was to find a mode of analysis which would recognize the functionality inherent in the operation of the total system under observation and would not subscribe to the various ideological orientations implicit in the procedures adopted by other social scientists to generate explanations. He was seeking an approach which would simultaneously offer a new interpretation of observed phenomena and be methodologically non-objectivist. In the second part of *Esquisse*, Bourdieu offers an outline of his alternative to existing intellectualist research – the generation of a theory of practice.

Bourdieu's foreword begins at once with a clear statement about the reflections which are to come in the text: 'This reflection on a scientific practice is undertaken to disconcert as much those who reflect on the human sciences without carrying out practical research as those who practise without reflecting.

Scientific practice is not exempted from the theory of practice which is proposed here' (Bourdieu, 1972a, 155). There is a clear echo of the opposition
expressed in *Le métier de sociologue* to 'theoretical theory' and to that text's
insistence that what is required of the epistemology of social science is that it
should enable practitioners to reflect on 'science in progress' (Bourdieu, Chamboredon and Passeron, 1968, 27; 1991, 8) rather than indulge in post hoc
scrutiny. Echoing the language of Panofsky, Bourdieu adds that this method
of continuous reflection releases understanding of the modus operandi inherent
in observed systems whereas the post hoc concentration on their opus operatum implies a 'systematic bias' (Bourdieu, 1972a, 155).

It is important to register the differences between *Esquisse* and the text
which, in 1977, was offered as its 'translation' – *Outline of a Theory of Practice*
(Bourdieu, 1977d). Following his foreword (which was not translated),
Bourdieu launched into a section entitled 'L'observateur observé' [the observer
observed] which, also, was not translated. He announces from the start that
he is aware of the risks of his project, that any questioning of objectivism is
doomed 'to appear initially to be a rehabilitation of subjectivism' and to play
into the hands of those who oppose 'the magic virtues of "participant observation"' (Bourdieu, 1972a, 157) to objectivist rigour or who suppose that 'practice is the only way to understand practice'. Importantly, Bourdieu adds that
this cognitive dilemma is mirrored socially, arguing that an analysis of the social
position of intellectuals would show that they are 'middlebrows'[2] or interme-
diaries between groups or classes. His intention, therefore, is not simply to
oppose theoretically the polarization of theory and practice, but also to introduce the conditions of possibility for adopting such a position in fact. In a
passage which is redolent of reflection on his personal situation, Bourdieu
elaborates that middlebrow intellectuals 'speak *for* others, that is to say in their
favour but also in *their place*: they are led to deceive, most often in good faith,
as much those of whom they speak as those to whom they speak. As for those
among them who have come from dominated classes, either transfuges or
upstarts, they can only speak because they have abandoned the wordless place
of those whose words they represent' (Bourdieu, 1972a, 158). For Bourdieu,
the necessary epistemological break must be correlative with a *social* break in
order to ensure that the theory of practice should not become the preserve of
a privileged class disposed to generate theories in themselves by 'forgetting the
social conditions of possibility of theory' (Bourdieu, 1972a, 158).

'L'observateur observé' is followed by a section entitled 'Les trois modes
de connaissance théorique' [the three modes of theoretical knowledge]. The
translation of this famous Bourdieu passage is exact for one and a half pages
of *Outline* (pp. 3–4). Bourdieu announces that 'the social world may be the
object of three modes of theoretical knowledge' (Bourdieu, 1972a, 162; 1977d,
3). It is important to stress that these three modes have only one thing in
common, which is that 'they are opposed to practical knowledge' (Bourdieu,

1972a, 162; 1977d, 3). Bourdieu calls the first knowledge '*phenomenological*', which he identifies with the approach of currently active schools ('interaction-ist' and 'ethnomethodological' in the French text and just the latter in the English). He states that this knowledge 'sets out to make explicit the truth of primary experience of the social world, i.e. all that is inscribed in the relation-ship of *familiarity* with the familiar environment, the unquestioning apprehen-sion of the social world which, by definition, does not reflect on itself and excludes the question of the conditions of its own possibility' (Bourdieu, 1972a, 163; 1977d, 3). The connotations of the French text are here more explicitly suggestive. The phrase 'the unquestioning apprehension of the social world' renders 'appréhension du monde social comme monde naturel et allant de soi', which emphasizes that the world of primary experience is one which is primarily of the taken-for-granted character of 'natural' existence, one exem-plifying, in other words, the kind of methexis advanced in Lévy-Bruhl's 'loi de participation' [law of participation] as characteristic of 'primitive mentality'.[3] It is a form of knowledge which does not require detachment.

Bourdieu calls the second knowledge 'objectivist', indicating that 'structur-alist hermeneutics' is a particular case of such objectivism, carefully implying a critique of the combination rather than structuralism per se. Objectivist knowledge 'constructs the objective relations (e.g. economic or linguistic) which structure practice and representations of practice' (Bourdieu, 1972a, 163; 1977d, 3), that is to say that it constructs the relations which are inherent in the familiar world but which are assumed and unconceptualized in that world. This construction 'presupposes a break with primary knowledge'. It involves an epistemological break reminiscent of Bachelard's injunction for the con-struction of science in general, but the French text makes it more clear that the break is seen as involving a *loss*: 'au prix d'une rupture avec cette con-naissance première' [at the cost of a break with this primary experience] (Bourdieu, 1972a, 163). The goal is to use objectivist analysis as a device to understand what obtains in primary experience but which that experience never articulates for itself. Although Bourdieu characterizes the first form of knowledge as 'phenomenological', it is rather a phenomenology of the natural attitude in the manner of Schutz, while objectivism performs the task proposed by Gurwitsch's constitutive phenomenology, deploying the equivalent of reduction to release the true structure of the primary world. Objectivism pre-supposes that observed, unreflecting agents operate within structural conditions of which they are unaware. Primary experience is characterized by its 'mécon-naissance' [misknowledge] of the real constraints or conditions within which it operates. Bourdieu therefore explains that 'in so doing, objectivist analysis does not, strictly speaking, contradict phenomenological analysis of primary experience ... It merely defines the limits of its validity by establishing the particular conditions within which it is possible, conditions which phenomeno-logical analysis ignores' (Bourdieu, 1977d, 198). Objectivism, in Bourdieu's view, presupposes that primary agency is not 'free' or 'self-expressive' but is always action within a constraining context which is not recognized. Objectivism reveals the total structural context of actions whereas the phenomenological analysis of the first order attends only to actions in themselves as phenomena. Bourdieu presupposes the primacy of consciousness. His post-structuralist theory is not a negation of structuralist insights and it is not based on assigning primacy to pre-logical, pre-predicative or pre-cognitive thought.

Bourdieu suggests that objectivist knowledge fails to do justice to primary experience. By asking the question which primary knowledge does not itself ask about the social conditions of its production, objectivist knowledge successfully defines negatively what primary knowledge 'lacks' (Bourdieu, 1972a, 164; 1977d, 4). To make this negative achievement positive, Bourdieu argues for a third kind of knowledge which he calls 'praxéologique' [praxeological] in the French text but to which he no longer gives this name in the English text. The purpose of this third kind of knowledge is to turn the table on objectivism. Praxeological knowledge reverses roles in that it reveals what objectivist knowledge lacks in not understanding the operations of practical knowledge as a consequence of complacently assuming the supremacy of its own perspective.

In *Esquisse/Outline*, Bourdieu proceeds to concentrate on demonstrating the analytical benefits of his objectivist recognition of immanent structures, in opposition both to Lévi-Straussian structuralism and to a form of phenomenological research which he identifies with the work of Mauss.[4] Praxeological analysis is announced but its practice is deferred.[5] Nevertheless, we have to be aware that in advancing his interpretation of Kabyle behaviour as a form of practice which operates on the basis of immanently internalized structures, Bourdieu is indirectly exploring the nature of behaviour in terms of which he will subject objectivism itself to scrutiny. Bourdieu elaborates his theoretical position in great detail in Part II of *Esquisse*, drawing on a wide literature to make his case. In doing so, he criticizes Saussure[6] and also Lévi-Strauss and Lévi-Strauss's reading of Mauss so as to demonstrate that analysis must shift from that of the opus operatum [past action] to that of the opus operandi [action in progress] (Bourdieu, 1972a, 174), or, in other words, must substitute analysis of 'rules' for that of 'strategies' (Bourdieu, 1977d, 9). This involves abandoning 'all the theories which explicitly or implicitly treat practice as a mechanical reaction directly determined by prior conditions' (Bourdieu, 1972a, 178). Recognition of the importance of time is crucial to appreciating how strategic actions differ from the static representation of exchange in objectivist analyses. In part, Bourdieu continues to expose the shortcomings of objectivist analyses, but he also elaborates his understanding of the way in which primary practice incorporates its structures. The first section is entitled 'Structures, habitus et pratiques' [structures, habitus and practices] in which he discusses the way in which in everyday activity the habitus for every individual mediates between primary experience and structural knowledge. He has recourse to Leibniz's discussion of how two clocks or watches agree precisely[7] to argue that group or class habitus are constituted by the convergent affinities of individuals accommodating to common situations. The habitus is an 'immanent law ... fixed in each individual by primary education' (Bourdieu, 1972a, 181). We may be duped into supposing that the harmonization of habitus indicates some extrinsic influence or that it confirms an objectivist reading of primary experience, but Bourdieu insists that corporate identities are constructed intrinsically. Whether they want or not, individual agents are producers and reproducers of meaning, participating in an 'objective intention' which surpasses conscious intentions. To support his argument Bourdieu significantly cites Gelb and Goldstein,[8] who derived from their work with aphasia patients their view that there exist acquired schemes of thought which operate as unconscious mechanisms for physiological repair. He explicitly rejects the notion, which he attributes to Schutz, that corporate assumptions are generated wholly in inter-personal interaction. It follows that Bourdieu turns attention to 'the incorporation of structures' and to the role of primary education in effecting the transition from primary experience to structured meanings. Again, Bourdieu disagrees with Schutz[9] (and, following him, the 'ethnomethodologists'), who supposes that the 'taken-for-granted' world of the 'natural attitude' possesses 'a collection of *formal and universal* presuppositions' (Bourdieu, 1972a, 199), whereas it should be understood as always being the product of particular cultural and political circumstances, both of which, to use the phrase adopted by Bourdieu and Passeron in *La reproduction*, are 'arbitrary' (Bourdieu, 1972a, 199). At the same time, Bourdieu is anxious to argue that the notion of habitus does not imply that individual agents are automatons. In a section devoted to consideration of 'stratégies, rituels et art de vivre' [strategies, rituals and the art of living] he begins by accepting that the theory of habitus 'raises a collection of questions which the notion of the unconscious has the effect of mystifying' (Bourdieu, 1972a, 200). Even if the practices produced by the habitus seem to 'present all the properties of instinctive conduct and, in particular, of automatism', it remains the case that 'a form of partial, lacunary, discontinuous consciousness always accompanies practices' (Bourdieu, 1972a, 200). He cites Merleau-Ponty's critique of reflex action in *La structure du comportement* to emphasize that agents can only have mastery over their own practices by operations which 'presuppose the structures which they analyse' (Bourdieu, 1972a, 201),[10] thereby suggesting that he is in sympathy with Gurwitsch's insistence on the primacy of consciousness prior to perception. Bourdieu devotes a section entitled 'Le corps géomètre' [the geometric body] to attempt to explain in a different way that, in his view, ritual is indicative of symbolic practice whereas the analysis of myths is redolent of an intellectualism which is unable to comprehend ritual as mythic practice. He acknowledges (Bourdieu, 1972a, 214)the influence of Jean Nicod's *La géométrie dans le monde sensible* [geometry in the sensible world] and he also quotes approvingly Heidegger's expression that '*Denken ist Handwerk*' [thinking is a craft] (Bourdieu, 1972a, 213). These references (and others, for instance notably to the work of Comte, Sartre, Jakobson, Mead, Prieto, Durkheim, Leach, Wittgenstein, Freud, Erikson, Klein, Boas, Pareto, Sapir, Weber, Bachelard, Husserl, Chomsky, Mauss, Benveniste and Marx) show that Bourdieu was attempting to work with different philosophical traditions to develop a theory of practice which would reconcile the perspective of mathematical logic with an emphasis on 'Being-in-the-World', insisting that practice operates in terms of its own consciousness.

Consolidation of Esquisse *and the emergence of 'field' projects*

Paradoxically, *Esquisse* was an intellectualist endeavour, marshalling a range of influences, to articulate a theory of practice. Bourdieu was advancing his own 'creative project' within the 'intellectual field' of his formation by challenging the ways in which intellectualist traditions in anthropology and sociology had denied the validity of the creative practices of ordinary people. Bourdieu was deploying the philosophical learning which he had acquired in a way which was exemplifying that commitment to the recognition of practice should not by definition be anti-intellectual. On the contrary, he was recognizing that there was a dialectic between his primary experience and the way in which his training in 'arbitrary' educational institutions had enabled him to conceptualize that experience. In short, there was a developing convergence between his objective analyses of situations within his immediate French social context and his incipient tendency to inspect his own thought and social trajectory in exactly the same terms. He was intent on subjecting his own objectivism to the second epistemological break which would disclose his own modus operandi as well as that of those whose behaviour he was observing.

Key factors in Bourdieu's attempt to harness the three modes of theoretical knowledge to articulate an understanding of underlying practices were, first, the way in which he orchestrated the activity of the group of researchers in the CSE, particularly after he became Director of the Centre[11] when Aron moved in 1970 to the Collège de France, and, secondly, the way in which he mobilized collective action by launching, in 1975, the journal entitled, significantly, *Actes de la recherche en sciences sociales* [research *acts* in the social sciences]. The motivation of his leadership of the Centre was to encourage research which would be *practice* and be communicated as such in the *Actes* rather than to contribute to sustaining intellectualist detachment from action, to stimulate a modus operandi rather than concentration on a modus operatum. The group would be instrumental in articulating its own class identity, representative of dominated sectors of French society. It would operate in accordance with its own subliminally absorbed structural regulations in opposition to the socially and intellectually dominant academic field which, in the view of the CSE team, used its authority to suppress the perspectives of dominated classes. The establishment of *Actes* was, therefore, an attempt to enact a retaliation to the kind of arbitrary cognitive control exercised pedagogically that Bourdieu and Passeron had analysed in *La reproduction*.

It is a constant feature of Bourdieu's work that scholarship and research practice advanced in tandem and that there was a continuous cross-reference and cross-fertilization between the two modes of activity. In 1964, Éditions de Minuit had established a series under his direction entitled 'Le sens commun'.[12] Initially, the series provided Bourdieu with an opportunity for the publication of his own books but, by the end of the decade, it was carrying relatively inaccessible foreign texts to which he had referred or was referring in his own writing.[13] As such, the series began to provide the means by which the French intellectual field could engage with his arguments by accessing some of his sources. In some cases, publications in the series enabled Bourdieu to represent classic texts which were susceptible to revision in accordance with his thinking.[14] Although Bourdieu was, therefore, disseminating his own texts and indirectly constructing a referential field of scholarship through the medium of an established publishing house with which he felt a socio-political affinity, the inauguration in 1975 of the *Actes* was a move of more direct field construction. The intention was that the medium and the message of the journal would be mutually reinforcing.

In the second half of the 1970s, the *Actes* published findings both from projects which had commenced in the early 1960s and from those which had commenced in 1972. In all cases, the researches and their published representations were now clearly informed by Bourdieu's realization that social scientific observation and the social behaviour which it observes are both forms of action which similarly operate by internalizing the structures within which they occur. This realization shaped the dual emphases of the new publications. They objectively analysed strategic practices within objective social reality but they also began to establish the grounds for understanding the analyses themselves as elements of the ongoing strategies of the observers. The important shift had occurred in two articles of the early 1970s which both reinforced the theory of practice theoretically outlined in *Esquisse*. 'Reproduction culturelle et reproduction sociale' [cultural reproduction and social reproduction] was a presentation that Bourdieu gave to a conference of the British Sociological Association in Durham, England, in April 1970, which was first published in 1971 (Bourdieu, 1971d; 1973b). It began by implicitly acknowledging the limitations of *La reproduction* (Bourdieu and Passeron, 1970; 1977) which, in outlining a theory of the system of education, had tended to isolate that system and to explore the internal processes of pedagogical transmission. In accordance with the argument advanced in 'Condition de classe et position de classe', Bourdieu was intent, rather, on exploring the nature of the educational system as a specific sub-system within the social system. 'Systèmes d'enseignement et systèmes de pensée' [systems of education and systems of thought] (Bourdieu, 1967) had, following Panofsky, tended to privilege the cultural transmission of the schooling system as the determinant of intellectual structures. Bourdieu was now disposed to treat the education system as one 'field' among others. It possessed its own rules and structures but these needed to be understood in relation to the whole social system. To use the terminology outlined by Bourdieu in 'Sur le pouvoir symbolique' [on symbolic power], a paper given at Harvard in 1973 and published in 1977 (Bourdieu, 1977c) to further clarify the meaning of the three forms of theoretical knowledge, pedagogical research operates in terms of the 'structured structure' of education whereas the proper sociology of education requires an analysis of the 'structuring structure' of education, problematizing or historicizing its character. He was insistent that he was talking about the need to understand the relations between *structures*. This would be the prologue to understanding how individuals act in relation to structures, but it was crucial for him to convey that commencing with analysis of the situations and behaviour of individuals without reference to the intrinsic structural constraints was liable to ensure that this inadequate sociology of education would reinforce the socio-political status quo. Bourdieu spells out this point immediately. He makes a plea for a 'science of the reproduction of structures'. This phrase defines the orientation of Bourdieu's work in the 1970s and he defines his meaning carefully. This science is to be understood 'as a system of objective relations which impart their relational properties to individuals whom they pre-exist and survive' (Bourdieu, 1971d, 45; 1973b, 71). In relation to the analysis of education as one field of cultural reproduction, Bourdieu clarifies that the science which he proposes 'has nothing in common with the analytical recording of relations existing within a given population' (Bourdieu, 1971d, 45; 1973b, 71), such as the relations between the academic success of children and the social position of their family. Such apparent fidelity to social reality in fact, in Bourdieu's view, makes an abstraction of the pedagogic process and ignores what that process is effecting within the social structure. It colludes in a view of the function of the education system which assumes what needs to be examined. He regards such 'realism' as a form of 'substantialist atomism' for which has to be substituted a form of relationalism, that is to say that we have to analyse how systems or fields relate to each other or compete with each other in determining the positions of individuals within society rather than starting with analysis of the behaviour of those individuals. 'Reproduction culturelle et reproduction sociale' reasserted the argument of 'La comparabilité des systèmes d'enseignement' that educational systems can only be usefully compared if they are understood systemically within the total social systems of different states. It offered a clarification of *La reproduction* in that it emphasized that the book provided an analysis of the process of transmission within an educational system. It showed the process of transmission in operation within one system, in terms of 'pedagogic authority' and 'pedagogic work', but it did not adequately suggest that the important social issue was the relative authority of that system in relation to other systems in society which reproduce themselves and their social groups by comparable procedures. To place this point alongside the argument advanced in *Esquisse*, Bourdieu was insisting that the important process to be understood is the one by which individuals in their practice internalize the structures by which they are constrained. The new emphasis emerging at the time of the publication of *Esquisse* was one in which Bourdieu began to analyse the ways in which constrained individuals are able to move between the constraints of competitive fields. Their practice remained constrained but Bourdieu was becoming primarily interested in the significance of the strategic deployment of fields in position-taking rather than in the process of initiation internal to fields. The interest shifted from a concentration on habitus as a process by which all structures are internalized to a concentration on the competition in society between the different fields within which habituses are constituted.

At this same period, Bourdieu restated his general theoretical approach by particular reference to Weber's sociology of religion. 'Une interprétation de la théorie de la religion selon Max Weber' [an interpretation of the theory of religion according to Max Weber] (Bourdieu, 1971b) was followed by 'Genèse et structure du champ religieux' [genesis and structure of the religious field] (Bourdieu, 1971c). In the first article, Bourdieu claims that Weber developed an interactionist theory 'in the sense in which we speak today of *symbolic interactionism*' (Bourdieu, 1971b, 5; 1987a, 121). For Bourdieu, Weber's 'ideal-typical' explanation of social relations superimposed 'definitions that are universal in scope' (Bourdieu, 1971b, 4; 1987a, 119) in denial of the motivations of the actors themselves, while his latent interactionism, including his emphasis of personal 'charisma', neglected the extent to which actors act within fields possessing specifically regulated practices. Bourdieu has sympathy with Schutz's critique of Weber's interpretative sociology but, equally, accepts Gurwitsch's critique of Schutz's concentration on the inter-personal, 'natural attitude' behaviour of actors which does not admit their dependence on pre-existing Gestaltist, structural constraints.[15] Bourdieu comments that symbolic interactionism, substantially derived from the work of Schutz, 'reduces relations between positions to the level of "inter-subjective" or "interpersonal" relations between the agents occupying these positions' (Bourdieu, 1971b, 5–6; 1987a, 121). 'Une interprétation de la théorie de la religion selon Max Weber' outlines a theory of the religious field which is equivalent to the analysis of the educational field offered in *La reproduction*.

'Genèse et structure du champ religieux' pursues the new emphasis by offering a complementary examination of the structure of the religious field itself in relation to other fields and the social totality. The article is devoted to an exploration of the means by which the religious field imposes itself on the socio-political field by concealing its own socio-political origins and by naturalizing its world-view 'as the natural-supernatural structure of the cosmos' (Bourdieu, 1971c, 300; 1991d, 5). Bourdieu discusses 'strictly religious interest' which, he argues, involves 'transmuting the *ethos* as a system of implicit schemes of action and appreciation into *ethics* as a systematized and rationalized ensemble of explicit norms' and which, in doing so, is 'predisposed to assume an *ideological function, a practical and political function of absolutization of the relative and legitimation of the arbitrary*' (Bourdieu, 1971c, 310; 1991d, 14). Bourdieu discusses 'political power and religious power', commenting that 'the church contributes to the maintenance of political order, that is, to the symbolic reinforcement of the divisions of this order, in and by fulfilling its proper function, which is to contribute to the maintenance of the symbolic order' (Bourdieu, 1971c, 328; 1991d, 31).

The combined effect of the two articles on Weber's theory of religion was that Bourdieu clarified his theoretical basis for analysing the functioning of the religious field both in its internal self-reproduction and in its structural relationship with other fields within the social system. The implication of this combined interest and the insistence that structural differentiation is constructed strategically was that Bourdieu was led to consider the mechanisms by which different fields might acquire socio-political domination. These theoretical discussions, related to anthropological interpretations of religion, coincided with a series of empirical investigations which sought to articulate the characteristics of different fields in French society and to explore the process by which power and influence transfer between fields. At first, this series of investigations acquiesced in privileging analysis of consecrated fields, but, with the establishment of *Actes*, Bourdieu explicitly acknowledged that this concentration on dominant fields reinforced their domination and should be counter-balanced by a willingness to analyse dominated cultural forms (see Bourdieu, 1975a).

The 'field' projects

The chronology of Bourdieu's 'field' analyses is complicated because the publications of one decade often deploy data assembled in an earlier period, but I am nevertheless arguing that the 'field' framework of interpretation began to be imposed in the early 1970s in new projects as well as on material preserved from earlier investigations (which had not been conducted in terms of this framework). 'Les stratégies de reconversion. Les classes sociales et le système d'enseignement' [strategies of reconversion. Social classes and the system of education] (Bourdieu, Boltanski and de Saint Martin, 1973) was the first article to draw on the emerging findings from a project on 'Le patronat' [company directors] which began in 1972. The findings from this project were published in 1978 as 'Le patronat' (Bourdieu and de Saint Martin, 1978), where it is presented as a contribution to the analysis of 'the field of economic power'

(Bourdieu and de Saint Martin, 1978, 9). The article indicates that the project had been an extension of an enquiry which had been undertaken in the CSE in 1966–67 on the grandes écoles and, subsequently, Bourdieu incorporated the findings of the project into his book on the grandes écoles published in 1989 as *La noblesse d'état. Grandes écoles et esprit de corps* [The state nobility. Elite schools and corporate spirit] (Bourdieu, 1989a). As this history suggests, 'Le patronat' began as an internal analysis of the place and function of grandes écoles within the French higher education system but, as Bourdieu comments in a footnote to the 1978 article, it became clear that 'it was not possible completely to understand and explain the system of the grandes écoles without a knowledge of the system of positions to which they give access' (Bourdieu and de Saint Martin, 1978, 78). Written at about the same time as *Esquisse*, 'Les stratégies de reconversion' begins to address the question of the relationship between the fields of education and employment, not just in terms of an abstract correlation between fields, but also in terms of the strategic behaviour of social actors deploying 'capital' acquired in one field to secure power within another. As such, the article represents a transition from an abstract, statistically objectivist analysis of 'field' relations to one which explores the nature of the practical actions of individuals constructing their trajectories within the constraints of their perceptions of those structural objectivities. Elsewhere at the time Bourdieu clarified that 'there are *general laws of fields*' such that, for instance, the fields of politics, philosophy and religion have 'functionally invariant laws' and such that, additionally, every study of any specific field contributes to an understanding of the 'universal mechanisms of fields' (Bourdieu, 1984a, 113; 1993c, 72).[16] Fundamentally, every field is the locus of a struggle between those in possession of authority who seek to conserve that authority by maintaining an orthodoxy and those possessing less capital who seek to subvert existing authority by courting heresy or heterodoxy. Nevertheless, both conservers and subversives maintain the structure of the field, which Bourdieu defines as 'a *state* of power relations between the agents or institutions engaged in the struggle' (Bourdieu, 1984, 114; 1993c, 72), that is to say, not a static, substantive state but rather one which is held in existence by continuous conflict. Bourdieu's interest in 'field' theory was twofold. He sought to analyse the internal mechanisms of a range of fields but, given that they are all subfields of the social system, he became increasingly preoccupied with the relations between fields and with the ways in which actors deploy those relations to maximize their positions within the social system. Once again, however, it is important to note that Bourdieu was not at all implying that the strategic investment of capital across fields is the action of free agents. On the contrary, he was intent on demonstrating that the capacity of individuals or groups to manage their field situations is dependent on the amount of capital at their disposal. 'Les stratégies de reconversion' opens with a precise sentence to this effect, the second half of which is missing from the English translation: 'The strategies of reproduction, by which members of capital-owning classes or class fractions tend, consciously or unconsciously, to maintain or improve their position in the structure of class relations by safeguarding or increasing their capital, constitute a system' (Bourdieu, Boltanski and de Saint Martin, 1973, 61; Bourdieu and Boltanski, 1977, 197–8). The omission in the translation is important because it transforms the article into an objectivist account of social reality, whereas Bourdieu was trying to analyse the mechanisms of reconversion at the disposal of participants. The strategic instruments available to them depend on their position on a continuum of knowledge which ranges from, at one extreme, unreflecting, primary, practical knowledge (unconscious strategy) to, at the other extreme, an immanent knowledge of statistical data which tends towards a coincidence with the objective information retrieved post hoc by objectivist analysts.

The methodological problem highlighted here applies similarly to the other products of Bourdieu's 'field' researches. Bourdieu confronted the issue directly at the same time in the last article which he published in the *Revue française de sociologie* entitled 'Avenir de classe et causalité du probable' [class future and causality of the probable] (Bourdieu, 1974). His field researches offered statistical information derived by the researchers from contemporary sources, but Bourdieu always struggled to communicate his conviction that the key issue in understanding the social phenomena under scrutiny was to analyse the consequences of the differential appreciation of this information on the part of the agents themselves, to analyse the degrees to which extrapolated statistical probabilities might differentially condition or cause the actual choices or aspirations of individuals or social groups.

In terms of the chronology of publication of Bourdieu's 'field' researches, the first article appeared in 1971, prior to the publication of *Esquisse*, as 'Champ du pouvoir, champ intellectuel et habitus de classe' [field of power, intellectual field and class habitus] (Bourdieu, 1971a). It was based on seminars which Bourdieu had given in the École Normale Supérieure for the previous three years on the sociology of texts and the sociology of culture for students aiming to specialize in literary studies. It continues the argument commenced in 'Champ intellectuel et projet créateur' in rejecting the post-Romantic tendency to regard art as self-expressive and in presenting the view that the disinclination to subject artistic production to sociological analysis is indicative of the continuing potency of that particular view of art. Bourdieu discusses in detail Sartre's interpretation of Flaubert, arguing that in spite of the apparent historicity of Sartre's account of Flaubert's family background it is predicated on an a-historical view of a transcendental self. Sartre's psychological analyses are 'redundant' (Bourdieu, 1971a, 24).[17] Instead, the artistic productions of the period between 1830 and 1914, including, in particular, those of the 'art for art's sake' movement, have to be seen as the consequence of the internalizations by individuals of their places within the intellectual field and, in turn, its place within the field of power. This article deserves attention because Bourdieu himself treats the 'field of power' as an abstraction. He observes that, 'at least since the Romantic epoque' (Bourdieu, 1971a, 16), writers have constituted 'a *dominated fraction of the dominant class*' (Bourdieu, 1971a, 17). He regards this as the position within the field of power which constitutes their habitus which he defines as the 'system of unconscious dispositions which is the product of the interiorisation of objective structures and which ... tends to the production of practices and, beyond that, of careers objectively adjusted to the objective structures' (Bourdieu, 1971a, 26). At this date, in other words, Bourdieu regards the field of power as a pre-constructed point of reference 'in reality' in terms of which he can distinguish between products of the intellectual sub-field. As the decade progressed, Bourdieu pursued his own logic in analysing this field of power and its class classifications as itself socially constituted, analysing it increasingly in terms of the field of politics.

'Le champ scientifique' [the scientific field] (Bourdieu, 1976a) is not con-fined to consideration of 'science' as a field but also raises the question of the social conditions for the development of rationality in Western civilization. It explores the processes by which domination is secured within the field of science without confronting epistemological questions about the explanatory value of any particular scientific account of reality. Implicitly, therefore, it examines, on the basis of an unstated phenomenological commitment, the way in which scientificity is constituted without embarking on any scrutiny of truth claims. Bourdieu considers the phenomenon of 'pure' science in the same way as he had analysed the emergence of 'art for art's sake'. In conform-ity with the interest expressed in 'Les stratégies de reconversion', Bourdieu uses his discussion of the scientific field to consider further the process of reconversion. In the terms set out in *Esquisse*, 'Le champ scientifique' is an exercise in praxeological analysis, subjecting objectivist science to scrutiny. As Bourdieu concludes:

> The sociology of science is so difficult only because the sociologist has a stake in the game he undertakes to describe (first, the scientificity of sociology and second, the scientificity of the form of sociology which he practices) and because he cannot objectify what is at stake, and the corresponding strategies, unless he takes as his object not simply the strategies of his scientific rivals but the game as such, which governs his own strategies too and is always liable to exert an insidious influence on his sociology. (Bourdieu, 1976a, 104; 1981c, 283)

'Le champ scientifique' was a particular 'field' study which logically entailed an incipient reflexivity, but this was not at the expense of the production of analyses of other fields, all of which were seen to be contributing to a general understanding of the generic operation of fields. These need to be mentioned briefly[18] in order to indicate the scope of Bourdieu's project.

'Anatomie du goût' was based on an enquiry undertaken in 1963 as part of the project from which findings in relation to students and culture and on photography had already been extracted and published respectively in *Les héritiers* and *L'art moyen*. The questionnaire which had been used (and which was re-used in a complementary survey in 1967–68) had been constructed on the assumption that positions within a field of tastes correlated uniformly with social positions. The categories of social position were derived from several surveys produced at the time by INSEE and other government agencies. Writing in 1976, Bourdieu found it necessary to guard against a 'positivist reading' of this schema. The use of classifications provided by the national statistical institute was only a necessary device to 'make sense of a particular collection of distributions, those defining life-styles' (Bourdieu and de Saint Martin, 1976, 13). Bourdieu was recognizing that the publication of material derived from an earlier research enquiry was in danger of reinforcing a static, objectivist view of correlations between class and culture. The article proceeds to discuss 'the hypothesis of the homology' between tastes and class positions and 'class tastes and life-styles', commenting that 'the correspondence which can be observed between the space of social positions and the space of life-styles results from the fact that similar conditions produce substitutable habitus which in their turn generate, according to their specific logic, infinitely diverse practices which are unpredictable in their singular detail but always confined within the limits inherent in the objective conditions of which they are the product and to which they are objectively adapted' (Bourdieu and de Saint Martin, 1976, 18). Bourdieu wants to insist that the perceived homologies are immanently constituted rather than imposed but, nevertheless, the mechanism of immanent constitution adheres to his interpretative formula. The article concludes with a postscript in which Bourdieu defends his use of statistical classifications, arguing that his intention is to present class as a 'synthetic factor', one enabling him not to classify for the sake of classifying but to 'make sense of a *particular* collection of distributions, those characterising life-styles' (Bourdieu and de Saint Martin, 1976, 80).

'Anatomie du goût' is of particular interest for two reasons. First, its publication in 1976 was indicative of the new determination of the *Actes* to subject ordinary social and cultural phenomena to analysis. It was consciously attempting to analyse dominated cultural forms and to publish that analysis in a journal which was itself seeking to present itself without any prior status or capital within a market of journals. Secondly, the article of 1976 was the precursor to one of the books on which Bourdieu's reputation rests – *La distinction. Critique sociale du jugement* [distinction. A social critique of the judgement of taste], published in 1979 (Bourdieu, 1979a; 1986a). In the transition from article to book, the text tended to offer substantive research findings in place of the original representation of research in progress. As such, the seeds were sown for the elevation of the book in its reception to canonical status. This outcome exacerbated the tension which Bourdieu always experienced between the logic of scientific discovery and the rhetoric of its communication, between rigorous science and popular transmission,[19] a tension which was to become acute in the coming decades when his texts began to be translated into other languages, particularly English.

Bourdieu confronts this problem head-on in the opening paragraph of Appendix 1 of *La distinction*, entitled 'Quelques réflexions sur la méthode' [some reflections on the method], but this is only a reproduction, now relegated to a methodological appendix, of the text which had constituted the preliminary section of 'Anatomie du goût', entitled 'les opérations de la recherche' [the research operations]. The sequence of presentation of *La distinction*, therefore, exacerbates its liability to the misrepresentation which Bourdieu had feared in introducing his article, in spite of the fact that he constantly points out that it has to be appreciated that the research perspective is situated within the phenomena which it purports to observe and that the actions of persons, groups or classes are all systemically prescribed rather than the consequences of freely adopted initiatives. In relation to the first point, for instance, Part I tackles the nature of the social critique of the judgement of taste in a way which suggests that there is an in-built partisanship in the way the research was conducted which itself has to be factored in. As Bourdieu puts it:

> It is now clear that the difficulty of the analysis was due to the fact that what the very tools of analysis – educational level and social origin – designate is being fought out in struggles which have the object of analysis – art and the relation to the work of art – as their prize in reality itself. These struggles are fought between those who are identified with the scholastic definition of culture and the scholastic mode of acquisition, and those who defend a 'non-institutional' culture and relation to culture. (Bourdieu, 1979a, 101; 1986a, 92)

Using statistics acquired in the early 1960s, Bourdieu is acknowledging here that the earlier work on education and culture of that time requires reinterpretation in the same way as *Esquisse* argued for a revision of the perspective adopted in 'La maison kabyle ou le monde renversé'. The objectivism of the earlier work has now to be analysed and incorporated into an account which, as a consequence, has the capacity to situate its own perspective within a total system of perspectives. At the same time, in relation to the second point, Part II is devoted to discussion of 'The Economy of Practices', where Bourdieu insists that the objectivism exposed in Part I can be rectified by accepting that 'culture' is analysed anthropologically rather than in the value-laden, prejudged terms of 'high' culture:

> the dispositions which govern choices between the goods of legitimate culture cannot be fully understood unless they are reintegrated into the system of dispositions, unless 'culture', in the restricted, normative sense of ordinary usage, is

reinserted into 'culture' in the broad, anthropological sense and the elaborated taste for the most refined objects is brought back into relation with the elementary taste for the flavours of food. (Bourdieu, 1979a, 109; 1986a, 99)

As always, Bourdieu emphasizes that the analysis of practices does not invite any relinquishing of understanding of the structural framework within which they are actualized. 'Distinction' is inherent in the objective structure of the system and it dictates the ways in which individuals define and position themselves by means of the habitus which accommodates their dispositions to their constraints. 'Aspiration' and 'pretension' as attitudinal dispositions, for instance, are defined through position-taking within structures. These terms have meanings which are assigned nominally in contexts. They are not the consequences of real, individual psychological characteristics, nor are they isolable outside of their contexts as universal.

La distinction is a hugely complex book and its argument is often advanced allusively or analogically through digressions and inserts, but the main point to make is that, paradoxically, Bourdieu celebrates practice while interpreting that practice within a conceptual framework which assumes that it is always constrained by its insertion within structural determinants, however 'soft' or subject to modifications (themselves circumscribed systemically). In establishing this model of social reality, Bourdieu's own practice was objectivist. Within the text he suggested the methodological necessity of reflexivity, but the book primarily conveys a view of the social world as an iron cage not susceptible to any unprescribed change, any changes other than those inherent in the functioning of the system qua system. Bourdieu asserts that his characterization of social space is an abstraction. The unresolved question, however, is what, in his own terms, might be the status of this abstraction. In 'The Habitus and the Space of Life-styles' (chapter 3 of *La distinction*) Bourdieu spells out his view on this, commenting that the fact that the book is able to present social space diagrammatically 'indicates that it is an abstract representation, deliberately constructed, like a map, to give a bird's-eye view, a point of view on the whole set of points from which ordinary agents (including the sociologist and his reader, in their ordinary behaviour) see the social world' (Bourdieu, 1979a, 189; 1986a, 169).

Bourdieu had referred in *Esquisse/Outline* to the way in which '"culture" is sometimes described as a *map*', commenting that this is the 'analogy which occurs to an outsider who has to find his way around in a foreign landscape and who compensates for his lack of practical mastery, the prerogative of the native, by the use of a model of all possible routes' (Bourdieu, 1972a, 159; 1977d, 2). There Bourdieu quoted from Poincaré[20] to prefer the corporeal cartography, denigrating the perspective of 'the "knowing subject"', as assumed in the idealist tradition. In *La distinction* Bourdieu sought to disown any suggestion of transcendentalism, any stance which might seem to equate with that of the detached 'knowing subject' of idealism, by asserting that 'the most crucial thing to note is that the question of this space is raised within the space itself – that the agents have points of view on this objective space which depend on their position within it and in which their will to transform or conserve it is often expressed' (Bourdieu, 1979a, 189; 1986a, 169), and by proceeding to launch into a critique of the practice of sociologists who, 'as if carried away by their quest for greater objectivity', classify their research objects and forget 'that the "objects" they classify produce not only objectively classifiable' practices but also classifying operations that are no less objective and are themselves classifiable (Bourdieu, 1979a, 189–90; 1986a, 169). Nevertheless, the analysis in *La distinction* seems to depend on the adoption of a stance which offers an overview of social practices and sociological interpretations without recognizing that this stance is only a more sophisticated form of objectivism and one which is as susceptible to analysis as much as the sociological objectivism which Bourdieu criticizes.

It is significant, therefore, that contemporaneously Bourdieu investigated the character of 'le sens pratique' [practical sense] in more detail, perhaps consciously complementing or counteracting the intellectualist excesses of *La distinction*. There is a sense in which Bourdieu advanced his position contrapuntally, sometimes erring towards the 'intellectualist' orientation of Gurwitsch and, at other times, erring towards the corporealism of the early Merleau-Ponty. The article entitled 'Le sens pratique' was published in the first number of 1976 of *Actes*, in February, before 'Anatomie du goût', which appeared in October in the fifth number. The book, also entitled *Le sens pratique*, was published in February 1980. Bourdieu notes in the article that it 'prolongs the analysis of the specific logic of practice' (Bourdieu, 1976b, 44, fn. 1) that he had presented in *Esquisse*. As a publication, 'Le sens pratique' falls between *Esquisse* and the revised text published in English as *Outline* and, therefore, is the first positive presentation of the post-structuralist position implicit in *Esquisse*. The discussion is a prolongation of the presentation in *Esquisse* because Bourdieu attempts to define *practice* as distinct from the first mode of *theoretical* knowledge which he had earlier described as the unreflecting primary experience of the world. He first reiterates his criticism of objectivism which 'constitutes the social world as a spectacle offered to an observer who takes "a point of view" on the action' (Bourdieu, 1976b, 43), but he implies that this attitude, which 'reduces all interactions to symbolic exchanges', is only relatively inappropriate. This point of view is the one 'which one takes in relation to elevated positions in the social structure where the social world is given as a representation ... and where practices can only appear as "executions"' (Bourdieu, 1976b, 43). Bourdieu argues that it is possible to give up the 'sovereign point of view' by situating oneself within 'real activity as such', that is, 'in the practical relation to the world, that quasi-corporeal aim which does not presuppose any representation either of the body or the world, and even less of their relationship, that active presence in the world by which the world imposes its presence, with its emergencies, its things to do or say, its things done to be said and said to be done [ses choses à faire ou à dire, ses choses faites pour être dites et dites pour être faites[21]], which directly govern gestures or words without them ever being displayed as a spectacle' (Bourdieu, 1976b, 43). Bourdieu insists that it is possible to 'admit that practice always implies a cognitive operation [opération de connaissance]' other than the execution of prescribed rules without making it into 'a purely intellectual construction' (Bourdieu, 1976b, 43). 'Practical knowledge is a practical operation of construction' which puts systems of classification into action which then structure practice. Without being overtly formulated, the schemes of perception and action which are imbibed in this way are 'produced by the practice of successive generations' and Bourdieu concludes with the summary statement that 'Practical taxonomies, instruments of knowledge and communication which are the condition for the establishment of sense and of consensus on sense [sens et du consensus sur le sens], only exercise their *structuring* effect in as much as they are themselves *structured*' (Bourdieu, 1976b, 43).

The form of this argument is not new. Bourdieu is describing the operation of the habitus. Juxtaposed with *La distinction*, however, what emerges is that Bourdieu seems to distinguish between the nature of the operation of the habitus within different kinds of social formation and acquiesces in the application of an analytical methodology on a scale from intellectualist to practical corresponding with a scale of social formation from 'inferior' or 'natural' to 'elevated' or 'cultured'. In the context of the culmination of his work on education and culture in mainland France, Bourdieu was prepared to celebrate 'vulgar taste' in opposition to the 'aristocracy of culture' but he did so by maintaining that ordinary people project their life-chances and tastes by internalizing, with different degrees of competence depending on their social position, the probabilities for themselves in terms of their class probabilities as identified objectively in statistical data, consciously or unconsciously available to them. By contrast, 'Le sens pratique' signals that, in the context of anthropological research and in relation to the anthropologically defined objects of that research, a methodology is required which recognizes that the habitus operates inter-generationally and semi-cognitively.

'Le sens pratique' has a section in which Bourdieu elaborates on 'the properties of practical logic' in which he starts by emphasizing that 'a logic must be recognized in practice which is not that of logic to avoid asking of it more logic than it can give' (Bourdieu, 1976b, 53). Much of the article is devoted to analysis of behavioural patterns imposed by natural phenomena, offering in particular a series of diagrammatic schemas indicating the correlations between the seasonal 'agricultural year' and the 'mythic year' and, relatedly, of the 'culinary cycle', the 'cycle of female work' and the 'diurnal rhythms' in winter and summer. The article is mainly designed to expose the intellectualist fallacy of interpreting myth and ritual as symbolic systems detached from their regulatory functions in everyday life, but Bourdieu targets more than just anthropological science. 'The ignorance of the truth of practice as learned ignorance [docte ignorance]', Bourdieu observes, is 'at the origin of occidental philosophy' (Bourdieu, 1976b, 85). Importantly, Bourdieu concludes by arguing that 'the fascination for some philosophers' with the texts of the Pre-Socratic philosophers is indicative of a sophisticated appropriation of practical sense by intellectualism. Bourdieu specifically mentions Heidegger who, he argues, appeared to deploy etymology to retrieve originary linguistic meanings but in fact was engaged in appropriating them within a literate discourse, situating within that discourse 'the principle of relations confusedly felt in the order of sense [sens]' (Bourdieu, 1976b, 86), deploying, in other words, the 'same words' for ideological purposes in the present rather than restoring them to their intrinsic practicality.

Summary

Bourdieu argued in *Esquisse* that there are three modes of theoretical knowledge, the third of which involves subjecting to sociological analysis the stance adopted by the second (objective science) in interpreting the first (primary experience). He also argued that individuals possess inherited dispositions to act (habitus) which they modify in relation to the structures, both social and intellectual, which impinge on them. These structures historically acquire autonomous existence, but the fact that they can be analysed within their own terms as 'structured structures' or 'fields' does not alter the fact that they are socially constructed structures whose autonomy can be challenged by recognizing their origins in the 'structuring structures' of the life-world from which they are derived. Bourdieu proceeded to manage a series of projects analysing 'fields'. These were of different kinds. Some provided statistical data, supported sometimes by prosopographical[22] information or interview transcripts, about the persons holding positions within fields ('Le patronat', 'La sainte famille', *Homo Academicus*), while others expatiated on the distinctive nature of the field in question ('La force du droit, 'Le champ littéraire', 'Le champ économique'). In particular, the process involved identifying cultural fields, other than those associated with established institutions, which Bourdieu defined as markets of symbolic goods, and these were analysed in 'Anatomie du goût' and *La distinction*. Often the research for these projects was started back in the 1960s and the presentations were revised in line with current thinking at the times of publication. However, it is possible to suggest that gradually Bourdieu released his model from the straitjacket which it had inherited from structuralism. Whereas initially Bourdieu used his accumulation of statistical data as a kind of neutral objectivism enabling him to analyse the ways in which individuals are differently able to project futures for themselves in relation to the avail-ability to them of such data about the class or group to which they belong, he gradually paid less attention to what was, in effect, a surrogate interpreta-tive objectivism, and more attention to the strategies adopted by individuals without apparent constraint. His difficulty was that, against Sartre (and tacitly pro-Merleau-Ponty), he wanted to continue to insist that no individuals possess absolute freedom of choice.

Notes

1 See Rancière, 2007 [1983], 239–88. For my defence of Bourdieu against this charge in terms which anticipate the argument of this book, see Robbins, 2015c.
2 In English in the French text and explicitly attributed to Virginia Woolf.
3 Chapter 2 of Lévy-Bruhl (1922) is entitled 'La loi de participation'.
4 Bourdieu makes this explicit in fn. 8 of the French text: Bourdieu, 1972a, 245.
5 I am suggesting that *Le sens pratique*, the article and the book (Bourdieu, 1976b and 1980a) attends to the question of practice as such, and that gradually Bourdieu's objectivist accounts of aspects of French social life evolved into a praxeological analysis of academicism in *Homo Academicus* (Bourdieu, 1984b) and thereafter into reflexive auto-analysis.
6 Reference to Saussure was constant in Bourdieu's early work. I cannot pursue this strand in Bourdieu's thinking in this book. I made some relevant comments in Robbins, 2000, and I discussed *Ce Que Parler Veut Dire* in some detail in Robbins, 2013.
7 Bourdieu cites Leibniz, 'Second éclaircissement du système de la communication des substances' (1696) [second elucidation of the system of communication of sub-stances], in *Œuvres philosophiques*, ed. P. Janet, vol. II, Paris, de Ladrange, 1866, 548.
8 See chapters 2 and 4 for the indebtedness of Gurwitsch and Merleau-Ponty to the work of, in particular, Goldstein. Bourdieu does not cite Gelb and Goldstein directly.
9 This time Bourdieu quotes from Schutz, from 'Husserl's Importance for the Social Sciences'. This article was first published in van Breda and Taminiaux, eds, 1959, but Bourdieu quotes from its publication in Schutz, ed. Natanson, 1962, 145.
10 Bourdieu in fn. 60 (Bourdieu, 1972a, 254), cites Merleau-Ponty, 1949, 131–5. This is a later edition of Merleau-Ponty, 1942. Bourdieu had already recognized in fn. 24 (Bourdieu, 1972a, 246) that Merleau-Ponty's book was congenial in that it exposed the errors of both intellectualism and empiricism.
11 In fact, Bourdieu became Director of a breakaway group from the CSE, entitled the Centre de Sociologie de l'éducation et de la culture (CSEC) [Centre for the Sociology of Education and Culture] in 1968. The title of CSE was restored in 1980 when Bourdieu was appointed Professor at the Collège de France. I refer to the work of the Centre throughout as the work of CSE.
12 The 'Le sens commun' series still continues. Bourdieu ceased to be the Director in 1992 when he transferred his allegiance to Éditions du Seuil (see Lescourret, 2008, 254).
13 The complete list is available at: www.leseditionsdeminuit.fr/collection-Le_sens_commun-49–1–1–0–1.html. This is offered alphabetically by author. It is informa-tive to make a chronological correlation between the texts published in the series and developments in Bourdieu's own work.

14 I am thinking particularly of the editions of the work of Mauss and Durkheim, both edited by Victor Karady (who was a member of the CSE): Mauss, ed. Karady, 3 vols., 1968, 1969, 1969, and Durkheim, ed. Karady, 3 vols., 1975.

15 Bourdieu does not make any reference here to either Schutz or Gurwitsch. I make the point to clarify the relation of the discussion to the exposition in Part I of this book.

16 These quotes are from a paper, entitled 'Quelques propriétés des champs' [some properties of fields] which Bourdieu gave in November 1976 at the École Normale Supérieure to a group of philologists and historians of literature. The paper was first published in Bourdieu, 1980b (2nd edition, 1984a).

17 For a more detailed account of Bourdieu and Sartre on Flaubert see Robbins, 2000, 67–79.

18 'La représentation politique. Éléments pour une théorie du champ politique' [political representation. Elements for a theory of the political field] 1981a will be considered in chapter 9.

19 This tension is also apparent in *Questions de sociologie* [Sociology in Question] (Bourdieu, 1980b; 1993c), where Bourdieu assembled earlier articles or talks and in each case provided references to publications in which he had made his argument more rigorously.

20 Henri Poincaré (1854–1912), mathematician and philosopher of science. Bourdieu does not give the reference for the quotation, but it is Poincaré, 1908, 80.

21 Note how this language anticipates Bourdieu's choice of title for the publication of a selection of his articles in 1987 entitled *Choses dites* [things spoken] (Bourdieu, 1987b), unhappily translated as *In Other Words* (Bourdieu, 1990c) as if Bourdieu were offering paraphrases rather than performances.

22 See Bourdieu, 1984b, 59; 1988a, 39.

8

The 1980s

Introduction

At the end of the last chapter I argued that, by the end of the 1970s, there was an obvious tension in Bourdieu's work, epitomized in *Le sens pratique* (Bourdieu, 1980a) on the one hand and *La distinction* (Bourdieu, 1979a) on the other. This was not an absolute tension but one which Bourdieu's system of thought enabled him to accommodate relativistically. In disciplinary terms, the tension equated with one between the explanatory parameters of anthropology versus those of sociology. More importantly, the tension correlated with changes in Bourdieu's personal trajectory. The analyses of 'Le sens pratique', largely replicated in *Le sens pratique*, offered interpretations of social practices based on observations in traditional peasant society in Algeria which, for Bourdieu, seemed to be corroborated by his experiences in his youth in his native Béarn. They were attempts to represent indigenous social self-understandings uncontaminated by the predispositions embodied in the traditions of occidental learned discourses. In an implicitly phenomenological manner, Bourdieu tried to 'bracket' the disciplinary discourse which he had acquired with a view to doing full justice to the alternative mode of social organization for which he felt affinity from his own indigenous, familial experience in rural, provincial France in the 1930s. In the same way that he believed that Marxist explanations of social reality are not universal but only possess varying validity relative to the situations of individuals or classes on a condition/position spectrum such that those holding high cultural capital are able to render themselves symbolically unsusceptible to the determinist economic explanation more legitimately applicable to the socially and culturally deprived, so Bourdieu was inclined to reconcile his practical and objectivist analyses by applying them to different target groups. His objectivist thought about education and culture was informed by his immersion in Western Enlightenment philosophy, particularly that of Leibniz, Kant and Cassirer. Partly through the work of these antecedents and through his familiarity with the arguments of the Scholastics about theology and empirical science, as well as through his knowledge of the Pre-Socratics and of Plato and Aristotle, Bourdieu developed a philosophical position which was formally intellectualist even while it was substantively sceptical about Western rationality (about itself).

The question at around 1980 (which was latent in the 1970s) was whether or how he could continue to ride these two horses. The 'field' projects undertaken within the CSE during the 1970s were attempts to characterize the objective structures of the French establishment and to present them as objectifications which owed their particularities to the ways in which dominant and dominated individuals and classes reproduced or modified their internalizations of pre-existing structures. Bourdieu was determined that these analyses should not be intellectualist and should not endorse the status quo but, equally, he was determined to reject the subjectivist libertarianism of Sartrean existentialism. Attachment to the objective status of statistical data (even though he meticulously tried critically to draw attention to its partisan provenance) enabled him to work with an objectivism which offered a functional and anti-humanist mediation between the structural interpretations imposed by intellectualist objectivists and the supposed immanently constrained constructivism of social agents. The effect of this device was to reinforce objectivism even though self-criticism was integral to it. Bourdieu needed to resolve whether his work would recommend a revival of 'practical sense' as a normative, ethical commitment or whether it would be understood to be providing exemplifications of a general model of self-critical, objectivist analysis to be absorbed into academic sociological tradition. In pertinent personal terms, he needed to resolve whether the intellectualist orientation which was a function of his educational formation could accommodate adherence to the practical values of his upbringing; whether he could pursue his intellectual career without becoming a 'transfuge'.

Texts

'La production de l'idéologie dominante', 1976

Monique de Saint Martin has recently recalled that, in the late 1960s, Bourdieu was approached by three American researchers to ask whether the CSE would participate in an international project they were proposing, an International Study of Opinion Makers (see Ducourant, 2014). The participation of CSE did not materialize but Bourdieu was interested in the topic. Indications of this interest are apparent in the work which he undertook with Boltanski leading to the publication of 'La production de l'idéologie dominante' (Bourdieu and Boltanski, 1976). The purpose of the project was to analyse the linguistic basis of the acquisition of power in the 1960s by a socially and intellectually connected group, how 'the economic and political thought which acquired ideological supremacy in the 1960s through institutions such as ENA[1], Sciences Po[2] or the Plan[3] had its roots in the new mood which developed after 1930' (Bourdieu and Boltanski, 1976, 32). Bourdieu analyses the mutually supportive intellectual and social movements between the wars, developing a dictionary of the use of terminology which almost subliminally moulded a conservative ideology. He considers the way in which the Sciences Po became complicit in legitimating as political science an ideological development which he calls 'reconverted conservatism' by which he suggests that it was a 'strategy of reconversion' whereby the politically dominant exploited the educational system to maintain their power, just as, contemporaneously, he was arguing, did 'le patronat'. The article was clearly a denunciation of the powers of persuasion deployed by those people, then holding political position, whom Bourdieu regarded as the enemy, but in launching this attack he was also reflecting, first, on the means to be adopted to counter the dominant ideology and, secondly and relatedly, on the implications of deploying the intellectual authority of university institutions in advancing a social philosophy. In the first respect, the article had a bearing on the thinking within CSE about the way in which *Actes* was attempting simultaneously to advance a form of analysis which recognized endemic social confrontations between dominant and dominated factions and, as a journal, itself to constitute a vehicle for the mobilization of a social movement, underpinned by a systematically inculcated collective consciousness. Bourdieu recognized that the historical situation analysed in 'La production de l'idéologie dominante' and his own situation both provided verification of the theory he had outlined earlier in 'Champ intellectuel et projet créateur' that every discourse is the product, differently realized, of a transaction between an expressive intention and the exigencies of the field within which it is offered. As a result of his recent analysis of strategies of reconversion, however, Bourdieu was now particularly interested in the way in which intentions expressed within one field can be suppressed or distorted by conversion to another field context. In 'La production de l'idéologie dominante' Bourdieu made reference (Bourdieu and Boltanski, 1976, 57) to the article which he had published the year before in which he had directly examined the way in which Heidegger had reconverted everyday language into philosophical discourse and, in doing so, had perverted the language of practical sense, deploying philosophical authority to reconvert the language of practice into ontology.

'*L'ontologie politique de Martin Heidegger*', 1975

Bourdieu had used Heidegger's notion of 'Handwerk'[4] to support his own account of practical sense and he had, therefore, some sympathy for Heidegger's anti-humanist ontology, but 'L'ontologie politique de Martin Heidegger' (Bourdieu, 1975e) is of interest because it enabled him to examine an objective correlative of his own dilemma, that of finding a medium to celebrate practice which would not distort it in transmission. The 1975 article on Heidegger was published in a number of *Actes* devoted to 'la critique du discours lettré' [the critique of learned language]. Bourdieu's article began in the following way: 'Learned jargons, official languages which specialists produce and reproduce by a systematic manipulation of ordinary language, are, like all discourse, the product of a compromise between an *expressive interest* and a *censure* consti-tuted by the very structure of the field in which the discourse is produced and circulates' (Bourdieu, 1975e, 109). This introduces the dominant theme of the article[5] which reinforces with respect to the discourse of philosophy the position which Bourdieu had adopted in relation to intellectual production in general in 'Champ intellectuel et projet créateur'.

The analysis of the work of Heidegger was, for Bourdieu, a case-study, in particular historical geo-political circumstances, of the general risks and dangers involved in transposing everyday language into philosophical discourse and, in particular, of the way in which this transposition legitimates an artificial repre-sentation of popular perspectives. The choice of the consideration of the work of Heidegger in its Weimar/Nazi contexts is significant. On the one hand, Bourdieu was attracted by the original philosophical content of Heidegger's *Sein und Zeit* [Being and Time], his ontological orientation,[6] but, on the other hand, he regarded its subsequent intellectualist appropriation of the language of practice as a salutary caution in his own situation.[7] Bourdieu tried to resolve this dilemma by emphasizing the point made by Heidegger himself, in his *Letter on Humanism*, that there had been a turning (Kehre) in his thinking somewhere in the 1930s (Heidegger, ed. Krell, 1977, 208). Bourdieu chooses to interpret this change of standpoint as a change from what he calls Heidegger I to Hei-degger II. Bourdieu analyses in detail some of the linguistic devices employed by Heidegger, arguing that 'it is by insertion in the system of philosophical language that the *denial* [*dénégation*] of primary meaning occurs'[8] (Bourdieu, 1975e, 112). Bourdieu describes this as 'false rupture' [fausse coupure], empha-sizing that, in his view, this is a completely different kind of break from those epistemological ruptures proposed, following Bachelard, in both *Le métier de sociologue* and *Esquisse*. Bourdieu insists that the transformation of language to suit the purposes of a consecrated discourse is not simply a linguistic transgres-sion. The philosophical formulation exists 'to mask *the primitive experiences of the social world*' (Bourdieu, 1975e, 112). Bourdieu attacks 'university aristocratism' apparent in 'philosophical distinction', arguing that they are mutually support-ive in effecting a '*break* which separates the authentically ontological meaning [sens] of ordinary and vulgar sense [sens]' (Bourdieu, 1975e, 113).

Two passages in the article suggest that Bourdieu was aware of the rele-vance of his consideration of the work of Heidegger to the tensions involved in his own attempt to advocate the values of practice within an academic context.

The last section of the article is entitled 'L'habitus de classe et le "métier" du philosophe' [class habitus and the philosopher's 'trade'].[9] Discussing Heidegger's attachment to peasant values, Bourdieu comments: 'And we should doubtless see in his exalted encounter [expérience exaltée] with an idealized peasant world rather a displaced and sublimated expression of his ambivalence towards the intellectual world, than an actual cause [le fondement] of this experience' (Bourdieu, 1991a, 51; 1988b, 62; 1975d, 152). Bourdieu was himself wrestling with his own uncertainty about his attitude towards the values of the peasants of the Kabyle and of his native Béarn in relation to the conceptual censure operated by the cosmopolitan values of the intellectual world within which he had become situated in Paris. Bourdieu was determined that his attachment to indigenous values should not be corrupted by elevated intellectual discourses in the way in which he thought Heidegger's thought had been.

Towards the end of the 1975 article, Bourdieu reflected on some of the influences which had corrupted Heidegger's thought.[10] Bourdieu wrote: 'Self-interpretation, which is the riposte of the author to those interpretations and interpreters which at once objectify and legitimize the author, by telling him what he is and thereby authorizing him to be what they say he is, leads Heidegger II to convert into a method the *schemata* of Heidegger I's stylistic and heuristic *practice*' (Bourdieu, 1991a, 101; 1988b, 115; 1975d, 155). It is no accident that Bourdieu wrote this of Heidegger at the time when his own work was beginning to become available in foreign-language translations, when, by analogy with fashion designers, he was conscious that he was in danger of losing grip on the practical meaning of his work as it was becoming absorbed and routinized in various fields of reception. More importantly, Bourdieu was becoming aware that, intrinsically in his own work and its reception, what he sought to offer as practice was in danger of becoming a schematized or routinized analytical formula. A sense emerges in the late 1970s that, in an attempt to retain his personal intentions and convictions, Bourdieu began to emphasize his personal trajectory rather more than the trajectory of the class formation which he had tried to represent and mobilize in CSE.

'Les trois états du capital culturel', 1979

In 1979, Bourdieu published a short piece in *Actes* entitled 'Les trois états du capital culturel' [the three states of cultural capital].[11] It was an abstract statement defining different meanings of the term which had developed functionally in his earlier work as he had tried to make sense of findings from research projects. In a footnote he recognizes that he is talking about 'concepts in themselves' rather than in relation to contexts where they might function, but he defends himself by claiming that his article is 'theoretical' in the ordinary sense of the word and not at all a contribution to a theoreticist literature (Bourdieu, 1979b, 3). This abstract discussion of concepts does, however, contribute theoretically to an understanding of the way in which Bourdieu sought, in terms which he had himself advanced, to understand the point at which he had arrived in his career. Bourdieu provides a framework for understanding the transition from Bourdieu I to Bourdieu II, from a Bourdieu who presented himself as an apologist for everyday practice to a Bourdieu who recognized that these apologies were in danger of gaining currency in fields of learned discourse which might neutralize them.

Bourdieu begins 'Les trois états du capital culturel' with a brief recapitulation of the origin of his use of the term. It had 'imposed itself' as 'an indispensable hypothesis' (Bourdieu, 1979b, 3) to account for the inequality in the performance of students from different social classes by reference to the notion of 'scholarly success'. When formulated in the 1960s, it had countered the contemporary inclinations either to attribute lack of success to lack of natural aptitude or to measure performance only as the consequence of economic investment. Specifically, Bourdieu reminds readers that the concept of 'cultural capital' was proposed in opposition to the theory of 'human capital' developed by Gary Becker (Becker, 1964). Bourdieu's representation in 'Reproduction culturelle et reproduction sociale' (1971d) of the task required of the sociology of education was that it should produce a 'science of the reproduction of structures' and not focus sociologically or social psychologically on the influence of family background. Bourdieu had argued that his hypothesis had tried to substitute an immanent economism, the calculations of individuals in relation to their perceptions of their objective future possibilities, for the imposed economism offered by Becker. Bourdieu's explorations of 'fields' in the 1970s were all predicated on a rejection of any sociological injection of subjectivist humanism into the analyses. Bourdieu's retrospection in 'Les trois états du capital culturel' seems to modify his original anti-humanism. The shift in emphasis apparent in Bourdieu's representation of the distinction between his position and that of Becker is confirmed by the way in which he proceeds to announce his current understanding that there are three kinds of 'cultural capital'. He writes:

> Cultural capital can exist in three forms: *in an incorporated state*, that is to say in the form of durable dispositions of the organism; *in an objectivated state*, in the form of cultural goods, paintings, books, dictionaries, instruments, machines, which are sketches or realisations of theories or of critiques of these theories, of problematics, etc.; and finally *in an institutionalised state*, a form of objectivation which must be kept separate because, as we see with *scholarly titles*, it confers completely original properties on the cultural capital which it is deemed to guarantee. (Bourdieu, 1979b, 3)

These three states need to be examined more closely. Bourdieu devotes about a page of explication to each. The incorporated state [l'état incorporé] is the fundamental form from which the majority of the properties of cultural capital derive. All cultural capital is '*bound to the body* and *presumes incorporation*'. The accumulation of cultural capital involves a process of inculcation and assimilation which takes time and personal investment, that is to say that it is a process of acquisition and not an innate state. Nevertheless, it is important that Bourdieu now emphasizes that the accumulation of cultural capital is a personal task, that 'the work of acquisition is the work of the "subject" on himself (we talk about "cultivating ourselves")' (Bourdieu, 1979b, 4). Cultural capital in its incorporated state is entirely personal: 'it perishes and dies with its bearer (with their biological capacities, memory etc.)' (Bourdieu, 1979b, 4). It is bound in many ways to people in 'their biological singularity' but its invisibility defies any attempt to define what is attributable to 'nature' or to 'nurture'. Bourdieu still emphasizes that the amount of economic capital possessed by a family determines the amount of time any individual might have to undertake the task of self-realization and that, therefore, the aspirations of individuals are constrained by their places within 'the system of strategies of reproduction' (Bourdieu, 1979b, 4), but his elaboration of the incorporated state emphasizes more than ever before the individuality of every incorporated state and its transient temporality. It is in this respect that it is most sharply differentiated from the objectivated state [l'état objective].

Objectivated cultural capital has some characteristics which derive from its relation to incorporated cultural capital but it has 'material props' [supports matériels] such as writings or paintings which mean that it is transmissible materially, operating as an autonomous market or field. Bourdieu spells this out clearly:

> Although it is the product of historical action, cultural capital in the objectivated state presents itself with all the appearance of an autonomous and coherent universe with its own laws, transcending individual wills, and which, as the example of language shows, remaining irreducible, on these grounds, to what each agent or even collection of agents can appropriate (that is to say to incorporated cultural capital). (Bourdieu, 1979b, 5)

As a reminder, Bourdieu adds to this statement the caveat that objectivated cultural capital can only exist and survive if it is activated. As such, it remains dormant or in constant potentiality until it is deployed by individuals, and the nature of the deployment at any given historical moment is dependent on the incorporated capital possessed by those effecting the activation. The paintings of Manet, for instance, are material props, the values of which are established in an apparently autonomous market of symbolic goods (see Bourdieu, 1971g), but that exchange value is ultimately dependent on the capacity of agents to recognize the validity of the market and of valuations within it.

Objectivated cultural capital, therefore, has an autonomy which is relative because it is *constituted* but not permanent because it is always susceptible to deconstitution. Just as incorporated cultural capital is the product of the work of self-production over time on the part of individuals over their life span, objectivated cultural capital is the product of social history. Institutionalized cultural capital has a different status altogether. Bourdieu takes the example of a 'scholarly title' [titre scolaire] such as, perhaps, the possession of a doctorate. Drawing tacitly on the distinction he had made in 'Le titre et le poste' (Bourdieu and Boltanski, 1975a) between 'titles' and 'positions', Bourdieu suggests that a title is a 'certificate of cultural competence which confers on its holder a conventional value which is constant and juridically guaranteed in respect of culture' (Bourdieu, 1979b, 5). Unlike the material props of objectivated cultural capital, titles exemplify the permanence of institutionalized cultural capital. Bourdieu states that the 'social alchemy ... *institutes* cultural capital by collective magic' and he supports his argument by referring to Merleau-Ponty's contention that 'the living *institute* their dead by mourning rites'. This is a significant reference. Merleau-Ponty had argued that 'to constitute ... is almost the opposite of to institute: the instituted has meaning without me, the constituted only has meaning for me and for the me of this moment. Constitution [means] continuous institution, i.e. never completed' (Merleau-Ponty, ed. Lefort, 2015, 48).[12] Merleau-Ponty had sought in the notion of 'institution' 'a remedy for the difficulties of the philosophy of consciousness' (Merleau-Ponty, ed. Lefort, 2015, 161) not unlike that proposed by Gurwitsch by announcing his theory of the 'field of consciousness'. Bourdieu comments that the institution of titles by 'collective belief' is the same process as the institution of any social group 'as a reality at the same time constant (that is to say transcendent to individuals), homogeneous, and differentiated, by the arbitrary institution, misrecognized as such, of a juridical frontier' (Bourdieu, 1979b, 5–6).

'Les trois états du capital culturel' appears to signal a significant shift of emphasis in Bourdieu's thinking. There appears to be a shift from an emphasis on the nominal to one on the real. Whereas in earlier work 'habitus' had functioned as a logical device for representing all 'subjective' internalizations of objective structures, it now appears to be actualized as a property which is indistinguishable from the incorporated state of cultural capital. The analytical practice of transposing the statistical data accumulated by researchers to constitute the mental framework constraining the behaviour of agents seems to be reduced and to be replaced by a willingness to understand the acquisition of symbolic goods (objectivated cultural capital) as dependent on the differential degree of incorporated capital held by actors. A disposition to circumscribe observed behaviour logically seems to have been replaced by one which is more sociological, or, rather, the logical disposition is consigned to the new category of institutionalized cultural capital, releasing understanding of objectivated capital as the locus of conflict between competing fields, all competitively constructed socially.

'Les trois états du capital culturel' can be seen to be an attempt to locate 'le sens pratique' as incorporated cultural capital within a schema of developmental cultural capitals which accommodates, in objectivated cultural capital, the phenomena analysed in *La distinction*. This is not simply a methodological development in Bourdieu's thinking. It coincides with the development in his career trajectory. The formulation of the schema of 'three states' enabled Bourdieu personally to try to accommodate his 'practical' convictions to the market of symbolic goods within which his own publications were becoming 'material props' both for himself and his readers. The objectified personal dimension of the presentation of the 'three states' became tangible when, very early in the 1980s, Bourdieu was a successful candidate for the Chair of Sociology at the Collège de France. His personal, incorporated cultural capital, deriving from his family background, had steadily become objectivated as he had intellectually absorbed the canon of Western European philosophy and had become self-objectivated in the production of his own texts within the intellectual field. However, he had left the École Normale Supérieure without a doctoral qualification and had spent most of the 1960s and 1970s trying to legitimate a research group which, paradoxically, was devoted to a subversion of existing legitimating authority. The vacancy in the Chair of Sociology at the Collège de France was announced in March 1981, and, on 1 February 1982, a decree of the President of the Republic (Mitterrand) named Bourdieu as the new incumbent, as from October 1981. As Professor in probably the most prestigious intellectual institution in France, Bourdieu had ascended his own scale of capitals, now thoroughly equipped with institutionalized capital, able to mobilize its permanently recognized status without any longer needing to establish himself or the research group under his direction.

There are several important consequences of this institutionalization which need to be explored. First, the Collège de France is not a teaching institution within the state system of higher education and its professors are primarily required to give courses of lectures accessible to the general public. Bourdieu was under professional obligation to behave magisterially as a public intellectual.[13] The appointment also affected the working relationships which he had developed since the beginning of the 1960s. It involved a removal from his base with the CSE and EHESS to offices in the Collège. Bourdieu took with him a small secretariat and, gradually, a group formed around him at the Collège to manage his own activities and, importantly, to organize the production of the *Actes*. Bourdieu maintained close relations with the CSE but, in 1985, Monique de Saint Martin became, with him, its co-Director. The change of location and of administrative responsibilities meant that Bourdieu's activities became more involved in the capitalization of his institutionalized capital than in the advancement of a counter-cultural collective movement, or, rather, it meant that he became more involved in personally publicizing his research than in practising it collaboratively with colleagues in the CSE.[14] Coincident with this change of milieu, there were consequences for the substance of Bourdieu's work as well as its form. Secondly, therefore, it seems as if Bourdieu began to release information about his life,[15] making public details, some of which would finally be accumulated selectively in his *Esquisse pour une auto-analyse* [sketch for a self-analysis] (Bourdieu, 2004b; 2007). He began to historicize his personal transition from incorporated to institutionalized cultural capital.[16] Thirdly, he seems to have become aware that he had acquired institutionalized capital specifically within the French state while his texts suddenly began to achieve objectivated status for others within an international intellectual field mainly as a result of the commencement, in 1984, of the English translations promoted by Polity Press in the UK. Whereas Bourdieu had earlier been interested in the process of conversion or reconversion of capital between competing fields within one state system, he revived his other earlier interest in the cross-cultural comparability of education systems of different political states to adapt his field studies such that they would become a model for understanding international competition – intellectual, social and political. Within a global framework, the institutionalized capital at the national level lost its transcendental permanence and became only a material prop in competition with others in an objectivated international culture. Bourdieu began to compete for international authority, to endeavour to ensure that his specific incorporated capital would still inform the version of his meaning which began to circulate internationally. Connected with this widening of the arena of field study, Bourdieu also began to be especially interested in the field of politics.

Le sens pratique, *1980*

Le sens pratique (Bourdieu, 1980a) was a revised representation of much of the content of 'Le sens pratique' (Bourdieu, 1976b), and, before that, of *Esquisse* (1972a), but it contained an important new preface and a new section/chapter entitled 'La croyance et le corps' [belief and the body]. The new chapter emphasizes the corporeality of practical sense whereas the article had been more concerned to identify the homologies between human behaviour and cycles in the natural world: 'Practical sense is a quasi-bodily involvement in the world which presupposes no representation either of the body or of the world, still less of their relationship' (Bourdieu, 1980a, 111; 1990d, 66). Bourdieu indicates specifically that *Le sens pratique* revisits both *Esquisse* and *La distinction* and, therefore, it is clear that he is attempting his own methodological break with the insights of his own earlier texts whereby he can more objectively reintegrate the texts which had oppositionally seemed to celebrate culture in its incorporated state on the one hand and in its objectivated state on the other. To carry out this attempt, Bourdieu provides in the preface a short history of the development of the conceptual framework which he had deployed in his Algerian fieldwork or in the transmission of his findings. He describes the influence of Lévi-Strauss within the French intellectual field at the end of the 1950s and the challenge of trying to produce a scientific analysis of Algerian society when the country was struggling for its independence. The normal preoccupations of traditional anthropological research with myth and ritual typified by orientalist work caused him initially to want to exclude ritual from his consideration and he turned to the work of statisticians to enable him to counteract the '"gratuitous" nature of purely ethnographic inquiry' (Bourdieu, 1980a, 11; 1990d, 3). Bourdieu's account is offered partly in the first person: 'I would never have come to study ritual traditions' and 'I took those photographs in the course of field-work' (Bourdieu, 1980a, 10; 1990d, 3) but it partly offers an account of the objective intellectual field in which he was operating and some reflections on three particular anthropological inter-pretations which influenced his thinking. He outlines the way in which his theory developed tentatively from a rough outline of a system towards a more refined understanding as a consequence of meticulous tabulation of published data. That refined understanding arose from a dissatisfaction with the attempt to construct diagrammatic representations of phenomena such as those of the agrarian calendar. Bourdieu became aware that the synoptic diagrams, derived methodologically from the procedures of structuralist anthropology, were pred-icated on assumptions of coherent rationality in observed practices whereas those practices themselves obeyed a different logic. Writing in 1980, therefore, Bourdieu makes explicit that his historical movement beyond structuralism was based on his realization of the *formal* inappropriateness of statistical modelling as much as on the sense that Western modes of thinking were being imposed on traditional cultural behaviour.

Modelling imposes a pattern on practices as much as structuralist interpreta-tion imposes meaning. The impossibility of producing one explanatory system covering behaviour and natural phenomena results 'from the fact that, without needing to establish the homology explicitly, but led by a practical understand-ing of the overall equivalence between a moment in the agrarian cycle and a moment of weaving ... agents apply the same schemes of perception and action to either situation' (Bourdieu, 1980a, 28; 1990d, 13). The main text of *Le sens pratique* proceeds to illustrate this point by reference to traditional Algerian society, but Bourdieu deliberately does not allow his position to be relegated by restricting its applicability only to anthropological discourse. He insists that the practical sense in operation in traditional society is 'no more and no less mysterious' (Bourdieu, 1980a, 28; 1990d, 13) than the sense enabling schemes of appreciation in taste, that is, making *distinctions* of taste. The opposition which is generally set up between the 'primitive' and the 'civilized', for Bourdieu, is only a particular case 'of the relationship between knowing and doing, interpreting and using, symbolic mastery and practical mastery' (Bourdieu, 1980a, 37; 1990d, 19). In each case, the former is not equipped to understand the latter. Bourdieu's book is only partially an attempted vindication of practical sense as observed in others. It also challenges the means adopted to make that vindication. Bourdieu poses the stark choice confronting the instituted academic: 'What is at stake is how far the objectifier is willing to be caught up in his work of objectification. The objectivist relation to the object is a way of keeping one's distance, a refusal to take oneself as an object, to be caught up in the object' (Bourdieu, 1980a, 37; 1990d, 19). Published before Bourdieu's appointment to the Chair at the Collège de France, this formulation articulates the tension which persisted for Bourdieu for the rest of his life. In the next twenty years he became increasingly inclined to present his diverse activities as mysterious manifestations of his incorporated state of cultural capital expressed in disparate objectivated or institutionalized forms. It is only possible to give an outline of this diversity of action in the 1980s which was evident as, nevertheless, Bourdieu concertedly presented his intellectual perspective as the particular form of practice which had evolved from his family background.

'Fieldwork in Philosophy'

The incipient tendency to become more auto-analytical that is evident in the preface to *Le sens pratique* developed further during the 1980s. In April 1985, Bourdieu was interviewed in Paris by Axel Honneth,[17] Hermann Kocyba and Bernd Schwibs. The interviewers elicited responses about his formation as a student at the École Normale Supérieure and about the development of his concepts, such as habitus. Importantly, the interview enabled Bourdieu to reflect on the nature and purpose of his account of his trajectory and also to comment on the effect of his recent institutionalization. In the first respect, he warns against retrospective distortions of the development of his thinking. The point, rather, of retrospection is to attempt to capture thought in its practical progression rather than to assume an a-temporal vantage point: 'I took the decision to tell the story of the path I have followed from this point of view, that is, by trying to supply the elements of a sociological analysis of the development of my work. If I have done so, it is also because this sort of self-analysis is part, I think, of the preconditions of the way my thinking has developed' (Bourdieu, 1987b, 37; 1990c, 25). Bourdieu suggests, in other words, that his release of material about his intellectual development is designed to enable him to present that development as essentially practical more than autonomously intellectual. It is part of a process by which he seeks to move away from an intellectual vindication of 'practice' towards a representation of his intellectuality as fundamentally practical.

'Fieldwork in Philosophy' offers a mixture of auto-analysis and, concomitantly, of conceptual reflexivity. Also in 1985, Bourdieu published 'The Genesis of the Concepts of Habitus and of Field'[18] (Bourdieu, 1985) in which he clarifies that the deployment of concepts mirrors self-development in that both are cumulative. Equally, each advances in reciprocal relation to the other. Categorically denying that his use of habitus was the introduction of a gratuitous 'neologism', Bourdieu insists instead that 'the treatment which consists of taking up, in order to reactivate it, a word belonging to a tradition, is inspired by the conviction that the work of conceptualizing can itself be cumulative' (Bourdieu, 1985, 14–15). Constantly, therefore, in moving towards reflexivity, Bourdieu was attempting to perform a balancing act. He recognized the power provided by institutional position but, at the same time, he struggled to ensure that his instituted cultural capital was perceived to be a logical extension from his incorporated state. The 'transcendent' force of the institutional state does not have a priori, ideal existence but is always the culmination of a process of construction. Bourdieu sought to exploit his own institutional capital precisely so as to demonstrate that his capacity to effect this exploitation and the authority of the effecting institution were both constructions made by individuals whose dispositions were also socially constituted rather than absolutely 'subjective'.

'La sainte famille. L'épiscopat français dans le champ du pouvoir', 1982, and Homo Academicus, 1984

Significantly, Bourdieu tried to illustrate the function of sociology as reflexive objectification by undertaking a 'field' study of the field within which he was operating – the 'academic field'. With Monique de Saint Martin, he also explored related issues in an analysis of French bishops. 'La sainte famille. L'épiscopat français dans le champ du pouvoir' [the holy family: French bishops in the field of power] (Bourdieu and de Saint Martin, 1982) was published in advance of *Homo Academicus* (Bourdieu, 1984b) and, taken together, the texts examined issues related to institutional authority and intellectual control in ways which informed Bourdieu's self-reflection. 'La sainte famille' was based on analysis of data primarily about the French episcopacy in 1972 in such a way as to generate comparison with the contemporary 'field' projects which were looking at the situations of business directors, professors and civil servants (Bourdieu and de Saint Martin, 1982, 7, fn. 1). The research extracted details of the social backgrounds, career trajectories and positions of ecclesiastical power of all the bishops in mainland France at that date, and the information gathered was complemented by in-depth interviews with fifteen bishops.[19] Bourdieu concludes with the contention that the analysis of the Church and the bishops 'equates, *mutatis mutandis*, with that of the State and State officials [hommes d'État]' (Bourdieu and de Saint Martin, 1982, 51) in that 'the Church (or the State) is truly that constituted body which exists in biological bodies and those biological bodies which exist in a constituted body' (Bourdieu and de Saint Martin, 1982, 51). Church and state are both institutions which, initially constituted, acquire an authority which has the capacity to constitute its adherents. The article is devoted to an analysis of the processes by which mind-controlling power is acquired and, in doing so, it exposes 'the roots of the fatal illusion that it is enough to seize the "gear levers" [leviers de commande] of the State Apparatus to change profoundly things and dispositions by which what we call the State is realised' (Bourdieu and de Saint Martin, 1982, 51). Bourdieu is not offering a secular critique of theological or ecclesiastical claims but is providing what he thinks is a generalizable case-study of power acquisition and imposition. One key component of the internal struggle within the Church which, nevertheless, the institution contrives to conceal in order to present itself homogeneously to the population is an opposition in recruitment between 'oblates' and inheritors. Bourdieu suggests that there is an opposition between the 'oblates' who, 'devoted to the Church since early infancy, invest totally in an institution to which they owe everything' (Bourdieu and de Saint Martin, 1982, 5) and the inheritors who, ordained relatively late in life, are already in possession of cultural capital acquired in other fields. The analysis of 'La sainte famille' is both self-reflective and also transferable. Bourdieu had already analysed the opportunities accorded to inheritors within the educational system in *Les héritiers* but his consideration of academic authority in *Homo Academicus* became more overtly auto-analytical. Within the French educational system he saw himself as an 'oblate', but part of the purpose of *Homo Academicus* was to analyse how other academics, as inheritors, reconverted cultural capital acquired outside the educational system to acquire power within it.

Much of the information for *Homo Academicus* was gathered at about 1968 when Bourdieu undertook an analysis of Parisian higher education. *Homo Academicus* revisited the early data in the light of the work of the 1970s, particularly the project on 'Le patronat' and the work on taste. The text of *Homo Academicus* superimposed the theoretical model articulated in 'Les stratégies de reconversion' (1973) on the primary data. The text was no longer a sociology of ideas but instead a sociology of the deployment of ideas in the position-taking of social agents – situating agents and ideas in the competing fields of power and economics. It was also a text which complemented statistical information with 'prosopographical' evidence. To achieve this, Bourdieu 'collected for each professor of the sample all of the information provided from written sources and from various enquiries already made for other purposes, usually administrative' (Bourdieu, 1984b, 59; 1988a, 39). Just as for 'La sainte famille', a range of sources of information were used to convey the sense that the statistically constrained behaviour of individuals is clarified by reference to their personal expressions of strategic intention or to the ways in which these are publicly represented. The methodology adopted here shows a disposition to understand persons as agents (although not 'free') rather than automata operating within a prescribed structural framework. As such, it reflects Bourdieu's inclination to place himself auto-analytically within his objectified model, which he does by situating himself (near to Foucault) in a diagram of the space of the arts and social science faculties provided at the end of an appendix in which he describes his use of correspondence analysis (Bourdieu, 1984b, 289; 1988a, 276).

Homo Academicus was not simply a text which now recognized the relationship between agency and structure within Parisian higher education (including Bourdieu's reflexive recognition of his own position and agency). It was much more. It was an instrument of Bourdieu's agency. With his appointment to the Chair of Sociology at the Collège de France, Bourdieu had become acutely aware that he was about to be associated with an institution which already possessed recognized 'institutional capital' and that this association could affect him ambivalently. On the one hand the institution strengthened his formal authority and his capacity to hold influential power but, on the other hand, the institution might symbolize an educational tradition which would seem to be at odds with the view of education that Bourdieu had developed in his empirical research of the 1960s. The issue which Bourdieu explored in an article of 1975 on fashion – 'Le couturier et sa griffe' (Bourdieu and Delsaut, 1975) – was relevant to his own intellectual situation. He wanted to be able to harness the power of the institution without forfeiting the convictions which arose from his personal habitus. From the mid-1980s, Bourdieu was conscious of the same tension in the relationship between his international label (griffe) and the specific social conditions which generated his research, his conceptual framework and his published findings. 'The Genesis of the Concepts of Habitus and Field' (1985) was an attempt to apply reflexively to his own concepts the approach which he had adopted in earlier articles such as 'Genèse et structure du champ religieux' (1971c). If, as Bourdieu argued in *Le métier de sociologue* (Bourdieu, Chamboredon and Passeron, 1968), concepts are tools, elements of an *ars inveniendi*, what happens to them when they become severed from the conditions in which they were instrumentally effective? What is the appropriate reaction to their being used pragmatically for different purposes in different contexts?

Bourdieu had written in 1984 a short preface to the English-language edition of *La distinction* (Bourdieu, 1986a, xi–xiv). This was followed by a much more detailed preface, in 1988, to the English edition of *Homo Academicus* (Bourdieu, 1988a). These both suggest that Bourdieu was aware of the need to situate his own thinking within an international intellectual field, to use his French institutional authority to safeguard the reception of his objectivated texts. Whereas his field researches had been inclined to assess the characteristics of various fields within the French state, his new institutional authority enabled him to consider the French state itself as a field within the international context. The interest in the field of politics as the tangible mani-festation of the field of power now became actualized internationally as he began to fight to defend his incorporated cultural capital as intrinsically 'French' in opposition to rival intellectual positions which correlated with different state systems. Bourdieu was now in a position to actualize the principles of com-parability which he had advanced earlier in his contribution to *Éducation, développement et démocratie* (Bourdieu and Passeron, 1967a).

Written primarily for American readers, the English preface to *Distinction* anticipates the expected response that the book will be considered 'very French'. Bourdieu acknowledges that it is French 'by virtue of its empirical object' (Bourdieu, 1986a, xi), as a result of its 'form' which, as in the case of all cultural products, 'depends on the laws of the market in which it is offered' (Bourdieu, 1986a, xiii), and, finally, to the extent that it exemplifies a specific characteristic of the French intellectual field in its 'immoderate ambition of giving a scientific answer to the old questions of Kant's critique of judgement' (Bourdieu, 1986a, xiii). Bourdieu assumes that in submitting the book to an American market he is offering it to an intellectual field which is alien in its disengagement from the traditions of Western European civilization. Never-theless, he insists that 'it is possible to enter into the singularity of an object without renouncing the ambition of drawing out universal propositions' (Bourdieu, 1986a, xi). In short, Bourdieu regards the publication of the transla-tion as potentially instrumental in enabling a socio-intellectual encounter rather than as a means to impose one social reality on another which, in his terms, would be a process of symbolic violence. The comparative method 'which treats its object as a "particular case of the possible"' is a means by which it is possible 'to avoid unjustifiably universalizing the particular case' (Bourdieu, 1986a, xi). Bourdieu's intention is relativist in order to release international invariants but this relativism is only achievable if a priori universalist models are discarded.

The preface to the English edition of *Homo Academicus* makes similar points but the discussion is inevitably more complex because Bourdieu is introducing cross-culturally a book whose empirical object is not only French but, more particularly, an institution (the academic field) which aspires to embody uni-versal values. As such, Bourdieu has to invite an extrinsic response to a book which fundamentally is about the intrinsic conditions of its own production. The book subjects the particular conditions of the French construction of academic identity to scrutiny and requests a reading which 'reflects the epis-temological intentions of this book' (Bourdieu, 1988a, xv) which requires that foreign readers should 'use it to lay the foundations of a self-analysis, either by concentrating on the invariants of the genus *homo academicus*, or, better still, by educating himself with what he may discover about himself through the objectification ... of one of the positions of *homo academicus gallicus* which is homologous to his own position in his own field' (Bourdieu, 1988a, xv).

In both English prefaces, Bourdieu asks for a reflexive response to be facilitated by his own analyses, an encounter which is pre-emptively circumscribed. Bourdieu embarked in the 1980s on encounters with other cultural contexts but there was always a tension as to whether these were open encounters or whether they were devices for imposing the supposed terms on which encounter might occur. He had indicated the principle to which he sought to adhere in the concluding paragraph of 'Le champ scientifique' in 1976 where he commented that 'the sociology of knowledge or of science is no more than the most irreproachable form of the strategies used to disqualify rivals, until it ceases to take as its object the rivals and their strategies and turns its attention to the *complete system of strategies*, i.e., the field of positions within which they are generated' (Bourdieu, 1976a, 104; 1981c, 283). It was this integrative function which he intended to fulfil in his intellectual encounters. Hence the apparent paradox that he fiercely advanced his own position while believing that he was enabling the emergence of a comprehensive, inter-national synthesis.

American encounters

Bourdieu had already spent a period in residence in the Institute for Advanced Study at Princeton in 1972–73, but it was in the 1980s that his 'voyages of conquest' (Bourdieu and Wacquant, 2014, 9)[20] began. He visited San Diego, Chicago (three times), Madison, New York and Princeton in the period between 1986 and 1989. There were three main effects of this development in Bourdieu's career and these can be illustrated by closer examination of three books which were published in the early 1990s as outcomes from conferences or seminars held in the late 1980s.

Wacquant has described in detail[21] the circumstances which led to the publication, in 1992, of both *An Invitation to Reflexive Sociology* (Bourdieu and Wacquant, 1992a) and *Réponses. Pour une anthropologie réflexive* [responses. For a reflexive anthropology] (Bourdieu and Wacquant, 1992b). I want to focus on the section of the 'Chicago Workshop' entitled 'The Personal is Social' in the English text and 'L'objectivation du sujet objectivant' [the objectification of the objectifying subject] in the French. Referring to a comment made by Bourdieu in his inaugural lecture at the Collège de France to the effect that every social science proposition ought to be applicable to the sociologist himself, Wacquant asks: 'Can we do a Bourdieusian sociology of Bourdieu? Can you explain yourself? If so, why this unwavering reticence to speak about the private person Pierre Bourdieu?' (Bourdieu and Wacquant, 1992a, 202; 1992b, 175). In the conversation which follows, Bourdieu contrives both to explain his reticence and also, for the first time in print, to overcome it. The explanation is in terms of a disinclination to provide material for a reductive relativization of his scientific findings. In respect to himself, he repeats his general, anti-subjectivist position: 'My sociological discourse is separated from my personal experience by my sociological practice, which is itself in part the product of a sociology of my social experience. And I have never ceased taking myself as an object, not in a narcissistic sense but as one representative of a category' (Bourdieu and Wacquant, 1992a, 203; 1992b, 175). Bourdieu applies to himself the distinction made in 'On symbolic power' between structuring and structured structures. He argues that his reticence has not been an attempt to defend 'myself, my identity, my privacy' but, rather, to protect the autonomy of his discourse 'in relation to the singular person I am' [la personne singulière que je suis] (Bourdieu and Wacquant, 1992a, 203; 1992b, 175). Accepting this response, Wacquant nevertheless pushed further to ask whether Bourdieu's sociology was 'an attempt to cope with the "social conversion" entailed by your trajectory and training' (Bourdieu and Wacquant, 1992a, 204; 1992b, 176). Bourdieu is forced to admit that there was a direct influence of his primary experience on his sociological thought and, in doing so, he articulates some consequences of spending his youth in a 'tiny and remote village of Southwestern France' and of his life as a 'boarder in a public school',[22] indicating that he 'could meet the demands of schooling only by renouncing many of my primary experiences and acquisitions' (Bourdieu and Wacquant, 1992a, 204–5; 1992b, 176–7).[23]

Bourdieu is slightly disingenuous in arguing for a rupture between his social experience and his participation in an autonomous field of sociological discourse when it is clear that it is precisely this conceptual separation that derives from his experience. This is suggestive of the dilemma which is apparent in the other two books which emanated from cross-cultural exchanges in the United States at the end of the 1980s. The books were the products of two conferences held within a week of each other at the end of March and early April 1989. The first was the outcome of discussions in the Center for Psychosocial Studies in the University of Chicago which culminated in a conference specifically about Bourdieu's work. The second was the outcome of a conference on 'Social Theory and Emerging Issues in a Changing Society', also held in the University of Chicago, which Bourdieu co-organized and co-presented with James Coleman.[24] The first led to the publication entitled *Bourdieu. Critical Perspectives* (Calhoun, LiPuma and Postone, eds, 1993) for which Bourdieu contributed 'Concluding Remarks', and the second led to the publication entitled *Social Theory for a Changing Society* (Bourdieu and Coleman, 1991) for which Bourdieu contributed an 'Epilogue'. Taken together, these publications, with Bourdieu's contributions, illustrate the problem Bourdieu was encountering in trying simultaneously to encourage the development of an international field of sociology while seeking to ensure that it would be a field which would respect the variety of contributing primary experiences.

In a footnote to his 'Epilogue' in *Social Theory for a Changing Society* Bourdieu states that his interest in the conference was that it brought together social scientists belonging to 'very different, if not antagonistic, theoretical and methodological traditions, who come from different countries and different intellectual traditions, and who sometimes root for opposed political visions of social science' (Bourdieu and Coleman, 1991, 373). He had wanted to open up a space of debate 'so as to demonstrate, experimentally as it were, that the progress of scientific reason in sociology hinges crucially on a transformation of the *social organization of scientific production and communication*' (Bourdieu and Coleman, 1991, 373). Borrowing his terminology from his earlier article on 'the specificity of the scientific field and the social conditions of the progress of reason', Bourdieu is clear that his involvement with the conference was intended as a practical test-case of his view that the possibility of establishing a 'field of world sociology'[25] depends on new mechanisms of conceptual exchange which recognize that intellectual debate has to be predicated on *social* encounter. Coleman's 'Prologue' to the publication sets out the basis of the debate as he sees it. Entitled 'Constructed Social Organization', Coleman's 'Prologue' gives an outline of his conception of the structural change occurring in modern society. He calls this 'a change from primordial and spontaneous social organization to constructed social organization' (Bourdieu and Coleman, 1991, 1) and he proceeds to clarify this distinction. Primordial social organization is characterized, perhaps consciously, in terms of the practical sense underlying traditional society as conceived by Bourdieu. This kind of organization 'is now coming to be supplanted by a differently based structure' (Bourdieu and Coleman, 1991, 2) which he calls 'constructed social organization', the expansion of which, he argues, became the 'preoccupation of Max Weber' who described it as 'the progressive "rationalization" of society' (Bourdieu and Coleman, 1991, 2–3). Coleman embraces this supposed demise of primordial organization. He has a clear view of the changed nature of social organization and, concomitantly, of the function of 'social theory'. In a passage which seems directly to oppose the kind of social theory represented by Bourdieu, Coleman says that 'It should be not merely theory that describes the transition from societies with a minimal division of labor to those with extensive division of labor. It should be theory developed to aid in the construction of social organization' (Bourdieu and Coleman, 1991, 8). Bourdieu's 'Epilogue' does not explicitly rise to the bait. Without directly challenging Coleman's view that 'primordial' social organization has now been superseded, Bourdieu argues instead that in general 'The scientific field is a social microcosm partially autonomous from the necessities of the larger social macrocosm that encompasses it' (Bourdieu and Coleman, 1991, 375) and that it cannot therefore be restricted to becoming an instrument for the realization of its conception of society. He makes the point that social science is a field in the same way as the other fields he had analysed and its characteristic is its tendency to be heteronomous, failing to distinguish between 'social' and 'sociological' issues. The substance of Bourdieu's 'Epilogue' becomes a socio-historical account of the evolution of American sociology, starting after 1945 when 'the ambition to give sociology full respectability by constituting it into a *profession* crystal-lized' (Bourdieu and Coleman, 1991, 378). With a glancing blow at Coleman's notion of 'constructed social organization' (Bourdieu and Coleman, 1991, 382) Bourdieu suggests that the institution of American sociology and its conception of its society have become mutually supportive, leaving American society itself inaccessible to proper sociology. Bourdieu concludes that the conference might introduce the possibility of a field of world sociology which, unlike dominant American sociology, might see its function not as to impose its world-view on the rest of the world but as to facilitate 'a *realpolitik* of reason armed with the rational knowledge of the social mechanisms that operate within the socio-logical field' (Bourdieu and Coleman, 1991, 384). Instead of confronting Cole-man's 'theory', Bourdieu subjects the social conditions of its production to scrutiny, implying that it is a form of special pleading and concluding that it is an inadequate model for realizing the socio-political potential of international social and sociological exchange.

In his 'Concluding Remarks' to *Bourdieu: Critical Perspectives*, he addressed the same disparity of sociological purpose by emphasizing the ways in which his own thought had been distorted within the (mainly) American intellectual field. The conference seems to have assembled (mainly) American scholars who were reputable and friendly towards Bourdieu's work. Published in 1993 by Polity Press in the UK, the book offers the first significant collection of critical essays on Bourdieu's work to that date. The contributors were primarily anthropologists, sociologists or philosophers. One contribution is from Hubert Dreyfus and Paul Rabinow, entitled: 'Can there be a Science of Existential Structure and Social Meaning?' Based on cited references only to four texts by Bourdieu[26] in English translation, the contribution epitomizes what Bourdieu regards as the shortcomings of attempts to relate to his work cross-culturally without the necessary analysis of the differences between the fields of produc-tion and reception of his texts. Once again, Bourdieu does not attempt to counter specific criticisms of his work directly. He implies that they are all offered within the 'structured structures' of various disciplines without coming to terms with the 'structuring structure' of his primary experience, as apparent in his social background and career trajectory. In general terms, Bourdieu's 'Concluding Remarks', sub-titled 'For a Sociogenetic Understanding of Intel-lectual Works', offer the criticism of his critics that, by 'synchronizing' or 'atomizing' his texts, they 'uncover apparent contradictions that would vanish if they replaced each of the theses or hypotheses in question back in the move-ment, or even better, in the progress of my work' (Calhoun, LiPuma and Postone, eds, 1993, 264). Put positively, Bourdieu asks that the '*sociogenetic point of view*' (Calhoun, LiPuma and Postone, eds, 1993, 264) should be adopted in relation to all his works and to all intellectual works. He uses his sympathy with elements of Dreyfus's ontological orientation (redolent of his suppressed sympathy for Heidegger I) because it recognizes that his work breaks with 'the philosophy of action which haunts the unconscious of most sociologists' (Calhoun, LiPuma and Postone, eds, 1993, 273) but he insists that he prefers to talk about an '*historicist ontology*' rather than an ontology. Stimulated by Dreyfus's commentary, Bourdieu therefore articulates the recommendation that all texts, including his own, should be understood historically as manifestations of the socially constrained trajectories of individuals rather than within the artificial rules of institutionalized discourses.

Summary

The publication of 'Les trois états du capital culturel' [the three states of cultural capital] (1979b) and *Le sens pratique* [*The Logic of Practice*] (1980a; 1990d) were key moments of a change of emphasis, coinciding approximately with Bourdieu's appointment to the Chair of Sociology at the Collège de France in 1981. I have argued that Bourdieu took the opportunity, offered by revisiting his fieldwork in Algeria, to affirm the primacy of practical sense as distinct from the three modes of 'theoretical' knowledge outlined in *Esquisse d'une théorie de la pratique* (1972a) and also to affirm that 'incorporated' cultural capital is the originator of subsequently acquired 'objectivated' and 'instituted' cultural capitals. This marked the beginning of Bourdieu's inclination to allow his conceptualizations to be seen as the extended products of his personal primary experience rather than as the consequences of his engagement with the debates within structured academic structures. As his publications were more and more quickly translated into foreign languages and, as texts, were becoming symbolic goods in an international market, Bourdieu became more determined that his meaning should be grounded in his experience and should not become disembodied. I have shown that, during the 1980s, his involvement with colleagues in the United States had the consequence that he became dissatisfied with the international circulation of ideas as it seemed to become predicated on a denial of the relational acquisition of knowledge and to assume an a priori universalism. This dissatisfaction reached an explicit conclusion with Bourdieu's response to several conferences in Chicago at the end of the 1980s and to the consequent publication of his 'Concluding Remarks' in *Bourdieu. Critical Perspectives* (Calhoun, LiPuma and Postone, eds, 1993) in which he advocated that his and all intellectual works should be understood sociogenetically, that is to say, by reference to their structuring structures, rather than in terms of the 'structured structures' of various disciplines.

Notes

1 The École Nationale d'Administration, an élite grande école founded in 1945 to train politicians and civil servants.

2 The Paris Institute of Political Studies, formerly the École libre des sciences politiques, founded in 1872.

3 The Commissariat général du Plan was a French institution which was established in 1946 by de Gaulle, responsible for defining the economic planning of the country, particularly through Five Year Plans.

4 See chapter 7.

5 It was relegated to chapter 4 of the book, entitled: 'Censorship and the Imposition of Form' (Bourdieu, 1988b, 83–100; 1991a, 70–87).

6 Bourdieu would have been in sympathy with Heidegger's critique of Sartre.

7 It is not possible to give here the detailed discussion of Bourdieu's response to Heidegger that the question demands.

8 Note that this correlates with Bourdieu's determination to analyse linguistic expression in terms of *Ce que parler veut dire* [what speaking means] (Bourdieu, 1982b) in *practice* rather than in terms of socio-linguistic theory.

9 This was incorporated into the second chapter of the book, called 'The Philosophical Field and the Space of Possibilities' (Bourdieu, 1988b, 51–65; 1991a, 40–54).

10 The reflections were reproduced in the final chapter of the book, entitled 'Self-interpretation and the Evolution of the System' (Bourdieu, 1988b, 113–19; 1991a, 99–105).

11 This is not to be confused with an article entitled 'Ökonomisches Kapital, kulturelles Kapital, soziales Kapital' (Bourdieu, 1983b) which was translated into German by R. Kreckel. I assume that it was the original French text of this article which was then translated by R. Nice into English as 'The Forms of Capital' (Bourdieu, 1986c). As the German title suggests, Bourdieu's discussion in this later article is not of the relations between incorporated, objectivated and institutionalized capitals but of those between economic, cultural and social capitals. The relationship between the 1979 and 1983 articles deserves close attention, taking into consideration the intermediary 'Le capital social. Notes provisoires' [social capital: provisional notes] (Bourdieu, 1980c).

12 I have not found the specific passage to which Bourdieu refers. The passage I quote comes from the published version of Merleau-Ponty's notes for his course of lectures at the Collège de France in 1954–55 entitled 'L'Institution dans l'histoire personnelle et publique' [the institution in personal and public history]. It seems probable that Bourdieu would have attended these lectures or have known the résumé of the course which was published in the *Annuaire* [annual review] of the Collège de France and then republished by Gallimard in 1966. See Merleau-Ponty, ed. Lefort, 2015, 6 and 41–198.

13 I do not directly pursue this 'magisterial' dimension. Those previously unpublished courses of lectures which Bourdieu gave at the Collège de France during his tenure of the Chair of Sociology are now gradually appearing in print. They deserve separate analysis as indications of one type of communication adopted by Bourdieu quite apart from consideration of their intellectual content. I refer to the courses given between 1981 and 1983 (Bourdieu, ed. Champagne, Duval, Poupeau and Rivière, 2015); those between 1983 and 1986 (Bourdieu, ed. Champagne and Duval, with the collaboration of Poupeau and Rivière, 2016); those between 1989 and 1992 (Bourdieu, ed. Champagne, Lenoir, Poupeau and Rivière, 2012); those of 1992–93 (Bourdieu, ed. Champagne and Duval, 2017) and those between 1998 and 2000 (Bourdieu, ed. Casanova, Champagne, Charle, Poupeau and Rivière, 2013).

14 These comments are based on my observations at the time.

15 In December 1982, Bourdieu wrote a brief obituary of Erving Goffman, praising him for having 'grasped the logic of the work of *representation*; that is to say, the

whole set of strategies with which social subjects strive to construct their *identity*, to shape their social image' (Bourdieu, 1983c, 113; 1982c).

16 Bourdieu began his inaugural lecture, given on 23 April 1982, by declaring: 'As a rite of incorporation [agrégation] and investiture, the inaugural lecture, *inceptio*, is a symbolic enactment of the process of delegation whereby the new master is finally [au terme duquel] authorized to speak with authority, and which establishes [institue] his words as a legitimate discourse' (Bourdieu, 1982a, 7; 1990c, 177). I have inserted some of the French text into the published English translation because the published translation confusingly uses the word 'incorporation' for 'agrégation' [admission] and 'establishes' for 'institue' [institutes], thereby missing that Bourdieu is *not* blurring his distinction between incorporated and institutionalized capitals. Less importantly, I humbly suggest that 'whereby' already covers 'au terme duquel' [in terms of which] which does not need to convey 'finally' at all.

17 Honneth was at that time research assistant to Jürgen Habermas. I have discussed the interview as an encounter between competing intellectual traditions in Robbins, 2016.

18 An abbreviated version of this article was published in French for the first time in Bourdieu, 1992a, 249–59.

19 Precise details of the information gathered are provided at the end of the article: Bourdieu and de Saint Martin, 1982, 52–3.

20 This is Wacquant's phrase in his introduction to the full text of what was originally published as Bourdieu and Wacquant, 1992a and b. I am indebted to this introduction for the detail of Bourdieu's visits to the United States.

21 See Bourdieu and Wacquant, 2014, 14–18.

22 Even this 'reminiscence' is 'objectified' by referring to Flaubert's analogous experience as a boarder and to Goffman's analysis of the effects of 'asylums'.

23 The passages quoted in this paragraph remain the same in Bourdieu and Wacquant, 2014, 260–3.

24 James Coleman (1926–95). He was Professor of Sociology at the University of Chicago from 1973.

25 This is the sub-title of his 'Epilogue'.

26 *Algeria 1960* (Bourdieu, 1979c); *In Other Words* (Bourdieu, 1990c); *Outline of a Theory of Practice* (Bourdieu, 1977d); and 'The Philosophical Establishment' (Bourdieu, 1983a).

9

The 1990s

Introduction

The last chapter argued that Bourdieu's engagement in the 1980s with the North American intellectual field reached a climax in two conferences in 1989. Wacquant records that Bourdieu visited New York in 1994 and Berkeley in 1996 (see Bourdieu and Wacquant, 2014, 10), but the intervention entitled 'Passport to Duke' which was delivered on his behalf at a conference on 'Pierre Bourdieu. Fieldwork in Culture' at Duke University in April 1995, repeats the same dismay at the misrepresentation of his work that he had articulated in the 'Concluding Remarks' to *Bourdieu. Critical Perspectives* (Calhoun, LiPuma and Postone, eds, 1993). It seems reasonable to suppose that he had begun to lose hope that the social construction of an international field of sociology might contribute to an amelioration of international relations and an equalization of life-chances between people living in different cultures. Instead, he seems to have wanted to become involved in direct action within his own country and to offer that activism as a paradigm for people in disadvantaged states. His actions were founded on previous sociological research, but, with a few exceptions, he was no longer himself closely involved in active research. He became more interested in processes of engagement and in actualizing those processes. He consolidated earlier thinking about the field of politics with a view to inserting himself within that field. He reasserted his earlier disquiet about the consecrated status of academic philosophy with a view to exemplifying the need, instead, for the exercise of thought in action. This chapter discusses Bourdieu's 'activism' of the 1990s.

The field of politics

Bourdieu had explicitly turned his attention to the field of politics at about the time he was developing the post-structuralist position first advanced in *Esquisse*. Bourdieu gave a paper entitled 'L'opinion publique n'existe pas' [public opinion does not exist] (Bourdieu, 1971e) at a conference in Arras in January 1971. He argued that opinion polls are instrumental in manufacturing 'public opinion'. The ways in which questions are phrased ensure that 'opinions' are elicited which endorse the predisposition of the pollsters. In this way, pollsters eliminate the practical reason of those who are not initiated into the discourse of politics who are left only with the option of giving 'no responses' which pollsters safely ignore. Opinion polls deploy political discourse to exclude the everyday opinions of the public. In this way, pollsters impose their intellectualist predispositions and perform a function which contributes to the production of the dominant ideology (the process analysed contemporaneously by Bourdieu and Boltanski leading to the publication of Bourdieu and Boltanski, 1976). 'L'opinion publique n'existe pas' was a sociological analysis of the domination of political discourse over primary social experience. Operating as if he were running a detached social observatory, Bourdieu offered an analysis of the process of attitudinal exclusion and also a socio-historical commentary on the contingency of the questions which pollsters chose to ask. Methodologically, Bourdieu deployed sociological analysis to undertake a second epistemological break which would enable him to expose the partisanship of objectivism and to liberate uninitiated primary attitudes. Bourdieu returned to the same kind of argument several times during the 1970s, particularly in 'Les doxosophes' (Bourdieu, 1972b), 'Questions de politique' (Bourdieu, 1977a) and the chapter of *La distinction* devoted to 'Culture and Politics' (Bourdeu, 1979a, 463–541; 1986a, 397–465), where, for the first time, he was prepared to countenance the significance of 'instituted' political parties in mediating between everyday and political discourses. However, it was not until 1981 that Bourdieu outlined a theory of the political field in 'La représentation politique. Éléments pour une théorie du champ politique' [political representation. Elements for a theory of the political field]. Whereas 'Anatomie du goût' (Bourdieu and de Saint Martin, 1976), 'Le patronat' (Bourdieu and de Saint Martin, 1978) and 'La sainte famille' (Bourdieu and de Saint Martin, 1982) had developed theories of, respectively, the fields of taste, business and religion by correlating data with surveys and interviews, 'La représentation politique' makes no attempt to provide specific characterizations of the attitudes or social backgrounds of holders of political position. The 'reality' of the political field, what gives it its identity at any given historical moment, derives from the fact that it is to be understood 'at the same time as a field of forces and as a field of conflicts aiming to transform the balance of power [le rapport de forces]' (Bourdieu, 1981a, 3). In different terminology, Bourdieu contends that the essence of the political field is that it is self-constituting. Unlike in the case of the fields of company directors and bishops, the hierarchy of political power is precisely what is at issue within the political field. In short, whereas Bourdieu examined the fields of company directors and bishops as structured structures, he argued that the political field was quintessentially one which revolved around the contest between electors and elected, 'the relation which electors, as a result of their differential distance from the instruments of political production, hold with their elected' and, also, around the relation which these latter hold with 'their organizations'[1] (Bourdieu, 1981a, 3). Bourdieu chose not to regard the field of politics as autonomous with its own rules by analogy with other fields but, instead, as the actual social locus for the fundamental confrontation between primary and intellectually excluding world-views, between 'practical sense' and objectivist knowledge. The professionalization of politics is, in Bourdieu's view, indicative of the attempt of the dominant to develop self-fulfilling and self-sustaining rules and procedures designed to exclude the dominated from participation.

At precisely the moment when Bourdieu was being appointed to the Chair of Sociology at the Collège de France, being 'instituted', he was reflecting specifically on the relationship between his accumulated intellectual endeavour and his inclination to put his own practical sense into action. The product was 'Décrire et prescrire. Note sur les conditions de possibilité et les limites de l'efficacité politique' [description and prescription. The conditions of possibility and the limits of political effectiveness] (Bourdieu, 1981b; Bourdieu, ed. Thompson, 1991, 127–36). In his concluding paragraph, Bourdieu reflects on the consequences of his earlier science of social mechanisms, notably the mechanisms exposed in the educational context (in *La reproduction*) and in the cultural market (in *La distinction*), fearing that these 'can be put to the service of an opportunistic *laisser-faire* approach' (Bourdieu, 1981b, 73; Bourdieu, ed. Thompson, 1991, 136). Just as Bourdieu's inaugural lecture at the Collège de France in April 1982 showed that he was conscious of the ambivalence of his new position, so, at the end of 'Décrire et prescrire', he additionally presented the positive hope that the findings of his earlier work might be the inspiration of future political effectiveness:

> But this science may just as easily serve as a foundation for a politics oriented towards completely different ends which, breaking just as much with the voluntarism of ignorance or despair as with the laisser-faire approach, would arm itself with the knowledge of these mechanisms in order to try to neutralize them; and which would find, in the knowledge of the probable, not an incitement to fatalistic resignation or irresponsible utopianism, but the foundation for a rejection of the probable based on the scientific mastery of the laws of production governing the eventuality rejected. (Bourdieu, 1981b, 73; Bourdieu, ed. Thompson, 1991, 136)

I argued in the last chapter that Bourdieu was engaged in a struggle in the 1980s in which he sought to defend the integrity of his intellectual work in the context of an international field of sociology which was developing, under the domination of American sociology, in ways which were antipathetic to his ambitions. He was driven to justify his version of sociology as the product of his personal social trajectory, arguing neither for intellectualism nor anti-intellectualism but, rather, for a recognition that his intellectual work should be understood as a progression from his primary experience, one which continuously absorbed the effects of contingent events as well as the independent logic of traditional modes of thought. Rather than renounce the accumulated knowledge which had made him a successful candidate for the Chair of Sociology, Bourdieu wanted to deploy it to 'neutralize' the effects of objectivated and instituted capitals which had become severed from their origins in incorporated capital.

In France in the 1980s, Bourdieu had used his institutional position to try to effect social and political change from the top down. In 1985, he had been largely responsible for the publication of *Propositions pour l'enseignement de l'avenir* [propositions for future education], a report from the professors of the Collège de France which had been commissioned by President Mitterrand. Similarly, Bourdieu co-presided on a commission set up in 1988 by Lionel Jospin as Minister for National Education which led to the publication of *Principes pour une réflexion sur les contenus d'enseignement* [principles for a reflection on the contents of education] (Bourdieu and Gros, 1989) which restated many of the ideas of the Collège de France report. Although these were attempts to exploit his institutional authority in the interest of changing the assumptions of the educational system in accordance with his principles, the mode of operation was not in tune with his disposition. To act in this way was to behave as a member of the 'noblesse d'état' [state nobility], deploying culturally accumulated capital patronizingly to manage the lives of the dominated rather than to promote the legitimate interests of all citizens.

La Noblesse d'état. Grandes Écoles et Esprit de Corps [The State Nobility. Élite Schools in the Field of Power] which Bourdieu published in 1989, the year of the bi-centenary of the French Revolution, was an attempt to analyse the mechanisms by which a new class of 'nobles' had emerged in French society, replacing the 'noblesse de robe' which had governed in pre-revolutionary France by hereditary authority. 'Le patronat' (Bourdieu and de Saint Martin, 1978) had analysed the ways in which the directors of the leading French companies had found it necessary to deploy educational qualifications to legitimate in the modern age the kind of inter-generational succession which had traditionally been the norm, supposedly accepting the transformation from hereditary to meritocratic inheritance. Bourdieu took the opportunity to incorporate the analyses of 'Le patronat' into the argument of the new book which sought to analyse the analogous process by which hereditary political power was clandestinely perpetuated by the exploitation of the spuriously neutral educational system. 'Le patronat' had emphasized the process of 'conversion' by which cultural capital possessed within one 'field' transferred inter-systemically into another. Bourdieu's reappropriation of his earlier research was designed to communicate an amended message. 'Le patronat' had analysed the relations between the fields of business and education, both as 'structured structures', in terms of their intrinsic and a-historical logics. By contrast, *La noblesse d'état* is concerned to situate the relations between fields understood in terms of the socio-historical structuring structures which generated them and continue to reproduce them. This revised emphasis correlated well with Bourdieu's inclination to understand the mechanisms by which he had personally attained 'noblesse'. The analysis was an enactment of the hope expressed at the end of 'Décrire et prescrire' that the exposure of social mechanisms of privilege might contribute to their elimination.

La noblesse d'état, *1989*

The prologue to *La noblesse d'état* boldly announces that the structure of the book reflects Bourdieu's intention to analyse the ways in which social change is the effect of a continuing encounter between 'social and mental structures'. Presentationally these are separated, such that Part I is 'constructivist' and Part III is 'structuralist', but, 'in good logic' (Bourdieu, 1989a, 7), they are inseparable. This is because constructivism cannot be posited on freedom. Distinguishing his position from that of the ethnomethodologists, Bourdieu clarifies that 'doubtless agents construct social reality, doubtless they enter into struggles and transactions aiming to impose their vision, but they always do this from points of view, interests and principles of vision determined by the position which they occupy in the very world which they aim to transform or conserve' (Bourdieu, 1989a, 8).

Bourdieu observes that the consequence of the ongoing reciprocity between social and mental structures is that the book provides numerous examples of the ways in which individuals come to 'possess' their mental internalizations of objective structures. They choose to become 'normaliens', to integrate for life the mental habits derived from their absorption of the ethos of the École Normale Supérieure. Bourdieu argues that this phenomenon requires a double scientific task. Rather than accept these forms of possession as things which 'go without saying because they are in the order of things', research must show that these passions have 'an arbitrary, unjustified, and, if you will, pathological character' (Bourdieu, 1989a, 11). At the same time, however, he insists that these passions, 'based on the *illusio*' (Bourdieu, 1989a, 11) themselves have to be analysed because they, too, are socially constructed pathologies. It is for this reason that Bourdieu comments that it is a fallacy to blame the ideological apparatus of a coercive state for problems which are historically and inter-subjectively constructed and which can be repaired by a process of reflexive scientificity.

Much of the text of *La noblesse d'état* can be read as an exercise in just such reflexive scientificity by which Bourdieu aimed to exorcise the consequences of the process by which he had become instituted. Bourdieu analyses the social characteristics of those who are deemed to have been 'successful' in the national Concours, and also the operation of the 'classes préparatoires' for entry into the École Normale Supérieure. Where we are accustomed to seeing in the educational process 'a rational training enterprise' (Bourdieu, 1989a, 163), Bourdieu contends that we should see a process of consecration which contributes 'to the distribution of powers and privileges and to the legitimation of this distribution' (Bourdieu, 1989a, 164). The education system is therefore complicit in the production of 'the state nobility, endowed with a universally recognized title' (Bourdieu, 1989a, 164). Parts I and II are devoted to the social constructivist processes of elite production in which Bourdieu was a participant. Part III offers an account of the structure of the 'grandes écoles', their relative standing within the system, followed by a history of their reputational changes within the previous thirty years. Part IV explores the relationship between the power acquired within the schooling system and state power, concluding with the historical observation that

> the state nobility, whose power and authority ... are founded ... on scholarly title, is the product of a labour of construction, inseparably practical and symbolic, aiming to institute positions of bureaucratic power relatively independent of already established temporal and spiritual powers (nobility of the sword, clergy, etc.,) and to create a hereditary body of agents skilled in occupying these positions in the name of a competence sanctioned by scholarly institutions especially established with a view to reproducing them. (Bourdieu, 1989a, 540)

The changing nature of the state had generated the complicity of the educational system. The way in which the educational system colluded in permanently defining citizens as separate and qualitatively different persons was, historically, the consequence of the rise of the modern state and the attempt of its perpetrators to substitute criteria of distinction for gradations of inherited privilege in ways which manufactured an alternative self-legitimation and exclusion of the majority.

In Part I, Bourdieu commented in respect of the institution of education that it cannot be properly thought about without 'operating a veritable conversion of the vision of itself that it comes to impose by the logic of its functioning' (Bourdieu, 1989a, 163). *La noblesse d'état* led Bourdieu remorselessly to the same conclusion about the state and to the view that the structures of the state itself were in need of transformation if society were to find ways of recognizing the practical sense of all its participants. It is no surprise, therefore, that the first lecture of his Collège de France course – *Sur l'état* [On the state] – given on 18 January 1990, opened with a discussion of the state as 'an unthinkable object' [Un objet impensable]. 'If it is so easy', he observes, 'to say easy things about this object, that is precisely because we are in a certain sense penetrated by the very thing we have to study' (Bourdieu, ed. Champagne,

Lenoir, Poupeau and Rivière, 2012, 13; 2014, 3). While Bourdieu pursued the logic of this problem in the public lectures which have now been post-humously published, at the same time he began to become involved in direct democracy. This was a major change in his career. He began to explore ways in which his concluding comments in 'Décrire et prescrire' could be actual-ized to resist the mind-controlling effects of the state as currently actualized. Initially this involved him in 'reconnoitring' the potential for change offered by various fields, now exploring them as fields of action for himself rather more than, abstractly, as analysable components of a conceptualized social system.

One exploration entailed the elimination of the 'philosophical field' as a context from which subversive action might be launched. Shortly after his appointment to the Chair of Sociology at the Collège de France, Bourdieu contributed a chapter to an English-language introduction to *Philosophy in France Today* (ed. Montefiore, 1983). Continuing his reflection on the social significance of 'institutions', Bourdieu's chapter was entitled 'The Philosophical Institution'. The fundamental shortcoming of 'philosophy' is, for Bourdieu, that 'If there is a question that philosophy, itself so questioning, manages to exclude, this is the question of its own socially necessary conditions' (Bourdieu, 1983a, 4). Any critique of philosophy which fails to ask this question, including a Marxist, materialist critique, is simply endorsing the autonomy which should be in dispute. What he proposes is 'the most radical form of a critique of theoretical reason' which involves both a proper recognition of 'practice' and a systematic attempt to understand, 'in order to transcend them', 'the limits inherent in all scholarly knowledge' (Bourdieu, 1983a, 5).

In making this last point, Bourdieu specifically referred the reader to his *Le sens pratique*. Just as that text was self-regarding in that Bourdieu related his intellectual development to his social trajectory, so, more precisely, in March 1988 Bourdieu gave a presentation[2] at a conference, mainly attended by phi-losophers, held in the Pompidou Centre, in which he analysed historically his original philosophical aspiration during the 1950s. His intention was to recall his own experience at the time, not 'personally' but as a socially constituted 'type':

> The exercise which I'm about to outline consists in trying to reconstruct the space
> of possibilities as it appeared to the member, which I was, of a particular category
> of adolescents, 'normalien philosophers', who all had in common a collection of
> properties linked to the fact of being situated at the heart and at the summit of
> the scholarly institution, and who could be separated from the rest by secondary
> differences, associated notably with their social trajectory. (Bourdieu, 1989c, 16)

Bourdieu asks himself why and how he was initially on course to become a philosopher. It was a social process: 'You became a "philosopher" because you had been consecrated and you consecrated yourself by making sure of the prestigious identity of the "philosopher"' (Bourdieu, 1989c, 17). Bourdieu offers two revealing reflections. First, he argues that he was subsequently able to objectify the process precisely because he had never been duped by it and, in a footnote, he compares himself in this respect with Paul Nizan, sharing with him the experience of the 'young oblate in anger against the deceitful seductions of the *Alma mater*' (Bourdieu, 1989c, 23, fn. 3). Continuing to situate himself in relation to the philosophical cohort of the École of the 1920s, Bourdieu, secondly, deliberately exonerates Merleau-Ponty. In his main text, Bourdieu discusses the 'death and resurrection of the philosophy without subject' between the 1950s and the 1970s, noting that the existentialists remained submissive to the 'dominant philosophical model' while those who reacted against existentialism in favour of 'subjectless philosophy' nevertheless kept the human sciences at a distance while employing some of their view-points within 'the most traditional philosophical discussion' (Bourdieu, 1989c, 22). Bourdieu asks whether it is possible 'to break with the dominant philosophy of the 1950s without breaking with the hegemonic ambition which was at the heart of its project and which was never so clearly expressed as in its claim to "found" the human sciences' (Bourdieu, 1989c, 22). At this point, Bourdieu inserts a footnote which indicates his respect for Merleau-Ponty's endeavour. Omitting to refer to the inaugural lecture which Merleau-Ponty had given at the Collège de France thirty years before his own (his *Éloge de la philosophie*), Bourdieu contradicts instead those of Merleau-Ponty's disciples who now make him 'the defender of philosophical elevation [hauteur]' (Bourdieu, 1989c, 24, fn. 13). On the contrary, Merleau-Ponty 'had used the instruments supplied by philosophy to confront the problems posed for him by the human sciences, and had asked the human sciences to help him resolve the problems posed for him by philosophy' (Bourdieu, 1989c, 24, fn. 13). Bourdieu states that Merleau-Ponty had 'known how to approach the political and social problems of his time (particularly the situation of "communist" regimes) with a methodological rigour which philosophers usually reserve for objects socially recognized as philosophical' (Bourdieu, 1989c, 24, fn. 13). Bourdieu recognizes that Merleau-Ponty was a special case, not representative of the general tendency of the previous fifty years for philosophers to seek to sustain the discourse as 'foundational'. Bourdieu recognizes that Merleau-Ponty sought to ground intellectual acitivity in inter-subjective experience. Substantively, Bourdieu was in agreement with Merleau-Ponty's inclination not to treat philosophy as a self-grounded discourse and respected the nature of his anti-Sartrean engagement with contemporary politics. Bourdieu makes no reference to Merleau-Ponty's late work or his posthumously published texts, but his representation of his earlier position suggests that Bourdieu regarded this as a model which he should enact fully by resisting Merleau-Ponty's late acquiescence in institutional philosophy.

In corroboration, the late 1980s was the period in which Bourdieu published in French (Bourdieu, 1987b, 13–46; 1990c, 3–33) the text of his earlier interview of 1985 with Axel Honneth and his colleagues, calling it 'Fieldwork in Philosophy', in which he further recalled the context of his early intellectual development and emphasized that his project was not 'philosophical' as understood in the German tradition. It was also the period in which he reissued, in revised form, the earlier article on Heidegger of 1975 as *L'ontologie politique de Martin Heidegger* [the political ontology of Martin Heidegger] (Bourdieu, 1988b; 1991a), emphasizing now the pernicious effects of Heidegger's appropriation of everyday language to sustain the academic discipline of philosophy, thereby denigrating practical sense. Bourdieu found it necessary to disown the contemporary manifestations of the discipline to which he had in his youth been an aspirant. His argument was with the social status which seemed to be an inevitable concomitant of the particularly philosophical form of intellectuality. His argument was with 'intellectualism' and he was intent on redefining the social function of intellectuals. The model which appeared to suit his intentions was not that of the detached philosopher but, rather, that of the creative writer, able to engage with social reality in ways which are not tightly prescribed by a pre-existing disciplinary framework.

'Le champ littéraire' 1991

Bourdieu released 'Le champ littéraire' [the literary field] in 1991 (Bourdieu, 1991c) although he notes in his introduction of that year that the piece had been written in 1982. A modified version was published in *Les règles de l'art* (Bourdieu, 1992a). Bourdieu draws attention in his introduction to the change of emphasis in his thinking in the decade between the text's original production and its publication. The article had originally exemplified a method of analysing cultural works analogous with that adopted in other 'field' projects. Now Bourdieu admits that his presentation risks appearing 'dogmatic and schematic' but he defends his use of tortuous language on the grounds that it was important to understand the social construction of the category of 'intellectual' rather than to suppose that it had a predefined meaning. This is the emphasis of the early 1990s. In seeking a political standpoint that was not already circumscribed by state structures, Bourdieu sought to promote the potential for effecting change possessed by writers as intellectuals unconstrained by political censure. Importantly, Bourdieu realized that this potentiality could only be released within a socially constructed intellectual sphere. There was a contemporary need to carry out the task of structuring an intellectual structure within society as well as of enabling it to sustain itself in its autonomous discourse. Whereas 'Champ intellectuel et projet créateur' (1966c) had predominantly emphasized that artistic and intellectual production is not 'self'-expressive but is constituted by its context, *Les règles de l'art* provides a reminder that the existence of a constituting intellectual sphere cannot be taken for granted but must itself be constantly regenerated. The intellectual field which had developed in France in the nineteenth century in opposition to the authority of the Church and the state and which had made possible the political intervention of a writer such as Zola in the Dreyfus Affair was now, in Bourdieu's view, in need of revivification.

Bourdieu was consistent in not seeking to promote a libertarian aestheticism but, instead, in seeking to construct politically alternative mechanisms which would allow for the articulation of politically subversive opinions. In tandem with making this case in his writing, Bourdieu became involved in activities which were attempts to actualize his thinking. In October 1989, he launched *Liber. Revue européenne des livres*, a periodical which was initially published simultaneously every three months in a collection of five European national newspapers,[3] as a supplement in their own languages. The *Revue* had a chequered publishing history.[4] Its last number (34) appeared in March 1998, by which time Bourdieu had contributed (short) articles to fifteen numbers. It was the intention that the periodical would create a space for the intra-European and international exchange of ideas, an exchange which would multilingually respect national expression while enabling a forum without national, political borders. Equally, the intention was that it should be a 'trojan horse' within the field of European journalism in that it was editorially independent while benefiting from the distributive stretch of major newspapers. For Bourdieu, the venture clearly had at least two key purposes. It was intended to revive the influence of European intellectuals in their cultural diversity and, by offering an independent forum for the exchange of ideas, it was intended to oppose the construction of a European 'identity' by the dominant administrators at work in the Commission.

Asked by Didier Eribon in a conversation for publication in *Le nouvel observateur* in September 1986 whether there were still any 'grand causes' to defend, Bourdieu had responded that, for his part, he thought that 'if there is a grand cause today, it is the defence of the intellectuals' (Bourdieu, 1986d, 38), and he proceeded to specify that in a situation where most Western countries had entered into a 'phase of conservative restoration', denigrating intellectuals, there was a need to 'invent new forms of action' which would stimulate a 'collective' or 'international' intellectual effort. He insists that his defence of intellectuals is not at all 'corporatist' but, rather, is derived from a French tradition, 'from Zola to Gide, from Sartre to Foucault', a 'mission of defending the universal' (Bourdieu, 1986d, 38) which is rooted in the historical particularity of French culture. He insists that such a regrouping of intellectuals is 'in progress' [c'est en cours] (Bourdieu, 1986d, 38). He also makes it clear that he is not advocating a seizure of power but only the seizure of 'counter-power': 'since power makes use of science, science must endow itself with a counter-power' (Bourdieu, 1986d, 38). It was this kind of argument which anticipated the launch of *Liber* as a new form of intellectual organization aiming to go beyond the traditional forms of counter-power, such as petitions.

Bourdieu's other main attempt in the early 1990s to actualize his vision of collective intellectual counter-power was his involvement in the establishment of the International Parliament of Writers. The link between Bourdieu's two initiatives is clear from his contribution to the second number of *Liber*, published in December 1989, entitled 'L'histoire se lève à l'Est' [history rises in the East]. Referring to the distortions of the meanings of words endemic in political discourse, Bourdieu argues that 'it is natural that the poet, the writer, the intellectual, whether it be Mircea Dinescu, Vaclav Havel or Christoph Hein, should regain the original role of spokesperson for the group or, more modestly, of public writer' (Bourdieu, 1989d, in Bourdieu, ed. Poupeau and Discepolo, 2002, 267–8). The parliament was founded in November 1993 in Strasbourg by Vaclav Havel who had recently been appointed President of the new Czech Republic. Among others involved in its establishment were Salman Rushdie, Jacques Derrida and Wole Soyinka. *Liber* 17 (March 1994) carried Rushdie's manifesto statement for the parliament, entitled 'A Declaration of Independence. For the International Parliament of Writers' in which he described the purpose of the parliament as being 'to fight for oppressed writers and against all those who persecute them and their work' (Rushdie, 1994, 29, quoted in Speller, 2011, 148). Bourdieu's conception of the parliament was clearly more ambitious in that he envisaged it as an instrument for consolidating counter-power right at the heart of the European project. The establishment of the Parliament of Writers was, for Bourdieu, a device for juxtaposing alternative European parliaments rather than simply one for protecting writers from oppression. Bourdieu wrote a rejoinder to Rushdie entitled 'Un parlement des écrivains pour quoi faire?' [a parliament of writers to do what?] which was published in *Libération* on 3 November 1994[5] (Bourdieu, 1994c, in Bourdieu, ed. Poupeau and Discepolo, 2002, 289–92) in which he outlined three principles to be adopted if the parliament were 'to exist collectively, as a force for solidarity, debates and proposals' (Bourdieu, ed. Poupeau and Discepolo, 2002, 289). These specified that the parliament should be completely independent of political, economic and media power; should be a new form of internationalism, based on the knowledge of diverse historical traditions; and should initiate new 'militant practices' (Bourdieu, ed. Poupeau and Discepolo, 2002, 290). Under this last principle, the parliament quickly inaugurated a practical policy of establishing an international network of 'villes-refuges' [asylum cities] which would guarantee the safety of writers in residence. As Vice-President of the International Parliament of Writers, Bourdieu gave an address at the end of May 1995 to a Congress of the Council of Europe. He explained the intentions of the parliament, typically emphasizing its practical goals. In October 1995, Bourdieu gave a talk at a round table organized by the Parliament of Writers at the Frankfurt Book Fair,[6] and in April 1996 he gave a speech at a public hearing of the Commission on Foreign Affairs of the European Parliament, outlining the 'asylum city' project, in which he concluded that 'the defence of the freedom to create and of free thought, the intensification of relations between European intellectuals and writers, are all inseparable from the struggle for democracy. ... This is not a tolerance conceded to writers and artists, but the very oxygen of democracy.'[7]

Bourdieu's emphasis in these contexts on 'freedom' is not typical. It seems possible that this was a strategic device to gain support and funding for an initiative which he was disposed to defend on rather different, social, grounds. By the end of 1995, Bourdieu's concern for the freedom of 'writers' as such was eclipsed by his sense of a more pressing need to find alternative strategies to defend social democracy. Two major projects commenced at the very end of the 1980s, both of which caused Bourdieu to emphasize the need to effect a social transformation as a *sine qua non* for political, cultural and educational change. The first project, on the housing market, led to six co-authored articles which appeared in a number of *Actes de la recherche en sciences sociales* of 1990 devoted to 'L'économie de la maison' [the economy of housing]. These were eventually assembled by Bourdieu and published in 2000 with an introduction and, in addition, a revised version of his 'Le champ économique' [the economic field] (Bourdieu, 1997b) as *Les structures sociales de l'économie* [the social structures of the economy] (Bourdieu, 2000b). The second project led to the publication, in February 1993, under Bourdieu's direction and after three years of research, of *La misère du monde* [the weight of the world] (Bourdieu, et al., 1993; 1999). Again, three elements of the final text were pre-published in *Actes* in a number of December 1990 devoted to 'La souffrance' [suffering/underclass France] which became the sub-title of the book.

One text of 1992 shows the way in which Bourdieu was beginning to concentrate on forms of deprivation in French society at the same time as he was seeking to mobilize a new form of intellectual engagement. 'Le sens de l'état' [the meaning of the state] was an interview which appeared in *Le Monde* in January 1992 (Bourdieu, 1992c), and was reproduced later as 'La main gauche et la main droite de l'état' [the left hand and the right hand of the state] in 1998 (Bourdieu, 1998a, 9–17; 1998b, 1–10). The original interview was provoked by the appearance shortly before of the first of the pre-publication extracts from what was to become *La misère du monde*. Bourdieu explains that it was becoming clear from the surveys being conducted by his research team that 'many people ... are caught in the contradictions of the social world' (Bourdieu, 1998a, 9; 1998b, 1), contradictions arising from the apparent opposition between the left hand of the state – 'the set of agents of the so-called spending ministries' (Bourdieu, 1998a, 9; 1998b, 2) such as social workers, youth leaders and teachers – and the right hand – 'the technocrats of the Ministry of Finance, the public and private banks and the ministerial *cabinets*' (Bourdieu, 1998a, 9–10; 1998b, 2). Bourdieu observes that 'the left hand of the state has the sense that the right hand no longer knows, or, worse, no longer really wants to know what the left hand does' (Bourdieu, 1998a, 10;

1998b, 2). In short, Bourdieu argues that the state no longer provides any conjunction between the 'social' and the 'economic'. In his interview responses Bourdieu still makes a plea for a revival of autonomous intellectuality, stating that he would 'like writers, artists, philosophers and scientists to be able to make their voice heard directly in all the areas of public life in which they are competent' (Bourdieu, 1998a, 17; 1998b, 9), but he also expresses his disquiet at the silence and corruption of politicians as well as at the malign consequences of television which 'has invited and projected on to the political and intellectual stage a set of self-promoting personalities' (Bourdieu, 1998a, 11–12; 1998b, 4). Bourdieu's articulation of this polarization of the social and economic worlds was his adaptation to the France of the 1990s of his earlier argument that there was an institutionalized disjunction between the primary experiences of ordinary people and the objectivist interpretations of them strategically presented by the established elite to maintain their distinction. While continuing to fight for the preservation of real intellectual values, the pursuit of a 'Realpolitik of reason', Bourdieu began to update his support for 'le sens pratique' of ordinary people inhabiting the left hand of the state.

La misère du monde, *1993*

La misère du monde is an important volume precisely because it was an attempt to offer a new kind of social science designed to represent the interests of those interviewed. The French text consists of sixty-nine articles or interviews.[8] The project involved twenty-four investigators. Bourdieu was author or co-author of twenty of the texts included in the volume. Bourdieu assembled a team of collaborators comprising individuals holding different professional positions, some from within the CSE but many from outside, who were not systematically united by a prior commitment to a standardized understanding of the nature of sociological research. A degree of uniformity of practice was constructed in team discussions of interviews which were held in Bourdieu's seminars in the Collège de France during 1991–92. Similarly, the establishment of the enquiry eschewed the conventional understanding of sociological researchers in respect of sampling techniques and interview procedures. As Bourdieu explains in his final, methodological chapter, entitled 'Understanding', 'we left investigators free to choose their respondents from among or around people they knew [*gens de connaissance*] or people to whom they could be introduced by people they knew' (Bourdieu, et al., 1993, 907; 1999, 610).

La misère du monde makes no attempt to justify the 'representativeness' of the findings. It provides no statistical contextualization of the accounts of interviewers and interviewed which, instead, are offered as particular case-studies of socio-analytic encounter, disclosing both the conceptual predispositions of the interviewers and primary experiences as articulated in their own linguistic manner by the interviewed. The book was designed so as to communicate in a special fashion. Most of the interview transcripts are dated from 1991. The production of the massive volume in February 1993 must have been the result of an arduous process of editing and textual organization during 1992. Many of Bourdieu's contributions attempt to explain the significance of the procedures adopted. In his introductory comment 'To the Reader', Bourdieu summarizes the point that he has reached after many years of research in which he had endeavoured to reconcile structuralist objectivity with subjectivist sensitivity. He emphasizes that the production of the book involves a process of rewriting 'that reconciles two doubly contradictory goals' and he elaborates these in the following way:

> On the one hand, the discussion must provide all the elements necessary to analyze the interviewees' positions objectively and to understand their points of view, and it must accomplish this without setting up the objectivising distance that reduces the individual to a specimen in a display case [curiosité entomologique]. On the other hand, it must adopt a perspective as close as possible to the individual's own without identifying with the alter ego (which always remains an object, whether one wants it or not) and turning into the subject of this world view. (Bourdieu, et al., 1993, 8; 1999, 2)

Bourdieu has forfeited the legacy of his earlier post-structuralism in that he now advocates a process of 'participant objectification' [objectivation participante] on the part of interviewers. The role of researchers is no longer to try to understand the statistical probabilities which constrain people's life-chances relative to their socially constructed capacities to internalize these objectivities, but, instead, reflexively to represent themselves as socially constructed persons in encounter with people who are different only to the extent that they have been socially constructed in different ways. The intention of the project was to operationalize egalitarian encounter. This was not simply an intention with respect to the relationship between interviewers and interviewed but, more importantly, the writing project of the book was to generate constructed encounters textually which were not physically possible, given the living conditions of those interviewed. In his introduction to the first group of interviews, Bourdieu makes it clear that all the interviews were conceived and constructed to be self-sufficient entities, but that in the presentation of the book 'they have been distributed in such a way that people belonging to groups who are likely to encounter each other, not to say confront each other, in physical space (like the custodians in low income housing projects and the residents, adults or adolescents, workers, craftsmen or shopkeepers, in this kind of housing) find themselves juxtaposed in the text' (Bourdieu, et al., 1993, 9; 1999, 3).[9] Bourdieu likens his procedure to that adopted by novelists such as Faulkner, Joyce or Woolf in that he fictively constructs pseudo-encounters in order to suggest the possible actual benefits which might follow from the recognition of 'multiple perspectives that correspond to the multiplicity of coexisting, and sometimes directly competing, points of view' (Bourdieu, et al., 1993, 9–10; 1999, 3).

La misère du monde was a huge success as a publication, selling 126,000 copies (see Lescourret, 2008, 503, fn. 75). In terms of Bourdieu's other involvements at the time with the Parliament of Writers and the publication of *Les règles de l'art*, the book was a very *literary* supplication on behalf of the disadvantaged, one which attracted politicians, writers and intellectuals but which exposed the inadequacy of those audiences to effect change and, equally, the similar inadequacy of its mode of presentation. The end of 1995 seems to have been the point at which Bourdieu decided to develop other means of communicating his message. There were two specific stimuli. First, on 15 November 1995, Prime Minister Alain Juppé announced to the National Assembly the details of a reform of social security, giving rise to the worst protests and strikes in France since the events of May 1968. The announcement provoked antithetical responses from French intellectuals. A petition entitled *Pour une réforme de fond de la Sécurité sociale* [for a fundamental reform of social security], emanating from the journal *Esprit*, was opposed by a petition entitled *Appel des intellectuels en soutien aux grévistes* [appeal of the intellectuals in support of the strikers], published on 4 December 1995. Bourdieu added his name to the list of signatories to the 'Grève' list of signatories. Before the final version of the 'Grève' petition went to press Bourdieu shortened it by about a quarter, emphasizing less the immediate complaints and arguing more for 'a radical reflection on the future of our society which (the movement) promises' (Duval, Gaubert, Lebaron, Marchetti and Pavis, 1998, 69). In effect, Bourdieu was trying to shift the protest movement away from the kind of procedure associated with 'petitions', which he had earlier considered to be superseded,[10] towards the development of a 'social movement' with a wider remit as a counter-political collective. In their history of social movements in France, Michel Pigenet and Danielle Tartakowsky suggest in their introduction to the period from 1980 until the present that the strikes and supporting petition of 1995 constituted a 'moment of return' to more traditional forms of protest which in the previous decade had been ousted by groups which were prepared to act illegally (Pigenet and Tartakowsky, eds, 2014, 583–4). Bourdieu's desire to remobilize intellectuals as a collective was an attempt to revitalize the revolutionary values of the first French Republic[11] in opposition to the 'Republican' party of which Juppé was leader, but he had no wish to encourage a proliferation of protest groups supporting specific interests.

The campaign against Juppé was a short-term 'success' in that, under duress, he was forced to withdraw his legislation, but Bourdieu was more concerned to consolidate mechanisms for longer-term counter-political movement. In the winter of 1995, he established an association entitled Raisons d'agir [reasons for acting]. The journal *Liber* ceased production in March 1998. While this was in decline, the new association launched a publishing initiative entitled Liber-Raisons d'agir. The first publication was Bourdieu's *Sur la télévision* [on television] (Bourdieu, 1996a; 1998f and 1998g) in which he enlarged on the critique of the media which he had mentioned in his 1992 interview in *Le Monde* in which he had distinguished between the left and right hands of the state. This was quickly followed by Serge Halimi's *Les nouveaux chiens de garde* [the new watch-dogs] (Halimi, 1997) in which he deliberately connoted Nizan's book,[12] updating it to suggest that the controllers of the media were now the kinds of oppressors of freedom of thought that academic philosophers had been in the 1920s and 1930s. Other ideologically like-minded publications followed, but the biggest impact of the edition was, initially, the collections of his speeches and interventions which Bourdieu published in 1998 and 2001 as, respectively, *Contre-feux. Propos pour servir à la résistance contre l'invasion néo-libérale* [Firing back. Conversations to serve in the resistance against the neo-liberal invasion] (Bourdieu, 1998a; 1998b),[13] and *Contre-feux 2. Pour un mouvement social européen* [Firing Back 2. For a European social movement] (Bourdieu, 2001a; 2003).[14]

Contre-feux, *1998 and 2001*

Bourdieu had emphasized the spoken word before (in *Questions de sociologie*, 1980b, and *Choses dites*, 1987b) and, posthumously, Franck Poupeau and Thierry Discepolo published a collection of Bourdieu's 'interventions' between 1961 and 2001 (Bourdieu, ed. Poupeau and Discepolo, 2002) in completion of a project which Poupeau had commenced in the autumn of 1999, but the *Contre-feux* publications were deliberate attempts to deploy a new publishing venture as a form of counter-political action.[15] *Contre-feux* contains seventeen interventions spanning the period from 1992 until 1998. In an address to the Reader at the beginning of *Contre-feux*, Bourdieu comments that he decided to bring together these spoken texts because he hoped that they might 'still provide useful weapons to all those who are striving to resist the scourge of neo-liberalism' (Bourdieu, 1998a, 7; 1998b, vii). Although it was Bourdieu's intention to stimulate opposition to neo-liberalism, he offers several tacit caveats against the appropriation of his texts for militant purposes. In a footnote, first, he specifies that the texts are presented chronologically 'so as to make clearer the historical context of remarks which, though they are not reducible to a given context, make no concessions to the vague and wordy generalities of what is sometimes called "political philosophy"' (Bourdieu, 1998a, 7, fn. 1; 1998b, viii, fn. 1). He is anxious to insist that his remarks should invite a 'socio-genetic understanding', that they are delicately balanced between a-temporal validity and contextual specificity in a way which guards against universalist objectivism without forfeiting intellectual engagement. Secondly, Bourdieu reinforces his claim that his interventions are not 'reducible' to contextual relevance by adding that his collection includes 'here and there some basic references to enable the reader to explore further the argument that is put forward' (Bourdieu, 1998a, 7, fn. 1; 1998b, viii, fn. 1).

The collected texts reflect, in tangible form, many of the arguments which Bourdieu had advanced in his research publications. In 'Le sort des étrangers comme schibboleth' [the status of foreigners. A shibboleth], a text first published in *Libération* in May 1995, based on the findings of a survey of the attitudes of presidential candidates to immigration, Bourdieu's argument reflects his earlier sense of the malign influence of opinion polls on political decision-making. The way in which politicians collude with opinion polls contributes to the diminished recognition of the practical good sense of ordinary people which Bourdieu celebrates in 'La parole du cheminot' [the train driver's remark] in which he comments on the absence of the xenophobia normally attributed to ordinary people in the reaction of a metro train driver to an explosion on his train attributed to the Algerian community. As the sub-title of *Contre-feux* indicates, the focus of the collection is on an attack on 'neo-liberalism'. Just as Bourdieu (with Boltanski) had, in the 1970s, exposed the methods by which an ideological counter-revolution was constructed in France after 1968, so Bourdieu now argues, in a talk first given to the Greek trade union confederation in Athens in October 1996, that the current view that 'there is nothing to put forward in opposition to the neo-liberal view' (Bourdieu, 1998a, 34; 1998b, 30), is the consequence of a concentrated process of inculcation of values such that they become 'taken for granted'. The essence of Bourdieu's opposition to neo-liberalism was that it enshrined the taken-for-grantedness of self-regulating economism. This is most powerfully expressed in an address which Bourdieu gave at the University of Freiburg in October 1996, in which he critically dissects a text written by Hans Tietmeyer, at that time President of the Bundesbank, which had appeared in *Le Monde* earlier in the month. His dissection concludes with the general assertion that 'Economics is, with a few exceptions, an abstract science based on the absolutely unjustifiable separation between the economic and the social which defines economism' (Bourdieu, 1998a, 57; 1998b, 51).

Contre-feux is dedicated to negating neo-liberal economism whereas *Contre-feux 2*, containing eight texts spanning the period from early 1999 to late 2000, is more preoccupied with mobilizing the social. This reflects a shift towards the end of the 1990s which is anticipated in a late text in *Contre-feux*, an intervention entitled 'La précarité est aujourd'hui partout' [job insecurity is everywhere now]. Summing up the discussions of the meeting, Bourdieu began by recommending the process: 'The collective thinking that has gone on here in the last two days is an entirely original undertaking, because it has brought together people who have little opportunity to meet and exchange their views – civil servants and politicians, trade unionists, economists and sociologists, people in jobs, often insecure ones, and people without jobs' (Bourdieu, 1998a, 95; 1998b, 81). Bourdieu believed that in such meetings he was involved in actualizing what he had only succeeded in representing as a literary device in *La misère du monde* – a real encounter between people whose paths would otherwise not cross. The French text of *Contre-feux 2* includes a virulent attack on the United States as the source of neo-liberal thought and as the agent for equating it with commitment to 'globalization'. Entitled 'L'imposition du modèle américain et ses effets' [the imposition of the American model and its effects], the paper was given at a conference of Raisons d'Agir which took place in Germany, with German partners, in October 1999. Bourdieu outlines five aspects particular to the social organization of the United States which have been disseminated globally in association with its political influence. These include the American idealization of individualism, its embodiment of the Weberian 'spirit of capitalism' and its fundamental neo-Darwinism. This text was suppressed in the Anglo-American translation of 2003 (Bourdieu, 2003) which, instead, adopts a more emollient tone in an introductory 'Letter to the American Reader'. The substance of *Contre-feux 2* is parochial in advocating the development of a European social movement. For instance, in a text dated from Paris, July 2000–January 2001,[16] entitled 'Contre la politique de dépolitisation' [against the policy of depoliticization] Bourdieu calls for 'the replacement of the European Commission by a genuine executive responsible to a parliament elected by universal suffrage' (Bourdieu, 2001a, 72; 2003, 52), and in a contribution to *Le monde diplomatique* of June 1999, entitled 'Pour un movement social européen' [for a European social movement], given prominence in *Contre-feux 2* but relegated in *Firing Back*, he criticizes the failure of the new social democrat leadership in several European countries (implicitly Blair, Jospin and Schröder) 'to conceive and carry out a genuine social policy together' (Bourdieu, 2001a, 14; 2003, 54). In the English text of 2003, Bourdieu tries to broaden his appeal for collective action, deliberately inviting the participation of 'American scholars and activists'. Such participation 'would strengthen the critique of and resistance to the neo-liberal doxa by showing that this critique can strike at, and radiate from, its very nerve center and global hub' (Bourdieu, 2003, 10).

Small paperback productions, *Contre-feux* and *Contre-feux 2* and the other texts issued by Liber-Raisons d'Agir transmitted Bourdieu's counter-political position to a wide audience, but Bourdieu had other strings to his bow. He continued to satisfy the requirements of his post at the Collège de France, and it seems likely that all the courses of lectures given to relatively restricted audiences during the 1990s will become available posthumously. In addition to the courses given in 1981–83, 1983–86 and 1989–92, we already have those on Manet given in 1998–2000 and those of 1992–93,[17] as well as the final course of 2000–1 (Bourdieu, 2001b; 2004a). He continued to edit *Actes de la recherche en sciences sociales*, contributing about thirty articles in the period between 1990 and his death, as well as the journal *Liber* until 1998. In 1997, he published *Méditations pascaliennes* [Pascalian meditations] (Bourdieu, 1997a;

2000d) in which he articulated an allegiance to the thought of Pascal under whose 'aegis' (Bourdieu, 1997a, 1; 2000d, 1) he had been empowered to present himself as an advocate of 'negative philosophy' (Bourdieu, 1997a, 15; 2000d, 7), and also *Les usages sociaux de la science. Pour une sociologie clinique du champ scientifique* [the social uses of science. For a clinical sociology of the scientific field] (Bourdieu, 1997c), in which he outlined to researchers and staff in the Institut national de la recherche agronomique [the National Institute for Agronomic Research] procedures which they might collectively adopt to ensure that they might resist political pressures controlling the orientation of their institute. In 1998, he published *La domination masculine* [Masculine domination] (Bourdieu, 1998c; 2001c) in which he referred back to his observations of gender relations in Algeria.to propose a perspective on feminist debates which would acknowledge the implications in this context of his usual recognition of the extent to which the behaviour of the dominated is the consequence of their internalization of the perceptions of the situation advanced by the dominated. In 1999, he wrote a preface to Sayad's *La double absence. Des illusions de l'émigré aux souffrances de l'immigré* (Sayad, 1999; 2004), substantially preparing the texts of his long-term friend for publication after his death and thereby sustaining analyses of immigration which would recognize that the experiences of emigrants and immigrants 'are completely different but indissociable' (Sayad, 2004, xi) just as are those of the dominant and the dominated, the masculine and the feminine. In 2000, he published *Propos sur le champ politique* [conversations on the political field] (Bourdieu, 2000a), the title he had chosen for a lecture and question–and–answer session which he gave at the University of Lyon 2 in February 1999.

In *Les usages sociaux de la science*, Bourdieu had tried to demonstrate how his objectivist/constructivist model might not simply be the means for understanding the situation of staff and researchers within a national research institute but could be a blueprint for stimulating constructivist action. In a similar way, the publication of *Les structures sociales de l'économie* in 2000, based on research undertaken at the beginning of the 1990s, was an attempt to move beyond the representation of the encounter between the fields of housing demand and those of housing provision towards an encouragement of means to be adopted in ensuring that social interests are not eclipsed by economic ones. The text offers a revision of 'Le champ économique' [the economic field] (Bourdieu, 1997b), now presented as 'Principes d'une anthropologie économique' [principles of an economic anthropology] (Bourdieu, 2000b, 235–70) which makes it clear that, for Bourdieu, the economic field is constituted in the same way as are all fields and that, as such, its current subordination to economistic thinking is reversible. The text becomes an adjunct to the campaigns reflected in the *Contre-feux* texts which emphasize the need to revive social control over the economic field, and Bourdieu both offers hints, in a case-study of 'the field of the firm' about how, at a micro level, management practices might become more socially responsive, and also reflections, in a 'post-script', on the new consequences at the macro level of the emergence of a 'global economic field'.

La sociologie est un sport de combat, *2001*

It is obvious that, during the 1990s, Bourdieu's activities and styles of self-presentation became more diverse and compartmented than had earlier been the case, even if this had always been a latent tendency. Nevertheless, it was important for him that he should show that his diverse activities were coherent and inter-connected. The affirmation that they possessed a necessary integrity derived conjointly from his primary experience and his constituted intellectuality became the central message of his last years. He tried to deal with the relationship between objective science and personal reflexivity in his final course of lectures at the Collège de France in 2000–1, and these concluded with a section entitled 'Esquisse pour une auto-analyse' [sketch for an auto-analysis] in which he attempted to objectify the conditions which had constituted his intellectual dispositions. It was this sketch that he elaborated in the last months of his life which was published posthumously as *Esquisse pour une auto-analyse* [Sketch for a Self-Analysis] (Bourdieu, 2004b; 2007). In similar vein, *Le bal des célibataires. Crise de la société en Béarn* [The Bachelors' Ball. The crisis of Peasant Society in Béarn] (Bourdieu, 2002; 2008) was an attempt to historicize his engagement with his native region by collecting together articles he had written about it at intervals of a decade from the early 1960s. Above all, however, it was the film made by Pierre Carles,[18] released as *La sociologie est un sport de combat* [sociology is a combat sport] in May 2001, after a period of three years in which he had followed Bourdieu's activities, which most comprehensively offered the kind of epitaph Bourdieu wanted by representing his endeavour as that of a total person, very different from that of a 'total intellectual'.

 La sociologie est un sport de combat presents twenty-nine episodes depicting Bourdieu's diverse activities.[19] In his introduction to the publication of *Sur la télévision* (Bourdieu, 1996a) which, originally, had been a televised interview issued by the Collège de France, Bourdieu had commented that a discourse about television would be less effective than the kind of visual scrutiny of the process given by Jean-Luc Godard or Pierre Carles (Bourdieu, 1996a, 7; 1998g, 11). In agreeing that Carles should make a documentary about his practices, Bourdieu was agreeing to a film which would *visually* represent the relations between televisual and personal communication. The film opens with a shot of the screen image, relayed to Chicago, of Bourdieu apologizing for his inability to attend in person as a result of illness the conference at which we are shown Edward Said introducing him to the audience as 'the major world figure in sociology'. We do not hear the address[20] but only Bourdieu's dissatisfaction with his performance as a result of his difficulty in communicating adequately in English. A few episodes later, Bourdieu is a guest on a radio station show. Asked whether social inequality serves a purpose and whether sociologists serve a purpose, Bourdieu produces a lucid summary of his ideas on social and cultural reproduction. There are scenes with Bourdieu in his office with his secretary, Marie-Christine Rivière and Rosine Christin, the co-editor of *Actes de la recherche en sciences sociales*. There is some badinage about their working relationships. We are then transported to Barcelona where Bourdieu is involved in a discussion of the recently published (2000) Spanish translation of *La domination masculine*. Bourdieu features as a European intellectual, at home in bilingual contexts, at ease in cross-national exchanges within the continent, a point which is reinforced when the film reproduces extracts of a televised conversation between Bourdieu and Günter Grass. We are next shown Bourdieu delivering one of his lectures on Manet at the Collège de France, representing his professorial performance and also conveying the essential points of his interpretation of Manet's art. There are episodes which show Bourdieu and his secretarial staff discussing editorial issues in relation to the publication of *Actes de la recherche*. There is an interview in which Bourdieu is asked details about his life where he and his interviewer comment on his school certificates and old photographs, one showing him as a member of a rugby team. There is a sequence in which Bourdieu is shown discussing Foucault with a group of students in a campus classroom. He is shown acting as mentor to Loïc Wacquant, advising him about what should be his priorities and exhorting him to set targets for publication. There is an episode in which Bourdieu is shown in discussion with colleagues at the Maison des Sciences de l'Homme, deciding how best to interpret research data, a discussion which considers important questions of analysis but which is also conducted with good humour. These scenes are often interrupted or interspersed by moments when Bourdieu is sleeping while travelling or, in mid-conversation, is disturbed by telephone calls.

Perhaps the most important sequence is the penultimate one. On 1 December 1999, Bourdieu was invited to Mantes-la-Jolie, a suburb thirty miles to the west of Paris with, then, a notoriously disaffected community. He was asked to give a radio broadcast in the early evening[21] and, later, to participate in a debate at the Centre culturel Le Chaplin du Val Fourré. Bourdieu is heckled from the floor and the film gives extensive cover to the hostile comments from the audience and to Bourdieu's attempts in response to offer himself as a sociologist concerned for the welfare of those with whom he is debating, differentiating himself from other sociologists whom he considers to be an insult to the profession. The debate is the climax of the film. It deliberately shows Bourdieu in his willingness to maintain his position in the rough and tumble of argument with disaffected youths, social workers and teachers. It is a visual actualization of the literary encounters of *La misère du monde*, now unchoreographed. The debate at Val Fourré is meant to epitomize the tension in Bourdieu's stance. On the one hand, the film is intent on 'showing *the man* before all else' (Truc, 2002). *La sociologie est un sport de combat* is an ultimate, licensed self-presentation. On the other hand, Bourdieu is shown in different situations constantly emphasizing the need to retain an intellectual perspective, culminating in his retort at Val Fourré, that 'c'est pas une maladie d'être intellectuel' [it isn't an illness to be intellectual]. Comparing Carles's documentary with another contemporary documentary based on a conversation with Alain Touraine, entitled *Parcours d'un sociologue* [career of a sociologist], Truc concludes that the question which arises in respect of the Carles documentary is 'the representativity of *this* portrait seeking to define sociology *itself* [*la* sociologie]' (Truc, 2004, 55). Paradoxically, it is the Carles representation of Bourdieu as a man which is an attempt to be prescriptive about the nature of the discipline. This is precisely the dilemma, seeking to reconcile human feeling with intellectual detachment, which caused in Bourdieu the strain and anguish which is apparent in the final shots of the film as, alone and silent, he slowly rubs his face, stretching his fingers over his creased brow, sick 'unto death'.[22]

Summary

During the 1990s, Bourdieu operated in different modes but essentially devoted himself to trying to preserve the social conditions which would continue to make possible the kind of reflexive, historicist ontology that he advocated. Although he tried to retain points of reference to his earlier scientific work in his political tracts, it increasingly seemed to become the case that his previous analyses were not so much integral to his current understanding of society as formal legitimations of his authority to speak and act. The logic of his absorption of his intellectualism into his practical sense was that he finally, in *La sociologie est un sport de combat*, allowed himself to be presented as an anguished human being. In *Méditations pascaliennes* [Pascalian Meditations] (1997a), he had admitted that his chosen stance as a 'negative philosopher' might run the risk of being 'self-destructive' [autodestructrice] (Bourdieu, 1997a, 15; 2000d, 7). The film showed an empathic human being who had wrestled all his life to retain intellectual commitment to a systematic anti-humanism, someone who, to the end, struggled to reconcile his primary experience with the intellectual apparatus which had cumulatively adhered to it.

Notes

1 In other words, Bourdieu here acknowledges that 'instituted capital' comes into the equation. The article devotes a section to 'the institutionalisation of political capital'.
2 Published as Bourdieu, 1989c. Bourdieu included a version of this text in Bourdieu, 1997a, 44–53; 2000d, 33–42. The comment on Paul Nizan is included in this text but the footnote on Merleau-Ponty is omitted.

3 These were: *Frankfurter Allgemeine Zeitung, El País, Le Monde, The Times Literary Supplement* and *L'Indice*.

4 For further details, see Delsaut and Rivière, eds, 2002, 85–6, fns.

5 This appeared first in *Littératures*, a Revue of the Parlement International des Écrivains, in October–November, 1994, 3–4 (Bourdieu, 1994c).

6 This was published in Bourdieu, 1998a, 25–6; 1998b, 19–20.

7 See www.europarl.europa.eu/hearings/19960425/droi/project_en.htm.

8 The English translation contained fifty-four of these articles. Fifteen were omitted 'for reasons of redundancy for a non-French audience' (Bourdieu, et al., 1999, ix).

9 I have modified slightly the translation given in Bourdieu, et al., 1999, 3 in order to try to bring out more clearly what Bourdieu was expressing.

10 See the discussion above of Bourdieu, 1986d.

11 He inserted a reference to the 'universal achievements of the Republic' in the 'Grève' petition in place of the 'general interest' invoked in the original text (Duval, Gaubert, Lebaron, Marchetti and Pavis, 1998, 68).

12 See chapter 4, pp. 109–10.

13 The title is translated for the English publication as *Acts of Resistance. Against the New Myths of Our Time*.

14 The title is translated for the English publication as *Firing Back. Against the Tyranny of the Market 2*, and it also is introduced by a 'Letter to the American Reader'.

15 I do not dispute that Bourdieu had intervened consistently throughout his career, but the *Contre-feux* publications were a different kind of engagement, emphasizing a new presentation of self, and the *Interventions* collection can be seen as an attempt to construct a pre-history so as strategically to endorse that new self-presentation.

16 These dates are only given in the English translation. It seems possible that the text was never published or delivered other than in *Contre-feux 2*.

17 See p. 208 fn. 13.

18 Pierre Carles (1962–). French documentarist who has been compared to Michael Moore.

19 For more detail about the background to the film, see Cyran, 2001.

20 It was published in *Contre-feux 2* (Bourdieu, 2001a, 33–41; 2003, 17–25).

21 This is probably the broadcast which features early in the film.

22 The three forms of despair: not being conscious of having a self, not willing to be oneself, but also despair at willing to be oneself. Despair is 'sickness unto death' (Kierkegaard, 1941 [1848]).

Postscript

Mais attention. Ce que nous appelons désordre et ruine, d'autres, plus jeunes, le vivent comme naturel et peut-être vont-ils avec ingénuité le dominer justement parce qu'ils ne cherchent plus leurs références où nous les prenions. Dans le fracas des démolitions, bien des passions moroses, bien des hypocrisies ou des folies, bien des dilemmes faux disparaissent aussi. Qui l'aurait espéré il y a dix ans? Peut-être sommes-nous à un de ces moments où l'histoire passe outre. Nous sommes assourdis par les événements français ou les épisodes bruyants de la diplomatie. Mais, au-dessous du bruit, un silence se fait, une attente. Pourquoi ne serait-ce pas un espoir? (Maurice Merleau-Ponty, 1960, *Signes*, Paris, Gallimard, Préface, 41)

But we should be careful. What we call disorder and ruin, others who are younger live as the natural order of things; and perhaps with ingenuity they are going to master it precisely because they no longer seek their bearings where we took ours. In the din of demolitions, many sullen passions, many hypocrisies or follies, and many false dilemmas also disappear. Who would have hoped it ten years ago? Perhaps we are at one of those moments when history moves on. We are stunned by French affairs or diplomacy's clamorous episodes. But underneath the clamor a silence is growing, an expectation. Why could it not be a hope? (Maurice Merleau-Ponty, trans. Richard C. McCleary, 1964, *Signs*, Northwestern University Press, Introduction, 23)

Only about six months after writing these sentences of cautious optimism, Merleau-Ponty died suddenly of a heart attack on 3 May 1961. Early in the same year, Pierre Bourdieu returned to Paris from Algeria to become secretary to Aron's research group. Just over ten years earlier, in 1950, Merleau-Ponty, aged forty-two, had been a member of the jury selecting entrants to the École Normale Supérieure which had admitted Bourdieu,[1] aged twenty. We can place Bourdieu among those 'others who are younger' who might 'seek their bearings' in new directions, and among those who offered Merleau-Ponty grounds for supposing that the 'many false dilemmas' which had troubled him throughout his career might 'disappear'.

Merleau-Ponty had realized late in life that the position which he was adopting, intellectually and professionally, was no longer tenable in terms of his own earlier arguments. One way of summarizing my discussion of Bourdieu's work is to state that I believe he relentlessly pursued the logic of the philosophical positions which Merleau-Ponty had balanced, pursuing them beyond the safe house of instituted philosophy into an active engagement with the real socio-political world effected by a sociological reflexivity which he refused to allow to be equated with a reflexive sociology. Did Bourdieu's work eliminate the 'false dilemmas' which had perplexed Merleau-Ponty? Did Bourdieu find 'new bearings' such that he provided the hope that Merleau-Ponty expected of the new generation? The answer to that question depends in part on the way in which his work is now used by the new next generation.[2]

Although Schutz and Gurwitsch were intellectually the products of continental gymnasium schooling, both initiated into the traditions of classical and post-Enlightenment humanist thought, they reacted differently in response to the different Austrian and German cultural situations. Schutz absorbed the work of Bergson and Husserl and others, but the attraction for him of phenomenology was that it methodologically legitimated his intention to subject inter-personal social relations to unprejudiced scrutiny, not that it supplied him with a valid 'philosophy'. This scrutiny involved understanding the agency of individual selves in constructing social reality. He did not conceive of these acting selves as themselves socially constituted and the constructed social reality was autonomously 'social' rather than comprehensively societal. Social scientists perform a role in society as particular agents and there are laws which regulate their activity but their role co-exists with other roles. There is no sense in which a prior consciousness inherent in communities establishes the grounds of possibility of all juxtaposed modes of action. Gurwitsch's endeavours were much more 'intellectual', grounded in doctoral and Habilitation theses which meticulously evaluated previous schools of thought in respect of philosophy and psychology. Paradoxically, however, Gurwitsch's intellectual project led him to reject any notion of a transcendent ego and to argue that intellectual 'fields' are constituted out of pre-rational community solidarity. Intellectual 'fields' have no transcendental priority or permanence. They are not 'idealist' but they function as objectivities which ensure, equally, that knowledge is never fully reducible to historically contingent subjective dispositions. The fact that he never felt integrated into a social context, either in Europe or in America, meant that he was never able to actualize his thinking. Instead, his theory of 'fields' became a theory within an intellectual discourse. Merleau-Ponty and Bourdieu were formed in lycées and at the École Normale Supérieure in much the same intellectual tradition as Schutz and Gurwitsch. Merleau-Ponty attempted to implement in political convictions the simultaneous rejection of idealism and existentialism which, in part, he absorbed theoretically from the work of Gurwitsch. In the immediate post-Second World War period in which French society sought to reconstitute itself, Merleau-Ponty turned away from dogmatic acceptance of Marxist ideology and advanced, instead, an approach to politics which was a form of applied phenomenology which, he hoped, would enable plural world-views to be reconciled through humanist inter-subjective encounter. This was the theoretical backdrop to Bourdieu's experience of the harsh clash of civilizations in Algeria. Bourdieu had already resented the social separation effected and consolidated by his privileged schooling and the conceptual dualisms, between mind and body, thought and experience, which seemed to be homologous with that separation. What he observed in Algeria showed him the consequences of the imposition of a colonial system on indigenous culture and provided him with a perspective on what he personally experienced within France. Nevertheless, Bourdieu was an 'oblate' who could never deny that it was his intellectual formation which had given him the language by which to understand the processes of social division about which he was passionately hostile.

I am an 'oblate'. Educated in the 1950s in a provincial English grammar school, analogous with the gymnasia or lycées attended by all the authors considered in this text, I was initiated into a scholarly tradition which was unfamiliar to my parents such that I gained admission to Cambridge University where my studies culminated in the completion of a doctoral thesis on the relationship between natural philosophy and literary fictions at the end of the eighteenth century, concentrating on the relations between the philosophy of Joseph Priestley and the poetry of Samuel Taylor Coleridge. I was on track to be an aspirant educator in the Humanities. Contingent events intervened and I became a lecturer in 1970 in the newly established North-East London Polytechnic, an institution which was in the vanguard of implementing policies for widening access to higher education and for developing a particular course which was designed to enable disadvantaged students to negotiate their curricula, a negotiation based upon an encounter between their dispositions and those of the staff who were professionally obligated to transmit the bodies of knowledge particular to their specialisms. I became a prime mover in the pedagogic innovation which led to the establishment of the School for Independent Study in 1974 which, with hindsight, could be said to have been attempting to institutionalize a negotiated knowledge construction by juxtaposing the habitus of students with the interests of staff as representatives of 'fields' of learning. The School lasted for sixteen years, during which time it had enabled students to build on their incorporated cultural capital to acquire objectivated capital which, in turn, became instituted through diploma and degree qualification. The School was disbanded in 1990 at the time when the institution felt obliged to safeguard the standardized acceptability of its graduates as it sought to acquire a brand image for itself within the new market of post-binary higher education institutions. During those sixteen years I had gradually found that Bourdieu's work of the 1960s provided me with a conceptual framework to analyse, justify and defend my pedagogic *practice*. The consequence of the abolition of the School for Independent Study was that I redefined the original intellectual interests which had been eclipsed by my involvement in innovation. My doctoral thesis had examined the competing truth claims of 'science' and 'literature'. I had no inclination to resurrect a career in the Humanities and found it possible to pursue my epistemological interests through an analysis of the development of the thinking of the person whose work had helped me interpret my practice. 1990 was a turning-point for Bourdieu as for myself. In late Thatcherite Britain I found that conditions were no longer propitious for the continuation of the practice with which I had been involved for almost two decades. As a substitute, I turned to the objective study of Bourdieu's work on the grounds that its representation would mentally keep alive possibilities which then appeared to be actually eliminated. At the same moment, Bourdieu's failure intellectually to prevail over the way in which American sociology was conceptualizing the modern world, and contributing to the imposition of that conceptualization on the world, caused him to realize that he needed to transform the conditions of possibility for the future by direct action as well as by intellectual endeavour. He turned to self-presentation at the moment when I wrote my first objective account of his work.[3] This book continues that objectification, now including consideration of the development of Bourdieu's work from 1990 until his death. As such, the book comes under scrutiny as a mode of communication in relation to the vision which Bourdieu attempted to actualize in his last decade.

Bourdieu had a vision of the world, partly nostalgic and partly utopian, partly derived from his observations of the social organization in his native Béarn and in traditional Algeria, and partly derived from his commitment to the ideals of the French Revolution. He was committed to an absolute egalitarianism, not 'equality of opportunity' nor 'social mobility', both of which were predicated on procedures of selection within a society in which hierarchical distinction remained unchallenged. He envisaged a society in which individuals might encounter each other socio-analytically, might recognize, that is, that differences can be understood and tolerated on the grounds that they are not absolute but are the consequences of differential social conditioning, thus removing the iniquities of 'symbolic violence'. He envisaged a society in which those in authority, whether politicians, judges or businessmen, would recognize that they held that authority by consent, that their authority was functional rather than absolute and always amenable to analyses which should continuously disclose the ways in which it was socially constituted and, therefore, reversible. He envisaged a society which would be comprehensively socio-centric such that 'sociological' research would be only one way of seeing the world operated by a minority of intellectuals whose perspective was subject to scrutiny in the context of a social ontology of all individuals. He envisaged a society which would not be beholden to 'public intellectuals' but would consist of an intellectual public.

As a result of my habitus and career trajectory I am disposed to be sympathetic to Bourdieu's vision and to share his sense, as expressed in the 1990s, that the likelihood of its realization is rapidly diminishing. The epigraphs which I have inserted at the beginning of the book indicate my orientation. In optimistic moments, I hope, like Tennyson's *Ulysses*, that 'Some work of noble note, may yet be done' to make Bourdieu's vision even conceivable again. This means implementing a historicist, ontological orientation which enables everyone to recognize, as Schelling put it, endorsed by Heidegger, the origins of the 'fundamental thought' of each other. In 'Classement, déclassement, reclassement' of 1978, Bourdieu argued that the young generation was 'une génération abusée' [an abused generation] (Bourdieu, 1978, 9) because it had been offered future prospects through education which were not actually available. This article was added as an epilogue to the English translation of *Les héritiers* which was published in 1979. Colourfully and memorably, Richard Nice rendered Bourdieu's phrase as 'The Bamboozling of a Generation' (Bourdieu and Passeron, 1979, 83), accurately capturing the spirit of Bourdieu's remark. Generations have been bamboozled for generations. The structural transformation of the public sphere needs to be re-transformed to accommodate mass democracy, or, as Thomas Mann's character says more generally, 'it's all up with the conventions currently considered prerequisite and obligatory'.

These are my mere opinions. There is, of course, the alternative view. As Aron said of the May Events of 1968, Bourdieu's vision was of 'une révolution introuvable' [an unrealizable revolution]. Societies need to be managed by bureaucracies. 'People' are quite happy to watch football matches or athletics, to participate in royal pageantry, to follow the behaviour of celebrities, all presented to them by the media. In Ibsen's *The Wild Duck*, written in 1884, one character, Gregers Werle, regards it as his mission to cause another, Hjalmar Ekdal, to confront the reality of his situation, to cease self-bamboozlement. The consequences are disastrous. Another character, Dr. Remming, reprimands Gregers, commenting: 'Take the saving lie from the average man and you take his happiness away, too' (Ibsen, 1964, 244). Perhaps this is an absolute truth or perhaps it is indicative of the continuing potency of a late nineteenth century bourgeois inclination to disparage average people.

There is, finally, a third possibility. The world is already very different from the one with which Bourdieu tried to deal in the 1990s. Facebook, for instance, was established in 2004, two years after his death. Social media have, perhaps, eclipsed 'incorporated' cultural capital such that social exchanges are becoming homogenized within a wholly 'objectivated' sphere. There are, perhaps, no more 'oblates' because the sense that education is an entitlement has removed the experience of indebtedness. Universal connectedness can be seen as the actualization of inter-subjectivity, especially if it becomes a vehicle for collective conversion rather than for the celebration of narcissistic subjectivity. In this view, Bourdieu's project and my discussion of it might both seem retrograde prolongations of the philosophical problematics which Merleau-Ponty hoped were in the process of being superseded.

Whatever the response of readers to my representation of Bourdieu's work in relation to some hypothetical antecedents, my intention has been to describe Bourdieu's intellectual trajectory in a way which will invite reflexive auto-analysis. It is fitting, therefore, to conclude with the sentence with which Bourdieu ends his own auto-analysis:

> And nothing would make me happier than having made it possible for some of my readers to recognize their own experiences, difficulties, questionings, sufferings, and so on, in mine, and to draw from that realistic identification, which is quite the opposite of an exalted projection, some means of doing what they do, and living what they live, a little bit better. (Bourdieu, 2004b, 142; 2007, 113)

Notes

1 See Bourdieu, 1989c, 17.
2 I am deliberately connoting here the book published by members of the Bourdieu Study Group of the British Sociological Association for which I wrote a preface (Ingram et al., 2015).
3 See Robbins, 1991.

References

Adams, R.M., 1994, *Leibniz: Determinist, Theist, Idealist*, New York, Oxford University Press.

Aiton, E.J., 1985, *Leibniz. A Biography*, Bristol/Boston, Adam Hilger.

Barber, M.D., 2004, *The Participating Citizen. A Biography of Alfred Schutz*, Albany, State University of New York Press.

Becker, G.S., 1964, *Human Capital*, New York, Columbia University Press.

Bergson, H., 1946 [1889], *Essai sur les données immédiates de la conscience*, Paris, Presses universitaires de France.

Bergson, H., 1948 [1907], *L'Évolution créatrice*, Paris, Presses universitaires de France.

Biemel, W., ed., 1972, *Phänomenologie heute. Festschrift für Ludwig Landgrebe*, The Hague, Martinus Nijhoff.

Beierswaltes, W., and W. Schrader, eds, 1972, *Weltaspekte der Philosophie. Rudolph Berlinger zum 26. Oktober 1972*, Amsterdam, Rodopi.

Boltanski, L., 2008, *Rendre la réalité inacceptable*, Paris, Demopolis.

Boschetti, A., 2006, 'Bourdieu's Work on Literature. Contexts, Stakes and Perspectives', *Theory, Culture & Society*, 23, 6, 135–55.

Bourdieu, P., 1958, *Sociologie de l'Algérie*, Paris, PUF.

Bourdieu, P., 1960, 'Guerre et mutation sociale en Algérie', *Études méditerranéennes*, 7, 25–37.

Bourdieu, P., 1961, 'Révolution dans la révolution', *Esprit*, 1, 27–40.

Bourdieu, P., 1962a, 'De la guerre révolutionnaire à la révolution' in Perroux, ed., 5–13.

Bourdieu, P., 1962b, 'Célibat et condition paysanne', *Études rurales*, 5–6, 32–136.

Bourdieu, P., 1962c, 'La hantise du chômage chez l'ouvrier algérien. Prolétariat et système colonial', *Sociologie du travail*, 4, 313–31.

Bourdieu, P., 1962d, *The Algerians*, Boston, Beacon Press.

Bourdieu, P., 1962e, 'Les sous-prolétaires algériens', *Les temps modernes*, 199, 1030–51.

Bourdieu, P., 1963, 'La société traditionnelle. Attitude à l'égard du temps et conduite économique', *Sociologie du travail*, 1, 24–44.

Bourdieu, P., 1964, 'The Attitude of the Algerian Peasant Toward Time', in Pitt-Rivers, ed., 55–72.

Bourdieu, P., 1965, 'The Sentiment of Honour in Kabyle Society' in Peristiany, ed., 191–241.

Bourdieu, P., 1966a, 'Condition de classe et position de classe', *Archives européennes de sociologie*, VII, 2, 201–23.

Bourdieu, P., 1966b, 'L'école conservatrice, les inégalités devant l'école et devant la culture', *Revue française de sociologie*, VII, 3, 325–47.

Bourdieu, P., 1966c, 'Champ intellectuel et projet créateur', *Les temps modernes*, 246, 865–906.

Bourdieu, P., 1967, 'Systèmes d'enseignement et systèmes de pensée', *Revue internationale des sciences sociales*, XIX, 3, 367–88.

Bourdieu, P., 1968a, 'Éléments d'une théorie sociologique de la perception artistique', *Revue internationale des sciences sociales*, XX, 4, 640–64.

Bourdieu, P., 1968b, 'Structuralism and Theory of Sociological Knowledge', *Social Research*, XXXV, 4, 681–706.

Bourdieu, P., 1970a, *Zur Soziologie der symbolischen Formen*, Frankfurt, Suhrkamp-Verlag.

Bourdieu, P., 1970b, 'La maison kabyle ou le monde renversé' in Pouillon and Maranda, eds, 739–58.

Bourdieu, P., 1971a, 'Champ du pouvoir, champ intellectuel et habitus de classe', *Scolies*, Cahiers de recherches de l'École normale supérieure, I, 7–26.

Bourdieu, P., 1971b, 'Une interprétation de la théorie de la religion selon Max Weber', *Archives européennes de sociologie*, XII, 1, 3–21.

Bourdieu, P., 1971c, 'Genèse et structure du champ religieux', *Revue française de sociologie*, XII, 3, 295–334.

Bourdieu, P., 1971d, 'Reproduction culturelle et reproduction sociale', *Information sur les sciences sociales*, X, 2, 45–99.

Bourdieu, P., 1971e, 'L'opinion publique n'existe pas', *Noroit*, 155.

Bourdieu, P., 1971f, 'Intellectual Field and Creative Project', in Young, ed., 161–88.

Bourdieu, P., 1971g, 'Le marché des biens symboliques', *L'année sociologique*, 22, 49–126.

Bourdieu, P., 1972a, *Esquisse d'une théorie de la pratique, précédé de trois études d'ethnologie kabyle*, Geneva, Droz.

Bourdieu, P., 1972b, 'Les doxosophes', *Minuit*, 1, 26–45.

Bourdieu, P., 1973a, 'The Three Forms of Theoretical Knowledge', *Social Science Information*, XII, 1, 53–80.

Bourdieu, P., 1973b, 'Cultural Reproduction and Social Reproduction' in Brown, ed., 71–112.

Bourdieu, P., 1974, 'Avenir de classe et causalité du probable', *Revue française de sociologie*, XV, 1, 3–42.

Bourdieu, P., 1975a, 'Méthode scientifique et hiérarchie sociale des objets', *Actes de la recherche en sciences sociales*, 1, 4–6.

Bourdieu, P., 1975b, 'L'invention de la vie d'artiste', *Actes de la recherche en sciences sociales*, 2, 67–94.

Bourdieu, P., 1975c, 'La spécificité du champ scientifique et les conditions sociales du progrès de la raison', *Sociologie et sociétés*, VII, 1, 91–118.

Bourdieu, P., 1975d, 'The Specificity of The Scientific Field and the Social Conditions of the Progress of Reason', *Social Science Information*, XIV, 6, 19–47.

Bourdieu, P., 1975e, 'L'ontologie politique de Martin Heidegger', *Actes de la recherche en sciences sociales*, 5–6, 109–56.

Bourdieu, P., 1976a, 'Le champ scientifique', *Actes de la recherche en sciences sociales*, 2–3, 88–104.

Bourdieu, P., 1976b, 'Le sens pratique', *Actes de la recherche en sciences sociales*, 1, 43–86.

Bourdieu, P., 1977a, 'Questions de politique', *Actes de la recherche en sciences sociales*, 16, 55–89.

Bourdieu, P., 1977b, 'Une classe objet', *Actes de la recherche en sciences sociales*, 17–18, 1–5.

Bourdieu, P., 1977c, 'Sur le pouvoir symbolique', *Annales*, 3, 405–11.

Bourdieu, P., 1977d, *Outline of a Theory of Practice*, Cambridge, Cambridge University Press.

Bourdieu, P., 1978, 'Classement, déclassement, reclassement', *Actes de la recherche en sciences sociales*, 24, 2–22.

Bourdieu, P., 1979a, *La distinction. Critique sociale du jugement*, Paris, Minuit.

Bourdieu, P., 1979b, 'Les trois états du capital culturel', *Actes de la recherche en sciences sociales*, 30, 3–6.

Bourdieu, P., 1979c, *Algeria 1960*, Cambridge/Paris, Cambridge University Press/ Maison des sciences de l'homme.

Bourdieu, P., 1980a, *Le sens pratique*, Paris, Minuit.

Bourdieu, P., 1980b, *Questions de sociologie*, Paris, Minuit.

Bourdieu, P., 1980c, 'Le capital social. Notes provisoires', *Actes de la recherche en sciences sociales*, 31, 2–3.

Bourdieu, P., 1981a, 'La représentation politique. Éléments pour une théorie du champ politique', *Actes de la recherche en sciences sociales*, 36–7, 3–24.

Bourdieu, P., 1981b, 'Décrire et prescrire. Note sur les conditions de possibilité et les limites de l'efficacité politique', *Actes de la recherche en sciences sociales*, 38, 69–73.

Bourdieu, P., 1981c, 'The Specificity of the Scientific Field' in Lemert, ed., 257–92.

Bourdieu, P., 1982a, *Leçon sur la leçon*, Paris, Minuit.

Bourdieu, P., 1982b, *Ce que parler veut dire. L'économie des échanges linguistiques*, Paris, Fayard.

Bourdieu, P., 1982c, 'Goffman, le découvreur de l'infiniment petit', *Le Monde*, 4 December, 1 and 30.

Bourdieu, P., 1983a, 'The Philosophical Institution' in Montefiore, ed., 1–8.

Bourdieu, P., 1983b, 'Ökonomisches Kapital, kulturelles Kapital, soziales Kapital', *Soziale Welt*, 2, 183–98.

Bourdieu, P., 1983c, 'Erving Goffman, Discoverer of the Infinitely Small', *Theory, Culture and Society*, 2, 1, 112–13.

Bourdieu, P., 1984a, *Questions de sociologie*, 2nd edn, Paris, Minuit.

Bourdieu, P., 1984b, *Homo Academicus*, Paris, Minuit.

Bourdieu, P., 1985, 'The Genesis of the Concepts of Habitus and Field', *Sociocriticism*, 2, 11–24.

Bourdieu, P., 1986a, *Distinction. A Social Critique of the Judgement of Taste*, London/New York, Routledge & Kegan Paul.

Bourdieu, P., 1986b, 'La force du droit. Éléments pour une sociologie du champ juridique', *Actes de la recherche en sciences sociales*, 64, 3–19.

Bourdieu, P., 1986c, 'The Forms of Capital', in Richardson, ed., 241–58.

Bourdieu, P., 1986d, 'D'abord défendre les intellectuels', *Le nouvel observateur*, 12–18 September, 82.

Bourdieu, P., with A. Honneth, H. Kocyba, B. Schwibs,1986, 'Der Kampf um die symbolische Ordnung', *Aesthetik und Kommunikation*, 16, 61–2 and 142–63.

Bourdieu, P., 1987a, 'Legitimation and Structured Interests in Weber's Sociology of Religion' in Whimster and Lash, eds, 119–36.

Bourdieu, P., 1987b, *Choses dites*, Paris, Minuit.

Bourdieu, P., 1988a, *Homo Academicus*, Cambridge, Polity Press.

Bourdieu, P., 1988b, *L'ontologie politique de Martin Heidegger*, Paris, Minuit.

Bourdieu, P., 1988c, 'Penser la politique', *Actes de la recherche en sciences sociales*, 71–2, 2–3.

Bourdieu, P., with H. Woetzel, 1988, "'… ich glaube, ich wäre sein bester Verteidiger". Ein Gespräch mit Pierre Bourdieu über die Heidegger-Kontroverse', *Das Argument* (Berlin), 171, 723–6.

Bourdieu, P., 1989a, *La noblesse d'état. Grandes écoles et esprit de corps*, Paris, Minuit.

Bourdieu, P., 1989b, 'The Corporatism of the Universal: The Role of Intellectuals in the Modern World', *Telos*, 81, 99–110.

Bourdieu, P., 1989c, 'Aspirant philosophe. Un point de vue sur le champ universitaire dans les années 50' in *Les enjeux philosophiques des années 50*, Paris, Centre Pompidou, 15–24.

Bourdieu, P., 1989d, 'L'histoire se lève à l'Est', *Liber*, 2, 3 (in Bourdieu, ed. Poupeau and Discepolo, 2002, 267–9).

Bourdieu, P., 1990a, 'La domination masculine', *Actes de la recherche en sciences sociales*, 84, 2–31.

Bourdieu, P., 1990b, 'Les conditions sociales de la circulation internationale des idées', *Romanistische Zeitschrift für Literaturgeschichte/Cahiers d'histoire des littératures romanes*, 14, 1–2, 1–10.

Bourdieu, P., 1990c, *In Other Words*, Oxford, Polity Press.

Bourdieu, P., 1990d, *The Logic of Practice*, Cambridge, Polity Press.

Bourdieu, P., 1991a, *The Political Ontology of Martin Heidegger*, Oxford, Polity Press.

Bourdieu, P., 1991b, 'Epilogue. On the Possibility of a Field of World Sociology' in Bourdieu and Coleman, eds, 373–87.

Bourdieu, P., 1991c, 'Le champ littéraire', *Actes de la recherche en sciences sociales*, 89, 3–46.

Bourdieu, P., 1991d, 'Genesis and Structure of the Religious Field' in Calhoun, ed., pp. 1–44.

Bourdieu, P., 1992a, *Les règles de l'art. Genèse et structure du champ littéraire*, Paris, Seuil.

Bourdieu, P., 1992b, 'Deux impérialismes de l'universel' in Fauré and Bishop, eds, 149–55.

Bourdieu, P., 1992c, 'Le sens de l'état', *Le Monde*, 14 January, 2.

Bourdieu, P., 1993a, 'L'Impromptu de Bruxelles', *Cahiers de l'École des sciences philosophiques et religieuses*, 14, 33–48.

Bourdieu, P., 1993b, 'Il n'y a pas de démocratie effective sans vrai contre-pouvoir critique', *Dossiers et Documents du Monde*, 87–9.

Bourdieu, P., 1993c, *Sociology in Question*, London, Sage Publications.

Bourdieu, P., 1994a, *Raisons pratiques. Sur la théorie de l'action*, Paris, Seuil.

Bourdieu, P., 1994b, 'L'emprise du journalisme', *Actes de la recherche en sciences sociales*, 101–2, 3–9.

Bourdieu, P., 1994c, 'Un parlement pour quoi faire?', *Littératures*, revue du Parlement international des écrivains, 3–4.

Bourdieu, P., 1995, 'La parole du cheminot', *Alternatives algériennes*, 1, 3.

Bourdieu, P., 1996a, *Sur la télévision*, Paris, Raisons d'Agir.

Bourdieu, P., 1996b, 'Passport to Duke', in Brown and Szeman, eds, 241–6.

Bourdieu, P., 1996c, *The State Nobility. Elite Schools in the Field of Power*, Cambridge, Polity Press.

Bourdieu, P., 1997a, *Méditations pascaliennes*, Paris, Seuil.

Bourdieu, P., 1997b, 'Le champ économique', *Actes de la recherche en sciences sociales*, 119, 48–66.

Bourdieu, P., 1997c, *Les usages sociaux de la science. Pour une sociologie clinique du champ scientifique*, Paris, Institut national de la recherche agronomique.

Bourdieu, P., 1998a, *Contre-feux. Propos pour servir à la résistance contre l'invasion néo-libérale*, Paris, Raisons d'agir.

Bourdieu, P., 1998b, *Acts of Resistance. Against the New Myths of Our Time*, Cambridge, Polity.

Bourdieu, P., 1998c, *La domination masculine*, Paris, Seuil.

Bourdieu, P., 1998d, 'Sur les ruses de la raison impérialiste', *Actes de la recherche en sciences sociales*, 121–2, 109–18.

Bourdieu, P., 1998e, *Practical Reason. On the Theory of Action*, Oxford, Polity.

Bourdieu, P., 1998f, *On Television and Journalism*, London, Pluto Press.

Bourdieu, P., 1998g, *On Television*, New York, The New Press.

Bourdieu, P., 1999a, 'The Social Conditions of the International Circulation of Ideas' in Shusterman, ed., 220–8.

Bourdieu, P., 1999b, 'On the Cunning of Imperialist Reason', *Theory, Culture & Society*, 16, 1, 41–58.

Bourdieu, P., 2000a, *Propos sur le champ politique*, Lyon, Presses universitaires de Lyon.

Bourdieu, P., 2000b, *Les structures sociales de l'économie*, Paris, Seuil.

Bourdieu, P., 2000c, 'Créez des réseaux' (interview with S. Keller and V. Mühlberger, trans. V. Gola), *Wochenzeitung*, 11 May.

Bourdieu, P., 2000d, *Pascalian Meditations*, Oxford, Polity Press.

Bourdieu, P., 2001a, *Contre-feux 2. Pour un mouvement social européen*, Paris, Raisons d'Agir.

Bourdieu, P. 2001b, *Science de la science et réflexivité*, Paris, Raisons d'Agir.

Bourdieu, P., 2001c, *Masculine Domination*, Oxford, Polity.

Bourdieu, P., 2002, *Le bal des célibataires. Crise de la société en Béarn*, Paris, Seuil.

Bourdieu, P., 2003, *Firing Back. Against the Tyranny of the Market 2*, London/New York, Verso.

Bourdieu, P., 2004a, *Science of Science and Reflexivity*, Oxford, Polity Press.

Bourdieu, P., 2004b, *Esquisse pour une auto-analyse*, Paris, Raisons d'Agir.

Bourdieu, P., 2005, *The Social Structures of the Economy*, Cambridge, Polity.

Bourdieu, P., 2007, *Sketch for a Self-Analysis*, Oxford, Polity Press.

Bourdieu, P., 2008, *The Bachelors Ball. The Crisis of Peasant Society in Béarn*, Cambridge, Polity.

Bourdieu, P., et al., 1993, *La misère du monde*, Paris, Seuil.

Bourdieu, P., et al., 1999, *The Weight of the World. Social Suffering in Contemporary Society*, Oxford, Polity Press.

Bourdieu, P., and L. Boltanski, 1975a, 'Le titre et le poste. Rapports entre le système de production et le système de reproduction', *Actes de la recherche en sciences sociales*, 2, 95–107.

Bourdieu, P., and L. Boltanski, 1975b, 'Le fétichisme de la langue', *Actes de la recherche en sciences sociales*, 4, 2–32.

Bourdieu, P., and L. Boltanski, 1976, 'La production de l'idéologie dominante', *Actes de la recherche en sciences sociales*, 2–3, 3–73.

Bourdieu, P., and L. Boltanski, 1977, 'Changes in Social Structure and Changes in the Demand for Education' in Giner and Scotford-Archer, eds, 197–227.

Bourdieu, P., and J. Coleman, 1991, *Social Theory for a Changing Society*, Boulder/San Francisco/Oxford, Westview Press.

Bourdieu, P., and A. Darbel, 1966, *L'amour de l'art, les musées d'art et leur public*, Paris, Minuit.

Bourdieu, P., with P.M. de Biasi, 1992, 'Tout est social', *Magazine littéraire*, 303, 104–11.

Bourdieu, P., and M. de Saint Martin, 1976, 'Anatomie du goût', *Actes de la recherche en sciences sociales*, 5, 2–112.

Bourdieu, P., and M. de Saint Martin, 1978, 'Le patronat', *Actes de la recherche en sciences sociales*, 20–1, 3–82.

Bourdieu, P., and M. de Saint Martin, 1982, 'La sainte famille. L'épiscopat français dans le champ du pouvoir', *Actes de la recherche en sciences sociales*, 44–5, 2–53.

Bourdieu, P., and Y. Delsaut, 1975, 'Le couturier et sa griffe. Contribution à une théorie de la magie', *Actes de la recherche en sciences sociales*, 1, 7–36.

Bourdieu, P., and F. Gros, 1989, *Principes pour une réflexion sur les contenus d'enseignement*, Ministère de l'Éducation nationale, de la jeunesse et des sports (in Bourdieu, ed. Poupeau and Discepolo, 2002, 217–26).

Bourdieu, P., and J.-C. Passeron, 1963, 'Sociologues des mythologies et mythologies de sociologues', *Les temps modernes*, 211, 998–1021.

Bourdieu, P., and J.-C. Passeron, 1964a, *Les étudiants et leurs études*, Paris/The Hague, Mouton. Cahiers du Centre de sociologie européenne, 1.

Bourdieu, P., and J.-C. Passeron, 1964b, *Les héritiers, les étudiants et la culture*, Paris Minuit.

Bourdieu, P., and J.-C. Passeron, 1967a, 'La comparabilité des systèmes d'enseignement' in Castel and Passeron, eds, 21–58.

Bourdieu, P., and J.-C. Passeron, 1967b, 'Sociology and Philosophy in France since 1945. Death and Resurrection of a Philosophy without Subject', *Social Research*, XXXIV, 1, 162–212.

Bourdieu, P., and J.-C. Passeron, 1968, 'L'examen d'une illusion', *Revue française de sociologie*, IX, 227–53.

Bourdieu, P., and J.-C. Passeron, 1970, *La reproduction. Éléments pour une théorie du système d'enseignement*, Paris, Minuit.

Bourdieu, P., and J.-C. Passeron, 1977, *Reproduction in Education, Society and Culture*, London/Beverley Hills, Sage Publications.

Bourdieu, P., and J.-C. Passeron, 1979, *The Inheritors. French Students and their Relation to Culture*, Chicago/London, University of Chicago Press.

Bourdieu, P., and J.D. Reynaud, 1966, 'Une sociologie de l'action est-elle possible?', *Revue française de sociologie*, VII, 4, 508–17.

Bourdieu, P., and A. Sayad, 1964a, *Le déracinement, la crise de l'agriculture traditionnelle en Algérie*, Paris, Minuit.

Bourdieu, P., and A. Sayad, 1964b, 'Paysans déracinés, bouleversements morphologiques et changements culturels en Algérie', *Études rurales*, 12, 56–94.

Bourdieu, P., and L. Wacquant, 1992a, *An Invitation to Reflexive Sociology*, Chicago/Cambridge, University of Chicago Press/Polity Press.

Bourdieu, P., and L. Wacquant, 1992b, *Réponses. Pour une anthropologie réflexive*, Paris, Seuil.

Bourdieu, P., and L. Wacquant, 2014, *Invitation à la sociologie réflexive*, Paris, Seuil.

Bourdieu, P., L. Boltanski and M. de Saint-Martin, 1973, 'Les stratégies de reconversion. Les classes sociales et le système d'enseignement', *Information sur les sciences sociales*, XII, 5, 61–113.

Bourdieu, P., J.-C. Chamboredon and J.-C. Passeron, 1968, *Le métier de sociologue*, Paris, Mouton-Bordas.

Bourdieu, P., J.-C. Chamboredon and J.-C. Passeron, 1991, *The Craft of Sociology*, New York, Walter de Gruyter.

Bourdieu, P., A. Darbel and D. Schnapper, 1990, *The Love of Art. European Art Museums and their Public*, Stanford, Stanford University Press.

Bourdieu, P., A. Darbel, J.-P. Rivet and C. Seibel, 1963, *Travail et travailleurs en Algérie*, Paris/The Hague, Mouton.

Bourdieu, P., L. Boltanski, R. Castel and J.-C. Chamboredon, 1965, *Un art moyen, essai sur les usages sociaux de las photographie*, Paris, Minuit.

Bourdieu, P., L. Boltanski, R. Castel, J.-C. Chamboredon and D. Schnapper, 1990, *Photography. A Middle-Brow Art*, Cambridge, Polity Press.

Bourdieu, P., ed. J. Thompson, 1991, *Language & Symbolic Power*, Oxford, Polity Press.

Bourdieu, P., ed. T. Yacine, 2013, *Algerian Sketches*, Cambridge, Polity Press.

Bourdieu, P., ed. P. Champagne and J. Duval, 2017, *Anthropologie Économique*, Paris, Raisons d'Agir/Seuil.

Bourdieu, P., ed. F. Poupeau and T. Discepolo, 2002, *Interventions, 1961–2001*, Marseille, Agone.

Bourdieu, P., ed. F. Schultheis and C. Frisinghelli, 2003, *Pierre Bourdieu. Images d'Algérie. Une affinité élective*, Actes Sud/Camera Austria/Fondation Liber.

Bourdieu, P., ed. P. Champagne, R. Lenoir, F. Poupeau and M.-C. Rivière, 2012, *Sur l'état*, Paris, Raisons d'Agir/Seuil.

Bourdieu, P., ed. P. Casanova, P. Champagne, C. Charle, F. Poupeau and M.-C. Rivière, 2013, *Manet: une révolution symbolique*, Paris, Raisons d'Agir/Seuil.

Bourdieu, P., ed. P. Champagne, R. Lenoir, F. Poupeau and M.-C. Rivière, 2014, *On the State. Lectures at the Collège de France, 1989–1992*, Cambridge, Polity.

Bourdieu, P., ed. P. Champagne, J. Duval, F. Poupeau and M.-C. Rivière, 2015, *Sociologie Générale*, volume 1, Paris, Raisons d'Agir/Seuil.

Bourdieu, P., ed. P. Champagne and J. Duval, with the collaboration of F. Poupeau and M.-C. Rivière, 2016, *Sociologie Générale*, volume 2, Paris, Raisons d'Agir/Seuil.

Brown, N., and I. Szeman, eds, 2000, *Pierre Bourdieu. Fieldwork in Cultures*, Lanham/Boulder/New York/Oxford, Rowman & Littlefield Publishers.

Brown, R., ed., 1973, *Knowledge, Education, and Cultural Change*, London, Tavistock.

Bryson, L., L. Finkelstein, H. Hoagland and R.M. MacIver, eds, 1955, *Symbols and Society*, New York/London, Harper and Brothers.

Bryson, L., L. Finkelstein, C.H. Faust and R.M. MacIver, eds, 1957, *Aspects of Human Equality*, New York, Harper.

Calhoun, C., ed., 1991, *Comparative Social Research*, 13, Bingley, Emerald Publishing.

Calhoun, C., E. LiPuma, and M. Postone, eds, 1993, *Bourdieu. Critical Perspectives*, Oxford, Polity Press.

Castel, R., and J.C. Passeron, eds, 1967, *Éducation, développement et démocratie*, Paris/The Hague, Mouton.

Chapsal, M., ed., 1960, *Les écrivains en personne*, Paris, Julliard.

Cléro, J.-P., 2001, 'Merleau-Ponty et la guerre. Un aspect des rapports de la philosophie de la perception et de la politique', *Études littéraires*, 333, 229–50.

Collot, C., 1987, *Les institutions de l'Algérie durant la période coloniale (1830–1962)*, Paris, CNRS.

Cyran, O., ed., 2001, interview of Pierre Carles and L. Wacquant, 15 February, Dossier de presse de *La sociologie est un sport de combat*, Paris, Groupement national des cinémas de recherche.

Delsaut, Y., and M.-C. Rivière, eds, 2002, *Bibliographie des travaux de Pierre Bourdieu*, Pantin, Le Temps des Cerises.

Ducourant, H., 2014, 'Entretien avec Monique de Saint Martin', *Revue Française de Socio-Économie*, 1, 13, 191–201.

Durkheim, E., ed. V. Karady, 1975, *Textes*, 3 volumes, Paris, Minuit.

Duval, J., C. Gaubert, F. Lebaron, D. Marchetti and F. Pavis, 1998, *Le 'décembre' des intellectuels français*, Paris, Liber-Raisons d'Agir.

Embree, L., 1977, 'Everyday Social Relevancy in Gurwitsch and Schutz', *Annals of Phenomenological Sociology*, 2, 45–61.

Embree, L., 1980, 'Merleau-Ponty's Examination of Gestalt Psychology', *Research in Phenomenology*, 10, 89–121.

Embree, L., 1981, 'Gurwitsch's Critique of Merleau-Ponty', *Journal of the British Society for Phenomenology*, 12, 2, 151–63.

Embree, L., 1991, 'Two Husserlians Discuss Nazism: Letters between Dorion Cairns and Aron Gurwitsch in 1941', *Husserl Studies*, 8, 77–105.

Embree, L., ed., 1984, *Essays in Memory of Aron Gurwitsch*, Center for Advanced Research in Phenomenology, Washington, D.C., University Press of America.

Engell, J., 1989, *Forming the Critical Mind. Dryden to Coleridge*, Cambridge, MA/London, Harvard University Press.

Farber, M., ed., 1940, *Philosophical Essays in Memory of Edmund Husserl*, Cambridge, MA, Harvard University Press.

Fauré, C., and T. Bishop, 1992, *L'Amérique des Français*, Paris, François Bourin.

Field, F., 1967, *The Last Days of Mankind. Karl Kraus and his Vienna*, London/ Melbourne/Toronto, Macmillan.

Fink, E., 1930, 'Vergegenwärtigung und Bild', *Jahrbuch für Philosophie und phänomenologische Forschung*, XI, 239–309.

Franzen, J., 2014, *The Kraus Project*, London, Fourth Estate.

Freedman, M., 2000, *A Parting of the Ways. Carnap, Cassirer, and Heidegger*, Peru, IL, Open Court Publishing.

Geraets, T.F., 1971, *Vers une nouvelle philosophie transcendantale. La genèse de la philosophie de Maurice Merleau-Ponty jusqu'à la Phénoménologie de la perception*, The Hague, Martinus Nijhoff.

Gerassi, J., 1989, *Jean-Paul Sartre. Hated Conscience of His Century*, Volume 1. *Protestant or Protester?* Chicago/London, University of Chicago Press.

Giner, S., and M. Scotford-Archer, eds, 1977, *Contemporary Europe. Social Structures and Cultural Patterns*, London, Routledge and Kegan Paul.

Goldstein, K., 1971, *Selected Papers/Ausgewählte Schriften*, The Hague, Martinus Nijhoff.

Grathoff, R., ed., 1978, *The Theory of Social Action. The Correspondence of Alfred Schutz and Talcott Parsons*, Bloomington/London, Indiana University Press.

Grathoff, R., ed., 1989, *Philosophers in Exile. The Correspondence of Alfred Schutz and Aron Gurwitsch, 1939–1959*, Bloomington/Indianapolis, Indiana University Press.

Gurwitsch, A., 1929, 'Phänomenologie der Thematik und des reinen Ich', *Psychologische Forschung*, 12, 279–381.

Gurwitsch, A., 1930, 'Hermann Cohen und der jüdische Zeitgeist', *Frankfurter Israelitisches Gemeindeblatt*.

Gurwitsch, A., 1931, 'Critical Study of Fritz Kaufmann, *Die Philosophie der Grafen Yorck von Wartenburg*', *Zeitschrift für Aesthetik und allgemeiene Kunstwissenschaft*.

Gurwitsch, A., 1932, Review of Edmund Husserl, 'Nachwort zu meinen *Ideen zu einer reinen Phänomenologie und phänomenologischer Philosophie*', *Deutsche Literaturzeitung*, 28.

Gurwitsch, A., 1933a, 'Zur Bedeutung der Praedestinationslehre für die Ausbildung des kapitalistischen Geistes', *Archiv für Sozialwissenschaft und Sozialpolitik*, LXVIII.

Gurwitsch, A., 1933b, 'Critical Study of Leo Strauss, *Die Religionskritik Spinozas als Grundlage seiner Bibelwissenschaft*', *Göttingische Gelehrte Anzeigen*.

Gurwitsch, A., 1934, 'La place de la psychologie dans l'ensemble des sciences', *Revue de Synthèse*, 8, 399–439.

Gurwitsch, A., 1935, 'Étude critique de *Psychologie du langage*', *Revue philosophique de la France et de l'Étranger*, CXX, 430–2.

Gurwitsch, A., 1936a, 'L'acquisition du langage d'après H. Delacroix', *Revue de Synthèse*, 12, 227–33.

Gurwitsch, A., 1936b, 'Quelques aspects et quelques développements de la psychologie de la forme', *Journal de psychologie normale et pathologique*, 33, 413–70 [In *Studies in Phenomenology and Psychology* (*SPP*), 3–55].

Gurwitsch, A., 1936c, 'Développement historique de la Gestalt-psychologie', *Thales*, 2, 167–76.

Gurwitsch, A., 1938, 'XI Congrès International de Psychologie', *Revue de Métaphysique et de Morale*, 50, 145–60.

Gurwitsch, A., 1939, 'Le fonctionnement de l'organisme d'après K. Goldstein', *Journal de Psychologie Normale et Pathologique*, 36, 107–38.

Gurwitsch, A, 1940a, 'La science biologique d'après K. Goldstein', *Revue philosophique de la France et de l'Étranger*, 129, 126–51 [*SPP*, 69–88].

Gurwitsch, A., 1940b, 'On the Intentionality of Consciousness', in Farber, ed., 65–83 [*SPP*, 124–40].

Gurwitsch, A., 1941, 'A Non-Egological Conception of Consciousness', *Philosophy and Phenomenological Research*, 325–38 [*SPP*, 287–300].

Gurwitsch, A., 1943, 'William James' Theory of the "Transitive Parts" of the Stream of Consciousness', *Philosophy and Phenomenological Research*, 3, 449–77 [*SPP*, 301–31].

Gurwitsch, A., 1945, 'On Contemporary Nihilism', *Review of Politics*, 7, 170–98.

Gurwitsch, A., 1946, review of Hans Kelsen: *Society and Nature*, *Isis*, 36, 142–6.

Gurwitsch, A., 1947, 'On the Object of Thought', *Philosophy and Phenomenological Research*, 7, 347–56 [*SPP*, 141–7].

Gurwitsch, A., 1949, 'Gelb-Goldstein's Concept of "Concrete" and "Categorial" Attitude and the Phenomenology of Ideation', *Philosophy and Phenomenological Research*, 10, 172–96 [*SPP*, 359–84].

Gurwitsch, A., 1951, 'Présuppositions philosophiques de la logique', *Revue de Métaphysique et de Morale*, 56, 395–405 [*SPP*, 350–8].

Gurwitsch, A., 1953, 'Sur une racine perceptive de l'abstraction', *Actes du XI. Congrès International de Philosophie*, volume 2, Amsterdam and Louvain, 43–47 [*SPP*, 385–9].

Gurwitsch, A., 1955, 'The Phenomenological and the Psychological Approach to Consciousness', *Philosophy and Phenomenological Research*, 15, 303–19 [reprinted in Natanson, ed., 1966, and in *SPP*, 89–106].

Gurwitsch, A., 1956, 'The Last Work of Edmund Husserl, Part 1', *Philosophy and Phenomenological Research*, 16, 370–98 [*SPP*, 397–418].

Gurwitsch, A., 1957a, 'The Last Work of Edmund Husserl, Parts 2–5', *Philosophy and Phenomenological Research*, 17, 370–98 [*SPP*, 418–47].

Gurwitsch, A., 1957b, *Théorie du champ de la conscience*, Bruges/Paris, Desclée de Brouwer.

Gurwitsch, A., 1959a, 'Beitrag zur phänomenologischen Theorie der Wahrnehmung' [contribution to the phenomenological theory of perception], *Zeitschrift für philosophische Forschung*, 13, 419–37 [*SPP*, 332–49].

Gurwitsch, A., 1959b, 'Sur la pensée conceptuelle', in Van Breda and Taminiaux, eds, 275–82 [reprinted in translation in Sayre and Crosson, eds, 1963, and in *SPP*, 390–6].

Gurwitsch, A., 1960, 'La conception de la conscience chez Kant et chez Husserl', *Bulletin de la Société Française de Philosophie*, 54, 65–96 [*SPP*, 148–74].

Gurwitsch, A., 1961, 'The Problem of Existence in Constitutive Phenomenology', *Journal of Philosophy*, 58, 625–32 [*SPP*, 116–23].

Gurwitsch, A., 1962, 'The Commonsense World of Social Reality. A Discourse on Alfred Schutz', *Social Research*, 29, 50–72.

Gurwitsch, A., 1964a, *The Field of Consciousness*, Pittsburgh, Duquesne University Press.

Gurwitsch, A., 1964b, 'Der Begriff des Bewußtseins bei Kant und Husserl', *Kant-Studien*, 55, 410–27.

Gurwitsch, A., 1966a, *Studies in Phenomenology and Psychology*, Evanston, Northwestern University Press.

Gurwitsch, A., 1966b, 'An Apparent Paradox in Leibnizianism', *Social Research*, 33, 47–64.

248   *References*

Gurwitsch, 1966c, 'Edmund Husserl's Conception of Phenomenological Psychology', *Review of Metaphysics*, 19, 698–727 [In *Phenomenology and the Theory of Science (PTS)*, 77–112].

Gurwitsch, A., 1967a, 'Husserl's Theory of the Intentionality of Consciousness in Historical Perspective', in Lee and Mandelbaum, eds, 388–401 [*PTS*, 210–40].

Gurwitsch, A., 1967b, 'Galilean Physics in the Light of Husserl's Phenomenology' in McMullin, ed., 388–401 [*PTS*, 33–59].

Gurwitsch, A., 1968, 'Bemerkungen zu den Referaten der Herren Patocka, Landgrebe und Chisholm', *Proceedings of the XIVth International Congress of Philosophy*, volume 2, Vienna, Herder Verlag, 209–15.

Gurwitsch, A., 1969, 'Social Science and Natural Science' in Heilbronner, ed., 37–55.

Gurwitsch, A., 1970, 'Problems of the Life-World' in Natanson, ed., 35–61 [*PTS*, 3–32].

Gurwitsch, A., 1971, 'Einleitung' in Goldstein, xi–xxiv.

Gurwitsch, A., 1972a, 'On the Systematic Unity of the Sciences', in W. Biemel, ed., 103–21 [*PTS*, 132–49].

Gurwitsch, A., 1972b, 'Zwei Begriffe von Kontingenz bei Leibniz', in Beierswaltes and Schrader, eds, 101–18.

Gurwitsch, A., 1973, 'Perceptual Coherence as the Foundation of the Judgment of Predication' in Kersten and Zaner, eds, 62–89 [*PTS*, 241–67].

Gurwitsch, A., ed. L. Embree, 1972, *Life-World and Consciousness. Essays for Aron Gurwitsch*, Evanston, Northwestern University Press.

Gurwitsch, A., ed. L. Embree, 1974, *Phenomenology and the Theory of Science*, Evanston, Northwestern University Press.

Gurwitsch, A., ed. L. Embree, 1984, *Marginal Consciousness*, Athens/Ohio/London, Ohio University Press.

Gurwitsch, A., ed. J. Garcia-Gomez, 2009, *The Collected Works of Aron Gurwitsch*, Vol. I. *Constitutive Phenomenology in Historical Perspective*, Dordrecht, Springer.

Gurwitsch, A., ed. J. Huertas-Jourda, 2002, *Esquisse de la phénoménologie constitutive*, Paris, Vrin.

Gurwitsch, A., ed. F. Kersten, 2010, *The Collected Works of Aron Gurwitsch*, Vol. II. *Studies in Phenomenology and Psychology*, Dordrecht, Springer.

Gurwitsch, A., ed. A. Métraux, 1976, *Die mitmenschlichen Begegnungen in der Milieuwelt*, Berlin, Walter de Gruyter.

Gurwitsch, A., ed. A. Métraux, 1979, *Human Encounters in the Social World*, Pittsburgh, Duquesne University Press.

Gurwitsch, A., ed. R.M. Zaner, 2010, *The Collected Works of Aron Gurwitsch*, Vol. III. *The Field of Consciousness. Theme, Thematic Field, and Margin*, Dordrecht, Springer.

Halimi, S., 1997, *Les nouveaux chiens de garde*, Paris, Liber-Raisons d'Agir.

Hartz, G., 2007, *Leibniz's Final System. Monads, Matter and Animals*, New York, Routledge.

Heidegger, M., 1927, *Sein und Zeit*, Tübingen, Niemeyer Verlag.

Heidegger, M., 1947, *Brief über den Humanismus*, Frankfurt am Main, V. Klostermann.

Heidegger, M., 1962, *Being and Time*, Oxford, Blackwell.

Heidegger, M., ed. D. Krell, 1977, *Basic Writings*, New York, Harper & Row.

Heilbronner, R.L., ed., 1969, *Economic Means and Social Ends*, Englewood Cliffs, Prentice-Hall.

Hume, D., 1961 [1748], *An Enquiry Concerning Human Understanding*, in *The Empiricists*, Garden City, Doubleday & Co.

Husserl, E., 1929, *Formale und transzendentale Logik*, Halle, Niemeyer.

Husserl, E., 1930, *Nachwort zu meinen 'Ideen zu einer reinen Phänomenologie und phänomenologischen Philosophie'*, *Jahrbuch für Philosophie und phänomenologische Forschung*, XI, 549–70.

Husserl, E., trans. W.R.B. Gibson, 1931, *Ideas: General Introduction to Pure Phenomenology*, Oxford, Macmillan.

Husserl, E., trans. G. Peiffer and E. Levinas, 1931, *Méditations cartésiennes. Introduction à la phénoménologie*, Paris: A. Colin.

Husserl, E., 1936, 'Die Krisis der europäischen Wissenschaften und die transzendentale Phänomenologie. Eine Einleitung in die phänomenologische Philosophie', *Philosophia*, 1, 77–176.

Husserl, E., 1960, *Cartesian Meditations*, The Hague, Martinus Nijhoff.

Husserl, E., 1970, *The Crisis of European Sciences and Transcendental Phenomenology*, Evanston, Northwestern University Press.

Husserl, E., ed. W. Biemel, 1954, *Die Krisis der europäischen Wissenschaften und die transzendentale Phänomenologie. Eine Einleitung in die phänomenologische Philosophie*, Husserliana Vol. VI, The Hague, Martinus Nijhoff.

Husserl, E., ed. E. Fink, 1939, 'Der Ursprung der Geometrie als intentional-historisches Problem', *Revue internationale de philosophie*, I, 2.

Husserl, E., ed. P. Soulez, 1988, 'Sur la mythologie primitive. Lettre de Edmund Husserl à Lucien Lévy-Bruhl 11 mars 1935', *Gradhiva*, no. 4, 63–72.

Husserl, E., ed. S. Strasser, 1973, *Cartesianische Meditationen und Pariser Vorträge*, The Hague, Martinus Nijhoff.

Ibsen, H., 1964, *Hedda Gabler and other Plays*, Harmondsworth, Penguin Classics.

Ingram, N., et al., eds, 2015, *The Next Generation. The Development of Bourdieu's Intellectual Heritage in Contemporary UK Sociology*, London/New York, Routledge.

Jankelevitch, V., 1985, *Libération*, 10 June and *Le Monde*, 11 June.

Jarausch, K., 1982, *Students, Society, and Politics in Imperial Germany*, Princeton, Princeton University Press.

Kersten, F., and R.M. Zaner, eds, 1973, *Phenomenology, Continuation and Criticism. Essays in Honor of Dorion Cairns*, The Hague, Martinus Nijhoff.

Kierkegaard, S., 1941 [1848], *The Sickness Unto Death*, Princeton, Princeton University Press.

Koestler, A., 1940, *Darkness at Noon*, London, Jonathan Cape.

Koestler, A., 1945, *Le zéro et l'infini*, Paris, Calmann-Lévy.

Kojève, A., ed. R. Quéneau, 1947, *Introduction à la lecture de Hegel*, Paris, Gallimard.

Koyré, A., 1931, 'Rapports sur l'état des études hégéliennes en France', *Revue d'histoire de la philosophie*, 5, 2.

Kurrild-Klitgaard, P., 2003, 'The Viennese Connection: Alfred Schutz and the Austrian School', *Quarterly Journal of Austrian Economics*, 6, 2, 35–66.

Kusch, M., ed., 2000, *The Sociology of Philosophical Knowledge*, Dordrecht/Boston/London, Kluwer Academic Publishers.

Lebaron, F., and G. Mauger, 1999, 'Raisons d'agir. Un intellectuel collectif autonome', *Journal des anthropologues*, 77–8, 295–301.

Lee, E.N., and M. Mandelbaum, eds, 1967, *Phenomenology and Existentialism*, Baltimore, Johns Hopkins Press.

Leibniz, G.W., ed. A.M. Schrecker, trans. P. Schrecker, 1965, *Monadology and Other Philosophical Essays*, Indianapolis, Bobbs-Merrill.

Leibniz, G.W., ed. P. Schrecker, 2001 [1959], *Opuscules Philosophiques Choisis*, Paris, Vrin.

Lemert, C., ed., 1981, *French Sociology. Rupture and Renewal since 1968*, New York, Columbia University Press.

Lescourret, M.-A., 2008, *Pierre Bourdieu. Vers une économie du bonheur*, Paris, Flammarion.

Lévy-Bruhl, L., 1922, *La mentalité primitive*, Paris, Alcan.

Lodge, P., 2003, 'Leibniz on Relativity and the Motion of Bodies', *Philosophical Topics*, 31, 277–308.

Lyotard, J.-F., 1991, *Phenomenology*, Albany, State University of New York Press.

Lyotard, J.-F., 1999 [1954], *La phénoménologie*, Paris, PUF.

Mariojouls, J., 2006, 'Pierre Bourdieu au Val Fourré. De quelques obstacles à la réception profane d'une sociologie critique', *Sociétés Contemporaines*, 4, 64, 115–33.

Mauss, M., 1950, *Sociologie et anthropologie*, Paris, PUF.

Mauss, M., ed. V. Karady, 1968–69, *Oeuvres*, 3 volumes, Paris, Minuit.

McMullin, E., ed., 1967, *Galileo, Man of Science*, New York, Basic Books.

Merleau-Ponty, M., 1935, 'Christianisme et ressentiment' (review of Max Scheler), *La Vie Intellectuelle*, XXXVI, 278–306, in Merleau-Ponty, ed. Prunair, 1997, 9–33.

Merleau-Ponty, M., 1936a, 'Être et Avoir' (review of Gabriel Marcel), *La Vie Intellectuelle*, 8, XLV, 98–109, in Merleau-Ponty, ed. Prunair, 1997, 35–44.

Merleau-Ponty, M., 1936b, review of J.-P. Sartre: L'Imagination, *Journal de Psychologie normale et pathologique*, 33, 9–10, 756–61, in Merleau-Ponty, ed. Prunair, 1997, 45–54.

Merleau-Ponty, M., 1942, *La structure du comportement*, Paris, PUF.

Merleau-Ponty, M., 1945a, *Phénoménologie de la perception*, Paris, Gallimard.

Merleau-Ponty, M., 1945b, 'La guerre a eu lieu', *Les temps modernes*, 1, 1, 48–66, in Merleau-Ponty, 1996 [1948], 169–85.

Merleau-Ponty, M., 1945c, 'La Querelle de l'Existentialisme', *Les temps modernes*, 1, 2, 344–56, in Merleau-Ponty, 1996 [1948], 88–101.

Merleau-Ponty, M., 1946a, 'Foi et bonne Foi', *Les temps modernes*, 1, 5, 769–82, in Merleau-Ponty, 1996 [1948], 209–20.

Merleau-Ponty, M., 1946b, 'L'Existentialisme chez Hegel', *Les temps modernes*, 1, 7, 1311–19, in Merleau-Ponty, 1996 [1948], 79–87.

Merleau-Ponty, M., 1946c, 'Marxisme et Philosophie', *Revue Internationale*, 1, 6, 518–26, in Merleau-Ponty, 1996 [1948], 152–68.

Merleau-Ponty, M., 1946d, 'Le Yogi et le Prolétaire, I', *Les temps modernes*, 2, 13, 1–29, in Merleau-Ponty, 1947c, 3–48.

Merleau-Ponty, M., 1946e, 'Le Yogi et le Prolétaire, II', *Les temps modernes*, 2, 14, 253–87, in Merleau-Ponty, 1947c, 48–75, 100–5, 111–41.

Merleau-Ponty, M., 1947a, 'Le Yogi et le Prolétaire, III', *Les temps modernes*, 2, 16, 676–711, in Merleau-Ponty, 1947c, 141–206.

Merleau-Ponty, M., 1947b, 'Le métaphysique dans l'homme', *Revue de Métaphysique et de Morale*, 52, 290–307, in Merleau-Ponty, 1966 [1948], 102–19.

Merleau-Ponty, M., 1947c, *Humanisme et terreur. Essai sur le problème communiste*, Paris, Gallimard.

Merleau-Ponty, M., 1948, *Sens et non-sens*, Paris, Nagel.

Merleau-Ponty, M., 1953, *Éloge de la philosophie*, Paris, Gallimard.

Merleau-Ponty, M., 1955, *Les aventures de la dialectique*, Paris, Gallimard.

Merleau-Ponty, M., 1960, *Signes*, Paris, Gallimard.

Merleau-Ponty, M., 1962, *Phenomenology of Perception*, London, Routledge & Kegan Paul.

Merleau-Ponty, M., 1964, *Signs*, Evanston, Northwestern University Press.

Merleau-Ponty, M., 1969, *Humanism and Terror*, Boston, Beacon Press.

Merleau-Ponty, M., 1970, *Themes from the Lectures at the College de France, 1952–1960*, Evanston, Northwestern University Press.

Merleau-Ponty, M., 1996 [1948], *Sens et non-sens*, Paris, Gallimard.

Merleau-Ponty, ed. J. Deprun, 1997, *L'Union de l'âme et du corps chez Malebranche, Biran et Bergson*, Paris, Vrin.

Merleau-Ponty, ed. M. Guéroult, 1962, 'Un inédit de Maurice Merleau-Ponty', *Revue de métaphysique et de morale*, 67, 4, 401–9.

Merleau-Ponty, ed. C. Lefort, 1964a, *Le visible et l'invisible*, Paris, Gallimard.

Merleau-Ponty, ed. C. Lefort, 1964b, *L'oeil et l'esprit*, Paris, Gallimard.

Merleau-Ponty, ed. C. Lefort, 1968, *Résumés de cours, Collège de France 1952–1960*, Paris, Gallimard.

Merleau-Ponty, ed. C. Lefort, 1969, *La prose du monde*, Paris, Gallimard.

Merleau-Ponty, ed. C. Lefort, 2015, *L'Institution, La Passivité. Notes de cours au Collège de France (1954–1955)*, Paris, Belin.

Merleau-Ponty, ed. S. Ménasé, 1996, *Notes de cours, 1959–1961*, Paris, Gallimard.

Merleau-Ponty, ed. J. O'Neill, 1970, *Themes from the Lectures at the Collège de France, 1952–1960*, Evanston, Northwestern University Press.

Merleau-Ponty, ed. S. Ménasé, 1997, 'Notes de lecture et commentaires sur *Théorie du champ de la conscience* de Aron Gurwitsch', *Revue de Métaphysique et de Morale*, 3, 321–42.

Merleau-Ponty, ed. S. Ménasé, 2001, 'Reading Notes and Comments on Aron Gurwitsch's the Field of Consciousness', *Husserl Studies*, 17,3, 173–93.

Merleau-Ponty, M., ed. J. Prunair, 1996, *Le primat de la perception et ses conséquences philosophiques*, Lagrasse, Verdier.

Merleau-Ponty, M., ed. J. Prunair, 1997, *Parcours 1935–1951*, Lagrasse, Verdier.

Merleau-Ponty, ed. J. Prunair, 2000, *Parcours deux, 1951–1961*, Lagrasse, Verdier.

Merleau-Ponty, ed. J. Prunair, 2001, *Psychologie et pédagogie de l'enfant, Cours de Sorbonne 1949–1952*, Lagrasse, Verdier.

Montefiore, A., ed., 1983, *Philosophy in France Today*, Cambridge, Cambridge University Press.

Morin, E., 1962, *L'esprit du temps. Essai sur la culture de masse*, Paris, Grasset.

Natanson, M., ed., 1966, *Essays in Phenomenology*, The Hague: Martinus Nijhoff.

Natanson, M, ed., 1970, *Phenomenology and Social Reality. Essays in Memory of Alfred Schutz*, The Hague, Martinus Nijhoff.

Nizan, P., 1960 [1931], *Aden Arabie*, Paris, Maspéro.

Nizan, P., 1998 [1932], *Les chiens de garde*, Marseille, Agone.

Otaka, T., 1932, *Grundlegung der Lehre vom sozialen Verband*, Vienna, Springer.

Panofsky, E., 1955, *Meaning in the Visual Arts*, New York, Doubleday and Co.

Panofsky, E., ed. P. Bourdieu, 1967, *Architecture gothique et pensée scolastique*, Paris, Minuit.

Passeron, J.-C., 2003, 'Mort d'un ami, disparition d'un penseur', *Revue européenne des sciences sociales*, xli–125, 77–124.

Passeron, J.-C., ed. D. Robbins, 2013, *Sociological Reasoning. A Non-Popperian Space of Argumentation*, Oxford, Bardwell Press.

Peristiany, J., ed., 1965, *Honour and Shame*, London, Weidenfeld and Nicholson.

Perroux, F., ed., 1962, *L'Algérie de demain*, Paris, PUF.

Pigenet, M., and D. Tartakowsky, eds, 2014, *Histoire des Mouvements Sociaux en France de 1814 à nos jours*, Paris, La Découverte.

Pitt-Rivers, J., ed., 1964, *Mediterranean Countrymen*, Paris/The Hague, Mouton.

Plaisted, D., 2002, *Leibniz on Purely Extrinsic Denominations*, Rochester, University of Rochester Press.

Poincaré, H., 1908, *La valeur de la science*, Paris, Flammarion.

Pouillon, J., 1966, 'Présentation. Un essai de définition', *Les temps modernes*, 246, 769–90.

Poupeau, F., and Discepolo, T., eds, 2002, *Bourdieu. Interventions, 1961–2001. Science sociale et action politique*, Marseille, Agone.

Principes pour une réflexion sur les contenus d'enseignement, 1989, Paris, Ministère de l'Éducation Nationale, de la Jeunesse et des Sports.

Propositions pour l'enseignement de l'avenir, 1985, Paris, Collège de France.

Puryear, S., 2012, 'Motion in Leibniz's Middle Years. A Compatibilist Approach', *Oxford Studies in Early Modern Philosophy*, 6, 135–70.

Rancière, J., 2007 [1983], *Le philosophe et ses pauvres*, Paris, Flammarion.

Richardson, J.G., ed., 1986, *Handbook of Theory and Research for the Sociology of Education*, New York/Westport/London, Greenwood Press.

Ricoeur, P., 1961, 'Hommage à Merleau-Ponty', *Esprit*, 29, 1115–20.

Ringer, F., 1969, *The Decline of the German Mandarins. The German Academic Community, 1890–1933*, Cambridge, MA, Harvard University Press.

Robbins, D., 1988, *The Rise of Independent Study. The Politics and the Philosophy of an Educational Innovation, 1970–1987*, Milton Keynes, Open University Press, co-published with the SRHE.

Robbins, D., 1989, 'Bourdieu in England, 1964–1977', *Higher Education Policy*, 2, 2, 40–6.

Robbins, D., 1991, *The Work of Pierre Bourdieu. Recognizing Society*, Milton Keynes, Open University Press.

Robbins, D., 2000, 'Bourdieu on Language and Linguistics. A Response to R. Hasan's "The Disempowerment Game; Bourdieu on Language in Literacy"', *Linguistics and Education. An International Research Journal*, 10, 4, 425–40.

Robbins, D., 2003, 'The Responsibility of the Ethnographer'. An introduction to Pierre Bourdieu on 'Colonialism and ethnography' with a co-translation (with R. Gomme) of the Bourdieu extract, *Anthropology Today*, 19, 2, 12–19.

Robbins, D., 2006, *On Bourdieu, Education and Society*, Oxford, Bardwell Press.

Robbins, D., 2009, 'Gazing at the Colonial Gaze: Photographic Observation and Observations on Photography based on a Comparison between Aspects of the Work of Pierre Bourdieu and Jean-Claude Passeron', *Sociological Review*, 57, 3, 428–447, Special Issue on 'Postcolonial Bourdieu', co-edited by Les Back, Azzedine Haddour and Nirmal Puwar.

Robbins, D., 2012, *French Post-War Social Theory. International Knowledge Transfer*, London/Thousand Oaks/New Delhi, Sage Publications.

Robbins, D., 2013, 'Response to Simon Susen's "Bourdieusian Reflections on Language: Unavoidable Conditions of the Real Speech Situation"', *Journal of Social Epistemology*, 27, 3–4, 261–74.

Robbins, D., 2014a, 'Religion and Cultural Politics. Islam and Bourdieu', *Journal of Classical Sociology*, 14, 3, 302–14.

Robbins, D., 2014b, 'Pierre Bourdieu and the Early Luc Boltanski (1960–1975). Collective Ethos and Individual Difference' in Susen and Turner, eds, 2014, 265–91.

Robbins, D., 2015a, review of Bourdieu, ed. T. Yacine, *Algerian Sketches*, for *Sociologica*, 3, 2014. Online publication: www.sociologica.mulino.it/doi/10.2383/79483.

Robbins, D., 2015b, *Cultural Relativism and International Politics*, Los Angeles/London/New Delhi/Singapore/Washington DC, Sage.

Robbins, D., 2015c, 'Pierre Bourdieu and Jacques Rancière on Art/Aesthetics and Politics. The Origins of Disagreement, 1963–1985', *British Journal of Sociology*, 66, 4, 738–58.

Robbins, D., 2016, Preface to Susen, 2016, 1–30.

Robbins, D., ed., 2016, *The Anthem Companion to Pierre Bourdieu*, London/New York, Anthem Press.

Ross, G. M., 1984, *Leibniz*, Oxford, Oxford University Press.

Rushdie, S., 1994, 'A Declaration of Independence. For the International Parliament of Writers', *Liber*, 17.

Sartre, J.-P., 1938, *La Nausée*, Paris, Gallimard.

Sartre, J.-P., 1946, *L'existentialisme est un humanisme*, Paris, Nagel.

Sartre, J.-P., 1960, *Critique de la raison dialectique*, Paris, Gallimard.

Sartre, J.-P., 1961, 'Merleau-Ponty vivant', *Les temps modernes*, 17, 184–5, 304–76.

Sartre, J.-P., 1996, *L'existentialisme est un humanisme*, Paris, Gallimard.

Sayad, A., 1999, *La double absence. Des illusions de l'émigré aux souffrances de l'immigré*, Paris, Seuil.

Sayad, A., 2004, *The Suffering of the Immigrant*, Cambridge, Polity Press.

Sayre, K., and F. Crosson, eds, 1963, *The Modelling of Mind*, Notre Dame, University of Notre Dame Press.

Schmitt, C., 2007, [1932], *The Concept of the Political*, London, University of Chicago Press.

Schnädelbach, H., 1984, *Philosophy in Germany 1831–1933*, Cambridge, Cambridge University Press.

Schopenhauer, A., 1818, *Die Welt als Wille und Vorstellung*, Leipzig, Brockhaus.

Schorske, C.E., 1979, *Fin-de-Siècle Vienna: Politics and Culture*, New York, Knopf, Vintage.

Schrecker, P., and A. Schrecker, eds, 1965, *G.W. Leibniz. Monadology and Other Philosophical Writings*, Indianapolis, Bobbs-Merrill.

Schutz, A., 1940, 'Phenomenology and the Social Sciences', in *Philosophical Essays in Memory of Edmund Husserl*, ed. M. Farber, Cambridge, MA, Harvard University Press, 164–86 [Schutz, ed. Natanson, 1962 (*CP I*), 118–39].

Schutz, A., 1941, 'William James's Concept of the Stream of Thought Phenomenologically Interpreted', *Philosophy and Phenomenological Research*, 1, 442–52 [Schutz, ed. I. Schutz, 1966 (*CP III*), 1–14].

Schutz, A., 1942, 'Scheler's Theory of Intersubjectivity and the General Thesis of the Alter Ego', *Philosophy and Phenomenological Research*, 2, 323–47 [*CP I*, 150–79].

Schutz, A., 1943, 'The Problem of Rationality in the Social World', *Economica*, New Series 10, 130–149 [Schutz, ed. Brodersen, 1964 (*CP II*), 64–88].

Schutz, A., 1944, 'The Stranger', *American Journal of Sociology*, 49, 499–507 [*CP II*, 91–105].

Schutz, A., 1945a, 'The Homecomer', *American Journal of Sociology*, 50, 363–76 [*CP II*, 106–19].

Schutz, A., 1945b, 'Some Leading Concepts of Phenomenology', *Social Research*, 12, 77–97 [*CP I*, 99–117].

Schutz, A., 1945c, 'On Multiple Realities', *Philosophy and Phenomenological Research*, 5, 533–76 [*CPI*, 207–59].

Schutz, A., 1946, 'The Well-Informed Citizen. An Essay on the Social Distribution of Knowledge', *Social Research*, 13, 463–78 [*CPII*, 120–34].

Schutz, A., 1948, 'Sartre's Theory of the Alter Ego', *Philosophy and Phenomenological Research*, 9, 181–99 [*CP I*, 180–203].

Schutz, A., 1950, 'Language, Language Disturbances and the Texture of Consciousness', *Social Research*, 17, 365–94 [*CP I*, 260–86].

Schutz, A., 1951a, 'Choosing among Projects of Action', *Philosophy and Phenomenological Research*, 12, 161–84 [*CP I*, 67–96].

Schutz, A., 1951b, 'Making Music Together. A Study in Social Relationship', *Social Research*, 18, 76–97 [*CP II*, 159–78].

Schutz, A., 1952, 'Santayana on Society and Government', *Social Research*, 19, 220–46 [*CP II*, 201–25].

Schutz, A., 1953a, 'Phenomenology and the Foundation of the Social Sciences (Edmund Husserl's *Ideas*, Vol. III)', *Philosophy and Phenomenological Research*, 13, 506–14 [*CP III*, 40–50].

Schutz, A., 1953b, 'Common Sense and Scientific Interpretation of Human Action', *Philosophy and Phenomenological Research*, 14, 1–38 [*CP I*, 3–47].

Schutz, A., 1954, 'Concept and Theory Formation in the Social Sciences', *Journal of Philosophy*, 51, 257–73 [*CP I*, 48–66].

Schutz, A., 1955, 'Symbol, Reality and Society', in *Symbols and Society*, ed. Bryson, Finkelstein, Hoagland and MacIver, New York, 135–204. [*CP I*, 287–356].

Schutz, A., 1956, 'La philosophie de Max Scheler', in *Les philosophes célèbres*, ed. Merleau-Ponty, 330–5, Paris, Lucien Mazenod [*CP III*, 133–44].

Schutz, A., 1957a, 'Equality and the Meaning Structure of the Social World', in *Aspects of Human Equality*, ed. Bryson, Faust, Finkelstein, and MacIver, New York, 33–78 [*CPII*, 226–73].

Schutz, A., 1957b, 'Max Scheler's Epistemology and Ethics. Part I', *Review of Metaphysics*, 11, 304–14 [*CP III*, 144–78].

Schutz, A., 1958a, 'Max Scheler's Epistemology and Ethics. Part II', *Review of Metaphysics*, 11, 486–501.

Schutz, A., 1958b, 'Some Equivocations in the Notion of Responsibility', in *Determinism and Freedom*, ed. S. Hook, New York, Collier-Macmillan, 206–8. [CP II, 174–276].

Schutz, A., 1959, 'Tiresias, or Our Knowledge of Future Events', *Social Research*, 26, 71–89 [*CP II*, 177–293].

Schutz, A., 1960, *Der sinnhafte Aufbau des sozialen Welt*, 2nd edn., Vienna, Springer Verlag.

Schutz, A., 1967, *The Phenomenology of the Social World*, Evanston, Northwestern University Press.

Schutz, A., ed. A. Brodersen, 1964, *Collected Papers II. Studies in Social Theory*, The Hague, Martinus Nijhoff.

Schutz, A., ed. M. Natanson, 1962, *Collected Papers I. The Problem of Social Reality*, The Hague, Martinus Nijhoff.

Schutz, A., ed. I. Schutz, 1966, *Collected Papers III. Studies in Phenomenological Philosophy*, The Hague, Martinus Nijhoff.

Schutz, A., ed., I. Schutz, 1971, *Gesammelte Aufsätze, Band I. Das Problem der sozialen Wirklichkeit*, The Hague, Martinus Nijhoff.

Schutz, A., ed. I. Srubar, 1981, *Theorie der Lebensformen*, Frankfurt, Suhrkamp.

Schutz, A., ed. H. Wagner, 1982, *Life Forms and Meaning Structure*, London, Routledge & Kegan Paul.

Schutz, A., ed. H. Wagner, G. Psathas and F. Kersten, 1996, *Collected Papers IV*, Dordrecht, Kluwer.

Shusterman, R., ed., 1999, *Bourdieu. A Critical Reader*, Oxford/Malden, Blackwell Publishers.

Speller, J.R.W., 2011, *Bourdieu and Literature*, Cambridge, Open Book Publishers.

Spiegelberg, H., 1976 [1960], *The Phenomenological Movement. A Historical Introduction*, 2 volumes, The Hague, Martinus Nijhoff.

Staiti, A., 2014, *Husserl's Transcendental Phenomenology. Nature, Spirit, and Life*, Cambridge, Cambridge University Press.

Stewart, J., ed., 1998, *The Debate between Sartre and Merleau-Ponty*, Evanston, Northwestern University Press.

Susen, S., 2016, *Pierre Bourdieu et la distinction sociale. Un essai philosophique*, Oxford/Bern/Berlin/Brussels/Frankfurt/New York/Vienna, Peter Lang.

Susen, S., and B.S. Turner, eds, 2014, *The Spirit of Luc Boltanski. Essays on the 'Pragmatic Sociology of Critique'*, London/New York, Anthem Press.

Tilliette, X., 1970, *Merleau-Ponty ou la mesure de l'homme*, Paris, Seghers.

Toadvine, T., ed., 2002, *Merleau-Ponty's Reading of Husserl*, Dordrecht, Kluwer.

Touraine, A., 1965, *Sociologie de l'action*, Paris, Seuil.

Truc, G., 2002, 'La sociologie est-elle un sport de combat? L'image de sociologie en Pierre Bourdieu (note critique)', *Terrains & Travaux*, 1, 3, 63–88.

Truc, G., 2004, 'Quand les sociologues font leur cinéma. Analyse croisée de *La sociologie est un sport de combat* et du *Parcours d'un sociologue*', *A Contrario*, 1, 2, 44–66.

Van Breda, H. L., 1962, 'Maurice Merleau-Ponty et les Archives-Husserl, Louvain', *Revue de métaphysique et de morale*, 67, 410–30.

Van Breda, H.L., and J. Taminiaux eds, 1959, *Edmund Husserl, 1859–1959*, The Hague, Martinus Nijhoff.

Wagner, H.R., 1977, 'The Bergsonian Period of Alfred Schutz', *Philosophy and Phenomenological Research*, 38, 2, 187–99.

Wagner, H.R., 1983, *Alfred Schutz. An Intellectual Biography*, Chicago/London, University of Chicago Press.

Welton, D., 2000, *The Other Husserl. The Horizons of Transcendental Phenomenology*, Bloomington, Indiana University Press.

Welton, D., ed., 2003, *The New Husserl. A Critical Reader*, Bloomington, Indiana University Press.

Whimster, S., and S. Lash, eds, 1987, *Max Weber, Rationality and Modernity*, London, Allen and Unwin.

Willinsky, J., ed., 1990, *The Educational Legacy of Romanticism*, Ontario, Wilfrid Laurier.

Young, M.F.D., ed., 1971, *Knowledge and Control. New Directions for the Sociology of Education*, London, Collier-Macmillan.

Index

CPSIA information can be obtained
at www.ICGtesting.com
Printed in the USA
BVHW040940180321
602887BV00002B/465